Accession no.
36038947

The Cambridge Companion to

This collection of specially commissioned essays by academics and practicing psychoanalysts explores key dimensions of Jacques Lacan's life and works. Lacan is renowned as a theoretician of psychoanalysis whose work is influential in many countries. He refashioned psychoanalysis in the name of philosophy and linguistics at a time when it was undergoing a certain intellectual decline. Advocating a "return to Freud," by which he meant a close reading in the original of Freud's works, he stressed the idea that the Unconscious functions "like a language." All essays in this *Companion* focus on key terms in Lacan's often difficult and idiosyncratic developments of psychoanalysis. This volume will bring fresh, accessible perspectives to the work of this formidable and influential thinker. These essays, supported by a useful chronology and guide to further reading, will prove invaluable to students and teachers alike.

THE CAMBRIDGE
COMPANION TO
LACAN

EDITED BY

JEAN-MICHEL RABATÉ

18C6424

LIBRARY

ACC. No.	DEPT.
36038947	
CLASS No.	

UNIVERSITY
OF CHESTER

CAMBRIDGE
UNIVERSITY PRESS

PUBLISHED BY THE PRESS SYNDICATE OF THE UNIVERSITY OF CAMBRIDGE
The Pitt Building, Trumpington Street, Cambridge CB2 1RP, United Kingdom

CAMBRIDGE UNIVERSITY PRESS
The Edinburgh Building, Cambridge, CB2 2RU, UK
40 West 20th Street, New York, NY 10011–4211, USA
477 Williamstown Road, Port Melbourne, VIC 3207, Australia
Ruiz de Alarcón 13, 28014 Madrid, Spain
Dock House, The Waterfront, Cape Town 8001, South Africa

http://www.cambridge.org

© Cambridge University Press 2003

This book is in copyright. Subject to statutory exception
and to the provisions of relevant collective licensing agreements,
no reproduction of any part may take place without
the written permission of Cambridge University Press.

First published 2003
Third printing 2006

Printed in the United Kingdom at the University Press, Cambridge

Typeface Sabon 10/13 pt.   *System* LATEX 2ε [TB]

A catalogue record for this book is available from the British Library

ISBN 0 521 80744 1 hardback
ISBN 0 521 00203 6 paperback

CONTENTS

NÉSTOR BRAUNSTEIN is a psychoanalyst, a professor and the director of the Center for Psychoanalytic Research and Studies (CIEP) in Mexico City, where he teaches. His books include *Psiquiatría, teoría del sujeto, psicoanálisis (hacia Lacan)* (1980), *Goce* (1990), *La jouissance: un concept lacanien (1992), Por el camino de Freud* (2001), and *Ficcioniaro de psicoanálisis* (2001). He has edited eleven volumes of the *Coloquios de la fundación.*

BERNARD BURGOYNE is a psychoanalyst and a member of the Ecole européenne de psychanalyse. He is professor of psychoanalysis and head of the Centre for Psychoanalysis at the Institute for Social Science and Health Research at Middlesex University. He co-edited with Mary Sullivan *The Klein-Lacan Dialogues* (1997) and edited *Drawing the Soul: Schemas and Models in Psychoanalysis* (2000).

TIM DEAN is a professor of English at the University at Buffalo, where he teaches psychoanalysis, queer theory, and poetic modernism. He is author of *Gary Snyder and the American Unconscious* (1991) and *Beyond Sexuality* (2000), as well as the co-editor of *Homosexuality and Psychoanalysis* (2001). His forthcoming book is *The Otherness of Art.*

JUDITH FEHER-GUREWICH is a psychoanalyst, the director of the Lacan Seminar at the Humanities Center at Harvard University, and a professor in the doctoral program for psychoanalysis and psychotherapy at New York University. She is also series editor at the Other Press, New York. She edited with Michel Tort *Lacan avec la psychanalyse américaine* (1996) and *Lacan and the New Wave of American Psychoanalysis* (1999), and is a member of Espace analytique, Centre de recherches freudiennes, in Paris.

DARIAN LEADER is a practicing psychoanalyst active in London. He is the co-author with Judy Groves of *Lacan for Beginners* (1995) and *Introducing Lacan* (1996). He has also published *Why Do Women Write More Letters*

Than They Send? A Meditation on the Loneliness of the Sexes (1996, published in the UK as *Why Do Women Write More Letters Then They Post?*), *Promises Lovers Make When It Gets Late* (1997), and *Freud's Footnotes* (2000).

CATHERINE LIU is a professor of French, cultural studies and comparative literature at the University of Minnesota. She is the author of *Copying Machines: Taking Notes for the Automaton* (2000). A first novel, *Oriental Girls Desire Romance* (1997) will be followed by *Suicide of an Assistant Professor* (2004). She is completing *Under the Star of Paranoia: Astrology, Conspiracy, Celebrity*.

DEBORAH ANNA LUEPNITZ is a member of the clinical faculty of the department of psychiatry at the University of Pennsylvania's School of Medicine. She is the author of *The Family Interpreted: Psychoanalysis, Feminism, and Family Therapy* (1988) and of *Schopenhauer's Porcupines: Intimacy and Its Dilemmas* (2002). She practices psychoanalysis in Philadelphia.

DANY NOBUS is a senior lecturer in psychology and psychoanalytic studies at Brunel University and a visiting scholar at the Boston Graduate School for Psychoanalysis. He is the editor of *Key Concepts of Lacanian Psychoanalysis* (1999) and the author of *Jacques Lacan and the Freudian Practice of Psychoanalysis* (2000).

JEAN-MICHEL RABATÉ is a professor of English and comparative literature at the University of Pennsylvania and has published books on Joyce, Pound, Beckett, modernism, and literary theory. Recent publications include the edited volume *Lacan in America* (2000), *James Joyce and the Politics of Egoism* (2001), *Jacques Lacan and the Subject of Literature* (2001), and *The Future of Theory* (2002).

DIANA RABINOVICH is a psychoanalyst and a professor at the University of Buenos Aires, where she has been the chair and founder of the department of psychoanalytical methodolology. Her books include *Sexualidad y significante* (1986), *El concepto de objeto en la teoría psicoanalítica* (1988), *Una clínica de la pulsión: las impulsiones* (1989), *La angustia y el deseo del Otro* (1993), *Modos lógicos del amor de transferencia* (1992), *El deseo del psicoanalista: Libertad y determinación en psicoanálisis* (1999).

ELISABETH ROUDINESCO is a psychoanalyst, a historian, and a director of studies at the University of Paris VII. Her books include *Jacques Lacan & Co.: A History of Psychoanalysis in France 1925–1985* (1990), *Jacques Lacan, Esquisse d'une vie, histoire d'un système de pensée* (1993; in English, *Jacques Lacan*, 1997), *Généalogies* (1994) and *Pourquoi la psychanalyse?*

(1999; in English, *Why Psychoanalysis?* 2002). She is the co-author with Michel Plon of the *Dictionnaire de la psychanalyse* (1997) and with Jacques Derrida of *De quoi demain . . . Dialogue* (2001).

CHARLES SHEPHERDSON, professor of English and comparative literature at the University of New York at Albany, is the author of *Vital Signs: Nature, Culture, Psychoanalysis* (2000). He has published numerous articles on phenomenology, theory, tragedy, and Lacan. He is completing a book on Lacan and Merleau-Ponty.

COLETTE SOLER, professor in philosophy, psychoanalyst, and doctor in psychology. She is a member of the International Association of the Forums of the Lacanian Field and of the Ecole de Psychanalyse du Champ lacanien. She has published *La maldición sobre el sexo* (2000), *L'Aventure littéraire ou la psychose inspirée: Rousseau, Joyce, Pessoa* (2001) and *Ce que Lacan disait des Femmes* (2003). She is the co-author and editor of *Psychanalyse, pas la pensée unique: Histoire d'une crise singulière* (2000).

JOSEPH VALENTE is a professor of English and critical theory at the University of Illinois. He is the author of *James Joyce and the Problem of Justice: Negotiating Sexual and Colonial Difference* (1992) and *Dracula's Crypt: Bram Stoker, Irishness and the Question of Blood* (2002). He is also the editor of *Quare Joyce* (1998) and the co-editor of *Disciplinarity at the Fin de Siecle* (2002). His work in critical theory has appeared in *Diacritics, Critical Inquiry, College Literature*, and *Gender and Psychoanalysis*.

ALENKA ZUPANČIČ is a researcher at the Institute of Philosophy, Scientific Research Center of the Slovenian Academy of Sciences and Arts. She is the author of *Ethics of the Real. Kant, Lacan* (2000), *Das Reale einer Illusion* (2001), and *Esthétique du désir, éthique de la jouissance* (2002).

After Freud, Lacan is arguably the most important theoretician of psycho-analysis. Like Freud, he has been endlessly discussed, and his controversial personality, his arcane style, and his huge claims on culture, ethics, philosophy, and sexuality, not to mention his unorthodox methods of teaching and of carrying out treatment, have elicited emphatic rejections as well as adulatory commendations. The controversy has not abated since his death in 1981 at the age of eighty. This may be due to the fact that his influence has not been limited to France, his native country, a country in which, thanks to his relentless efforts at pedagogy, the number of psychoanalysts per capita is the highest in the world. His teachings and philosophy have spread worldwide, first to Latin countries like Italy, Spain, Argentina, Brazil, then to North America, before reaching Asian countries, especially China. This has happened precisely at a time when one can observe a general decline in traditional psychoanalytic practice throughout the world.

Lacan was one of the first theoreticians of psychoanalysis to take note of what Herbert Marcuse has called the "obsolescence" of psychoanalysis, an obsolescence that was perceptible by the middle of last century and undeniable by the end of the century, when psychoanalysis had been incorporated and trivialized by popular culture on the one hand, while caught between incompatible scientific claims and aims on the other, tempted either by biological neuro-scientism or adaptive psychological meliorism. Lacan's originality consisted in refusing to "modernize" psychoanalysis by updating medical treatment or relying on new chemical drugs or even using a simplified therapy, allegedly more adapted to the needs of modern society. Instead, he raised the stakes, firmly positing post-Freudian psychoanalysis first as a therapy based on a particular use of language in which the analyst's measured silence would call up radical otherness, then as a rigorous discourse that could only find true conceptual bearings in the writings of its inventor and that would benefit from new scientific advances in domains like linguistics, mathematics, or symbolic logics. He saw the unconscious not as a dark dungeon full of libidinal imps hiding behind rational volition and planning unwholesome incursions, but as the "discourse of the Other," that is, as a systemic social formation, a hoard of words, names, and sentences out of which collective utterances are made; this hoard of words also accounts for my own singularity, thanks to the agency of the specific condensation of signifiers that appears as a symptom, that is, *my* symptom.

Lacan has often been called a "philosopher of psychoanalysis" but it is clear that he could never have achieved the radical re-foundation of psychoanalysis he envisaged if he had not been a psychiatrist first, someone who had been trained in the French school that produced Charcot, Janet, Babinski, and Gatian de Clérambault – the latter still claimed as a "master" by Lacan in 1966, next to the only other "master" he named, the Russian-born philosopher Alexandre Kojève. It is because of a solid clinical base in the reality of hospitalized madness that Lacan was able to make inroads into Hegel's speculative philosophy, just as it is because of his training as a philosopher that he was able to denounce the lack of culture and conceptual rigor among his contemporaries who were active in psychiatry or in psychoanalysis. The outcome of this double postulation was the relentless exploration of a single field, that of the speaking id – in other words, the interaction between the suffering body in its manifold symptoms and the suffering mind when it stumbles in parapraxes and unconscious delusions. True to this central insight, Lacan always considered that the body and the "soul" (let us not forget that "psychoanalysis" etymologically at least implies addressing the diseases of the soul) were connected not via Descartes' pineal gland but simply by language. Lacan is often associated with a "linguistic turn" in psychoanalysis, that is to say, a turning away from biology in therapy and metapsychology so as to stress the element of language as dominant both in clinical practice and in theory. The linguistic turn initiated by Lacan was prompted by a refusal of the psychologization of psychoanalysis that dominated at the time of Freud's death, especially under the influence of Freud's daughter Anna (Lacan's *bête noire*). In that sense, what he did for post-Freudianism was parallel to the revision of Husserlian phenomenology accomplished by Heidegger – who also exerted a lasting influence on Lacan. However, Heidegger's vision of a poetic language leading to a site where ontology turns into language was soon replaced by a more technical perspective that freely adapted Ferdinand de Saussure's structural linguistics to sharpen and systematize Freudian insights into language. Saussurean linguistics is not the only science adduced by Lacan, who peppered his seminars with references to anthropology, comparative religion, logic, mathematics, topology, or set theory. One may say that there is a very strong myth of science in Lacan, although this science is not at all identical with the science that Freud took as a model.

His aim was thus to revitalize psychoanalysis by epistemology, which evokes another important theoretician of psychoanalysis who attempted to provide the same type of conceptual clarification, but within the field mapped out by Melanie Klein, W. R. Bion (1897–1979, Lacan's exact contemporary). Like Bion, Lacan invented idiosyncratic concepts made up of elements that he borrowed from different traditions, but his references remained Freudian. Like Bion, he believed that he needed to formalize his concepts in a particular theoretical shorthand (Bion used Greek letters and a conceptual grid appended to all his books, while Lacan invented a whole battery of schemata, "graphs," and "mathemes") in order to transmit them as faithfully as possible. Like Bion, he stressed the need for a different method of training and a new pedagogy; he saw himself more as a "teacher" who would form a new generation of intelligent psychoanalysts. Lacan took very seriously Freud's admonitions against the medicalization of psychoanalysis in *The Question of Lay Analysis* (1926). There, Freud advises his ideal students to take up not only psychiatry and sexology, but also "the history of civilization, mythology, psychology, the psychology of religions, literary history and literary criticism" (*SE* 20, p. 246). Indeed, a mere glance at Freud's library suggests that he was not only interested in technical books on psychiatry and psychology, but was also a voracious reader in the fields of world literature, archaeology, ancient history, and mythology. As Lacan explains, psychoanalysis should belong to the "liberal arts" and avoid reductive scientism or medical normativization (*E/S*, p. 76). Such a view should force a psychoanalyst to realize that the objects of the "talking cure," that is, my symptoms, resemble the study of cultural history – as Lacan develops it, these are the "monuments" of my body, the "archival documents" of my childhood memories, the "semantic evolution" of my idioms and personal style, the "traditions" and "legends" that carry my heroic stories, and finally the distortions and obliterations rendered necessary by the need to "finish the story" and make it somewhat palatable (*E/S*, p. 50).

This literary or humanistic drift, as well as his original practice of variable (in fact, much shorter) sessions, led Lacan into a series of battles with the International Psychoanalytic Association until he decided to found his own school. This complex institutional history is not finished, which makes it hard, even today, to find the required distance and to keep the institutional and ideological detachment needed just to introduce Lacan's works, while not losing the enthusiasm and passions he elicited. Since we are reaching the date of a quarter of a century after a personality's death, a clear discussion of his works, free of jargon and prejudice seems possible. As most contributions in this volume will show, there is still a lot to untangle and explicate in Lacan's complex theories. If Lacan is difficult, he is perhaps not *so* difficult.

One might distinguish between three types of difficulty. The first is stylistic: Lacan is a notoriously obscure writer who loves witty epigrams, puns, drawn-out metaphors, recondite allusions, baroque disquisitions, and paradoxical pronouncements. As early as 1938, the editors of an encyclopedia felt the need to rewrite his scientific contribution several times. The second is genetic: Lacan's concepts were elaborated (often in groups and seminars) over five decades of intense research and experimentation; they thus underwent important transformations, which is why a good "introductory dictionary" to his concepts has been obliged to distinguish historical layers and periods when discussing terms like "desire," "jouissance," the "phallus," the "*objet a*" – to name only fundamental concepts. A loaded term like the "big Other" (*le grand Autre*) will not carry the same meaning in 1955 as in 1970, for instance, and it would be very hard to reintroduce the "barred Other" or the "jouissance of the Other" into the canonical texts from 1953 or 1957. Lacan, on the other hand, would claim that he had never swerved from a straight route, and thanks to Jacques-Alain Miller's clever use of structural schemata and thematic recurrences, managed to make *Ecrits*, a collection of very different texts written from 1936 to 1966, look almost like a coherent system. A third difficulty will hence be more contextual than conceptual: given the high frequency of references to other writers and Lacan's close association with thinkers as diverse as Claude Lévi-Strauss, Roman Jakobson, Martin Heidegger, Maurice Merleau-Ponty, Françoise Dolto, Jean Genet, Philippe Sollers, or Julia Kristeva, not to mention the younger philosophers and mathematicians he worked with in the seventies, quite often one needs to reconstruct a whole intellectual atmosphere to read a single seminar. It is not only the fact that his work presupposes the kind of familiarity with the history of philosophy that most French students are forcefully fed at high-school level, but also that the network of his arcane references would imply a whole education of its own. Thus it is not only a knowledge of Aristotle, Kant, and de Sade that will be needed to grasp the intricacies of a really "seminal" text like *The Ethics of Psychoanalysis* but also, for instance, an idea of twelfth-century courtly love, a familiarity with the writings of female mystics, or with Bataille's concept of *dépense*.

However, a number of recent guides, introductions, dictionaries, commentaries, close readings of individual texts, and seminars have paved the way to a more realistic appraisal of Lacan's work. The time of simple exegesis has passed; we do not need yet another account of Saussure's binaries or a summary of ternaries like Imaginary, Symbolic, and Real. Although these notions obviously need to be understood, what matters today is how productive they are. It is less a matter of defining deliberately elusive concepts like "the Other" than of understanding their dynamic usage in several contexts.

Indeed, by a curious twist, Lacan's fortune in the English-speaking world was due to literary critics or to writers dealing with visual culture, who saw, for instance, in the theory of the gaze developed in *Seminar XI* the best way of talking about film, more often than not in the context of the American *film noir*. The impact of a philosopher like Slavoj Žižek on cultural studies has systematized the theories of a later Lacan, more gnomic and paradoxical, who could be adduced to address issues of post-communism, racism, terrorism, and the political upheavals of a world undergoing a fast and painful globalization.

What was lost as a consequence, or seen as dated at best, was the reference to a psychoanalytic "experience" that is recurrent in Lacan's texts. After I had asserted that some knowledge of Freud was a prerequisite for understanding Lacan, and that Lacan himself would spend a lot of time seeing patients, one of my students noted that she had forgotten when reading Lacan and Žižek that one could indulge in such an old-fashioned thing as having people lying upon a couch to chat to a psychoanalyst. She cried out in desperation: "I thought that this was only done in the nineteenth century!" Indeed, all this may send us back to a superannuated mythology, what with the beard, the quizzical stare behind glasses, the fat cigar, strange clothes, and sick jokes, not to mention the Bela Lugosi accent from Transylvania that is absolutely necessary for pseudo-Viennese jokes like "Vat is dhere between Fear and Sex? . . . – *Fünf*!" – a mythology to which Lacan added his own bizarre arithmetic, claiming that he could only count to four in his interlocked Borromean knots. For those who may not know German, *vier*, pronounced like "fear," is four, *fünf* is five, and *sechs* (pronounced "zex" or, in Austrian German, "sex") is six. But even jokes force us to revisit the same ground, and lead us to explore anew the crucial interaction between the clinical and the theoretical. This is why the majority of contributors to this volume are psychoanalysts who also teach and write. By exploring Lacanian concepts such as the "mirror stage," the "letter," the "mathemes," the "symptom," "desire," "jouissance," "the phallus," or the "formulas of sexuation," they will guide us on the many paths of Lacan's map of the modern soul. In their different ways and styles, they remind us that if the unconscious exists, it is not simply located in our brains, in packs of neurons or chemical reactions triggered by hormones, but more fundamentally, because we are born into language and are therefore what Lacan called *"parlêtres"* – speaking, suffering, and desiring beings.

ACKNOWLEDGEMENTS

I want to thank Ray Ryan, who believed in the project from the start and greatly contributed to the consistency of this *Companion*, and Paul Kintzele, who has helped me edit most of its contributions.

ABBREVIATIONS

Note: English translations quoting texts without any mention of a published English-language translation are from the French original and provided by the contributors.

AE   Jacques Lacan, *Autres écrits*, edited by Jacques-Alain Miller (Paris: Seuil, 2001).

E   Jacques Lacan, *Ecrits* (Paris: Seuil, 1966).

E/S   Jacques Lacan, *Ecrits, A Selection*, translated by Alan Sheridan (London: Tavistock Publications, 1977).

PP   Jacques Lacan, *De la psychose paranoïaque dans ses rapports avec la personnalité, suivi de Premiers écrits sur la paranoïa* (Paris: Seuil, 1975).

S I   Jacques Lacan, *Seminar I, Freud's Papers on Technique*, edited by Jacques-Alain Miller, translated and annotated by John Forrester (New York: Norton, 1998).

S II   Jacques Lacan, *Seminar II, The Ego in Freud's Theory and in the Technique of Psychoanalysis*, edited by Jacques-Alain Miller, translated by Sylvana Tomaselli and annotated by John Forrester (New York: Norton, 1998).

S III   Jacques Lacan, *Seminar III, Psychoses*, edited by Jacques-Alain Miller, translated and annotated by Russell Grigg (New York: Norton, 1993).

S VII   Jacques Lacan, *Seminar VII, The Ethics of Psychoanalysis*, edited by Jacques-Alain Miller, translated and annotated by Dennis Porter (New York: Norton, 1992).

S XI   Jacques Lacan, *Seminar XI, The Four Fundamental Concepts of Psychoanalysis*, edited by Jacques-Alain Miller, translated by Alan Sheridan (London: The Hogarth Press and the Institute of Psycho-Analysis, 1977).

S XX Jacques Lacan, *On Feminine Sexuality, the Limits of Love and Knowledge 1972–1973. Encore, the Seminar of Jacques Lacan, Book XX*, edited by Jacques-Alain Miller, translated and annotated by Bruce Fink (New York: Norton, 1998).

SE Sigmund Freud, *The Standard Edition of the Complete Psychological Works of Sigmund Freud*, translated from the German under the general editorship of James Strachey, in collaboration with Anna Freud, Alix Strachey, and Alan Tyson, 24 vols. (London: The Hogarth Press and the Institute of Psycho-Analysis, 1955).

T *Television*. Edited by Joan Copjec, translated by Denis Hollier, Rosalind Krauss, and Annette Michelson, and *A Challenge to the Psychoanalytic Establishment*, translated by Jeffrey Mehlman (New York: Norton, 1990).

1901	*13 April* Birth of Jacques-Marie Emile Lacan, the first child of Alfred Lacan (1873–1960) and Emilie Baudry (1876–1948). The middle-class Roman Catholic family has settled at 95 boulevard Beaumarchais in Paris. The father is overseeing a prosperous food business that his family started a century earlier with a reputed vinegar company, expanding later into the commerce of pickled goods, mustard, brandy, rum, and coffee.
1902	Birth of Raymond, Lacan's brother, who dies two years later.
1903	*25 December* Birth of Madeleine, Lacan's sister.
1907	Lacan enters the very select Collège Stanislas, a Marist college catering to the Parisian bourgeoisie, a year earlier than Charles de Gaulle, who is a student there in 1908–9. At Collège Stanislas, Lacan receives a solid primary and secondary education with a strong religious and traditionalist emphasis. He completes his studies in 1919.
	25 December Birth of Marc-Marie, Lacan's second brother.
1915	During the war, Alfred Lacan is drafted as a sergeant, and parts of the Collège Stanislas are converted into a hospital for wounded soldiers. Lacan starts reading Spinoza.
1917–8	Lacan is taught philosophy by Jean Baruzi, a remarkable Catholic thinker who wrote a dissertation on Saint John of the Cross.
1918	Lacan loses his virginity and starts frequenting intellectual bookshops like Adrienne Monnier's Maison des amis des livres and Sylvia Beach's Shakespeare and Company at rue de l'Odéon. New interests in Dadaism and the avant-garde.
1919	*Autumn* Lacan enters the Paris medical faculty and studies medicine.
1920	Lacan meets André Breton and acquaints himself with the Surrealist movement.

1921	Lacan is discharged from military service because of excessive thinness. *7 December* Lacan hears the lecture on Joyce's *Ulysses* by Valéry Larbaud with readings from the text, an event organized by La maison des amis des livres, and at which James Joyce is present.
1925	*January 20* Madeleine, Lacan's sister, marries Jacques Houlon. Soon after, they move to Indochina.
1926	*4 November* The first French Freudian society, the Société psychanalytique de Paris, is created. By a curious coincidence, it is the day of Lacan's first clinical presentation in front of Théophile Alajouanine and other doctors. Lacan co-authors his first paper with Alajouanine and Delafontaine on the Parinaud syndrome, published in the *Revue neurologique*.
1927–8	Clinical training in psychiatry at the Clinique des maladies mentales et de l'encéphale, a service linked with the Sainte-Anne hospital in Paris and directed by Henri Claude.
1928	Lacan co-authors with M. Trénel an article on "Abasia in a case of war trauma" in the *Revue neurologique*. He publishes with J. Lévy-Valensi and M. Meignant a paper on "hallucinatory delirium." Altogether, between 1928 and 1930, he co-authors five more neurological studies based on psychiatric cases. Engagement to Marie-Thérèse Bergerot, to whom he will dedicate his 1932 doctoral thesis with a line of thanks in Greek, the other dedicatee being his brother. Clinical training at the Paris Police Special Infirmary for the Insane under the supervision of Gaëtan Gatian de Clérambault, whose unconventional style of teaching will exert a lasting influence on Lacan.
1929	In spite of Lacan's disapproval, his brother enters the Benedictine order at the abbey of Hautecombe on the Lake Bourget. He takes his vows on 8 September 1931, and changes his first name to Marc-François.
1929–31	Clinical training at the Hospital Henri Rousselle.
1930	*July* Arranges to meet Salvador Dalí who has published "The rotten donkey" in July 1930. His poetic praise of paranoia has attracted Lacan's attention. Lacan and Salvador Dalí remain friends all their lives. Friendship with the novelist Pierre Drieu La Rochelle. From 1929 to 1933 Lacan is the lover of Olesia Sienkiewicz, Drieu's estranged second wife. *August–September* Lacan takes a two-month training course at the Burghölzli clinic in Zürich.

1931   *18 June* Lacan examines Marguerite Pantaine-Anzieu, who has been admitted to Sainte-Anne hospital after stabbing the actress Huguette Duflos. Lacan calls her Aimée and makes her case the cornerstone of his doctoral dissertation.

1932   Publication of Lacan's translation of Freud's "Some neurotic mechanisms in jealousy, paranoia and homosexuality" for the *Revue française de psychanalyse.*
    June Lacan begins his analysis with Rudolph Loewenstein.
    November Lacan defends his thesis on paranoia, published as *De la psychose paranoïaque dans ses rapports avec la personnalité* (Paris: Le François, 1932).

1933   Lacan publishes a sonnet, "Hiatus Irrationalis," in *Le Phare de Neuilly* 3/4. He meets Marie-Louise Blondin, the sister of his friend Sylvain Blondin.
    October Lacan attends Alexander Kojève's seminar on Hegel's *Phenomenology of Spirit* at the Ecole pratique des hautes études. There he meets Georges Bataille and Raymond Queneau, both of whom will remain friends. He publishes "The problem of style and the psychiatric conception of paranoiac forms of experience" and "Motivations of paranoid crime: the crime of the Papin sisters" in the Surrealist journal *Le Minotaure* 1 and 3/4.

1934   Lacan sees his first patient.
    29 January Marriage with Marie-Louise Blondin.
    November Lacan becomes a candidate member of the Société psychanalytique de Paris.

1936   *3 August* Lacan attends the 14th congress of the International Psychoanalytic Association at Marienbad, where he presents his paper on the mirror stage. After ten minutes, he is brutally interrupted by Ernest Jones. Quite upset, Lacan leaves the conference. He will never submit his text for publication.

1937   8 January Birth of Caroline, first child of Lacan and Marie-Louise Blondin.

1938   Lacan writes a long article on the family for the *Encyclopédie française*. The essay, commissioned by Henri Wallon and Lucien Febvre, is found too dense and has to be rewritten several times. Its final title is "Family complexes in the formation of the individual. An attempt at analysis of a function in psychology" ("Les Complexes familiaux dans la formation de l'individu. Essai d'analyse d'une function en psychologie", *AE*, pp. 23–84).

Lacan starts a relationship with Sylvia Maklès-Bataille, who has separated from Georges Bataille in 1934.
December Lacan finishes his analysis with Loewenstein and is made a full member of the Société psychanalytique de Paris.

1939 *27 August* Birth of Thibaud, second child of Lacan and Marie-Louise Blondin.

1940 *June* When the Vichy regime is put in place, the Société psychanalytique de Paris (despite some efforts at imitating the German Psychoanalytic Society) suspends all its activities.
26 November Birth of Sybille Lacan, third child of Lacan and Marie-Louise Blondin.

1941 *Spring* Lacan moves to 5 rue de Lille, where his office will be located until his death. After his death, a commemorating plaque was put on the façade.
3 July Birth of Judith Bataille, daughter of Lacan and Sylvia Maklès-Bataille.
15 December Lacan and Marie-Louise Blondin are officially divorced.

1944 Lacan meets Jean-Paul Sartre, Maurice Merleau-Ponty and Pablo Picasso. He will remain very close to Merleau-Ponty.

1945 *September* Lacan travels to England, where he stays five weeks to study the practice of British psychiatry during the war. He meets W. R. Bion and is very impressed by him. Two years later, writing about this meeting, Lacan will praise the heroism of the British people during the war.

1946 The Société psychanalytique de Paris resumes its activities.
9 August Sylvia Maklès-Bataille and Georges Bataille are officially divorced.

1948 Lacan becomes a member of the teaching committee of the Société psychanalytique de Paris.
21 November Death of Lacan's mother.

1949 Lacan meets Claude Lévi-Strauss. Beginning of a long friendship.
17 July Lacan attends the 16th congress of the International Psychoanalytic Association in Zürich. He presents the second version of his paper on the mirror stage (*E/S*, pp. 1–7). In a climate of ideological war between the British Kleinians and the American "Anna-Freudians" (a clear majority), the French second generation, following the philosophy of Marie Bonaparte, tries to occupy a different space. Dissident

luminaries include Daniel Lagache, Sacha Nacht, and Lacan, often assisted by his friend Françoise Dolto. Lacan dominates the French group and gathers around him brilliant theoreticians such as Wladimir Granoff, Serge Leclaire, and François Perrier. He gives a seminar on Freud's Dora case.

1951   Lacan introduces psychoanalytical sessions of variable length in his practice, a technical innovation which is condemned as soon as it becomes known to the other members of the Société psychanalytique de Paris. He begins to give weekly seminars at 3 rue de Lille.

2 May Lacan reads "Some reflections on the ego" to the members of the British Psycho-Analytical Society. This will be his first publication in English in the *International Journal of Psychoanalysis* (1953).

1951–2   Lacan gives a seminar on Freud's Wolf-Man case.

1952   Sacha Nacht, then president of the Société psychanalytique de Paris, proposes that a new training institute be established. He resigns as director of the institute in December and Lacan is elected interim director.

1952–3   Lacan gives a seminar on Freud's Rat-Man case.

1953   20 January Lacan is elected president of the Société psychanalytique de Paris.

16 June Lacan resigns as president of the Société psychanalytique de Paris. Creation of the Société française de psychanalyse (SFP) by Daniel Lagache, Françoise Dolto, and Juliette Boutonnier. Soon after, Lacan joins the SFP.

July The members of the SFP learn that they have been excluded from the International Psycho-Analytical Association. Introduced by Lagache, Lacan gives the opening lecture at the SFP on the three registers of the Imaginary, the Symbolic, and the Real.

17 July Lacan and Sylvia Maklès are married.

26 September In his "Rome discourse," Lacan presents "Function and field of speech and language in psychoanalysis" (*E/S*, pp. 30–113, original talk in *AE*, pp. 133–64), a veritable manifesto. In this pyrotechnical display showing all the facets of his culture, Lacan introduces the doctrine of the signifier. Among many crucial theoretical pronouncements, the "Rome discourse" justifies the practice of the variable-length session. Françoise Dolto speaks after Lacan and Lagache and expresses her support for the new movement.

18 November Lacan starts his public seminar at Sainte-Anne hospital with a close reading of Freud's papers on technique (later *S I*). He also conducts weekly clinical presentations of patients.

1954   Lacan visits Carl Gustav Jung in Küssnacht near Zürich. Jung tells Lacan how Freud had declared that he and Jung were "bringing the plague" to America when they reached New York in 1909, an anecdote subsequently often repeated by Lacan.

1955   *Easter* Accompanied by his analysand Jean Beaufret, a disciple and translator of Heidegger, Lacan pays a visit to Martin Heidegger in Freiburg and Beaufret acts as an interpreter between the two thinkers.

July The International Psycho-Analytical Association rejects the SFP's petition for affiliation.

September At the occasion of the Cerisy conference devoted to the work of Heidegger, Lacan invites the German philosopher and his wife to spend a few days in his country house at Guitrancourt.

7 November Lacan reads "The Freudian Thing, or the meaning of the return to Freud in psychoanalysis" at the Neuro-psychiatric clinic of Vienna (*E*, pp. 401–36).

1956   *Winter* Publication of the first issue of *La Psychanalyse* with Lacan's "Rome discourse" and his translation of the first part of Heidegger's essay "Logos," a commentary on Heraclitus' fragment 50.

1957   *9 May* Lacan presents "The agency of the letter in the unconscious; or, Reason since Freud" (*E/S*, pp. 146–78) to a group of philosophy students at the Sorbonne, later published in *La Psychanalyse* (1958). Less Heideggerian and more linguistic, the paper sketches a rhetoric of the unconscious based on the relationship between signifier and signified and generates the algorithms of metaphor and metonymy corresponding to Freud's condensation and displacement.

1958   Lacan presents in German "Die Bedeutung des Phallus" ("The signification of the phallus" in *E/S*, pp. 281–91) at the Max-Planck-Institut in Munich.

1959   *July* The SFP renews its request for affiliation to the International Psycho-Analytical Association, which nominates a committee to investigate the issue.

1960   *15 October* Death of Lacan's father.

1961   *August* A progressive reintegration of the SFP within the International Psycho-Analytical Association is accepted on the condition that Françoise Dolto and Lacan be demoted from their positions as training analysts.

1963   *April* Lacan publishes "Kant with Sade" in *Critique*, one of his most important theoretical essays devoted to desire, the law, and perversion (*E*, pp. 765–90).

August 2 The International Psycho-Analytical Association reaffirms that the SFP will lose its affiliated status if Lacan remains as a training analyst.

19 November The majority of the SFP analysts accept the International Psycho-Analytical Association's ultimatum. After ten years of teaching his seminar at Sainte-Anne, Lacan is obliged to stop. He holds a final session on "The names of the father" (*T*, pp. 80–95).

1964   *January* Lacan starts his seminar at the Ecole normale supérieure, rue d'Ulm, under the administrative control of the Ecole pratique des hautes études. Claude Lévi-Strauss and Louis Althusser have intervened on his behalf to secure the room. This seminar, devoted to the *Four Fundamental Concepts of Psychoanalysis*, finds a broader and more philosophical audience.

June Lacan founds the Ecole française de psychanalyse. His "Act of foundation" dramatizes his sense of heroic solitude ("I hereby found – as alone as I have always been in my relation to the psychoanalytic cause – the Ecole française de psychanalyse, whose direction, concerning which nothing at present prevents me from answering for, I shall undertake during the next four years to assure"). Three months later it changes its name to the Ecole freudienne de Paris. Lacan launches a new associative model for his school; study groups called "cartels," made up of four or five people, are constituted, including one person who reports on the progress of the group.

1965   *19 January* Dissolution of the SFP.

June Lacan arranges a meeting with Marguerite Duras after the publication of *The Ravishing of Lol V. Stein*, a novel that describes psychosis in terms similar to his. When they meet up late one night in a bar, he says to her enthusiastically, so as to congratulate her: "You don't know what you are saying!"

1966   *January* First issue of the *Cahiers pour l'analyse*, a review
        produced by younger epistemologists of the Ecole normale
        supérieure who publish serious articles on Lacan's concepts.
        February–March Lacan gives a series of lectures at six North
        American universities, including Columbia, Harvard, and MIT.
        18–21 October Lacan attends an international symposium
        entitled "The Languages of Criticism and the Sciences of Man"
        at Johns Hopkins University. He participates actively in the
        debate on Structuralism and presents his paper "Of structure as
        an inmixing of an Otherness prerequisite to any subject
        whatever." In a text as dense as its title, Lacan quotes Frege and
        Russell, explaining that his motto that the unconscious is
        "structured as a language" is in fact a tautology, since
        "structured" and "as a language" are synonymous. He states
        memorably: "The best image to sum up the unconscious is
        Baltimore in the early morning."
        November Publication of *Ecrits*. Surprisingly, the thick (924
        pages) book sells very well.
        December Marriage of Judith Lacan and Jacques-Alain Miller.

1967   *9 October* Lacan launches the new procedure of the "pass"
        (*la passe*) as a final examination allowing one to become a
        training analyst in his school.

1968   *Autumn* Publication of the first issue of *Scilicet*, a journal whose
        motto is "You can know what the Ecole freudienne de Paris
        thinks" and in which all articles are unsigned except Lacan's.
        December The department of psychoanalysis is created at the
        University of Vincennes (later Paris VIII) with Serge Leclaire as
        its director.

1969   *March* The introduction of the practice of the "pass" as a sort
        of final examination provokes a rebellion at the Ecole
        freudienne de Paris and a splinter group is created by Lacanian
        "barons" such as François Périer and Piera Aulagnier.
        November Having been forced to leave the Ecole normale
        supérieure, Lacan now holds his weekly seminar at the law
        faculty on the place du Panthéon. It draws even bigger crowds.

1970   *September* Leclaire resigns as head of the department of
        psychoanalysis of Paris VIII and Jean Clavreul replaces him.

1972   *9 February* Lacan introduces the Borromean knot during his
        seminar, and starts pondering ways in which three interlocking
        circles can be tied together.

1973   Publication of *Seminar XI*, the first of a series edited by
Jacques-Alain Miller, at Editions du Seuil.
March Prodded by a growing number of feminists among his
students, Lacan introduces in his seminar the "formulas of
sexuation," which demonstrate that sexuality is not determined
by biology, since another, so-called "feminine" position (i.e. not
determined by the phallus) is also available to all speaking
subjects next to the phallic law giving access to universality.
30 May Death of Caroline Lacan-Roger in a road
accident.

1974   The department of psychoanalysis is reorganized with
Jacques-Alain Miller as its director.

1975   First issue of the journal *Ornicar?* It publishes Lacanian articles
and the texts of some seminars.
16 June Invited by Jacques Aubert, Lacan gives the opening
lecture at the Paris International James Joyce Symposium. He
proposes the idea of "Joyce le sinthome."
November–December Second lecture tour in the United States.
Lacan goes to Yale, Columbia, and MIT, where he has
discussions with Quine and Chomsky.

1978   *Autumn* After a minor car accident, Lacan appears tired and is
often silent for long periods of time even in his seminars, in
which his discourse tends to be replaced by mute
demonstrations of new twists on Borromean knots.

1979   Creation of the Fondation du champ freudien, directed by
Judith Miller.

1980   *January* Lacan dissolves the Ecole freudienne de Paris by a
"Letter of Dissolution" mailed to all members and dated 5
January 1980. It presents Lacan as a "père sévère" (strict father)
who can "persévérer" (persevere) alone. All the members of the
school are invited to write a letter directly to him if they want to
follow him in the creation of a new institution. He mentions the
price Freud has "had to pay for having permitted the
psychoanalytic group to win over discourse, becoming a
church" (*T*, p. 130). The Cause freudienne is created.
12–15 July Lacan presides at the first International Conference
of the Fondation du champ freudien in Caracas.
October Creation of the Ecole de la cause freudienne.

1981   *9 September* Death of Lacan in Paris at the age of eighty, from
complications of cancer of the colon.

1985   Jacques-Alain Miller wins a legal battle confirming his rights as editor of Lacan's *Seminars* and sole literary executor. Twenty years after Lacan's death, France has the highest ratio of psychoanalysts per capita in the world, with some five thousand analysts. There are more than twenty psychoanalytic associations in France, at least fifteen of which are Lacanian in their inspiration.

I

JEAN-MICHEL RABATÉ

Lacan's turn to Freud

Since we are talking about Lacan, therefore about psychoanalysis, I will begin with a personal reminiscence, almost a confession. It could borrow its title from Milan Kundera's novel *The Joke*, for it all started with a silly practical joke. In the fall of 1968, when I was a new student at the Ecole normale supérieure, I overheard friends preparing one of the idiosyncratic pranks that used to be one of the privileges of that French cathedral of learning. They had espied with some nervous envy how the famous psychoanalyst would be driven to the school's entrance to emerge with a beautiful woman on his arm and make his way to the office of Louis Althusser, who was then the Ecole's administrative secretary. By contrast with the nondescript student style of the school, Lacan was known to draw crowds from the city's select quarters, a medley of colorful intellectuals, writers, artists, feminists, radicals, and psychoanalysts. It was easy to rig the speakers connected with his microphone. A tape consisting of animal squeals and pornographic grunts had been rapidly put together. Now was the moment to see how the master and his audience would react to this insolence; not having had time to finish lunch, still clutching an unfinished yogurt pot, I followed the conspirators. We arrived late (our X-rated tape was to be aired close to the end of the seminar) into a crowded room, in which dozens of tape recorders had been set on the first row of tables in front of a little stage. There Lacan was striding and talking to the forest of microphones; behind him was a blackboard on which was written: "The essence of psychoanalytic theory is a discourse without words." Clearly, he was begging for our rude interruption! Precisely as I entered the room, Lacan launched into a disquisition about mustard pots, or to be precise, *the* mustard pot, *l'pot d'moutard'*. His delivery was irregular, forceful, oracular. The first sentences that I managed to jot down despite my postprandial stupor are the following:

> This pot, I called it a mustard pot in order to remark that far from necessarily containing any, it is precisely because it is empty that it takes on its value as a

mustard pot. Namely that it is because the word "mustard" is written on it, while "mustard" means here "must tardy be" [*moult me tarde*], for indeed this pot will have to tarry before it reaches its eternal life as pot, a life that begins only when this pot has a hole. Because it is in this form that throughout the ages we find it in excavation sites when we search tombs for something that will bear witness to us about the state of a civilization.

This sounded deep, Dadaist, and hilarious, and yet no one laughed or even smiled. Here I was, facing an aging performance artist (Lacan was sixty-seven then) whose very garb had something of the cabaret comedian's outfit, with a dandiacal Mao costume, a strange shirt, and the most tortured elocution one could imagine, broken by sighs, wheezes, and sniggers, at times slowing down to a meditative halt, at times speeding up to culminate in a punning one-liner. Curiously, he was being listened to in utmost silence by an audience intent on not missing one word. I had forgotten my own yogurt pot, embarrassingly half-full or half-empty in my hand: it had turned into an urn. I vaguely knew the popular etymology of the word *moutarde*, which was supposed to derive from *que moult me tarde* (attributed to one of the Dukes of Burgundy, as I would verify a few years later when I started teaching in Dijon, a first academic post no doubt programmed by these ominous sentences), but did not know that Lacan came from a dynasty of vinegar makers and that one of their specialties was fine mustard. In the seminar, I had just witnessed a typical series of virtuoso associations taking off from mustard pots to engage with funerary vessels as they characterize entire civilizations. Lacan obliquely quoted Heidegger's meditation on jugs allegorizing the work of art, then climaxed with the Danaids and compared Pan's musical flutes to empty barrels, all this in a few breathtaking sentences. His words circled around in freewheeling thematic glides rendered more startling by a very particular enunciation: it systematically elided mute *e*'s (*e muets*) and thus, in an accent that sounded old-fashioned but full of stage-Parisian *gouaille*, endowed with new echoes homely phrases such as *l'pot d'moutard'*. Much later, I found out that Lacan had punned not only on mustard and vinegar but also on the broader conceptual category of "condiment," a word he would always use with the demonstrative *ce*, thus uttering "ce condiment," a phrase which could be heard as *ce qu'on dit ment*: what one says is lying, we only say lies. Lies and truth passed through the hole in the mustard pot, thanks no doubt to the obscene echo of *con* ("cunt"). By way of the mustard pot, I had been introduced to the devious logic of the signifier.

By the time our little prank came up, I had been captured by the master's voice and was really paying attention to what he was saying: that he still considered himself a Structuralist even if the tide of fashion had started to turn (this was 13 November 1968), that he was busy constructing a model in which Freudian concepts like *Lust* were combined with Marxist concepts like *Mehrwert* (surplus value), so as to produce the new concept of *Mehrlust* or "surplus enjoyment." He hoped that such a concept would account for the social function of symptoms while, of course, indulging in rhyming slang and knotting the *mère verte* (or "green mother," whoever she was) to *Mehrwert*. Thus, when the grunts and groans finally came, no one seemed to be particularly disturbed, Lacan even smiled approvingly as if he had expected such banter as a greeting, if not feared something more offensive. The squeals were quickly switched off and he resumed his talk. Needless to say, the following week, I came on time to the salle Dussane and added my microphone to the others. Little did I know then that I was following a general trend that in a matter of months would bring most of the May 68 generation, all those political baby boomers who had fought their war on the barricades, to Lacanian seminars, reading groups, and couches. Lacan's voice, his exaggerated posturing, his outrageous rhetoric that was not above obscenities or risqué jokes, all this connects him in my mind with the old leader who had been rejected by the young, who after a period of intense doubt had survived the political tempest before deciding it was time to retire. Particularly when seen with the benefit of hindsight, Lacan's life shows many parallels with that of de Gaulle, although his reliance on the "young guard" in the movement he had created means that he may be seen as the anti-de Gaulle of psychoanalysis.

Founders of discursivity

At the second meeting of the seminar, Lacan commented on the political upheaval of the previous spring. Assessing the May "events," he said that what had taken place was a *prise de parole* (speaking out) – even though no Bastille had been "taken." What was at stake when the students "took" the streets was Truth, a truth that might be uttered collectively. But, he insisted, Truth only speaks through the staged prosopopeia of fiction (Lacan would mime this trope by saying "The Truth has said: 'I speak'" on a number of occasions). Because the truth can never be completely accessible, the students of May 68 had wanted to stage a "strike of truth" and expose the way social truth is produced. Lacan remained skeptical and cynical, telling the young audience (he noted that those who were twenty-four understood him better than their elders) that they, too, would soon participate in the reproduction of academic knowledge, knowledge that was fast turning into a commodity. A few meetings later, Lacan saluted the new year with some flourish – as he said, "69" was a much better number than "68" – by calling attention to an article penned by a professor of linguistics, Georges Mounin, who had published in the *Nouvelle revue française* a critical examination of Lacan's own style.

This short essay is worth examining because, despite barbs and snide put-downs from an expert in linguistic theory (on the whole, Lacan is accused of not having understood Saussure's theories), it hit home in some cases. The article, entitled "Some features of Jacques Lacan's style,"[1] justifies its decision to approach Lacan via linguistic and rhetorical analysis by quoting Lacan's equation of "style" with "personality." It seemed therefore legitimate to analyze Lacan's deviations from standard usage and to infer from these a whole method. To describe what had already often been called Lacan's "mannerism," a labyrinthine syntax that its author had preemptively defended as "Gongorism," a poetic manner that would force his readers to be attentive while immersing them in the fluid equivocations of unconscious discourse, Mounin listed a number of oddities in the psychoanalyst's use of vocabulary and syntax. He began with French prepositions like *à, de*, and *pour* that were used quite idiosyncratically: Lacan would systematically replace the usual "because," *parce que* by the ambiguous *de ce que* or, as often, *pour ce que*. For a long time, even after his death, one could immediately spot a Lacanian by a peculiar use of *sauf à* followed by the infinitive instead of *sauf si* followed by a conjugated verb to mean "except if . . . ," and also by the use of the verb *pointer* instead of *désigner* to mean "to point," "to point out," and "to refer to." In his wish to modalize at any cost, Lacan relished syntactic periphrases like *pour autant que* (meaning "in so far as," "in as much as") often reduced to ambiguous phrases like *à ce que* or *de ce que*.

On the whole, Lacan, so Mounin continued, loved nothing more than obscure archaisms, poetic inversions, or unusual turns of phrase borrowed either from German or Latin. Guessing wrongly that these deviations were due to early bilingualism, and naming Mallarmé as an obvious literary model (like Lacan's, Mallarmé's idiosyncratic style owed nothing to a family's bilingualism but a great deal to a lifetime of reading the works of German and English writers), Mounin observed a dramatic increase in the frequency of these circumlocutions; for him, the 1966 preface to *Ecrits* verged on self-parody. Mounin wished to take seriously not only the meaning but the baroque language of one of Lacan's most important and programmatic essays, "The Freudian Thing," subtitled "or the meaning of the return to Freud in psychoanalysis," a highly rhetorical text delivered in Vienna in 1955 and published in 1956. In this lecture, we discover not only a three-page-long speech in which Truth speaks in person but also a highly wrought conclusion finishing on a paragraph that conceals in dense prose a submerged quatrain in classical rhyming alexandrines:

Actéon trop coupable à courre la déesse,
proie où se prend, veneur, l'ombre que tu deviens,
laisse la meute aller sans que ton pas se presse,
Diane à ce qu'ils vaudront reconnaîtra les chiens . . .

(*E*, p. 436)[2]

Mounin's worry seemed justified, even inevitable: was Lacan a frustrated poet, a post-Heideggerian thinker progressing by opaque epigrams, a psychoanalyst wishing to revolutionize a whole field of knowledge, or just a charlatan?

To be honest, Mounin was contrasting what he saw as the excessive theatricality of a fustian style suggesting the image of a hamming buffoon with what he knew of Lacan's personal openness, professional rigor, and availability. Such a style was above all meant to provoke and thus forced commentators to be as excessive as the persona they saw looming behind. In Mounin's outline, the flaunting of style as style underpinned a program summed up by three main claims: a claim to science, since Lacan was transforming Freud's thinking into an algebraic system (Mounin wondered whether mathematical or logical models were only metaphors); a claim to philosophy, whether post-Hegelian or neo-Marxist – Mounin pointed to the recurrent but inconsistent use of the term "dialectic"; and a claim to a new systemic rigor in the discourse of psychoanalysis thanks to the importation of the main concepts of linguistics – and this was what Mounin, anxious about his own field, lambasted. Not only had Lacan misunderstood Saussure's concept of the sign, but he unduly privileged the signifier and collapsed it with the symptom through what Mounin thought was a submerged pun on "significant" (any symptom was thought to be *significatif,* hence *signifiant*). Mounin showed how late Lacan had come to structuralist linguistics, only to embrace it with the blind fervor of a neophyte who distorts what he has not assimilated fully. The Parthian shaft came at the end when Mounin deplored the fact that Lacan's influence on young philosophers of the Ecole normale supérieure had been condoned or encouraged by their institution. According to him, because of Lacan's undue prestige, ten or fifteen years of solid foundational research in linguistics had been wasted. The last remark was to have repercussions, for indeed, at the end of the spring of 1969, Lacan's seminar was canceled. Flacelière, the new director of the Ecole normale supérieure, had declared him *persona non grata*. The last session of the seminar was devoted to scathing political remarks denouncing the director's double game, which led to a chaotic sit-in in his office, a fitting emblem of Lacan's conflicted relations with almost all official institutions. Lacan, following more in the steps of Chairman Mao, who repeatedly used the younger generations as a weapon against the old guard, than in those of de Gaulle, who had haughtily dismissed France as ungovernable, was no doubt starting his own cultural revolution.

Lacan's revolution was waged more in the name of Freud than of Marx, however, although Lacan strove for a while to reach a synthesis of Marx and Freud after he trumpeted his "return to Freud" at the beginning of the 1950s. Typically, when he mentioned Mounin's essay in public, Lacan did not try to defend or explain himself. He jokingly reminisced that he had started his career by writing about the problem of style[3] and should re-read his own text to be enlightened. He dismissed the whole article and kept his equanimity; however, there was one remark that hit a raw nerve. Mounin wrote: "Let us savor the tranquil Bretonian majesty [*la majesté tranquillement bretonnienne*, referring to André Breton] with which Lacan says: Freud and I" (*SJL*, p. 87). There he was not quoting Lacan but summing up the gist of a page of "Science and Truth" in *Ecrits*, a theoretical tract read to the same students – no doubt the source of Mounin's critical remark about Lacan's negative influence on the *normaliens*, the students of the Ecole normale supérieure. In his text, Lacan sounds even more pretentious: he not only claims that he alone "tells the truth about Freud, who lets truth speak under the name of the unconscious," but adds his name just after that of Freud as those of the true founders of psychoanalysis: "But there is no other truth about the truth on this most vivid point than proper names, the name of Freud or mine . . ." (*E*, p. 868). Mounin had been rather sarcastic when he was inciting his readers to open *Ecrits* and see in a passage taken out of its context another symptom of Lacan's indurate grandiosity.

Lacan debunked Mounin's reproach as coming from an envious rival, someone who would object: "Well, that guy doesn't take himself for no-body!" Then he wondered why Mounin, who had confessed in the article that he did not understand Freud or care for him in the least, should show such an exaggerated respect for the founder of psychoanalysis. To convey his point more strongly, Lacan quoted a story he had narrated earlier, during the first seminar he had given at the Ecole normale supérieure in March 1964, the famous anecdote of the tin can floating on water. In 1964, Lacan had engaged in a digression about the difference between the eye and the gaze, a new conceptual couple that had been suggested to him by the publication of Merleau-Ponty's posthumous book, *The Visible and the Invisible*. To provide a personal illustration, he evoked a vignette, the story of an outing in a boat when, as a young man, he had accompanied a group of fishermen. One of them pointed to an empty sardine can floating in the water, glittering in the sun. Then he said to Lacan, "You see that can? Do you see it? Well, it doesn't see you!" and burst out laughing (*S XI*, p. 95). Lacan, quite aware that the fisherman's jibe implied that he, the bourgeois tourist, was the odd man out among a group of active workers, added that, to be more precise, even if the can did not see him (*voir*), it was in fact gazing at him (*regarder*) all the time. The sardine can condensed the light without which we cannot see anything, while allegorizing the idea of an Other gaze looking at us when, because we just see objects in our field of perception, we do not pay attention to the gaze that frames them and us from outside.

In January 1969, by a bold reworking of the allegory, the sardine can encapsulated Freud's gaze, for Lacan offered the following as a retort to Mounin: "The relation between this anecdote and 'Freud and I' leaves the question open of where I place myself in this couple. Well then be reassured, I place myself always in the same place, in the place where I was, and where I still remain, alive. Freud does not need to see me (*me voir*) in order to gaze at me (*me regarder*)."[4] Lacan was not simply asserting that Freud was dead while he was alive, which would have been an inelegant triviality. "Alive" in this context implies keeping something alive within a tradition that is in danger of becoming mummified. It is against this risk that Lacan constantly evoked the living "experience" of psychoanalysis. And what is it that is being kept alive? Speech, language, the medium without which psychoanalysis does not exist, a medium that has to be understood by splicing together Freud's insights and those of linguistics. Being alive in a world whose epistemologies have changed, Lacan "sees" new things by elaborating new concepts like *objet a* (this is the object as defined by psychoanalysis, as in "object of fantasy" or "object of desire"). However, this could only succeed if one acknowledged that the field had been opened by another whose gaze and signature should not be elided. The name of an Other who had, above all, written texts is the name of an Author to whom Lacan vowed to return constantly but not slavishly. He could see and speak truly because Freud was still "regarding" him.

A month and half later, a different event in Paris allowed Lacan to probe deeper his link to Freud. On 22 February 1969, Michel Foucault gave his influential lecture "What is an Author?" at the Collège de France. Lacan heard it with interest and took part in the general debate that followed. He then referred to it at some length in his seminar four days later. In a typical burst of *que* and *de*, Lacan evoked his *Seminar on Ethics*, a seminar whose publication he had considered although it was postponed until after his death. In his talk, Lacan quoted phrases used by Foucault, such as "the Freud event" and "the Author function,"[5] as he summed up his discussion with the philosopher. Such terms derive from Foucault's masterful mapping of authority. Foucault was trying to distinguish his position, a position rather close to new historicism, from that of critics like Roland Barthes, who had argued in

1968 that authors were "dead" since they only played the part of bourgeois owners of meaning. Without acknowledging any individual author's right to the ownership of meaning, Foucault explains that it is necessary for certain names to serve as points of reference, thus defining the Author function, particularly when dealing with "inventors of discursivity" or "initiators of discursive practices," among whom Freud and Marx figure preeminently.[6] Foucault, who as early as 1962 evinced some familiarity with Lacan's theses,[7] is clearly alluding to Lacan when he states that it is "inevitable that practitioners of such discourses must 'return to the origin' " (*LCP*, p. 134). Foucault explains that recourse to foundational texts does not simply indicate inadequacies or gaps but transforms the discursive practice governing a whole field: "A study of Galileo's works could alter our knowledge of the history, but not the science, of mechanics; whereas a re-examination of the books of Freud or Marx can transform our understanding of psychoanalysis or Marxism" (*LCP*, pp. 137–8). In his seminar, Lacan states with some pride that "no individual alive today has contributed more than I to the idea of the 'return to,' particularly in the context of Freud."[8] However, he does not engage with an argument made more trenchant by Foucault's keen epistemological assessment: if Marxism and psychoanalysis do not have the status of hard sciences, it is because they are still in debt to the texts of a founder, a founder who left a legacy of future strategies that are both marked by future resemblances and future differences:

> They [Marx and Freud] cleared a space for the introduction of elements other than their own, which, nevertheless, remain within the field of discourse they initiated. In saying that Freud founded psychoanalysis, we do not simply mean that the concept of libido or the technique of dream analysis reappear in the writings of Karl Abrahams or Melanie Klein, but that he made possible a certain number of differences with respect to his books, concepts, and hypotheses, which all arise out of psychoanalytic discourse. (*LCP*, p. 132)

Unlike scientific inventors, the "founders of discursivity" cannot be accused of error – Foucault even writes that "there are no 'false' statements in the work of these initiators" (*LCP*, p. 134) – but precisely for this reason their theories demand a constant reactivation; they are productive because of the many "constructive omissions" that demand endless returns to the origin. Such an origin is not defined by truth procedures or verification; on the contrary it is porous, full of gaps and holes: the return "is always a return to a text in itself; specifically, to a primary and unadorned text with particular attention to those things registered in the interstices of the text, its gaps and absences. We return to those empty spaces that have been masked by omission or concealed in a false and misleading plenitude" (*LCP*, p. 135).

Foucault makes it clear that the "return to" does not entail respectful imitation but a type of reading that is also a rewriting. Much as Althusser was wondering how one could read Marx "symptomatically," that is, by separating what is really "Marxist" and what is merely "Hegelian" in his writings, Lacan wonders where and how Freud may be said to be properly "Freudian." The issue is thus not that of a greater or lesser fidelity to Freud. It is the critical diagnosis of a loss of vitality, a weakening of the original "cutting edge" of a discourse and practice. Thus it is no surprise to see Lacan comment on his own return to Freud in the recapitulative introduction he wrote for a number of early texts on psychoanalysis in the 1966 edition of *Ecrits* by saying that this meant his taking Freud "against the grain" or "in reverse": "an inverted reawakening [*reprise par l'envers*] of the Freudian project characterized our own" (*E*, p. 68). This is to be found in "Of our antecedents," a preface to canonical Lacanian texts such as "The mirror stage." Some ten years earlier, when presenting Freud's work to a Viennese audience in the essay on "The Freudian Thing" quoted above, Lacan complains about the failure of Austria to honor the revolutionary discoverer of psychoanalysis. Given the betrayal of the founder by his own disciples, any "return to" will have to function as a "reversal": he denounces a "psychoanalytical movement in which things have reached such a state that the *mot d'ordre* of a return to Freud means a reversal."[9] This is what the back cover of *Ecrits* dramatizes as a drawn-out struggle between "obscurantism" or "prejudice" and a new "dawn" or "enlightenment": "No surprise, then, that one should resist, still now, Freud's discovery – a phrase that can be extended by amphibology: the discovery of Freud by Jacques Lacan." What this suggests is that the exploitation of the ambiguity between a subjective and an objective genitive leads to the redoubling of Foucault's paradox: if there has been a Freudian discovery, it has been forgotten, and one needs the rediscovery of the discovery; thus Lacan is not simply pointing to Freud as too soon forgotten by the International Association of Psychoanalysts (whose faulty memory is an equivalent of the murder of the father). If we want to understand Freud's discovery we must grasp how the discovery of the unconscious, of the signifier, of an Other place for desire could have been rediscovered by Jacques Lacan.

Freud's discovery by Lacan

Unlike Freud, Lacan was never a self-conscious "author," although like Freud he knew the difference between "a book by ..." and "a book from ..." an author. In a passage of *The Interpretation of Dreams*, Freud mentions a fragment of a dream he had forgotten. In that fragment, Freud spoke in English, saying of one of Schiller's works, "*It is from . . . ,*" then noticing the mistake and correcting it to: "*It is by* . . ." (*SE* 5, p. 456 and p. 519). This dream of books, travels, and defecation (Freud links texts with titles such as Clerk-Maxwell's *Matter and Motion* with literary glory but also anal excretion) called the "Hollthurn dream" is analyzed in two passages of *The Interpretation of Dreams*, and shows how crucial the publication of books and their related claims to authority were for Freud. In another dream, Freud mentions lending a novel by Rider Haggard to a female friend who wants to read some of Freud's books instead. He replies simply: ". . . my own immortal works have not yet been written" (*SE*, 5, p. 453). That same dream had presented the rather horrific picture of his lower body open by dissection and showing tangled viscera but also silver paper, containing, as he explains, an allusion to a book on the nervous system of fishes (a topic that had interested Freud before his psychoanalytic discoveries). Freud's imaginary body was partly made up of books, and his discovery of psychoanalysis via dreams and hysteria was based upon a process of self-analysis that required writing as a technique and medium. Besides, we know that he would often tell his patients about his latest findings and urge them to read his papers as they appeared. Whereas we see Freud engaged quite early in the rigorous writing schedule he observed throughout his life even when his fame brought more patients, Lacan always boasted of his teaching and the interactive space of his seminar while dismissing his "writings" as being just that: matter, anal writing – what he repeatedly called *poubellification* (garbage-publishing) for "publication." Later, he would often quote Joyce's pun in *Finnegans Wake* on *letter* and *litter*, even using it as a starting point for a meditation on writing.[10] If Lacan's writings are now available in two dense collections, *Ecrits* and *Autres écrits*, totaling some fifteen hundred pages, the seminars make up a larger but more problematic sequence of oral texts partly edited or rewritten. Besides, the kind of interactive performance I have described makes it impossible to produce a definitive version of these seminars. What stands out is that in both his writings and his seminars, Lacan's style, even when it does not consciously mimic an oral delivery, keeps a strong flavor of oratory. In his Viennese talk, "The Freudian Thing," Lacan suggests that his writings condense the gist of his doctrine while the seminars present a continuous commentary on Freud. This view turned out to be misleading for, after 1964 and the move to the Ecole normale supérieure, the seminars moved on from Freud and began to probe and develop Lacan's own concepts. Thus "The Freudian Thing" lauds Freud:

> Will I surprise you if I tell you that these texts, to which for the past four years I have devoted a two-hour seminar every Wednesday from November to July, without having covered more than a quarter of the total, if indeed

my commentary presupposes their totality, have given me and those who have attended the seminars the surprise afforded only by genuine discoveries? Discoveries ranging from concepts that have remained unused to clinical details uncovered by our exploration that prove how far the field investigated by Freud extended beyond the avenues that he left us to tend, and how his observations, which at times suggest exhaustiveness, were never enslaved to what he wanted to demonstrate.   (E/S, pp. 116–17)[11]

But in what precisely does Freud's discovery consist? If we go back to two texts already quoted, it is clear that Lacan is never reluctant to give his version of the discovery, although his definition varies hugely. On the back cover of the 1966 *Ecrits*, we read that Freud's discovery was that "the unconscious is determined by pure logic, in other words by the signifier." Eleven years earlier, in "The Freudian Thing," a no less memorable statement is provided: "One took to repeating after Freud the word of his discovery: it speaks [*ça parle*], and, no doubt, where it was least expected, namely, where there is pain [*là où ça souffre*]" (E/S, p. 125).[12] An important decade has elapsed, a decade that produced a shift in Lacan, who moved from the pathos of the suffering subject of the unconscious (albeit in a neutral mode, since one may wonder whether it is "it speaks" or "the id speaks") to a logical or linguistic mode of apprehension via the signifier.

Thus it would be wrong to believe that Lacan's discourse in his seminars restricts itself to close readings of Freud's texts, even if most of them, at least in the first decade, do just that, and very well,[13] before boldly exploring the new avenues he mentions – but the gesture is less that of modesty than a wish to be a founder above all, that is, a founder re-discovering the Freudian truth, and much less an author. This is why Lacan constantly foregrounds a practical dimension in his doctrine and always refers to an "analytic experience" that must be taken as the sole foundation for this type of discourse. Such an experience of language, of possible healing by words and silence, locking in a curious duo two persons, each of whom projects ghosts of many others and of the Other, often leaves a simple alternative: either to stress purely clinical issues, or to focus on the politics of new institutions. This does not mean that theory is left lagging behind: all of this is done in the name of theory.

Once more, it was Althusser who perceived keenly the underlying unity of what Lacan had been doing for some time. His position on Lacan had been a mixture of personal resistance to a man he saw captivated by effects of power and seduction, and fascination for a theoretical effort that was never produced in the voids of pure ideas but on the contrary was buttressed by concrete political gestures like foundations, exclusions, dissolutions. In an illuminating letter to René Diatkine, who had expressed personal reservations against Lacan, Althusser stressed Lacan's historical role: "Lacan's claim and his unique originality in the world of psychoanalysis lie in his being a *theoretician*. Being a theoretician . . . means producing a *general system* of the theoretical concepts, rigorously articulated with each other and capable of accounting for the *total set* of facts and of the field of analytic practice."[14]

When did Lacan become a theoretician, then? Probably as early as 1932 with a thesis that not only flaunted philosophy by quoting Spinoza in Latin in an epigraph culled from *The Ethics* ("Therefore desire in one individual differs from desire in another individual only in so far as the nature or essence of the one differs from the nature or essence of the other"[15]) but also offered a "dogmatic" solution to age-old dilemmas: the third part of the thesis on paranoia presents "dogmatic conclusions" (*PP*, p. 346–9) and dismisses facts that are not based upon a theory ("It is the postulate that creates science and the doctrine facts" [*PP*, p. 308, n. 1]), while praising psychoanalytic knowledge for having discovered the "laws" that determine the links between subjective and objective phenomena (*PP*, p. 248). Lacan not only stood out among his immediate contemporaries and colleagues in psychiatry as a philosopher who could read Greek and German fluently and who put to good use his knowledge of the classics, but also as someone who had the nerve and the ambition to "re-found" a whole field. In that context, one should not forget that Lacan came to Freudian psychoanalysis via French psychiatry even if his doctoral thesis, *Of Paranoid Psychosis in Its Connection with Personality*, does not hesitate to criticize the then dominant psychiatric discourse in France, from Babinski's "pithiatism" (a term that he intended to replace "hysteria") to Janet's notion of automatism. Lacan's thesis undertakes a major shift from French psychiatry to Freudian psychoanalysis, and it is worth taking a closer look at this, his first published book. The thesis has been denigrated as belonging to a pre-Lacanian Lacan, much in the same way as Freud's pre-psychoanalytic works on aphasia, cocaine, and eels are still not included in the *Standard Edition*. Even if it has received some critical attention,[16] it has not been translated into English yet. It nevertheless presents a foundational moment for Lacan's oeuvre despite a few crucial hesitations.

What makes this work distinctive is not simply the rich methodology or the culture deployed but the fact that the central part of the thesis reads like a novel. It rests on a systematic exploration of one case of paranoia. When the woman he called Aimée (quoting a character from one of her novels) was brought to Lacan's attention in June 1931, it was after a dramatic incident: on 10 April 1931, she had attempted to stab a theatrical actress. The actress was wounded in the hand but did not press charges, as her attacker was clearly insane. Two months later she was brought to Lacan's care at Sainte-Anne and he confirmed the previous diagnosis of paranoid psychosis. After having worked intensively with her for about a year, he refined the diagnosis, downplayed the elements of erotomania and persecution and stressed the "auto-punitive" structure (and to do so, he needed Freud's concepts). Before the crisis, Aimée's erotomaniac delusions had focused on two male figures, the Prince of Wales and Pierre Benoit, a popular novelist, but the latter infatuation was soon directed at the novelist's mistress, the very visible actress Huguette Duflos, who had become a dangerous alter ego for Aimée. Aimée was also a frustrated self-taught writer, whose beautiful texts were confiscated and then amply quoted by Lacan. The two novels Aimée had written in a frenzy of inspiration in the months preceding her assault are summed up and partly transcribed. Lacan provides a diagnosis of a particular type of delirium based partly upon a written archive and his insight into the structure of a personality. What is then a "personality"?

Lacan uses the term "personality" rigorously and criticizes approaches to what he calls a "psychological personality" (*PP*, p. 31). For him, personality must be approached on three levels: as a biographical development (he needed to reconstruct Aimée's story); as the conception one has of oneself, a reflexive measure that is "dialectical" and can be gauged in dialogue, eventually modified and acted on; and finally as a "tension" between social values implying an ethical participation (*PP*, p. 42). Personality implies a dynamic dialogue between social determinations, personal fate, and reflexive revisions. Before giving his definition, Lacan reviews the theories of personality from traditional metaphysics to scientific psychology and then clearly opts for a phenomenological approach: the philosophical references in the thesis (beyond the debt to Spinoza) are mostly to Scheler, Husserl, and Jaspers. He uses "intentionality" not as an intuitive capture of subjective intentions but as a focus on a subject defined as a speaking being: "But one still has to explain the *phenomenological* existence of these intentional functions, like the fact that the subject says 'I,' believes he acts, promises, asserts" (*PP*, p. 39). A footnote mentions the derivation from the Latin *persona*, the mask with a hole to let the voice of the actor resound: even if philologists are divided on this point, Lacan approves "the significant intention" of the etymology (*PP*, p. 34, n. 6). This insight will not be lost, even after the turn to Structuralism. In a long theoretical essay criticizing Daniel Lagache (he read Lagache's work in 1958, wrote the essay in 1960, and published it in 1961), Lacan attacks the latter's "personalism" and fusion of psychology and psychoanalysis. He writes: "We can say that with the *per-sona* the person begins, but what of the personality? Here an ethics announces itself, hushed into silence not by fear but by desire: the whole question is to know whether the way through babble of psychoanalytic experience will lead us there." (E, p. 684).

Because it forces us to consider issues of social relations and ethics, "personality" cannot be reduced to a vague equivalent of the "self" or the "ego." Precisely because of this dangerous proximity, Lacan has to distinguish personality from the "ideal image of the ego" – and this is where Freud comes into play for the first time when a footnote refers to "Freudian theories" that have pointed out the partly unconscious mechanisms presiding over the constitution of this image and its links with affective identification (PP, p. 39, n. 18). A second footnote sends us to Freud's Das Ich und das Es (1923) when invoking the clash between the Ich and Über-Ich (both left in German). What is remarkable here is Lacan's prudence in refusing to translate hastily Ich as "ego" ("id" was then translated into French as soi, a usage adhered to in the thesis). In addition, Lacan refuses to moralize personality, just wonders what we mean when we say that so-and-so has "personality" (PP, p. 41): the term suggests moral autonomy or a sense that a person can make promises that will be held. Often though, under the promises and suggestions of moral autonomy, we discover resistances that arise to oppose a limit to the encroachments of reality (PP, p. 41). What is presented as a "phenomenological" analysis of personality in the first part appears in the synthetic third part of the thesis as a thoroughly Freudian theory of the subject, even if the subject or je is not yet opposed to the ego. In the last part, Lacan explains that he had been using Freudian categories all along, especially when he was talking of resistance, even if he notes that most moralists, from La Rochefoucauld to Nietzsche, had described this mechanism before (PP, p. 320). In fact, what he needs above all is Freud's notion of the super-ego.

The last and synthetic part of the thesis makes it clear that Lacan's intention is not to complement Freudian psychoanalysis, which has stayed cautiously within the confines of treatment of neurotics, with a bolder approach to psychosis: his aim is to use what he has learned from the treatment of psychosis to redefine Freud's topological model of the subject, a model articulating the id, the ego, and the super-ego. Lacan limits his direct borrowings from psychoanalytic doctrine to two "dogmatic postulates": first, that there is a strict overlapping between genesis and structure in personality; second, that there is a common yardstick by which we can measure the various features composing personality, and which is found in psychic energy, or libido (PP, p. 320). These postulates are instrumental in criticizing theories of psychosis based upon a doctrine of innate "constitutions" – as Lacan adds, the only issue that remains in such doctrines is to know when to lock up the patient! (PP, p. 308). This is why he can state his reliance on "historical materialism"

(*PP*, p. 309 n. 2), for it is at the social level that the approach to a structure like the difference between neurosis and psychosis and the deluded "idealism" of each person's self-reflection can cohere (*PP*, p. 314). The "science of personality" combines the intentionality of phenomenology and an account of social forces as they are replayed in the psyche. Aimée is a good example of this social determination: she chose an actress for her crazy attack because she had been caught up in the phenomenon of the "star" (*la vedette*) which provides, as Lacan glosses, a modern form of social participation (*PP*, pp. 317–18). Aimée was an uprooted woman of peasant extraction who had polarized on this fascinating image all her ideals and all her hatred. The actress embodied her *Ich-Ideal*, Freud's expression with which Lacan will grapple for decades. In the thesis he expresses his dissatisfaction with the Freudian notion of a "narcissistic fixation" often adduced to account for psychosis; he asks: "Is narcissistic *libido* produced by the Ego or the Id?" (*PP*, p. 321). He queries Freud's hesitations about the exact status of the *Ich*: is the ego purely identified with the function of perceptive consciousness, the *Wahrnehmungsbewusstsein*, or it is "partly unconscious" (*PP*, p. 322)? After having quoted Fenichel, Abraham, and Freud, he concludes this survey on a skeptical note: "In fact, narcissism appears in the economy of psychoanalytic doctrine as a *terra incognita* whose borders have been delimited by investigations born from the study of neuroses but whose interior remains mythical and unknown" (*PP*, p. 322). This maps out the terrain that Lacan would keep on exploring over the next decade via the mirror stage.

Was Freud more timid in accounting for the social factors of his patients' neuroses? Lacan hints that this is the case, and his diagnosis of a psychosis of self-punishment for Aimée culminates with the global category of the "psychoses of the super-ego." Thus Aimée's case ties together three levels, the intentional level rife with the subject's personal tensions, the structural level determined by the function of the ideal of the ego and the super-ego, and the social level with a dialectic of social alienation and desired ethical participation. And finally it is desire that provides a key to the totality of Aimée's personality (*PP*, p. 311). Because of the determining factor of desire, personality cannot be reduced to the "ego," whether as a philosophical or a psychoanalytical concept. But Lacan too seems to hesitate, for in the conclusion to the discussion of Aimée (perhaps in view of all the personal details amassed) he writes that the best approach to the case is via the patient's resistances and that a "psychoanalysis of the ego" is sounder than a "psychoanalysis of the unconscious" (*PP*, p. 280). This sounds like the dominant Freudian orthodoxy that Lacan would attack in the fifties. However, this was not just a distortion introduced by Freud's followers; in a late essay like "An outline of psychoanalysis" (1938), Freud had written typically: "The analytical physician and the weakened ego of the patient, basing themselves upon the real external world, are to combine against the enemies, the instinctual demands of the id and the moral demands of the consciousness of the super-ego" (*SE* 23, p. 173). In the synthetic part of the thesis, however, Lacan stressed both the sadistic function of the super-ego and the fact that the term "personality" allowed him to overcome the individual ego. The "new science" of personality was condensed as "the development of man's intentional functions linked to tensions that are proper to social relations" (*PP*, p. 328). In fact, all these tensions, intentions, and relations pave the way for the realm of what Lacan would start calling the "symbolic system" of culture in the fifties.

In spite of the classical transparency of its language, Lacan's thesis offers some difficulties. It is packed with questions, questions that aim at expanding the Freudian field concerning paranoia and leading to a more precise description of the structure of subjectivity. After the thesis, Lacan continued the discussion of Freudian concepts. As early as 1936, we find an article entitled with some bravura "Beyond the 'reality principle.'" Its sub-title is revealing: "Around this fundamental principle of Freud's doctrine, the second generation of his school can define its debt and its task" (*E*, p. 73). There Lacan opposes the concern for truth (evinced by philosophy) and the concern for reality. A phenomenological stance still dominates, but this time phenomenology yields a different insight: Freud's reverence for reality as a principle leads to the awareness that psychoanalysis only works with language. "The given of this experience is first of all language, a language, that is to say a sign" (*E*, 82). Much later, Mounin will quote this equation ironically, hinting that Lacan did not know much about linguistics. But we are in 1936, and what matters is how he stresses two important notions, all the more important as they are linked: the impact of unconscious knowledge and a concern for language as such.

As Lacan reminisced in "Of our antecedents," the lesson of this conceptual knot was conveyed to him once and for all by Aimée. By "clinical exhaustion," systematically and exhaustively examining one single case, he had reached a "paranoid knowledge" that finally forced him to take creativity into account: "For fidelity to the formal envelope of the symptom – the only true clinical trace we may acknowledge – led us to this limit which turns into pure creativity. In the case of our thesis (the Aimée case), these were literary effects, and with enough merit to have been quoted by Eluard under the (reverential) heading of involuntary poetry."[17] Thus one might say that "Aimée" played for Lacan the role Nadja had played for Breton or Anna O. for Freud and Breuer: a figure of inspiration, a brilliant failure despite extraordinary artistic and linguistic gifts, and finally an allegory of femininity granting access, without any need of "theory," to a different truth concerning the unconscious. This is why we need to explore once more Lacan's not so tranquil "Bretonian majesty" when he speaks of "Freud and I."

Lacan's paranoid modernity

Mounin's remark about Lacan's "Bretonian" majesty contains an element of truth, less because it denounces Lacan's arrogance or delusion of grandeur than because Breton's notoriously ambivalent attitude to Freud was repeated by the French psychoanalyst some ten years later. Breton had launched Surrealism as a quasi-Freudian movement that trusted the spontaneous dictation of the unconscious, but when, in October 1921, he paid a visit to Freud that should have been a reverent pilgrimage, he was severely disappointed by the meeting. "Interview with Professor Freud" (1922) describes Freud pitilessly as "an old man without elegance" whose shabby consulting room is worthy of an impoverished local generalist. The Viennese MD stubbornly refuses to engage in meaningful dialogue and hides behind polite generalities. He concludes tongue-in-cheek by quoting Freud's tepid endorsement: "Happily, we do count a lot upon the young."[18] This painful sense of a discrepancy between Freud the man and Freudian ideas, or between the inventor of psychoanalysis caught in all his human and social limitations and the empowering invention of psychoanalysis itself was to mark the attitude of the French intelligentsia in the following years.

Thus Breton's second *Manifesto of Surrealism* (December 1929) quotes Freud rather distantly and with critical asides about the term of "sublimation," while reasserting that a dose of dialectical materialism would do wonders for Freud. As we have noted, in his thesis Lacan had saluted dialectical materialism as a way of avoiding both spiritualism and "mechanistic materialism" or any behaviorism (*PP*, p. 309, n. 2). Moreover, for Breton, Freud was suspected of lending arguments to what he saw as Georges Bataille's "non-dialectical" materialism. In this ideological conflict, Dalí's theory of paranoia emerged as a new watershed in Surrealist groups. Dalí had been the object of a tug of war between Bataille and Breton; Bataille initially took to Dalí and wrote a passionate article on the 1929 painting called "The Lugubrious Game." In his commentary, Bataille interpreted the painting as representing castration and emasculation; he saw a sign of this in the way one male figure is portrayed in breeches stained with excrement. Immediately Dalí refused permission to reproduce the painting, and then attacked Bataille in "The rotting donkey" (July 1930) for his "senile" ideas. As Dalí wrote, Bataille's mistake derived from an incorrect interpretation of Freud, a "gratuitous use of modern psychology."[19] All this brought grist to the mill of what appeared as Dalí's object, the definition of his paranoid-critical method. Aligning himself with Breton's Second Manifesto, Dalí explained that next to going into the street with a revolver and shooting people at random (as Breton said, this was the purest Surrealist act), his proselytizing activity aimed at propagating the "violently paranoid will to systematize confusion" (OU, p. 110). Anticipating Lacan, Dalí adds that since Freudian ideas have been watered down he means to use paranoia to give them back their "rabid and dazzling clarity." He then launches into a description of the method he has devised to see reality differently, a method that took its bearings in paranoia:

> The particular perspicacity of attention in the paranoiac state must be insisted upon; paranoia being recognized, moreover, by all psychologists as a form of mental illness which consists in organizing reality in such a way as to utilize it to control an imaginative construction . . . Recently, through a decidedly paranoiac process, I obtained an image of a woman whose position, shadow and morphology, without altering or deforming anything of her real appearance, are also, at the same time, those of a horse.   (OU, p. 112)

This passage leads to a new method for the avant-garde and provides a new foundation for Rimbaud's program of a "systematic deregulating of all senses" leading to the automatic production of spontaneous hallucination and the multiplication of delirious sign-systems. In "The rotting donkey," Dalí pushes his thesis further by collapsing conventional systems of representation and paranoid delirium. The woman who is at the same time a horse and a lion forces us to conclude that "our images of reality themselves depend upon the degree of our paranoid faculty" (OU, pp. 116–17). If paranoia opens a door into other kinds of visual perception, it also turns into a principle that replaces any idea of the material world by simple hallucination – a view leading to Lacan's later distinction between reality and the real. Here reality is just a type of simulacrum. This might be why Dalí had chosen Breton's rather than Bataille's camp. Both criticize Freud's dualism while rewriting his insights in a monist discourse stressing either the materiality of the body leading to excess, waste, and excrement (Bataille), or a series of simulacra underpinned by a universal and productive desire (Breton). Bataille appears stuck in "vulgar materialism" while Breton tends to stress the creative imagination. In this context, Lacan's relationships with Bataille and Breton appear loaded with transference and counter-transference, from his marriage to Bataille's estranged wife, Sylvia, up to a much later stress on jouissance, a notion that translates Bataille's concepts of waste, expenditure, erotic excess, and trangression.

Dalí's ideas gave a jolt to Lacan, who chanced upon them just as he was working on his doctoral dissertation. Elisabeth Roudinesco thinks that it was the impact of Dalí's "The rotting donkey" that allowed Lacan to break with classical psychiatric theories and revisit Freudian meta-psychology with a new agenda.[20] Indeed, at the time of his thesis, Lacan was translating Freud's article on "Certain neurotic mechanisms in jealousy, paranoia and homosexuality," a text in which Freud restates the theory underlying his main analysis of paranoia, that is the Schreber case: for him, the creation of a paranoid system of delusions aims at allowing the return of a repressed homosexuality. Freud mentions a case of jealous delirium in a heterosexual patient, noting how delusional attacks would follow successful sexual relations in the couple; by inventing imaginary male lovers and creating delirious recriminations, the husband projected his own desire for men. This theory is clearly not the route followed by either Dalí or Lacan in the early thirties. Lacan already relied on an analysis of the signifer. It was also at that time that he co-authored "Inspired writings" (1931), an essay analyzing the psychotic ramblings of a young teacher who had been hospitalized at Sainte-Anne. The stylistic analysis of the grammar of mad utterances acknowledges Surrealism. The authors quote Breton's first *Manifesto of Surrealism* and look for a model of interpretation in Breton's and Eluard's imitations of different types of delirium in *The Immaculate Conception* (1930).[21]

Thus, quite logically, the Surrealists were the first to greet the thesis with exuberant praise: Crevel's 1933 "Notes toward a psycho-dialectic"[22] expressed the hope that Lacan's work would provide a new foundation for psychoanalysis at a time when Freud appeared reactionary, idealistic, or pusillanimous. It was not only that Lacan dared to treat psychosis but also that his work was firmly grounded in the social world. In spite of himself, Lacan was thus enlisted in the cause of a Surrealist Freudo-Marxism. But as Dalí later insisted,[23] Crevel's suicide in 1935, partly brought about by his inability to reconcile Surrealism, psychoanalysis, and communism, was one of the bad omens that announced the demise of the movement. It may not have helped that Dalí was investing more and more paranoiac activity into fantasies about Hitler on the one hand and high fashion on the other. Conversely, Lacan had already taken some distance from Surrealism and from left-wing politics; he only elaborated his own version of Freudo-Marxism in the late sixties.

If Lacan's theory of paranoia has little to do with Dalí's concept of a beautifully multiple hallucination,[24] it does leave room for artistic creation, since, as we saw, Aimée was a gifted writer looking for recognition from the press and novelists. The Aimée case forced him to make inroads into mirrored doubles and the release of aggression they elicit in paranoids. This would soon provide a bridge to the construction of the alter-ego as a dangerous rival and the need for fabricating delirious paternity systems that resemble the symbolic. Above all, thanks to the convergence of interests between Bataille, Dalí, Breton, Eluard, Crevel, and Lacan, the second decade of Surrealism was dominated by the concept of paranoia exactly as the first had been by automatism and hysteria. Breton's comprehensive memoir *Mad Love* (1937) affirms his belief in desire as the main spring of all our dreams and actions but also leaves room for paranoia. Desire is not just unleashed by hysteria in a distorted pastiche of artistic creation but it is structured like paranoia – that is, it produces knowledge. Close to the end, Breton uses Freud's *A Childhood Memory of Leonardo da Vinci* to expound the principle of paranoiac criticism. Even if the vision of a vulture hidden in the Virgin's dress was only Pfister's hallucination and not the direct product of Freud's meditations, once an interpretation has produced a new image in a previous one, it remains there, hovering between objectivity and subjectivity.[25] What Leonardo had stumbled upon was the "objective chance" in which any artist or person will learn to read the half-erased letters of a text written by desire. Breton continues his musings:

> The purely visual exercise of this faculty which has at times been called "paranoiac" allows us to conclude that if a single spot on a wall or elsewhere will almost always be interpreted differently by different individuals acted upon by distinct desires, this does not imply that one will not manage to make the other see what he has perceived.[26]

Even when Polonius humors Hamlet's feigned madness by agreeing to see a whale in the clouds, his calculated acceptance suggests the possibility of a verbal communication. Breton's view of paranoia is weaker than Lacan's because, unlike Lacan, he does not try to think systematically but magically; he avoids Spinozist "essences" that provide Lacan with a firmer conceptual grid, since these essences are not substances but the relations provided by language. Paranoia creates a system of signs that function as "images" or pure signifiers before being held accountable to so-called objective truth. Thus they betray the creative function of desire that underpins their production. Such a desire can lead to murderous attacks, at times with the objective of putting oneself under the domination of the sadistic super-ego through an expected punishment but also with a view of getting rid of an idealized image of oneself projected in another person.

Lacan's first deliberate critique of Freudian logic came much later with the *Seminar on Hamlet*, but it is based on insights provided by Aimée. Freud's main argument about the Oedipal structure of Hamlet's desire (Hamlet cannot strike his uncle because the uncle has enacted his own incestuous and murderous wish) is not based on a secure foundation, since, after all, Hamlet might want all the more to get rid of such a successful Oedipal rival! What for Lacan accounts for the riddle of the play lies on the side of the impenetrable desire of the mother, or the hidden source of Gertrude's jouissance.[27]

However, desire remains a mythical notion that will contain all tensions and contradictions; like Breton and like Freud, Lacan dreamed of an essential and foundational libido that would be identical with the substance of nature. One can verify this by perusing one of Lacan's earliest texts, a sonnet based upon his reading of Alexandre Koyré's book on Boehme, *La Philosophie de Jacob Boehme* (1929). Lacan's sonnet was written in 1929 under the title "Panta Rhei" and was slightly rewritten for publication in *Le Phare de Neuilly* (1933) as "Hiatus Irrationalis."[28] A paraphrase of Lacan's opening and concluding lines of the final version could be the following: "Things, whether sweat or sap flows in you, / Forms, whether begotten from forge or flood, /Your stream is not denser than my dream, /And if I do not strike you with unceasing desire, // I cross your water and fall to the shore / Brought down by the weight of my thinking genie . . . // But, as soon as all words have died in my throat, / Things, whether begotten from blood or forge, / Nature, – I lose myself in elementary flux: // He who smolders in me, the same lifts you up, / Forms, whether sweat or sap flows in you, / It is the fire that makes me your eternal lover . . ." Beyond echoes of Rimbaud's famous "It is the fire that rises again with its damned soul" (from *Season in Hell*),[29] Lacan posits desire as a universal principle running through nature like a Heraclitean stream and Boehme's fire. However, to reach the *mysterium magnum*, the subject has to be mute: the central lines point to a moment of speechlessness: "But, as soon as all words have died in my throat, / Things, whether begotten from blood or forge, / Nature, – I lose myself in elementary flux . . ." Boehme's mystical discourse foreshadows the function of an absolute Other whose silence lets nature disclose its most hidden secrets.

Lacan's sonnet is contemporary with his first attempts at letting the "insane" or the "psychotic" speak. If he has discovered that everyday language is structured as poetry through the "inspired speech" of raving patients, it is not to say like Freud that he has "succeeded where the paranoiac fails."[30] Freud was referring to the Schreber case, hinting that Freud himself had managed to sublimate his homosexual inclinations (all needed for the elaboration of his system when he was in correspondence and transference with his friend Fliess). Does this apply to Lacan? Did he use Aimée to sublimate his own erotomania and erect in its stead what could be called a theoretical monument of paranoid modernism? In fact, Lacan would probably not say that the paranoiac failed! When Aimée replaces Schreber, she is always right, even when she sees the kingdom of peace as the future realm of the just . . . Lacan's displacement entails a much needed feminization of those who try to write down the discourse of the Other – which is also why Freud's castrating father will yield some ground to Lacan's big Other, mostly embodied by the Mother. Paranoia is always right, especially when it forces us to elaborate a parallel system of thoughts underpinned by desire. Here, Lacan's Freudo-Lacanism reaches its limit. Lacan, one of the first to warn against the duplicity of religious piety for the creed's founder, is ready to rewrite and to contest Freud, in short to fail where the paranoiac succeeds. Hence the added difficulties and the heavier burden of a theoretical legacy: an endless task of re-reading.

NOTES

1. Georges Mounin, "Quelques traits du style de Jacques Lacan," *La Nouvelle revue française* (1 January 1969), pp. 84–92. Hereafter cited in text as *SJL*. The cover of the review mistakenly calls the essay "Quelques extraits du style de Jacques Lacan."
2. I have reproduced the text as poetry, but it is laid out as prose in the original. Sheridan's translation cannot render the mock heroic tone and its deliberate preciosity, which is not above a low pun on "reconnaîtra les siens / les chiens": "Actaeon, too guilty to hunt the goddess, the prey in which is caught, O huntsman, the shadow that you become, let the pack pass by without hastening your step, Diana will recognize the hounds for what they are . . ." (*E/S*, p. 145).
3. Lacan was alluding to his 1933 essay "Le Problème du style et la conception psychiatrique des formes paranoïaques de l'expérience," published in the first issue of *Le Minotaure* (Paris, June 1933) and taken up in *De la psychose paranoïaque dans ses rapports avec la personnalité suivi de Premiers écrits sur la paranoïa* (Paris: Seuil, 1975), pp. 383–8. Hereafter cited in text as *PP*.
4. Personal notes, session of 1 January 1969.
5. Personal notes, session of 26 February 1969.
6. Michel Foucault, "What is an Author?" in *Language, Counter-Memory, Practice*, ed. Donald F. Bouchard, trans. Donald F. Bouchard and Sherry Simon (Ithaca: Cornell University Press, 1977), pp. 113–38. Hereafter cited in text as *LCP*. There is another and markedly different translation based on another version of the essay by Josué V. Harrari in *The Foucault Reader*, ed. Paul Rabinow (New York: Pantheon Books, 1984), pp. 101–20. What Harrari translates as "founders of discursivity" Bouchard and Simon translate as "initiators of discursive practices."
7. See his review of Jean Laplanche's book, *Hölderlin and the Question of the Father*, entitled "The father's no" (*LCP*, especially pp. 81–3). For a comprehensive assessment of the links between Foucault and Lacan, see Christopher Lane, "The experience of the outside: Foucault and psychoanalysis," *Lacan in America*, ed. Jean-Michel Rabaté (New York: The Other Press, 2000), pp. 309–47.
8. Personal notes, session of 26 February 1969.

9. Lacan, *E*, p. 402. Because of an unfortunately interpolated "not," Sheridan's translation says the exact opposite (*E/S*, p. 115).

10. Jacques Lacan, "Lituraterre," *Autres écrits* (Paris: Seuil, 2001), p. 11.

11. Translation modified. For the original, see Lacan, *E*, p. 404.

12. Translation modified. See Lacan, *E*, p. 413.

13. However, a few critics have pointed out some errors and misreadings. See for instance Paul Roazen's "What is wrong with French psychoanalysis? Observations on Lacan's First Seminar," *Lacan in America*, pp. 41–60.

14. Louis Althusser, "Letter to D." (18 July 1966), *Writings on Psychoanalysis: Freud and Lacan*, trans. Jeffrey Mehlman (New York: Columbia University Press, 1996), pp. 48–9.

15. Benedict de Spinoza, *The Ethics*, trans. R. H. M. Elwes (New York: Dover, 1955), p. 170. Lacan concludes his thesis with a translation of the sentence and a generalizing gloss that seems to inscribe the whole work in a Spinozist perspective. See on this issue Elisabeth Roudinesco, *Jacques Lacan & Co.: A History of Psychoanalysis in France 1925–1985*, trans. Jeffrey Mehlman (Chicago: University of Chicago Press, 1990), pp. 52–6.

16. See Jean Allouch's thorough examination in *Marguerite ou l'Aimée de Lacan* (Paris: EPEL, 1990) and Elisabeth Roudinesco's reconstruction of the file in *Jacques Lacan*, trans. Barbara Bray (New York: Columbia University Press, 1997), pp. 31–60.

17. Lacan, *E*, p. 66. Lacan is alluding to Eluard's book called *Poésie involontaire et poésie intentionnelle* (1942), in which he quotes on the left-hand page "involuntary" poetic creations found in newspapers, stray utterances, novels, or texts of psychotic patients. Aimée's passage appears as "quoted by Lacan" without further reference. Her fragments conclude with: "Those who read books are not as dumb as those who write them: they add to them." See Paul Eluard, *Oeuvres complètes*, vol. 1 (Paris: Gallimard, 1968), pp. 1166 and 1168.

18. André Breton, *Les Pas Perdus, Oeuvres complètes*, vol. 1 (Paris: Gallimard, 1988), p. 256.

19. Salvador Dalí, "The rotting donkey," *Oui: The Paranoid-Critical Revolution. Writings 1927–1933*, ed. Robert Descharnes, trans. Yvonne Shafir (Boston: Exact Change, 1998), p. 117. Hereafter cited in text as *OU*. See also the essay by Félix Fanès, "Une toile à destination secrète: Le Jeu lugubre," *Revue des Sciences Humaines: Lire Dalí*, 262 (Lille, 2001), pp. 163–85.

20. See Elisabeth Roudinesco, *Jacques Lacan & Co.*, pp. 110–12 for an account of their meeting.

21. See Jacques Lacan (with J. Lévy-Valensi and P. Migault), "Ecrits 'inspirés': Schizographie" (*PP*, pp. 379–80).

22. René Crevel, "Notes en vue d'une psycho-dialectique," *Le Surréalisme au service de la révolution* 5 (Paris: 15 May 1933), pp. 48–52.

23. See Dalí's foreword to René Crevel's *Difficult Death*, trans. David Rattray (San Francisco: North Point Press, 1986), pp. vii–xiv.

24. See Hanjo Berressem, "Dalí and Lacan: Painting the imaginary landscapes," *Lacan, Politics, Esthetics*, ed. Willy Apollon and Richard Feldstein (Albany: State University of New York Press, 1996), pp. 275–90.

25. André Breton, *L'Amour fou, Oeuvres complètes*, vol. 2 (Paris: Gallimard, 1992), p. 753.

26. Breton, *L'Amour fou*, p. 754.
27. I have developed this point in my *Jacques Lacan, Psychoanalysis and the Subject of Literature* (Houndmills: Palgrave, 2001), pp. 54–68.
28. See the discussion by Annick Allaigre-Duny, "A propos du sonnet de Lacan," *L'Unebévue* 17 (Paris: Spring 2001), pp. 27–48. The two versions are presented side by side. My paraphrase uses single slashes for line endings and double slashes for stanzas. Koyré's elucidation of Boehme's system should be read carefully, as its theory of monism, which may be seen as the reconciliation of all opposites, influenced Lacan's Spinozism (Koyré quotes Boehme's "*In Ja und Nein bestehen alle Dinge*" – All things consist in Yes and No). Fire is the key image of this atonement. See Alexandre Koyré's *Jacob Boehme* (Paris: Vrin, 1929), pp. 393–4.
29. Arthur Rimbaud, *Collected Poems*, trans. Oliver Bernard (London: Penguin, 1986), p. 317, modified.
30. Quoted by Peter Gay, *Freud: A Life for Our Time* (New York: Norton, 1988), p. 275. See also the lively discussion in David Trotter, *Paranoid Modernism: Literary Experiment, Psychosis and the Professionalization of English Society* (Oxford: Oxford University Press, 2001), pp. 51–73.

2

ELISABETH ROUDINESCO

The mirror stage: an obliterated archive

Why speak of the "mirror stage"[1] as an archive that has been obliterated? The reason is both simple and complex. First, there is no existing original of the lecture on this subject delivered by Jacques Lacan at the 16th congress of the International Psychoanalytical Association (IPA), which took place in Marienbad between the second and eighth of August 1936. After he had been speaking for minutes, Lacan was interrupted by Ernest Jones, the chairman, who considered that this French participant, of whom he had never heard, was exceeding the time allotted to each speaker. At this time, the rule regulating the duration of each spoken contribution was already being applied at international conferences. Lacan, who regarded the interruption as a humiliation, quit the conference and went on to the Olympic Games in Berlin to see at close quarters what a sporting event manipulated by the Nazis was like. One might well see some connection between the forceful manner in which Jones interrupted Lacan's talk and Lacan's notorious invention of "variable sessions" marked by radical brevity and a sense of deliberate suspension. All his life, Lacan would struggle with an impossible control over time, as evinced by the masterful analysis presented in his 1945 essay on "logical time."

The Marienbad incident arose out of a serious misunderstanding. In the eyes of the then leaders of the IPA, Lacan was not yet the Lacan known to history, but merely a modest, anonymous clinician belonging to the Société psychanalytique de Paris (SPP), with no claim to any special privileges. In France, on the other hand, Lacan was already recognized in literary circles as an important thinker. He often was put on a par with Henri Ey, whom many saw as the leader of a new school of psychiatry, even though his reputation was not high among psychoanalysts. As for Lacan himself, he already considered himself as important enough to find it intolerable to be treated so dismissively at an IPA congress. As a result, he did not hand in his text for publication in the conference proceedings.

We have nevertheless two records of the August 1936 text. The first is to be found in the notes Françoise Dolto took at a preliminary lecture that Lacan delivered to the SPP on 16 June 1936, notes that are undoubtedly a faithful reflection of the missing August text. The second trace is to be found in the draft of an article by Alexandre Kojève, with whom Lacan was to have collaborated in the summer of 1936. The article did not see the light of day in final form and was never mentioned by Lacan himself, who probably forgot about it. But it is a pointer to the genesis of his later ideas about Descartes' cogito, the subject of desire, and the origin of madness.[2]

These notes should be compared with another text by Lacan that was included in a famous article on the family commissioned by Henri Wallon and published in 1938 in the *Encyclopédie française*. According to Lacan himself, this long article, reprinted in 1985 under the title of "Family complexes," reproduces the content of the 1936 Marienbad lecture.[3] The passage in question occurs in the second part of the article, entitled "The intrusion complex." It is followed by a paragraph on "Jealousy, archetype of social feelings," which has sub-paragraphs bearing on "Mental identification," "The imago of fellow beings," and "The meaning of primal aggression." The paragraph on the mirror stage is divided into two parts: (1) The secondary power of the mirror image; (2) The narcissistic structure of the ego.

As Françoise Dolto's notes show, on that day at Marienbad Lacan expounded not only the "stade du miroir" paragraph that was taken up again later in the *Encyclopédie* but also a large number of the themes developed in the 1938 article. Her notes show that the lecture was divided into nine parts: (1) The subject and the I (*je*); (2) The subject, the I (*je*) and the body; (3) The expressivity of the human form; (4) The libido of the human form; (5) The image of the double and the mirror image; (6) Libido or weaning and the death instinct, Destruction of the vital object, Narcissism; (7) Its link with the fundamental symbolism in human knowledge; (8) The rediscovered object in the Oedipus complex; (9) The values of narcissistic symptoms: twins. All this probably reflects, with a few variants, the paper written by Lacan for the Marienbad congress: a text too long for the IPA authorities, and one neither in the style of Freud nor of Melanie Klein, but influenced by Alexandre Kojève's seminar on Hegel's *Phenomenology of Spirit*.

Lacan's lecture, transcribed by Dolto, is followed by a discussion in which Marie Bonaparte, Daniel Lagache, Georges Parcheminey, Rudolph Loewenstein, René Laforgue, Paul Schiff, and Charles Odier take part. The lecturer then answers them all. The lecture is so obscure that the SPP audience finds it hard to understand what Lacan means. They ask him to define his attitudes more clearly, in particular his view of the relation between weaning and the death impulse, and his conception of the link between the I (*je*), the body and fantasy. Is the I (*je*) one's body? Is fantasy the specular image? Another question asked is: what is the relationship between the I (*je*) and the ego (*moi*), and between the I and the personality?

This raises a major theoretical issue. As is well known, in Freud's works the notion of the subject is not fully conceptualized, even though he does use the term. At this point in time, Lacan is trying to introduce the concept as it has been used in classical philosophy rather than in psychology: the subject is man himself, inasmuch as he is the foundation of his own thoughts and actions. Man is the subject of knowledge and law. Lacan is trying to link not Freud's second topography of the id, the ego, and the super-ego with a theory of the I, but to connect together a philosophical theory of the subject and a theory of the subject of desire derived from Freud and from Hegel via Kojève. From this he will pass to the notion of the subject of the unconscious.

It is from an article published by Henri Wallon in 1931 that Lacan borrows the term of the "mirror stage" (*stade du miroir*).[4] However, Lacan neglects to cite his main source. Wallon's name is not mentioned either in Lacan's lecture or in the bibliography of the *Encyclopédie française*. As I have had occasion to show, Lacan always tried to obliterate Wallon's name so as to present himself as the inventor of the expression. For instance, Françoise Bétourné has found some sixty examples of the use of the term "mirror stage" in Lacan's work. Lacan always insists on the fact that it was he who introduced the term. In his seminar on *L'Acte psychologique* (session of 10 January 1968), he says: "Everyone knows that I entered psychoanalysis with the little brush that was called the 'mirror stage' . . . I turned the 'mirror stage' into a coat rack."[5]

In order to understand what happened in 1936, we need to know that Lacan was then still unacquainted with the work of Melanie Klein, whose theories were as yet little known in France. In the discussion that followed the SPP lecture, no one mentioned her work, concerned though it was with ideas on object relations, weaning, and character formation in infants. In fact, Lacan, in his own way – a "French" way, that is – was providing an interpretation of Freud that ran parallel to Klein's own interpretation of the master at the same period. Lacan's specific reading of Freud arose out of his attendance at Kojève's seminar on *The Phenomenology of Spirit* and follows directly from questions asked in the review *Recherches philosophiques*, of which Kojève was one of the leading lights. Kojève's generation had been marked by the "three H's" of phenomenology, Husserl, Heidegger, and Hegel. This generation was seeking in philosophy a way of apprehending a world that saw the rise of dictatorships, that was haunted by the problems of anxiety, fragmented consciousness, doubts hanging over human progress, and all the forms of nihilism deriving from the fear that history might be coming to an end. Lacan belonged to this group.

Documents from this period show that in July 1936 Lacan intended to collaborate with Kojève in writing a study dealing with the same philosophical principles as those found in the Marienbad lecture and later in the article in the *Encyclopédie*. The study was to be entitled "Hegel and Freud. An attempt at a comparative interpretation." The first part was called "The genesis of self-consciousness," the second, "The origin of madness," the third, "The essence of the family." In the end, the study was never written. But in the fifteen pages that survive in Kojève's handwriting we find three of the major concepts used by Lacan in 1936: the I as subject of desire; desire as a revelation of the truth of being; and the ego as site of illusion and source of error. These concepts would also be present, mixed in with the two theories on the origin of madness and the essence of the family, in all the texts Lacan published between 1936 and 1949. They are to be found in "Beyond the reality principle" and "Family complexes," as well as in "Observations on psychic causality" and in the second version of the "mirror stage," a lecture delivered at the 16th IPA congress in Zürich.[6]

There can be no doubt that Lacan drew inspiration from Kojève's handwritten pages, in which their author suggested that to be up-to-date the thirties would need to progress from Descartes' philosophy based on "I think" to Freud and Hegel's philosophy based on "I desire," on the understanding that desire is the Hegelian *Begierde* rather than the Freudian *Wunsch*. *Begierde* is the desire through which the relation of consciousness to the self is expressed: the issue is to acknowledge the other or otherness insofar as consciousness finds itself in this very movement. The other is the object of desire that the consciousness desires in a negative mirror-relationship that allows it to recognise itself in it. *Wunsch*, or desire in the Freudian sense, is more simply an inclination, an aspiration, the fulfilment of an unconscious wish. Thus in the transition from a philosophy of "I think" to a philosophy of "I desire" there is, according to Kojève, a split between the true I of thought or desire and the ego (*moi*), seen as the source of error and the site of mere representations.

This shows us the evolution of Lacan's interpretation of Freud between 1932, when the thesis on Aimée and the paranoia of self-punishment was published,[7] and 1936, when the lost first version of the "mirror stage" was written. The analogy between Lacan and Klein consists above all in the way they both contributed at almost the same time to an internal overhaul of psychoanalytical thinking. Like Melanie Klein, Lacan approaches Freud's second topography with an opposition to any form of ego-psychology. Two choices were possible after the overhaul aimed at by Freud himself in 1920–3. One was to make the ego the product of a gradual differentiation of the id, acting as representative of reality and charged with containing drives (this was ego-psychology); the other turned its back on any idea of an autonomous ego and studied its genesis in terms of identification.

In other words, if one chose the first option, which was to some extent the path followed by psychoanalysis in the United States, one would try to remove the ego from the id and make it the instrument of the individual's adaptation to external reality. If one chose the second option, which was that of Klein and Lacan and their respective followers, and later of Self Psychology (that of Heinz Kohut, for example), one brought the ego back toward the id to show that it was structured in stages, by means of imagos borrowed from the other through projective identifications.

To understand this development, we must define the idea of narcissism in the Freudian sense of the term. Although Freud's position changed several times after the publication in 1914 of his famous article "On introducing narcissism,"[8] we can give a more or less firm definition of the distinction he drew between primary and secondary narcissism. Primary narcissism is a first state, prior to the constitution of the ego and therefore auto-erotic, through which the infant sees his own person as the object of exclusive love – a state that precedes his ability to turn towards external objects. From this ensues the constitution of the ideal ego. Secondary narcissism results from the transfer to the ego of investments in objects in the external world. Both primary and secondary narcissism seem to be a defence against aggressive drives.

In 1931 Henri Wallon gave the name *épreuve du miroir* (mirror test) to an experiment in which a child, put in front of a mirror, gradually comes to distinguish his own body from its reflected image. According to Wallon, this dialectical operation takes place because of the subject's symbolic comprehension of the imaginary space in which his unity is created. In Wallon's view, the mirror test demonstrates a transition from the specular to the imaginary, then from the imaginary to the symbolic. On 16 June 1936, Lacan revised Wallon's terminology and changed the *épreuve du miroir* into the *stade du miroir* ("mirror stage") – that is, mixing two concepts, "position" in the Kleinian sense and "phase" in the Freudian sense. He thus eliminated Wallon's reference to a natural dialectic. In the context of Lacan's thinking, the idea of a mirror stage no longer has anything to do with a real stage or phase in the Freudian sense, nor with a real mirror. The stage becomes a psychic or ontological operation through which a human being is made by means of identification with his fellow-being.

According to Lacan, who borrowed the idea from the Dutch embryologist Louis Bolk,[9] the importance of the mirror stage must be linked to human prematurity at birth, which is demonstrated objectively by the anatomical incompleteness of the pyramidal system in infants and their imperfect powers of physical coordination during the early months of life. From this date, and increasingly as time goes by, Lacan distances himself from Wallon's psychological design by describing the process in terms of the unconscious rather than of consciousness. Basing himself on one of Kojève's theories, he declares that the specular world, in which the primordial identity of the ego is expressed, contains no alterity or otherness. Hence the canonic definition: the *stade du miroir* is a "phase" – that is, a state structurally succeeding another state, and not a "stage" in the evolutionary sense. The distinction is not negligible, even if Lacan retains the Freudian terminology and the idea of historicity.[10] The mirror phase, occurring between the sixth and eighteenth month of life, is thus the time when the infant anticipates mastery of his bodily unity through identification with the image of a fellow being and through perceiving his own image in a mirror. Henceforth, Lacan bases his idea of the mirror phase on the Freudian concept of primary narcissism. Thus the narcissistic structure of the ego is built up with the *imago* of the double as its central element. When the subject recognizes the other in the form of a conflictual link, he arrives at socialization. When on the contrary he regresses to primary narcissism, he is lost in a maternal and deathly imago.

In abandoning himself to death he seeks to rediscover the maternal object and clings to a mode of destroying the other that tends toward paranoia. Like Melanie Klein, Lacan favours the archaic link to the mother in the construction of identity, but unlike her he retains the Freudian idea of a stage with a beginning, an end, and a precise state within a duration. As we know, Melanie Klein abandoned the idea of "stage" or "phase" for that of "position" (*Einstellung* in German, *position* in French). According to her view, "position" (depressive or paranoid/schizoid) occurs at a certain point in the subject's existence, a point in his development, but this moment, internal to his fantasy life, may be repeated structurally at other stages in his life. Another difference between Lacan and Melanie Klein is that she rejects the idea of primary narcissism and postulates the early existence of object relations as a constituent factor in the appearance of the ego. We can see how Lacan, through the notion of the mirror phase, works out his first conception of the Imaginary and constructs a concept of the subject, distinct from the ego, which has nothing to do with that of Freud.

Maurice Merleau-Ponty was the first to comment on Lacan's idea, in his 1949–51 lectures on child psychology. While paying tribute to Wallon, he showed that Lacan had a much firmer grasp of the essential Narcissus myth,

beyond what Freud said of it, thus opening the way to a more phenomenological approach to the problem: "Lacan revises and enriches the myth of
Narcissus, so passionately in love with his image that he plunges into the
water and is drowned. Freud saw the sexual element of the myth first and
foremost, the libido directed towards the subject's own body. Lacan makes
full use of the legend and incorporates its other components." [11]

The question of the subject becomes central in the second version of the
lecture on the mirror stage, delivered in Zürich at the 16th IPA congress in
1949. Ernest Jones was again the president, but this time he let Lacan read his
paper through to the end. The positions Lacan adopted now were different
from those of 1936. What he was concerned with in 1949 was a plan for
constructing the notion of the subject in psychoanalysis and in the history
of science – a topic already touched on under the influence of Kojève. The
title of Lacan's lecture reflects his new preoccupation: "The mirror stage as
formative of the function of the I as revealed in psychoanalytic experience."

Before arriving at this new formulation, Lacan had been careful to enter
the psychoanalytical movement through the front door. After the humiliation at Marienbad he published an article in *L'Évolution psychiatrique*
entitled "Beyond the reality principle," in which he called for the creation
of a second psychoanalytical generation able to bring about the theoretical
"revolution" necessary for arriving at a new interpretation of Freud. As is
well known, Lacan belonged to the third world-wide generation, but he saw
himself as the spokesman of a second generation vis-à-vis the pioneers of
the first French generation, whom he accused of not having understood the
master's discoveries. He made a point of dating his text as precisely as possible: "Marienbad-Noirmoutier, August–October 1939." The dating is not
without significance. It was at Noirmoutier that Lacan spent the summer of
1936 with his first wife, Marie-Louise Blondin, then five months pregnant.
At the age of thirty-five, about to become a father for the first time, he hails
the triumphant advent of a generation of whom he now sees himself as the
intellectual leader, and which he charges with the task of "reading Freud"
against and independently of all ego-psychology.

On the theoretical plane, this call to rebellion is a continuation of Lacan's
formulation of the first version of the mirror stage and of the article in
which he was to have collaborated with Kojève. Lacan distances himself
from the idea that an individual might adapt to reality. Thus he makes
mental identification a constituent factor in human knowledge. Hence the
proposal to identify "imaginary posts (*postes*) of personality," the three elements in Freud's second topography (ego, id, and super-ego), and then to
make out a fourth, the I, which he describes as the function by means of
which the subject can recognize himself. This, Lacan's first formulation of

the concept of the Imaginary, by which the genesis of the ego is assimilated, as with Melanie Klein, to a series of operations based on identification with imagos, is accompanied by an even vaguer mention of the notion of symbolic identification. Needless to say, this idea was to be expanded later.

When Lacan was preparing his new lecture on the mirror stage for the Zürich congress, he was no longer advocating the same positions as those he had put forward before the war. He had now read the work of Melanie Klein and discovered that of Claude Lévi-Strauss. He was also adapting the principles of Saussurean linguistics for his own purposes, though he had not yet made use of them. He was interested in the logics of the Cartesian cogito, and still fascinated by the psychogenesis of madness. The theme of the cogito, which was absent from the 1936 text, became central in that of 1949, when Lacan set forth a theory of the subject. To understand its significance we must examine the lecture he gave at Bonneval in 1946, "Observations on psychic causality."

In answer to Henri Ey, who suggested combining neurology and psychiatry so as to provide the latter with a theory that could incorporate psychoanalytical concepts, Lacan advocated a revision of psychiatric knowledge based on the model of the Freudian unconscious. However, as against the scientists who reduced man to a machine, both men shared the belief – as did most psychiatrists at that time – that psychoanalysis restored a humanist meaning to psychiatry, in that it rejected the idea of a classification of diseases isolated from the everyday experience of madness.

It was in this context that Lacan advocated the need for a return to Descartes – not to the philosophy of the cogito but to a philosophy capable of apprehending the causality of madness. In a few lines he commented on the famous sentence in the first part of the *Meditations* that later became the subject of a polemic between Michel Foucault and Jacques Derrida.[12] Descartes wrote: "And how could I deny that these hands and this body are mine, were it not perhaps that I compare myself to certain persons, devoid of sense, whose cerebella are so troubled and clouded by the violent vapors of black bile, that they constantly assure us that they think they are kings when they are really quite poor, or that they are clothed in purple when they are really without covering, or who imagine that they have an earthenware head or are nothing but pumpkins or made of glass. But they are mad, and I should not be any more the less insane were I to follow examples so extravagant."[13] Thus in 1946 Lacan suggested, as Derrida did later, that Descartes' founding of modern thought did not exclude the phenomenon of madness.

If we compare this attitude with that of 1949 concerning the mirror stage, we see that Lacan has changed his point of view. Having appealed to Descartes in 1946, he now rejects Cartesianism and points out that the experience of psychoanalysis "is fundamentally opposed to any philosophy deriving from the cogito." In the 1966 version, the one included in *Ecrits*, he corrects the lecture by reinforcing his criticism of the cogito: he says that the mirror stage is "an experience that leads us to oppose any philosophy directly issuing from the cogito" (*E*, p. 1). We can therefore see how Lacan evolves between 1936 and 1949. At first he constructs a phenomenological theory of the imaginary while distancing himself from the biological notion of "stages." Then he appeals to Cartesian rationality to show that madness has its own logic and cannot be apprehended independently of the cogito. And lastly he invents a theory of the subject that rejects not only the Cartesian cogito but also the tradition of ego-psychology that derives from the cogito. His criticism was directed as much at Daniel Lagache, who was anxious to set up in France a psychological unit that would include psychoanalysis, as at the American advocates of ego-psychology, who, it may be said in passing, were no Cartesians.

As for the 1949 lecture, it is quite simply splendid in its style and tone. We are a long way now from the 1936 version of the mirror stage. Thirteen years after his humiliating failure to enter the arena of the psychoanalytical movement, Lacan invites us to partake in a genuinely tragic vision of man – a vision derived from a baroque aesthetic, from Theodor Adorno's and Max Horkheimer's views on Auschwitz,[14] and a conception of time influenced by Heidegger. He turns psychoanalysis into a school for listening to the passions of the soul and to the malaise of civilization, the only school capable of counteracting the philanthropic but deceptive ideals of happiness therapies that claim to treat the ego and cultivate narcissism, while really concealing the disintegration of inner identity.

Translated by Barbara Bray

NOTES

1. Jacques Lacan, "Le Stade du miroir comme formateur de la fonction du Je, telle qu'elle nous est révélée dans l'expérience psychanalytique" (1949), *Ecrits* (Paris: Seuil, 1966), pp. 93–101. Translated by Alan Sheridan as "The Mirror Stage as formative of the function of the I as revealed in psychoanalytic experience" (*E/S*, pp. 1–7).

2. Françoise Dolto, "Notes sur le stade du miroir," 16 June 1936, unpublished. On the notes by Alexandre Kojève, see Elisabeth Roudinesco, *Jacques Lacan. Esquisse d'une vie, histoire d'un système de pensée* (1993), translated by Barbara Bray as *Jacques Lacan, Outline of a Life, History of a System of Thought* (New York: Columbia University Press, 1997). The unpublished document was communicated to me by Dominique Auffret.

3. Jacques Lacan, *Les Complexes familiaux* (1938), reprinted in *Autres écrits* (Paris: Seuil, 2001), pp. 23–84. See also Emile Jalley, *Wallon, lecteur de Freud et de Piaget* (Paris: Éditions sociales, 1981) and Emile Jalley, *Freud, Wallon, Lacan, l'enfant au miroir* (Paris: EPEL, 1998).

4. Henri Wallon, "Comment se développe chez l'enfant la notion de corps propre," *Journal de psychologie* (November–December 1931), pp. 705–48; *Les origines du caractère chez l'enfant* (Paris: PUF, 1973).

5. As quoted by Françoise Bétourné, *L'insistance des retours du Un chez Jacques Lacan*, doctoral thesis in fundamental psychopathology and psychoanalysis, University of Paris VII, 23 February 2000, vol. 3, pp. CVIII–CIX. Emile Jalley rightly notes that Lacan mentions authors cited by Wallon without knowing them directly himself. See *Freud, Lacan, Wallon*, p. 151.

6. See in particular: Jacques Lacan, "Au-delà du 'principe de la réalité'" (1936), *Ecrits* (Paris: Seuil, 1966), pp. 73–93; "Le Temps logique et l'assertion de certitude anticipée" (1945), pp. 197–215; and "Propos sur la causalité psychique" (1946), pp. 151–97.

7. Jacques Lacan, *De la psychose paranoïaque dans ses rapports avec la personnalité* (1932) (Paris: Seuil, 1975). See pp. 12–16.

8. *SE* 14, pp. 67–102.

9. Louis Bolk, "La Genèse de l'homme" (Jena, 1926), in *Arguments* 1956–1962, vol. 2 (Toulouse: Privat), pp. 1–13.

10. In English the terms "phase" and "stage" are often used interchangeably. In German, *Stufe* is used to mean "stage" in the Freudian sense, while *Stadium* translates the Lacanian concept.

11. Maurice Merleau-Ponty, *Merleau-Ponty à la Sorbonne, résumé de cours 1949–1952* (Grenoble: Cynara, 1988), pp. 112–13. See also Emile Jalley, *Freud, Wallon, Lacan*.

12. See Jacques Derrida, "Cogito and the history of madness," *Writing and Difference*, trans. Alan Bass (Chicago: University of Chicago Press, 1978), pp. 31–63.

13. René Descartes, *The Philosophical Works*, vol. 1, trans. Elizabeth S. Haldane and G. R. T. Ross (Cambridge: Cambridge University Press, 1967), p. 145.

14. Max Horkheimer and Theodor W. Adorno, *Dialectic of Enlightenment* (New York: Herder, 1972).

3

DARIAN LEADER

Lacan's myths

Freud's work has been both praised and maligned for its frequent introduction of myths and narratives which attempt to map out the archaeology of the human psyche. These range from classical myth to the invention of new myths, from the use of the Sophoclean Oedipus to the strange story about the origin of society set out in *Totem and Taboo*. Critics of Freud have pointed out the limitations of these models, their historical contingency, and the implausibility of their claims in terms of evidence taken from other fields in the human sciences. As historical narratives, their weaknesses are taken as impeachments of Freudian theory as a whole. Hence the psychological theories of the Oedipus complex or the castration complex become, in their turn, mere myths, fictions that collapse once their historical underpinnings undergo scrutiny.

Even to those sympathetic to psychoanalysis, many of Freud's narratives seem quaint and far-fetched, and yet, as the recently published text on the importance of the ice age for human development makes clear, such apparent flights of fancy formed an integral part of Freud's procedure.[1] A search for origins was characteristic of much early twentieth century thought, as it had been in the Enlightenment, and Freud's commitment to a form of phylogeny was shared by many other Continental thinkers. While this is not the place to go into the details of Freud's use of classical myth and mythic constructions, we can ask whether Lacan's methods of exposition have anything in common with Freud's. Can we, indeed, speak of "Lacan's myths" in the same way that we can speak of Freud's?

Lacan's use of narratives is certainly very different from Freud's. After the late 1950s, he tended to avoid developmental schemas and was also quite sparing in the use of the sort of analogies that were dear to Freud. The difficulty of his style is consonant with this. The theory of the mirror stage is probably one of the most accessible of Lacan's concepts, and its developmental flavor is perhaps why it is often misconstrued. Its "easiness" generates a range of problems, and Lacan's reformulations of it after its introduction in the 1930s testify to his effort to undermine quick assimilations of his concepts. It might also be argued that developmental schemas share something in common with myths, and that Lacan's avoidance of the one is what entails his avoidance of the other. If we understand myths less as fictions with a low truth value than as attempts to make sense of contingent and perhaps traumatic sets of events by means of a narrative, then all developmental schemas have a mythic character.

Freud, after all, introduces myths like the *Totem and Taboo* story or the struggles of Eros and Thanatos at the moments when he is trying to articulate clinical problems linked to the psyche's difficulties in accommodating excessive pain or pleasure. In Lacanian terms, myth is inserted as a way of approaching the real, which resists symbolization. If a basic tenet of psychoanalytic theory is that there exists a nonsymbolizable and nonrepresentable aspect of human reality, it follows that attempts to access it theoretically will involve possibly discontinuous modes of presentation. One could think here not only of Freud's use of myth but also of Lacan's use of mathematical and logical formalizations.

As we will see, this is a thread that runs throughout Lacan's work and it will allow us to situate the sense of myth particular to him. Although his gravitation towards logical problems and modes of exposition may be interpreted as the effort to contest the imaginary pull to assimilate new ideas to recognizable and familiar sets of meanings, it is part of a larger project to find mathematical structures for the psyche. In this sense, the avoidance of Freud's appeal to narrative and his search for origins is understandable. In their place we find a wide range of logical and mathematical apparatus, from the early paper on the problem of logical time to the later concern with knots that would characterize his final works. And with this, we find a particular theory – and use – of myth.

To approach this thread of Lacan's work, we need to focus on two motifs that are central to psychoanalysis: impossibility and contradiction. In Freud's early work on systems of defense in the psyche, he argues that certain representations will be deemed incompatible with others, and barriers established to separate them. These separations arise out of the experience of pain, and generate oppositions and contradictions: for example, the representation of the mother as a sexual being might be deemed incompatible with that of the mother as an object of love, to produce the famous splitting in love life whereby a woman who is loved cannot be desired sexually and a woman who is desired sexually cannot be loved. The current in love life derives from the experience of pain – that of considering the mother to be both a love and a sexual object – and it results in the manufacture of an impossibility: once the separation is made, a woman cannot be both loved and desired at the same time.

Freud also claimed that in the archaic link of infant to caregiver, there is a dimension of the relation between them that is separated from the field of linguistic predication, in which representations involving qualities and attributes is constructed. These linguistic chains will circle around the primary object without ever accessing it. Freud's early theories thus suggest that there are at least two different forms of impossibility encountered by the subject: the impossibility of symbolizing a primordial real, and the impossibilities generated by the network of representations themselves.

These encounters are also at the heart of Freud's exploration of infantile sexual theories. The child is unprepared for and unable to make sense of such troubling and enigmatic phenomena as the sexual relation between the parents, childbirth and the first sexual stirrings of its own body. There is no knowledge, in the sense of a signifying web of representations, that can subsume them in any simple way. Hence the child constructs, painfully, sexual theories to inject meaning and representation, to generate a knowledge around these points of impasse (SE 9, pp. 209–26). Freud noticed how skeptical children were about the usual explanations offered by parents, preferring instead to invent their own versions, using material supplied by their signifying environment. The fact, however, that these inventions tended to fall into a limited number of forms suggested that certain organizing laws were at play. This would allow Freud to enumerate a limited number of infantile sexual theories.

It was exactly this sort of contrast between elements of an individual's biographical vocabulary and formal, organizing principles that would interest the anthropologist Claude Lévi-Strauss. Although the constituents of a biography or a myth were infinite, why should the forms they took turn out to have a limited number of structures? In his paper "The effectiveness of symbols," published in 1949, he argued that whereas the preconscious consisted of an individual lexicon "where each of us accumulates the vocabulary of his personal history," the unconscious "structures it according to its laws and thus transforms it into language." The unconscious "is as alien to mental images as is the stomach to the foods which pass through it. As the organ of a specific function, the unconscious merely imposes structural laws upon inarticulated elements which originate elsewhere – impulses, emotions, representations and memories."[2]

Lévi-Strauss's article was important to Lacan in a number of ways. As well as introducing the idea of what Lévi-Strauss called an "empty unconscious," it elaborated a subtle comparison of the work of the psychoanalyst and the shaman. The shaman appeals to myth to reintegrate what a patient may experience as arbitrary and incoherent physical pain. The appeal to the symbolic system of myth can serve to situate this in a framework of meaning, giving the patient a language in which to express his or her psychic state. But whereas the shaman's patient receives a social myth which does not correspond to a "former personal state" (a physical disorder), the Western neurotic starts out with "an individual myth" made up of elements drawn from his or her past.

This myth would consist of elements from the patient's personal history – their vocabulary – structured by the symbolic function of the organizing principles of the unconscious. "The form of myth," says Lévi-Strauss, "takes precedence over the content of the narrative."[3] This would explain the fact that, following Freud, there are a limited number of complexes, although the diversity of patients' experiences is obviously unlimited. The complex moulds the multiplicity of cases, and is equivalent to what Lévi-Strauss calls the individual myth.

This tension between the level of what Lévi-Strauss calls personal vocabulary and formal structure corresponds to and perhaps had an influence on Lacan's notion of the unconscious as the imposition of the signifier. Lacan would in fact adopt Lévi-Strauss's term, "individual myth," and it formed an important part of his research program in the 1950s. However, what made Lévi-Strauss's concept so workable for Lacan was the addition, over the next few years, of a mathematical substructure. Lacan's project of finding the mathematical substratum of psychoanalysis owes something perhaps to the general optimism of the time that mathematical techniques and structures could be fruitfully applied in the human sciences. When Lévi-Strauss came up with just such a model to formalize the structure and function of myths, Lacan immediately put it to use.

The 1940s and 50s had seen the introduction of mathematical models into anthropology, primarily algebraic structures, structures of order, and topology. Lévi-Strauss had been using algebraic ideas from group theory as early as 1945 in his essay, "Structural analysis in linguistics and anthropology," and he would develop these some four years later in *The Elementary Structures of Kinship* in collaboration with the mathematician André Weyl. The key moment for Lévi-Strauss came when he realized that although myths seemed to be made up of certain basic building blocks, in the same way that words were made up of phonemes, these should be seen less as isolated elements than as bundles of relations. When he had first asked Weyl if he had any interest in studying the mathematics of the various operations that constituted marriage, Weyl had replied that he had no interest in marriage, only in the relation between marriages.[4]

This crucial step of prioritizing relational structures informed Lévi-Strauss's work on both kinship systems and myth. Moreover, seeing myth as made up of sets of relations was well-suited to the mathematics of group theory, which allows an equation to be identified with a group of permutations. All the known variants of a myth could be placed into a set which formed the permutation group. The elements would consist of relations between terms or sets of terms. Now, we might well ask what all this has to do with psychoanalysis, and especially with clinical practice. The answer to this question shows us why myth mattered so much to Lacan.

We saw earlier how Freud had interpreted the sexual theories of children as responses using signifying material to the painful problems of sexuality and family dynamics. What seemed like a contradiction or an impossibility could be made sense of using the sexual theories. A myth could be seen in the same way. Long before Lévi-Strauss, myths were often understood as the way that a society might give meaning to the question of its origins or the mysteries of birth and death. Like a sexual theory, a myth is a way of treating an impossibility. But Lévi-Strauss went much further than this. He argued that myth responds to the initial situation of impossibility or contradiction not with a solution but by finding new ways of formulating it logically. One contradiction replies, as it were, to another.

In his analysis of the Oedipus myth, for example, the initial contradiction is between the theory of the autochthonous origin of man (born from one) and the knowledge that man is in fact born from two. Although this problem cannot be solved, Lévi-Strauss argues, the Oedipus myth provides a "logical tool" which relates this initial problem to a secondary problem, "to be born from different or born from same." The key here is the link between the two sets of relations, to give a basic functional formula: the overrating of blood relations (e.g. incest) is to the underrating of blood relations (e.g. parricide) as the attempt to escape autochthony is to the impossibility to succeed in it. We have thus moved from a theory of the Oedipus myth as the disguised representation of repressed wishes to a structural model which sees it as the response to a logical problem.

In one of his first formulations of myth, Lévi-Strauss defined it in the following way: "The inability to connect two (contradictory) relationships is overcome (or rather replaced) by the positive statement that contradictory relationships are identical inasmuch as they are both self-contradictory in a similar way."[5] A myth takes an initial contradiction between A and B and shows that a further contradiction between C and D is contradictory in a similar way. Lacan adopted this definition of myth as a working model, using it in the early seminar held at his home on Freud's case histories, and then during the later 1950s. Myth, in Lacan's very Lévi-Straussian terms, was "a way of confronting an impossible situation by the successive articulation of all the forms of impossibility of the solution."[6]

These developments in structural anthropology had brought together two projects fundamental to Lacan: the study of mental structure as a response to an encounter with contradictions and impossibilities, and the study of mathematical structure as the underlying structure of the psyche and the symbolic order. Although his use of the Lévi-Strauss model is usually assumed to start with his 1956 commentary on the case of Little Hans, the earlier paper on "The neurotic's individual myth" conceals quite a strict use of Lévi-Strauss's schema applied to the case of the Rat Man.[7] Lacan does not reproduce the mathematical formula that Lévi-Strauss gives in his paper on myth, but refers to it implicitly throughout the article.

Lacan focuses on the situation that seems to precipitate the Rat Man's neurosis. He loses some glasses while on military maneuvers and wires for another pair from Vienna, which he receives soon after. But whereas he knows perfectly well to whom he owes the money for their receipt, he concocts an obsessional scenario involving a certain Lieutenant A paying the money to a lady at the post office, this lady then passing on the money to a Lieutenant B, and then himself giving the sum to Lieutenant A. In his discussion on the case, Lacan puts an emphasis on this absurd scenario, rather than on the more sensational account of the rat torture so often evoked by commentators. What interests him, following Lévi-Strauss, is the system of relations involved, and, as with myth, the constellation that preceded the patient's birth.

This constellation, Lacan suggests, has a "transformational formula," which becomes crystallized in the scenario involving the glasses. The two key relations concern (1) the Rat Man's father's marriage to a wealthier woman of higher station, superseding his attachment to a poor but pretty girl, and (2) a gambling debt from which the father was saved by a friend, whom he subsequently fails to repay. He had in fact gambled away the regimental funds and was only saved from disgrace by the intervention of his friend. These two debts form a first contradiction and Lacan claims that there is "a strict correspondence between these initial elements of the subjective constellation and the ultimate development" of the obsessional scenario.

The Rat Man is trying to reformulate the impossibility of bringing together (1) and (2), the two debts which function at different levels in his family history, and the convoluted set of exchanges that make up the repayment scenario are a functional variant of the initial contradiction. They are a new version of the inaugural relation between the father, the mother, and the friend. "This phantasmic scenario," writes Lacan, "resembles a little play, a chronicle which is precisely the manifestation of what I call the neurotic's individual myth."[8]

Lacan's reading of the Rat-Man case goes on to elaborate a differentiation of the symbolic and imaginary functions of the father, and it was the use of these registers that he added soon afterwards to the Lévi-Strauss model. A myth was still understood as the reformulating of contradiction or impossibility, but now it was the symbolic work of reformulating or "reshuffling" that responded to some emergence of the real via the permutation of imaginary elements. Since this sort of reorganization would in fact characterize the early life of the child, Lacan's argument suggests that the construction of myths is a central feature of entry into the symbolic order. This would be illustrated clearly in Lacan's reading of the case of Little Hans.

Confronted with the initial question of his position in relation to his mother, Hans has to deal with two further problems: the experience of his first erections and the birth of a sister. These constitute real elements, and to situate them in a new symbolic configuration, the imaginary elements of Hans's world have to be reshuffled. This results in the proliferation of stories, ideas, dreams, and scenarios that Hans comes up with, which use a limited number of elements in different configurations (the horse, other children, trams, etc.). Lacan sees this sustained production of material as a "mythic activity," the effort to pass from a world dominated by imaginary relations to one organized around symbolic principles and places.

This reshuffling is equivalent to the transformational formula of myth provided by Lévi-Strauss. Myth is now defined as the use of "imaginary elements in the exhaustion of a certain exercise of symbolic exchange" and as "the response to an impossible situation by the successive articulation of all the forms of the impossibility of the solution."[9] The passage from the imaginary to the symbolic consists, for Hans, in an "organization of the imaginary in myth,"[10] an idea that allows Lacan to link the theory of myth to the theory of neurosis that he was elaborating in the early 1950s.

Lacan had taken Heidegger's notion that human existence consists fundamentally in a question, and used it to define neurosis as a question posed by the subject concerning not only its existence but its sex. As he discusses Hans's mythic constructions, he argues that they respond to the question of his place between his mother and his father, experienced by him as an impasse. By running through the different forms of possible and impossible modes of reshuffling the components of his world, he reaches the point where "the subject has placed itself at the level of its question." Hence Hans is positioned within the field of neurosis, and his use of myths is formally equivalent to the process of responding to and elaborating a question. The phobia, construed as a mythic activity, has functioned, to use Lévi-Strauss's phrase, as a "logical tool."

One of the striking features of the case of Little Hans is the fact that Freud's own myth of Oedipus functions as an element that Hans uses in his constructions. When Hans and his father go to visit Freud, he tells Hans that "Long before he was in the world . . . I had known that a little Hans would come who would be so fond of his mother that he would be bound to feel afraid of his father because of it . . ." (*SE* 10, p. 42). The Oedipus complex is presented here as an a priori schema, and hence as a purely symbolic narrative rather than the consequence of a set of empirical relations. When critics of Freud argued that they failed to find any evidence of an Oedipus complex in their own fields of experience, they missed this crucial point: that as a myth, the Oedipus was a formal structure that a child could aspire to, and hence, in a certain sense, a fiction as such.

In Hans' case, where the father is failing to function in a way appropriate to introduce the Oedipal myth, the son introduces the logical tool of his phobia to get things moving. When Malinowski and others criticized Freud's theory of the Oedipus complex in the light of anthropological data in which the father's role in the family was clearly weak and devalorized, they missed this basic point: that the starting point for Hans's Oedipus was precisely such a failing at the level of his father, to which the Oedipal myth provided a form of response, albeit in a rather particular way with Hans. If there were a necessary discrepancy between real fathers and the symbolic function of the father, the Oedipus complex could be elaborated *as a myth* to allow the child a positioning in the symbolic. The Freudian father, in this sense, is less the authoritarian figure caricatured by Malinowski than a benign one.[11]

Lacan's focus on myth shows how a fiction should not be understood simply as something "false" but as something that can be *used* to organize disparate and traumatic material. This is not to say that it is entirely arbitrary, as Lévi-Strauss had indicated when he drew attention to the limited number of complexes described by Freud. Indeed, Freud makes the same claim in his analysis of the Wolf Man, when he equates the Oedipus complex with an inherited schema: inherited schemata, he says, are like the categories of philosophy, placing impressions derived from experience into a pre-existing framework (*SE* 17, p. 119). When experiences fail to fit into such schemata, they become remodeled, and "it is precisely such cases that are calculated to convince us of the independent existence of the schema."

Thus, in the case of the Wolf Man, the threat of castration was attributed to the father when it had actually arisen elsewhere. Subjective experience was being reinvented to incarnate the symbolic schema. The schema functions to structure the experience, and, Freud writes, the Oedipus complex is a prime example of such a process. Where Freud sees the disparity between the schema as a phylogenetic inheritance and lived experience, Lacan sees it as concerning symbolic structures and the imaginary and real elements that make up our world: but for both, a disparity exists between formal schema and the rest of experience, and both Freud and Lacan evoke Kant during the course of their explanations. The Oedipus is thus not the result of experience, and its structure must be sought elsewhere.

Seen in this light, Hans is making a sustained effort to constitute a fictional Oedipus complex, even if, in the end, he is not entirely successful. It is thus less a question of finding a "real" Oedipus complex in the material than of seeing how a child might try to manufacture one, and how the elements of his or her environment may either encourage or hinder such a construction. Lacan is claiming that the Oedipus is certainly a myth, but that the basic question is to understand what myths are and how they are put to use.

Lacan did not go on to elaborate his ideas about myth as a set of permutations in any systematic way after his seminar on object relations and it is a pity that this aspect of his research program remained undeveloped. The use of the Lévi-Strauss model in the cases of Little Hans and the Rat Man is extremely fruitful, yet today the notion of equating a neurosis with an individual myth is often taken to have merely historical interest. As far as I know, there is no published clinical case in the Lacanian literature which uses the model proposed by Lacan to make sense of the material in anything more than a perfunctory way.

Despite this waning of the more programmatic approach that characterized Lacan's work in the 1950s, the two central threads of mathematical structure and the encounter with impossibilities run throughout his subsequent seminars. In his seminar of 1969–70, *L'Envers de la psychanalyse*, Lacan returns to Lévi-Strauss's theory of myth in the context of a discussion of truth. It shows, he argues, how truth can only be half-said, and that "half-saying is the internal law of any kind of enunciation of the truth."[12] Truth here is linked to desire, and will emerge "in the alternance of strictly opposed things." We find here a clear statement of the Structuralist principle that what cannot be given form as a meaningful proposition will take on the form of a relation, exactly the principle that Lévi-Strauss emphasized in his study of myth.

A literary example can clarify this idea. The play-within-a-play in *Hamlet* has always constituted something of a puzzle. The main plot concerns a son commanded to avenge his murdered father and in the midst of his indecision and hesitancy, he hits on the idea of staging a play before his guilty uncle Claudius in which the murder scene is played out. The mini-play, however, makes of the nephew the king's murderer, not the brother, as in the main narrative. Countless interpretations of this episode have been put forward in the literature on *Hamlet*, but the first question that we can ask is why it was necessary to add the extra play at all: what, structurally, is its function?

To be suitably dogmatic, suppose for a moment the presence of some Oedipal material, the kind of thing that the best and the worst psychoanalytic commentators on the play have always emphasized. Little boys want to murder their daddies, so when someone else actually does, all the unconscious currents become especially reanimated: the uncle, in this sense, is in the place of the unconscious desire of Hamlet himself. We don't find such an Oedipal desire expressed as such in the play. What we have instead are two contradictory plots, and it is this very contradiction which can suggest that when an unconscious wish is impossible to assume, it will take the form of pieces of material that cannot be fully superimposed the one on the other. Desire, in this sense, is not to be identified with one or the other piece of material, but with the relation between them. Two stories thus cipher an initial point of impossibility, something that cannot be thought because it is so unbearable: that the son is himself in the place of the father's murderer. In other words, what the play-within-a-play shows us is that when a wish cannot be expressed as a proposition ("I want to kill daddy"), it will take the form of a relation, a relation in which the "I" is missing.

We can find the same principle at work in the formation of "dream pairs," the occurrence of two related but separate dreams on the same night. Referring to a paper by Alexander, Freud writes that "If a dream-wish has as its content some piece of forbidden behavior towards a certain individual, then that person may appear in the first dream undisguised, while the behavior is only faintly indicated. In the second dream it will be the other way round. The behavior will be openly shown, but the person will be made unrecognizable, or else some indifferent person will be substituted for him . . ." (*SE* 22, p. 27). The forbidden point thus emerges not in one or the other dream but in the relation between the two.

Lacan's argument, following Lévi-Strauss, is much stronger. It is not that the forbidden thought is simply disguised, hidden behind the dream material, but rather that it only exists, in a sense, as the slippage between the one and the other. Another example can illustrate this principle. A man has two dreams on the same night. In one, he loses a blood-soaked tooth and stares at it in absolute horror. In the other, his penis is being examined in a medical test and no problems are found. Neither of the dreams represents castration as such, but it is in the relation between the two that the reference to castration is situated. In Lacanian terms, it is being half-said.

Does Lacan's use of the myth-as-impossibility model give us a clue to his own use of myth in his seminars? Let's look at two examples, one from the

Seminar on *Transference*, one from the *Four Fundamental Concepts*. In the first example, Lacan is elaborating his commentary on Plato's *Symposium*, and discussing the schema in which, through an exchange of places, the beloved becomes a lover. "To materialize this in front of you," he tells his audience, "I have the right to complete any image, and to turn it into a myth." Love for the object can be compared to "the hand stretching out to reach a ripe fruit or an open flower, or to stoke the log that has suddenly caught alight. But if at the moment that the hand gets close to the fruit or the flower or the log another hand emerges to meet your own, and at this moment your own hand freezes in the closed plentitude of the fruit or the open plentitude of the flower – what's produced then is love."[13]

Although Lacan does not cite the reference, this odd metaphor is in fact adapted from the work of the thirteenth-century mystic Ramon Lull. The emergence of the other hand may seem miraculous, but what Lacan stresses here is the lack of symmetry in the scene depicted: the hand, after all, is not initially reaching out for another hand but for an object (the flower, the fruit). There is thus a basic lack of symmetry behind what seems to be a perfectly symmetrical relationship – exactly what Lacan will elaborate in the rest of his seminar, where he is trying to emphasize the disparity between the object of desire and the demand for love. In the *Symposium*, Alcibiades may seem to love Socrates, but the latter's intervention in the final scenes shows that Alcibiades' desire is in fact directed to the poet Agathon. Likewise, although love may seem to involve the symmetrical relation between two partners, Lacan gives a crucial role to the partial object or *agalma* as the principle of the dynamics of love.

If this object is a real one, the use of the myth of the two hands shows how, as Lacan puts it, "a myth here is understood as responding to the inexplicable nature of the real."[14] The image in question, however, seems to lack the qualities of myth that Lacan made so much of in his earlier work: it shows perhaps how it is not so much the content of the image that matters than its place within the context of a theoretical elaboration. It is introduced at a point where Lacan is trying to show the relations of the imaginary to the real in the field of love – and hence of something ungraspable simply in terms of the imaginary and its field of symmetry.

The story of the lamella, introduced a few years later, has enjoyed a far greater popularity than that of the two hands. Like the latter story, it is situated in the context of a series of references to the *Symposium*, in particular, to the Aristophanic myth of the egg-like being split in two by the gods which then searches to reconstitute itself. Imagine, says Lacan, that this separation has a surplus, like the afterbirth lost at human birth. This large, flat being would move around like an amoeba, sliding under doors,

LIBRARY, UNIVERSITY OF CHESTER

45

led by a pure life instinct. What would it be like, Lacan muses, to find that this hideous being had draped itself over one's face while one slept (*S XI*, p. 197).

This organ is the libido, and the "new myth" has been introduced because, like all other myths, its function is to provide a "symbolic articulation," rather than an image, of something that has a direct relation with the real. The libido is understood here as pure life instinct, what the living being loses in becoming subject to the cycle of sexed reproduction. The *objets a* are the representatives of this lamella, standing in for that part of him or herself that the subject has lost. The relation of the subject to these objects is the drive. Just as Freud had described the drives as situated on the frontier of the somatic and the psychic, here Lacan tackles this limit phenomenon in a Freudian way: he inserts a myth. In other words, a response to a point of contradiction or impossibility, here between the symbolic and the real, the life instinct, and the mortal side of reproduction.

Although Lacan does not explain his choice of term, the reference follows many of his other comments on ancient burial practice. Lamellae were thin gold plates or foils buried with a cadaver and containing instructions and passwords for use in the next world. These have been linked to both Orphic and Pythagorean currents by historians of classical culture, but what matters here is the opposition between the mortal body and an enduring, separate life substance that is linked to it. Lacan often refers to this duality, and will later identify the objects buried with the dead with the objects of jouissance, in other words, with a form of libido.[15] Note once again how the reference to myth comes at a point where Lacan is dealing with a disparity of registers: the mortal body, reduced to a signifier, and the real, the objects of enjoyment around it.

Beyond this internal consistency in Lacan's thinking about the libido, the first thing to be said about this story of the lamella is that it is not a myth in the strict sense: it has no set of variants, and it does not seem to be linked to a series of successive mythic constructions. In fact, it is similar to some of Freud's similes, and functions to present a quite complicated theoretical development with the aid of a nightmarish image. One might see this passage as in fact symptomatic of exactly the kind of expository technique that Lacan usually did his best to avoid. It is continually rehashed in commentaries on Lacan's theory of the libido and tends to act as a block to any serious consideration of the theory itself.

Curiously enough, the story of the lamella carries a mathematical shadow. In a footnote to the *Ecrits* that once attracted some interest, Lacan proposes a mathematical model for the relation of the libido to the surface of the body, taken from physics.[16] The reference to Stokes' theorem occurs just after a discussion of the lamella, yet unfortunately its value as a model is limited: the mathematics evoked adds little to Lacan's argument and it presupposes a particular, metaphorical interpretation of what a vector space is. If we interpret the footnote, however, as more than a rhetorical device to generate transference to some supposed mathematical knowledge, it testifies first of all to Lacan's effort to give a mathematical backbone to his theorizing, following the belief that the structures at play in the analytic field are mathematical structures, and secondly that what he is aiming to access theoretically cannot be simply formulated as a proposition.

We see the same principle at work in the equally famous commentary on Poe's story "The purloined letter." Lacan uses a fiction to develop his theory of the signifier and the function of the symbolic order, but then adds a difficult appendix introducing mathematical models, which usually passes without too much commentary. Why did Lacan choose to add this section to his work? Perhaps for the same reasons as the Stokes reference follows his use of the lamella story. He is aiming to access the structure of the relation of the subject to the signifier, and believes that this will be most clearly mapped out in mathematics.

We might find here the very principle that organizes Lévi-Strauss's work on myth that Lacan took up in the 1950s: when something cannot be expressed as a meaningful proposition, it will take the form of a relation between two sets of elements. In this case, the lamella story and the Stokes theorem, the commentary on Poe and the mathematical appendix. Rather than interpreting these textual juxtapositions as indicating that the "truth" of the "Purloined letter" commentary or the lamella story lies in the mathematics, it suggests that, for Lacan, there is a real involved which can only emerge in between these two modes of presentation. As Lévi-Strauss's work on myth showed, the real is only present as the result of a signifying combinatory of oppositions.

This tension between the use of fictional models and logical or mathematical ones is also present in Lacan's various perspectives on the Oedipus myth. In *L'Envers de la psychanalyse*, he claims that he only ever spoke about the Oedipus complex in terms of the paternal metaphor, that is, a formalized structure which concerns a normative set of relations.[17] His various accounts of the Oedipus complex as a narrative are likewise shadowed by attempts to establish formal structures. This would eventually involve an application of the old Lévi-Strauss method: the Oedipus myth is treated as one bundle of relations, set in a relation of opposition to the other bundle of relations that constitutes the myth of *Totem and Taboo*.

In the story of Oedipus, access to the enjoyment of the mother has to pass via the murder of the father. In *Totem and Taboo*, it is after the brothers murder the father that they decide to forbid themselves the women that the murder was supposedly intended to allow them to access. The contradiction between these two sets of relations leads Lacan to equate the dead father and enjoyment: in other words, an impossibility emerges out of the opposition between the two stories. This impossibility will frame Lacan's famous "formulas of sexuation," discussed elsewhere in this volume, in which male and female sexuation is given a logical formalization involving two sets of contradictions. On a more general level, we see here the passage of the Oedipus myth as a narrative transformed into a set of abstract logical relations embodying different forms of impossibility.

We could conclude our discussion by asking whether Lacan created any new myths. Given the popular sense of the term as designating merely a fictional narrative dealing with a question of origins, our answer must be negative. But in the particular sense to which Lacan subscribed, there is no dearth of mythic activity: his continuous effort to grapple with psychoanalytic problems involving a real or point of impossibility led him to the construction of relational modes of exposition involving stories, images and fictions caught up with logical and mathematical models. If classical myth aimed "to give an epic form to structure," Lacan was also after the structure, yet he chose logic rather than epic to do so.

Lacan's emphasis on relational models was a central direction of research, and can be linked to the basic Structuralist notion that what cannot be formulated as a proposition can take on the form of a relation. As we have seen, this is why Lacan could refer to "the kinship of logic and myth."[18] And this is perhaps the key difference between Lacan's and Freud's myths: where Freud uses a mythic narrative to account for some contradictory or impossible real, Lacan looks to the *relation between* mythic narratives to access this same point. Hence his reading not of the Oedipus story or of the *Totem and Taboo* story as separate narratives, but as two oppositional poles of a formula.

Although it has been fashionable for many years to try to dispel the idea of a Structuralist Lacan, this aspect of his orientation is fundamental and extends into even his final seminars. What we need is less the well-worn critique of the aspects of Structuralism that are clearly antithetical to Lacan's work than a reappraisal of the Structuralism that focuses on impasse and impossibility, and the introduction of logical structures as a response to this. Despite their many differences, there is thus a current in the work of both Lacan and Lévi-Strauss that constitutes a part of the same, relentless mythic activity. And if this activity involves what can only be half-said, how could reading Lacan ever be easy?

NOTES

1. Sigmund Freud, *A Phylogenetic Fantasy* (1914), ed. Ilse Grubrich-Simitis (Cambridge, Mass.: Harvard University Press, 1987).
2. Claude Lévi-Strauss, *Structural Anthropology*, trans. Claire Jacobson and Brooke Grundfest Schoepf (New York: Basic Books, 1963), p. 203.
3. Lévi-Strauss, *Structural Anthropology*, p. 204.
4. Lévi-Strauss, personal communication, 1997.
5. Lévi-Strauss, *Structural Anthropology*, p. 216.
6. Jacques Lacan, *Le Séminaire IV. La Relation d'objet, 1956–1957*, ed. Jacques-Alain Miller (Paris: Seuil, 1994), p. 330.
7. Jacques Lacan, "The neurotic's individual myth" (1953), trans. Martha Noel Evans, *Psychoanalytic Quarterly* 48 (1979).
8. Lacan, "The neurotic's individual myth," p. 414.
9. Lacan, *Le Séminaire IV. La Relation d'objet*, p. 330.
10. *Ibid.*, pp. 266–7.
11. Melford Spiro, *Oedipus in the Trobriands*, 2nd edn. (New Brunswick: Transaction Press, 1993).
12. Jacques Lacan, *Le Séminaire XVIII. L'Envers de la psychanalyse, 1969–1970*, ed. Jacques-Alain Miller (Paris: Seuil, 1991), p. 126.
13. Jacques Lacan, *Le Séminaire VIII. Le Transfert, 1960–1961*, ed. Jacques-Alain Miller (Paris: Seuil, 1991), p. 67.
14. Lacan, *Le Séminaire IV. La Relation d'objet*, p. 67.
15. Jacques Lacan, "Radiophonie," in *Scilicet* 2/3 (Paris: Seuil, 1970), pp. 61–2.
16. Jacques Lacan, *Ecrits* (Paris: Seuil, 1966), p. 847.
17. Lacan, *Le Séminaire XVIII. L'Envers de la psychanalyse*, p. 129.
18. Jacques Lacan, "Ou pire," seminar of 14 June 1972. Unpublished.

4

DANY NOBUS

Lacan's science of the subject: between linguistics and topology

Many students of the arts and humanities probably first encounter the name of Jacques Lacan in one of the numerous studies of the French Structuralist movement, an intellectual paradigm which attained the zenith of its public success during the 1960s, and which has since occupied many an Anglo-American scholar's critical spotlight, either as a fashionable esoteric creed or as an original explanatory doctrine. Invariably associated with the contributions of Claude Lévi-Strauss, Roland Barthes, Michel Foucault, and Louis Althusser – the central quadrivium of Structuralism – Lacan's oeuvre has indeed frequently appeared as another influential instance of how Structuralist ideas managed to change the face of many research areas in the human and social sciences, in his case the field of Freudian psychoanalytic practice. Whereas his companions have been hailed or vilified for their Structuralist approaches to anthropology, literary criticism, philosophy, and politics, Lacan has entered history as the quintessential defender of the Structuralist cause in psychoanalysis, an acolyte so militant that he did not shrink from making the claim that Freud himself had always been an inveterate structuralist *avant la lettre*.[1]

The main reason for Lacan's recognition, and his intermittent self-identification as a Structuralist is situated in his allegiance to the basic principles of Structuralist linguistics, as inaugurated by Ferdinand de Saussure in his famous *Course in General Linguistics*, published posthumously in 1916, and as elaborated from the late 1920s by Roman Jakobson, founding member and chief representative of the Prague Linguistic Circle.[2] As Jakobson explained in his *Six Lectures on Sound and Meaning*, a series of epoch-making presentations at the *Ecole libre des hautes études* in New York during the autumn of 1942, Saussure cleared the path for an innovative conception of language, focusing more on the meaningful function of sounds than on their anatomo-physiological basis, investigating language as a socially regulated, universal human faculty rather than a culturally diverse and historically evolving collection of words, and viewing language as a complex system of relationships between a basic repertory of sounds instead of the sum total of all the elements employed for conveying a message. To substantiate his revolutionary outlook on language, Saussure brought an impressive array of new concepts to his object of study, many of which were couched in dual oppositions. In this way he distinguished between the language system (*langue*) and individual speech acts (*parole*) (*CGL*, pp. 17–20), between synchronic (static) and diachronic (evolutionary) linguistics (p. 81), and between syntagmatic (linear) and associative (substitutive) relationships within a given language state (pp. 122–7). Yet Saussure's greatest claim to fame no doubt stems from his definition of the linguistic sign as a dual unit composed of a signifier (*signifiant*) and a signified (*signifié*) (pp. 65–70).

Against the realist perspective on language, according to which all words are but names corresponding to prefabricated things in the outside world, Saussure argued that within any language system the linguistic signs connect sound-images to concepts, instead of names to things. The sound-image, or signifier, coincides with the vocal production and sensory perception associated with a verbal utterance. It therefore possesses acoustic and material (physical) qualities, the phonic aspects of which could, in principle, be registered and measured. The concept, or signified, coincides with the idea in the individual's mind, a thought-process occuring as a result of a particular sensory impression, or seeking to express itself through a verbal utterance. Unlike the signifier, the signified possesses mental and semantic (meaningful) qualities, the psychological and social aspects of which could, in principle, be referred to the individual's family background, education, social identity and nationality.

In Saussure's linguistics the relationship between the signifier and the signified is completely arbitrary, whilst the two constitutive elements of the linguistic sign remain fully interdependent. An example may clarify this proposition. The concept (signified) of "the male individual who was born as my parents' child before or after me" is linked in the English language to the sound-image (signifier) of "brother." Yet nothing whatsoever within this concept predisposes it to being conveyed by this specific signifier. Proof is that the same concept is linked to very different signifiers in other languages: "frère" in French, "broer" in Dutch, "hermano" in Spanish, "bhai" in Hindi, and so on. Conversely, nothing within the signifiers "brother," "frère," "broer," "hermano," and "bhai" makes them intrinsically well-suited for conjuring up the concept of "the male individual who was born as my parents' child before or after me." The fact that they do is purely accidental and a matter of convention. Any other signifier could have been connected as effectively with the same signified within a certain language. In one and the same language a single signifier may even be linked with various non-overlapping

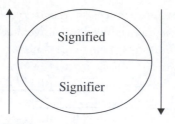

Figure 4.1 Schema showing the relationship between the signifier and the signified

concepts. In English, for instance, the signifier "brother" is not exclusively tied up with the concept of "the male individual who was born as my parents' child before or after me." When Roman Jakobson sent an offprint of one of his papers to Claude Lévi-Strauss with the inscription "To my brother Claude,"[3] he evidently did not mean to imply that a blood-relationship of biological fraternity existed between them, but presumably wished to show his gratitude to a kindred spirit. In addition, that one amongst an infinite number of sound-images is being used for conveying a concept does not alter the arbitrariness of the relationship between signifier and signified; it merely shows that language is a fraudulent game or, to use Saussure's designation, a "stacked deck" (*CGL*, p. 71). For on the one hand we are free to choose whichever signifier we want for expressing a particular signified, whereas on the other hand the choice has already been made (be)for(e) us and there is nothing we can do to change it. The language system thus sanctions specific connections between the signifier and the signified, excluding all others, which prompted Saussure to aver that the linguistic sign is a dual unity of separate yet mutually dependent elements, and to adduce the well-known schema (*CGL*, p. 114).

From the mid 1950s, Lacan started to integrate the principal tenets of Saussurean linguistics into his own theory of psychoanalytic practice. The first article in which he discussed at length the relevance of Saussure's ideas for psychoanalysis was published in 1957 as "The agency of the letter in the unconscious or reason since Freud" (*E/S*, pp. 146–78), and this was, incidentally, also Lacan's first paper to be translated into English. Putting his trust in structural linguistics as the harbinger of a scientific revolution, Lacan posited that its entire edifice rests on a single algorithm, which he formalized as $\frac{S}{s}$ (*E/S*, p. 149). Although explicitly conceding that this formula appears nowhere as such in the whole of the *Course*, Lacan nonetheless acknowledged Saussure as its mainspring, simultaneously promoting the Swiss scholar as the indisputable source of inspiration for modern linguistic science. In Lacan's pseudo-Saussurean schema, S stands for signifier and *s* for signified, and the line between the two terms symbolizes the "barrier resisting signification"

(*E/S*, p. 149). In response to some erroneous interpretations of the latter definition, especially that which had been advanced by Jean Laplanche and Serge Leclaire in their 1960 text on the unconscious, Lacan later pointed out that the bar between the signifier and the signified ought not be understood as the barrier between the unconscious and the preconscious, thus representing the psychic mechanism of repression, nor as a proportion or fraction indicating a ratio between two variables.[4] Instead, he pointed out that the bar should be read as a "real border, that is to say for leaping, between the floating signifier and the flowing signified."[5]

Much has been written about Lacan's distortion of Saussure's basic schema of the relationship between the signifier and the signified. One of the earliest and most trenchant critical assessments of Lacan's operation is included in *The Title of the Letter*, a meticulous deconstruction of his 1957 paper by Jean-Luc Nancy and Philippe Lacoue-Labarthe, which he himself praised in his 1972–73 seminar as "a model of good reading."[6] Encouraged by the vigor of Jacques Derrida's attack on Western logocentrism in *Of Grammatology* and *Writing and Difference*, Nancy and Lacoue-Labarthe set out to demonstrate that Lacan's linguistic turn in psychoanalysis, however far it reportedly removed itself from traditional philosophical notions, epitomized an implicit return to the age-old metaphysical concepts of subjectivity, being, and truth.[7] Comparing Lacan's algorithm of the signifier and the signified to Saussure's original notation, the authors discerned a number of crucial differences, which prompted them to conclude that instead of taking his bearings from Saussurean linguistics, Lacan had spitefully destroyed one of the cornerstones of his alleged theoretical foundation in view of its potential appropriation for his own psychoanalytic purposes.

The most conspicuous difference between Saussure's and Lacan's diagrams concerns the positions of the signifier and the signified relative to the bar that separates them. Whereas in Saussure's schema, the signified and the signifier are located above and beneath the bar respectively, in Lacan's version their position has been interchanged. Secondly, whereas Saussure's diagram suggests if not an equivalence, at least a parallelism between the signified and the signifier, owing to the similarity with which they are graphically inscribed above and beneath the bar, Lacan's algorithm underscores visually the incompatibility of the two terms. For in Lacan's formula the signifier is written with an upper-case letter (S) and the signified appears in lower-case type (s), and is italicized (*s*). Additionally, the ubiquitous ellipse encapsulating the signifier and the signified in Saussure's diagrams is absent from Lacan's rendering, and so are the two arrows that link the terms. For Saussure, both the ellipse and the arrows symbolize the unbreakable unity of the sign; the signifier does not exist without the signified, and vice versa, despite the arbitrariness of their connection. Lacan's deletion of the ellipse and arrows thus already suggests that in his account of the relationship between the signifier and the signified the unity of the linguistic sign is seriously put into question. Finally, whereas for Saussure the line distinguishing the signifier and the signified expresses at once the profound division and the strict solidarity of the two terms, for Lacan the line constitutes a genuine barrier – an obstacle preventing the smooth crossing from one realm to the other.

These four differences between Saussure's linguistic sign and Lacan's algorithm of the signifier and the signified raise a number of important questions concerning the motives and corollaries of Lacan's distortion and the general affinities between his theory of psychoanalysis and structural linguistics. Did Lacan subvert Saussure's model because he deemed it imprecise – as indeed Jakobson had already surmised in his 1942 lecture series – from a linguistic point of view, or rather because he considered it unsuitable as a workable construct for psychoanalysis? If it was his psychoanalytic experience that inspired Lacan to revise Saussure's schema, which aspects of this experience urged him to implement the revision in this particular fashion? And what are the consequences of Lacan's subversion for the way in which language is held to function both outside and within psychoanalytic treatment? More generally, what are its implications for Lacan's perceived allegiance to the Structuralist paradigm? Does it invalidate Lacan's role as one of the key players within the Structuralist movement, or does it open the door to a more radical, super-Structuralist approach?

The first thing to note when assessing Lacan's motives for modifying Saussure's schema of the linguistic sign is that instead of discovering the Swiss linguist's lectures all by himself, he was exposed to them indirectly, through the structural anthropology of Claude Lévi-Strauss. The latter's knowledge of Saussure and structural linguistics had in turn been mediated by somebody else's comments, notably those of Roman Jakobson, whose New York course Lévi-Strauss attended in the autumn of 1942.[8] As the anthropologist admitted on numerous occasions, it was Jakobson who had provided him with a solid theoretical framework for interpreting his observations and who had encouraged him to engage in the project of *The Elementary Structures of Kinship*, the book which announced the birth of structural anthropology.[9] Thus, Lacan initially read Saussure through the eyes of Lévi-Strauss, whose own reading had passed through the critical filter of Roman Jakobson.

In his *Six Lectures on Sound and Meaning*, Jakobson was generally appreciative of Saussure's work, commending it as one of the most significant steps for the study of language sounds in their functional aspects, yet he also believed that the *Course* remained deeply entrenched in a "naive psychologism," similar to many nineteenth-century treatises on linguistics.[10] In Jakobson's reading, Saussure had failed to draw the radical conclusions from his novel conception of language, emphasizing psychic impressions over the strictly linguistic functional value of sounds, and re-introducing psychic and motor aspects of sound articulation rather than advancing the formal characteristics of a phonological system. Following this criticism, Jakobson did not adjust Saussure's concepts, but decided to elaborate on his own structural approach to language in keeping with the theses formulated by the Prague Linguistic Circle during the late 1920s.

When Lévi-Strauss dipped into Saussurean theory in *The Elementary Structures of Kinship*, and more markedly in his extraordinary *Introduction to the Work of Marcel Mauss*, his was already much more a critical re-interpretation of Saussure's ideas than an accurate presentation of their impact. For example, Lévi-Strauss declared in the latter text that structural linguistics has "familiarised us with the idea that the fundamental phenomena of mental life . . . are located on the plane of unconscious thinking," adding that the "unconscious would thus be the mediating term between self and others."[11] Inasmuch as Saussure and Jakobson were interested in the unconscious at all, to the best of my knowledge they had never formulated anything as specific and decisive about its importance within mental functioning. And whereas Lévi-Strauss's first statement may still leave some doubt as to the exact nature of his viewpoint – "unconscious" could be a mere quality of certain thoughts – the second statement makes it crystal-clear that he conceived of the unconscious as a mental system, akin to how Freud had defined it in his so-called "first topography" of the unconscious, the pre-conscious, and consciousness. Further in the same section of the *Introduction to the Work of Marcel Mauss*, Lévi-Strauss argued that social life and language share the same autonomous reality, whereby symbols function in such a way that the symbolized object is much less important (and real) than the symbolic element that conveys it. This observation emboldened him to posit, challenging the basic principle underlying the Saussurean linguistic sign, that "the signifier precedes and determines the signified."[12] Needless to say, this proposed primacy of the signifier could still be conceivable alongside a Saussurean-type interdependence of the signifier and the signified. But Lévi-Strauss dismantled the unity of the linguistic sign as swiftly as the other components of Saussure's theory. Substituting "inadequation" for equivalence and "non-fit" for adequacy, he claimed that no signifier ever "fits" a signified perfectly, human beings doing their utmost to distribute the available signifiers across the board of signifieds without ever creating a perfect match.[13]

In light of Lévi-Strauss's singular espousal of structural linguistics, Lacan's alleged distortion of the Saussurean sign becomes evidently more considerate and less idiosyncratic, less erratic and more deliberate. In defending the "primordial position of the signifier" and defining the line separating the signifier and the signified as a "barrier resisting signification" (E/S, p. 149), Lacan simply reiterated and formalized the ideas that Lévi-Strauss had already professed some seven years earlier. Although he did not mention his friend-anthropologist by name in his seminal 1957 article on the value of Saussure's theory for psychoanalysis, Lacan attributed to the Swiss linguist what was in reality a Lévi-Straussian conception of the relationship between the signifier and the signified. And until the end of his intellectual career, Lacan did not budge an inch on the supremacy of the signifier and the "inadequation" of its relationship with the signified, the two hallmarks of Lévi-Strauss's take on structural linguistics. Even when these axioms came under serious attack, towards the end of the 1960s, from Derrida's deconstructionist critique of the Western metaphysical tradition, Lacan remained adamant that the letter (writing) cannot overthrow the signifier (speech) as the primary force of language, and that the greatest achievement of structural linguistics consists in the imposition of a barrier between the signifier and the signified.[14]

Lacan's formalization of the constitutive linguistic algorithm, along the lines suggested by Lévi-Strauss, was not just indicative of his eagerness to rescue the ailing body of psychoanalysis through an injection of the latest scientific developments. His integration of clinical psychoanalysis and structural linguistics à la Lévi-Strauss was not merely inspired by a desire to accelerate the *aggiornamento* of Freud's legacy. For Lacan was equally keen to underscore that Freud himself had anticipated the premises of Saussure's doctrine and those of the Prague Linguistic Circle, so that instead of infusing psychoanalysis with a foreign substance he could safely argue that structural linguistics entailed the most advanced continuation of Freudian psychoanalysis. In the 1971 text "Lituraterre" Lacan even went so far as to recognize the signifier in the notion of *Wahrnehmungszeichen*, literally "perception sign," which Freud had introduced in a letter to his friend Wilhelm Fliess of 6 December 1896.[15] Remarkably, when trying to find evidence for the presence of Saussure's concepts in Freud's writings, Lacan never took advantage of the terminology suffusing Freud's 1891 book On Aphasia, in which the founder of psychoanalysis had decomposed "word-representations" into four distinct images, dubbing the most important one *Klangbild*, that is to say "sound image," or precisely what Saussure would later elect to designate as the signifier.[16]

Over and above the question as to whether it makes sense to claim that Freud had foreshadowed the principal propositions of structural linguistics, it may seem self-evident to many a reader for Lacan to attempt a revaluation of psychoanalysis through the systematic accounting of language and its functions. After all, Anna O., one of the most famous patients in the history of psychoanalysis, could not have described the treatment regime to which she had been subjected by Josef Breuer more accurately than that of a "talking cure" (*SE* 2, p. 30). And when Freud decided to leave the so-called hypno-cathartic method behind, in order to access more fully the pathogenic vicissitudes of representations and their effects in the unconscious mind of his patients, language became even more the privileged playground of psychoanalytic treatment. Trying to substantiate a clinical practice which relies exclusively on the effects of a verbal exchange through the promotion of linguistics may thus appear to be an act of common sense rather than a revolutionary undertaking.

However, Lacan's main rationale for merging psychoanalysis with structural linguistics lies elsewhere. Throughout his career, he ventured to explain how Freud had demonstrated in *The Interpretation of Dreams*, *The Psychopathology of Everyday Life*, and *Jokes and their Relation to the Unconscious* that the modus operandi of the unconscious and its formations (dreams, slips of the tongue, jokes) cannot be understood without taking account of the role of the signifier and the structure of language. For instance, in his notorious 1953 "Rome discourse," Lacan explicated at length how Freud's tactics of interpretation ought to be conceived as a practice of reading, deciphering, and translation (*E/S*, pp. 57–61). In Lacan's understanding, Freud had recourse to these procedures because the formations of the unconscious are themselves the outcome of an intense rhetorical labor – as opposed to, say, the simple transformation of words into images or the transmission of psychic energy to the biological substratum of the body. Freud's extensive probing of word-connections in the analysis of his own forgetting of the name Signorelli thus proved to Lacan that psychoanalytic interpretation is tantamount to a reading process, and that this method is invaluable, owing to the linguistic nature of the unconscious (*SE* 3, p. 287).

Lacan's discovery of a linguistic breeding-ground in Freud's psychoanalytic theory and practice equipped him with a powerful argument against the ego-psychological tradition in contemporary psychoanalysis, whose representatives were more concerned with rebuilding their analysands' personalities as well-adapted, competent citizens than with the dissection of unconscious formations, and in whose clinical field language functioned more as an obstacle than a necessary means. Yet, similar to his distortion of Saussure's concept of the linguistic sign, Lacan found additional support for his personal rendering of the Freudian unconscious in the work of Lévi-Strauss. Indeed, as early as 1949, in an influential paper on "The effectiveness of symbols" the anthropologist had already proclaimed that the unconscious is synonymous with the symbolic function, which operates in every human being according to the same laws, regardless of individual idioms and regional dialects.[17] Combining this insight with his own re-reading of Freud's books on dreams, slips, and jokes, Lacan subsequently adduced the formula which would gain prominence as the single most important emblem for his entire work: "The unconscious is structured as a language."[18] The only reservation he ever made pertaining to the value of this statement concerns the tautological nature of its wording. As such, he indicated to an international audience of scholars gathered in Baltimore during the autumn of 1966 that the qualification "as a language" is entirely redundant because it means exactly the same as "structured."[19]

Armed on the one hand with the idea that the signifier prevails over the signified and on the other with the formula that the unconscious is structured (as a language), Lacan devoted all his energy during the 1950s and 60s to the careful deployment of a version of Freudian psychoanalysis which simultaneously vindicated its loyalty to the founder's original inspiration and justified its enlightened character through the principles of structural linguistics. For many of his fellow-analysts, Lacan's interpretation of Freud was exactly the opposite of what he himself wanted it to be: they saw it as a potentially dangerous and fundamentally flawed aberration which needed to be exposed and exterminated, rather than a strictly orthodox elaboration which ought to be regarded as the only true account of the original texts. Who is the honest defender of the Freudian cause and who is the impostor? Lacan or ego-psychology? These are the issues that have divided the international psychoanalytic landscape since Lacan's occupation of the intellectual scene as a contested, yet hugely influential *maître-à-penser*.

Looking back at these questions twenty years after Lacan's death, and in a contemporary climate of newly erupting conflicts between Lacanians and the International Psychoanalytic Association (IPA), it would be ridiculous to maintain that Lacan merely sought to regurgitate the naked truth of Freud's doctrine. As he openly declared in "The Freudian Thing" (1955), the meaning of his so-called "return to Freud" was no more and no less than "a return to the meaning of Freud," but this admission did not preclude this meaning being refracted by the prism of Structuralism advocated in Lévi-Strauss's new paradigm of anthropological research (E/S, p. 117). In Lacan's amalgamation of structural linguistics and psychoanalysis, both disciplines were simultaneously preserved and modified, according to the Hegelian principle of sublation (*Aufhebung*). If Lacan's espousal of Saussure's linguistic sign encompassed a fruitful distortion of its underlying tenets, then his interpretation of Freud's work also entailed a radicalization of its main thrust. If

Lacan's psychoanalytic course supported his modification of Saussurean linguistics, however influential Lévi-Strauss's ideas may have been, his linguistic interest also inflamed his recuperation of Freudian psychoanalysis as a clinical practice based on the power of speech and the structure of language.

After his excommunication from the IPA in November 1963, Lacan engaged in an even more vehement campaign for the recognition of his approach, solidifying its foundations and exploring its significance for the epistemological differentiation between psychoanalysis, religion, and science. Concerning the latter debate, he suggested in "Science and Truth" that the structural approach constitutes a necessary and sufficient condition for guaranteeing the scientificity of psychoanalysis, thus scorning those psychoanalysts who try to redress the legitimacy of their discipline by tailoring its logic to the requirements of empirical science, and ultimately refusing to relinquish the notion that psychoanalysis is an unscientific, speculative "depth-psychology" concerning the illogical, irrational and ineffable aspects of the mind.[20] Invigorated, once again, by Lévi-Strauss's take on the nature of a scientific praxis as detailed, for instance, in *The Savage Mind*, Lacan argued that the psychoanalytic delineation of the mental invariants governing the empirical diversity of the formations of the unconscious suffices to define psychoanalysis as a scientific enterprise – not a science in the traditional (positivistic, experimentalist) sense of the term, but a science nonetheless.[21] Hence, the Structuralist project also offered Lacan the opportunity to realize Freud's ardent wish to see psychoanalysis included among the sciences.[22]

The aforementioned differences between Saussure's formula of the linguistic sign and Lacan's algorithm of structural linguistics indicate how Lacanian psychoanalysis no longer puts the signifier and the signified on an equal footing (considering its reliance on the primacy of the signifier), and how it repudiates the possibility of a self-contained, unitary relationship between a sound-image and a concept (considering its emphasis on the barrier between the two components). In a sense these two key characteristics of Lacanian theory sustain each other, because the imposition of a cut between the signifier and the signified increases the autonomy of the signifier, and the latter's separation from the signified is directly proportional to its symbolic autonomy.

The direct implication of these two characteristics for clinical psychoanalysis is that it ought to concentrate on the existing relationships *within* the network of signifiers rather than on the relationship between a signifier and a signified *outside* its sphere of influence. Lacan believed that analysts ought to target their interpretations at the connections between the signifiers in their analysands' associations, and not at the meaningful links between signifiers and signifieds (*S XI*, p. 250). Put differently, he urged the analyst neither to ratify or condemn the meaning of an analysand's symptoms (as it has taken shape in his or her own mind), nor to try to alleviate these symptoms by suggesting a new meaning (as it appears in the mind of the analyst), but to elicit analytic effects through the intentional displacement of the analysand's discourse.[23] The notion "displacement" is synonymous here with the shifting connection between signifiers and also with the rhetorical trope of "metonymy," which Lacan extracted, alongside that of "metaphor," from the work of Roman Jakobson (E/S, pp. 156–8, 163–4).[24] By demanding that the analyst formulate metonymical interpretations – undoing and not fortifying meaning, revealing and not concealing it – Lacan championed a purportedly more effective tactic for psychoanalytic treatment than any of the other, accepted techniques of interpretation (explanation, clarification, confrontation, reassurance, etc.). For Lacan insisted that all these techniques somehow rely on the substitution of the analyst's signifiers for those of the analysand, that is to say, they all function within the dimension of metaphor, which invalidates their power over the symptom, because the latter is a metaphor in itself (E/S, p. 175). Indeed, because the symptom is a metaphor – the exchange of one signifier for another signifier or, in Freudian terms, the replacement of one repressed unconscious representation with another representation – it cannot subside by means of an analytic intervention that is metaphorical too.[25]

The clinical issues I am highlighting here are by no means marginal, much less alien to Lacan's Structuralist project of psychoanalysis. On the contrary, the peculiarities of clinical psychoanalytic practice inform every single aspect of Lacan's trajectory, from his earliest contributions on the family and the mirror stage to his final excursions on the intertwining of the real, the symbolic, and the imaginary. It is precisely this relentless clinical questioning rather than, say, the impact of Lévi-Straussian Structuralism, which triggered some of Lacan's supplementary modifications of Saussure's linguistic model. The most significant of these adjustments no doubt concerns his critique of the superiority of the language-system (langue), to the detriment of speech (parole) in the Course.[26] In his ambition to devise a new scientific theory of language as an abstract system of signs embedded within a social context of human interactions, Saussure needed to make abstraction of the utterance, in which individuals employ the language code for expressing their thoughts and in which they rely on psycho-physical mechanisms of motor production and sensory reception. For Saussure, the only possible object for linguistics proper is therefore the language system (CGL, pp. 14, 20). As a psychoanalyst, Lacan disagreed with Saussure's decision to relinquish the study of speech, because within psychoanalytic treatment the function of the analysand's speech is more important than anything else. The signifier thus appeared in Lacan's version of structural linguistics not as an element of the general language system but as the key element of the analysand's speech.

Lacan's emphasis on speech and his relative disregard for the language-system coincided with a sustained reflection upon the status of the subject in relation to the law of the symbolic order, or what Lacan designated as the Other. The subject should not be understood here as the unified, self-conscious being or the integrated personality so dear to many a psychologist, but as the subject of the unconscious – a subject that does not function as the center of human thought and action, but which inhabits the mind as an elusive agency, controlling yet uncontrollable.[27] The reason for Lacan's "subversion" of the classical, psychological notion of the subject is that during psychoanalytic treatment the analyst is not supposed to be concerned with how the analysand wittingly and willingly presents him- or herself in the twists and turns of his or her verbal productions, nor in the content of the analysand's speech (what somebody is saying), but in the fact that something is being said from a place unknown to the analysand. "*It speaks*, and, no doubt, where it is least expected, namely, where there is pain," Lacan stated in 1955 (*E/S*, p. 125). In keeping with Freud's formula that patients suffer from "thoughts without knowing anything about them," Lacan subsequently stipulated that the unconscious is a body of knowledge which expresses itself in various formations (dreams, slips, symptoms) without this knowledge being operated by a conscious regulator. Analytic treatment rests on the manipulation of the analysand's unconscious thoughts and as such it should reach beyond what is said and how it is being said, towards an investigation of where things are being said from and who, if anybody, is actually saying it. What the analysand says is but a semblance and cannot be dissociated from what the analyst hears in his or her own understanding of the words; the very process of saying is much more important than the form of the productions in which it results.[28] Throughout his work Lacan insisted on this point, deploring the fact that many analysts just continued to devote all their attention to understanding the content of the analysand's message.

Borrowing another set of concepts from Jakobson's research, Lacan also mapped out the antagonism between self-conscious identity and unconscious subject across the two poles of the opposition between the subject of the statement (*sujet de l'énoncé*) and the subject of the enunciation (*sujet de l'énonciation*). Freud's famous joke of the two Jews who meet at a station in Galicia still serves as an excellent example of what Lacan was trying to demonstrate here. When the first Jew – let us call him Moshe – asks the second, who will go by the name of Mordechai, "So where are you going?" Mordechai says, "I am going to Cracow." This message instantly infuriates Moshe, who exclaims: "You're a dirty liar, Mordechai, because you are only telling me you're going to Cracow in order to make me believe that you're going to Lemberg, but I happen to know that you *are* going to Cracow!" (*SE* 8, p. 115). Of course, the joke is that Moshe accuses Mordechai of being a liar, whereas what Mordechai says is a truthful description of his journey plan. Moshe acknowledges that the subject of the statement is telling the truth about himself – "I know you're going to Cracow" – but he also pinpoints the deceitful intention behind Mordechai's statement, which reveals the subject of the enunciation: "Your true intention is to deceive me." Mordechai may or may not have been aware of his intention, the fact of the matter is that Moshe acknowledges the presence of another subject behind the subject of the statement.

As a postulate, the subject of the enunciation implies that the subject of the statement (the personal pronoun or name with which the speaker identifies in his or her message) is continuously pervaded by another dimension of speech, another location of thought. However strongly somebody may identify with the subject of the statement, we have good reason to believe that the utterance is also coming from somewhere else than the place which the message has defined as the locus of emission. More concretely, if an analysand says, "I am doomed to ruin every relationship I am engaged in," the analyst need not bother very much about the grammatical structure and semantic value of the message, but ought to concentrate on the fact that something is being said from a particular place, the exact source and intention of which remain unclear and require further exploration. When the analysand is saying, "I am doomed, etc.," the subject of the enunciation is not necessarily herself. The statement may very well represent the discourse of her mother and she may easily produce these words for the analyst to believe that they are hers and for him to try to convince her that she is not doomed at all.

When Lacan embraced structural linguistics to advance the practice of Freudian psychoanalysis, he was hardly concerned with the type of questions Saussure and Jakobson were interested in, namely those related to the study of language as an abstract functional system linking sound and meaning. And despite his high regard for Lévi-Strauss's structural anthropology, it is fair to say that he was neither involved in the study of how rules of kinship, the classification of natural phenomena, and the deployment of myths reflect the organization of the human mind and vice versa. What mattered more than anything else to Lacan, considering the specific nature of psychoanalytic praxis, was the establishment of a science of the subject – not the self-contained subject of consciousness but the ephemeral subject of the unconscious.

It probably does not come as a surprise, then, that as his work progressed Lacan became more and more skeptical about the value of linguistics for psychoanalysis. In December 1972, during a crucial session of his seminar *Encore*, which was notably attended by Jakobson, he eventually admitted that in order to capture something of the Freudian unconscious and its subject, linguistics does not prove very helpful. Insofar as language is indeed of the utmost importance to the psychoanalyst, what is needed, Lacan quipped, is not the science of linguistics, but "linguisteria" (*linguisterie*), a certain (per)version of linguistics which takes account of the process of saying and its relation to the (subject of the) unconscious (*S XX*, p. 15).[29] In "L'Etourdit," the message was even more provocative: "For linguistics on the other hand does not open up anything for analysis, and even the support I have taken from Jakobson isn't . . . of the order of retrospective effect [*après-coup*], but of repercussion [*contrecoup*] – to the benefit, and secondary-sayingly [*second-dire*], of linguistics."[30] In other words, instead of conceding that psychoanalysis had progressed by virtue of its marriage to structural linguistics, Lacan claimed that linguistic science itself would benefit from his psychoanalytic espousal of Structuralist ideas.

It is tempting to entertain the idea that Lacan's gradual departure from structural linguistics and his concurrent divergence from the Structuralist paradigm in general, fostered the ascendancy of topological investigations in his work. Topology is a branch of mathematics which came to prominence towards the end of the nineteenth century and which deals with those aspects of geometrical figures that remain invariant when they are being transformed. As such, a circle and an ellipse are considered topologically equivalent because the former can be transformed into the latter through a process of continuous deformation – that is, a process which does not involve cutting and/or pasting.[31] References to topology abound in Lacan's texts, and topological surfaces such as the Möbius strip, the Klein bottle, the torus, and the cross-cap emerged intermittently in his seminars from the early 1960s until the early 1970s. Yet during the last decade of his life, from 1971 to 1981, Lacan spent more time than ever studying the relevance of these surfaces for the formulation of a scientific theory of psychoanalysis. After having discovered the so-called "Borromean knot" during the winter of 1972, Lacan would often spend hours and hours weaving ends of rope and drawing complicated diagrams on small pieces of paper.[32] His preoccupation with topological transformations became so overwhelming that during his seminar of 1978–79 he even silenced his own voice in favor of the practice of writing and drawing, treating his audience to the speechless creation of intricate knots on the blackboard.

Does topology supplant Structuralism in Lacan's intellectual itinerary? Does topology address the problems Lacan identified within structural linguistics? Does it constitute a more scientific approach to the practice of psychoanalysis than the doctrine of Structuralism? Is it more in tune with the subject of the unconscious than the linguistic research tradition? Within the space of this paper, I can only touch the surface of these issues, due to the fact that they put at stake the entire epistemology of Lacanian psychoanalysis, the transmission of psychoanalytic knowledge within and outside clinical practice, and the conflictual relationship between speech and writing. Lacking the space for developing the long reply to the above questions, I shall restrict myself to giving the short answer, which can only be "yes and no."

Let me start with the affirmative side of the answer. Topology does indeed replace structural linguistics within Lacan's theoretical advancements of the 1970s. To verify this claim one need not look further – although I can imagine that many readers of Lacan will already situate this point way beyond their intellectual horizon – than his 1972 text "L'Etourdit." Juxtaposed to his explicit devaluation of linguistics is the affirmation that topology constitutes the essential reference and prime contributing force to the analytic discourse. Unlike linguistics, Lacan contended, topology is not "made for guiding us" in the structure of the unconscious. For topology is the structure itself, which entails that (unlike linguistics) it is not a metaphor for the structure.[33] It should be noted here that Lacan did not define topological transformations in general as the equivalent of unconscious structure, but only those that apply to non-spherical objects, such as the torus and the cross-cap (projective plane). Topology's advantage over linguistics thus comes exclusively from its non-spherical applications, that is to say those transformations implemented on objects without a center. If Lacan's critique of structural linguistics stemmed largely from the latter's inherent presupposition of a total and totalizing language system centered around the primordial incidence of the signifier, his recourse to topology was meant to account for the very absence of a nodal point in the unconscious. Whereas linguistics did make ample room for the study of structural transformations – as exemplified by Lévi-Strauss's massive, four-volume "science of mythology" series – it was, at least according to Lacan, incapable of explaining the occurrence of these transformations without continuing to presuppose the presence of a creative or transformative agency. In the unconscious, however, the subject is real; it is the very absence of being that rules the organization and transformation of knowledge. This is what Lacan endeavored to demonstrate with his non-spherical topology.

The negative side of the answer is slightly more difficult to explain. Topology does not replace structural linguistics within Lacan's theoretical advancements of the 1970s, partly because topology emphasizes writing to the detriment of speech, partly because topology is equally at risk of functioning as a mere metaphor for the mechanisms of speech and language in the unconscious. During the early to mid 1970s Lacan engaged in a lengthy paean to the virtues of writing, because he believed that, by contrast with the signifier, writing operates within the dimension of the real and is therefore able to guarantee a complete transmission of knowledge.[34] In his seminar *Encore*, Lacan confessed unreservedly to his faith in the ideal of mathematical formalizations, because he considered them to be transmitted without the interference of meaning (*S XX*, pp. 108, 100). For many years, writing in its various avatars (the letter, algebraic formula, topological figures, drawings of Borromean knots) was Lacan's preferred mode of demonstration, and he relentlessly imbued his followers with his latest achievements in the realm of knot theory. Yet what he seemed to forget at this stage is that psychoanalytic practice does not rely on an exchange of letters, but on the production of speech. Topology may have taken Lacan to the real heart of the psychoanalytic experience, it also drove him away from its necessary means and principal power.

At the same time when Lacan expressed his confidence in formalization, he also divulged that mathematical formulae cannot be transmitted without language, so that the re-emergence of meaning presents an ongoing threat to the possibility of an unambiguous, integral transmission of knowledge. Nonetheless, Lacan continued to step up his campaign for the acknowledgement of writing, mathematical formalization, and topology until the end of his 1976–7 seminar, when he admitted that the entire project was likely to fail in light of the inevitable interference of meaning.[35] Towards the very end of his career, Lacan expressed this failure even more strongly, when formulating the most trenchant self-criticism of his entire life's work and admitting to the fact that instead of conveying the real of psychoanalytic experience the Borromean knot had just proved to be an inappropriate metaphor. In this way, he opened up new avenues for a return to the study of speech and language in the unconscious, not via the rejuvenation of structural linguistics, but possibly via another, more psychoanalytically attuned theory of language. Unfortunately, Lacan did not live long enough to embark on this new, challenging project.

NOTES

1. The reader will find the best analysis of Lacan's position within the Structuralist movement in François Dosse, *History of Structuralism*, 2 vols. (Minneapolis: University of Minnesota Press, 1997). For other informative accounts, see Malcolm Bowie, "Jacques Lacan," *Structuralism and Since: From Lévi-Strauss to Derrida*, ed. John Sturrock (Oxford: Oxford University Press, 1979), Richard Harland, *Superstructuralism: The Philosophy of Structuralism and*

Post-Structuralism (London: Methuen, 1987), and (less recent but still valuable) Fredric Jameson, *The Prison-House of Language: A Critical Account of Structuralism and Russian Formalism* (Princeton: Princeton University Press, 1972).

2. See Ferdinand de Saussure, *Course in General Linguistics*, ed. Charles Bally and Albert Séchehaye in collaboration with Albert Riedlinger, trans. Wade Baskin (London: Peter Owen, 1960). Hereafter cited in the text as *CGL*. Saussure's book is also available in a more recent translation by Roy Harris, yet owing to its idiosyncratic rendering of some of Saussure's key terms, the reader will find this version quite difficult to use, especially in light of the fact that the bulk of the secondary literature on Saussurean linguistics has not adopted Harris' options.

3. Dosse, *History of Structuralism*, vol. 1, p. 76.

4. See Jean Laplanche and Serge Leclaire, "The unconscious: A psychoanalytic study," trans. Patrick Coleman, *Yale French Studies* 48 (1972), pp. 118–75. For Lacan's criticism of this text, see his "Position of the unconscious," *Reading Seminar XI: Lacan's Four Fundamental Concepts of Psychoanalysis*, eds. Richard Feldstein, Bruce Fink, and Maire Jaanus, trans. Bruce Fink (Albany: State University of New York Press, 1995), pp. 259–82, "Preface by Jacques Lacan," Anika Lemaire, *Jacques Lacan*, trans. David Macey (London: Routledge & Kegan Paul, 1977), pp. vii–xv, and "Radiophonie," *Scilicet* 2/3 (1970), pp. 55–99.

5. Lacan, "Radiophonie," p. 68.

6. See Jean-Luc Nancy and Philippe Lacoue-Labarthe, *The Title of the Letter: A Reading of Lacan*, trans. François Raffoul and David Pettigrew (Albany: State University of New York Press, 1992).

7. See Jacques Derrida, *Of Grammatology*, corrected edition, trans. Gayatri Chakravorty Spivak (Baltimore: Johns Hopkins University Press, 1997), and *Writing and Difference*, trans. Alan Bass (London: Routledge, 1977).

8. See Claude Lévi-Strauss, "Preface," Roman Jakobson, *Six Lectures on Sound and Meaning*, trans. John Mepham (Hassocks: Harvester Press, 1978).

9. See, for example, Didier Eribon, *Conversations with Claude Lévi-Strauss*, trans. Paula Wissing (Chicago: University of Chicago Press, 1991).

10. See Lévi-Strauss, "Preface," p. xx.

11. Claude Lévi-Strauss, *Introduction to the Work of Marcel Mauss*, trans. Felicity Baker (London: Routledge & Kegan Paul, 1987), p. 35.

12. *Ibid*, p. 37.

13. *Ibid*, p. 62.

14. See Jacques Lacan, "Lituraterre," *Autres écrits* (Paris: Seuil, 2001), p. 14, and "Radiophonie," p. 55.

15. *The Complete Letters of Sigmund Freud to Wilhelm Fliess 1887–1904*, ed. and trans. Jeffrey Masson (Cambridge, Mass.: Harvard University Press, 1985), p. x.

16. See Sigmund Freud, *On Aphasia*, trans. Erwin Stengel (New York: International Universities Press, 1953). For a judicious discussion of this book and its historical context, see Valerie D. Greenberg, *Freud and his Aphasia Book: Language and the Sources of Psychoanalysis* (Ithaca: Cornell University Press, 1997). For a more encompassing yet equally astute evaluation of the importance of Freud's linguistic ideas for the emergence of psychoanalysis, see John Forrester, *Language and the Origins of Psychoanalysis*, 2nd edn. (London: Palgrave, 2001). For an

in-depth treatment of Freud's general theory of symbolism in relation to the analysis of unconscious productions, see Agnes Petocz, *Freud, Psychoanalysis and Symbolism* (Cambridge: Cambridge University Press, 1999).

17. Claude Lévi-Strauss, "The effectiveness of symbols" (1949), *Structural Anthropology*, trans. Claire Jacobson and Brooke Grundfest Schoepf (New York: Basic Books, 1963), pp. 186–205.

18. The formula appeared for the first time, in rudimentary form, in Lacan's seminar of 1955–56: "Translating Freud, we say – the unconscious is a language" (*S III*, p. 11).

19. Jacques Lacan, "Of structure as an inmixing of an otherness prerequisite to any Subject whatever" (1966), *The Languages of Criticism and the Sciences of Man: The Structuralist Controversy*, eds. Richard Macksey and Eugenio Donato (Baltimore: Johns Hopkins University Press, 1970), p. 188.

20. Jacques Lacan, "Science and Truth" (1965), trans. Bruce Fink, *Newsletter of the Freudian Field* 3, nos. 1/2, pp. 4–29.

21. Claude Lévi-Strauss, *The Savage Mind* (*La Pensée sauvage*) (1962) (London: Weidenfeld and Nicolson, 1966).

22. For Freud's position on the scientific status of psychoanalysis, see in particular Lecture 35, "The question of a *Weltanschauung*," *New Introductory Lectures on Psycho-Analysis* (*SE* 22, pp. 158–82).

23. Lacan, "Radiophonie," p. 59.

24. See also Roman Jakobson, "Two aspects of language and two types of aphasic disturbance," Roman Jakobson and Morris Halle, *Fundamentals of Language* (The Hague: Mouton, 1956), pp. 55–82.

25. For a more detailed discussion of these principles, see my *Jacques Lacan and the Freudian Practice of Psychoanalysis* (London and Philadelphia: Brunner-Routledge, 2000), pp. 153–83.

26. The reader should note that Baskin has translated the term *parole* as "speaking," reserving "speech" rather confusingly for *langage*. Harris has adopted "speech" for *parole*, but fails to distinguish consistently between *langue* and *langage*. Sometimes he translates *langue* as "the language itself," and sometimes as "a language system" and "language structure," thus introducing a notion (that of structure) which has no conceptual status in Saussure's work. At other times he also renders *langue* erroneously as "individual languages."

27. For Lacan's distinction between the subject of psychoanalysis and the subject of psychology, see the opening pages of "The subversion of the subject and the dialectic of desire in the Freudian unconscious" (*E/S*, pp. 292–325). For more detailed discussions of Lacan's concept of the subject, see Bruce Fink, *The Lacanian Subject: Between Language and Jouissance* (Princeton: Princeton University Press, 1995), and Paul Verhaeghe, "Causation and destitution of a pre-ontological non-entity: On the Lacanian subject," *Key Concepts of Lacanian Psychoanalysis*, ed. Dany Nobus (New York: The Other Press, 1999), pp. 164–89.

28. Jacques Lacan, *Le Séminaire XIX . . . ou pire* (1971–72), session of June 21, 1972. Unpublished. Also, see Jacques Lacan, "L'Etourdit" (1972), *Scilicet* 4 (1973), pp. 5–52. In the latter text Lacan launched the formula "What one may be saying remains forgotten behind what is being said in what is heard."

29. While Fink has translated *linguisterie* as "linguistricks" and mentions "linguistrickery" as another solution (see *S XX*, p. 15, n.3) in opting for "linguisteria" I have tried to render what I believe to be the gist of Lacan's portmanteau word: a combination of linguistics and hysteria or, even better, a hysterical transformation of linguistics. For a more extensive discussion of Lacan's alternative linguistics, see Jean-Claude Milner, "De la linguistique à la linguisterie," *Lacan, l'écrit, l'image*, ed. Ecole de la cause freudienne (Paris: Flammarion, 2000), pp. 7–25, and Cyril Veken, "La Linguistique de Lacan," *La Célibataire – Revue de psychanalyse* 4 (2000), pp. 211–28.

30. Lacan, "L'Etourdit," p. 46.

31. For a concise description of the history of topology and its place within Lacanian theory, see Nathalie Charraud, "Topology: the Möbius strip between torus and cross-cap," *A Compendium of Lacanian Terms*, eds. Huguette Glowinski, Zita M. Marks, and Sara Murphy (London: Free Association Books, 2001), pp. 204–10.

32. For an excellent discussion of Lacan's "affair" with the Borromean knot, see Luke Thurston, "Ineluctable nodalities: On the Borromean knot," *Key Concepts of Lacanian Psychoanalysis*, ed. Dany Nobus (New York: The Other Press, 1999).

33. Lacan, "L'Etourdit," pp. 28, 40.

34. See, for instance, Jacques Lacan, "Yale University, Kanzer Seminar (24 novembre 1975)," *Scilicet* 6/7 (1976), pp. 7–31.

35. See Jacques Lacan, "Le Séminaire XXIV: L'insu-que-sait de l'une bévue s'aile à mourre" (1976–77), *Ornicar?* 17/18 (1979), pp. 7–23. For a more detailed account of Lacan's contrived engagement with writing and formalization during the 1970s, see Dany Nobus, "Littorical reading: Lacan, Derrida and the analytic production of chaff," *JPCS: Journal for the Psychoanalysis of Culture and Society* 6/2 (2001), pp. 279–88.

5

BERNARD BURGOYNE

From the letter to the matheme: Lacan's scientific methods

I

How can we ask questions about the language in which we have our intellectual being as it were?

Georg Kreisel in *Gödel Remembered*[1]

The book of nature is written in a mathematical script. Human nature finds itself called upon to decipher this text, and it is perhaps more deeply implicated in this activity than a mere external reader would be. The idea that there is a text outside that demands attentive and renewed reading fails to do justice to the complexities postulated by Freud, for whom the unconscious is equipped with its own inner text. Any reading that is to be done then presupposes the existence of a relation between these interiorities and an exterior that they are engaged with. There is a question here of giving an interpretation of a text, but there is also a question of whether a mathematician may be needed in order to address these questions of exterior, interior, and the frontier between them.

The psychoanalyst is called on to be a poet – or, as Jacques Lacan occasionally phrased it, to be a poem. Analytical work, at the same time, "scientifically" purifies the subject. Lacan held to both these opinions, and he was not alone in the analytical movement in wanting to bridge the gap between them. Such themes were present from the beginnings of psychoanalysis. Freud put forward claims on both sides of this divide; on the one hand, he described how words have a magical power, and on the other, he suggested that psychoanalysis can be formalized as a science.[2] Making such a transition – from literary text to mathematics and its proofs – may seem at first glance to be beyond the power of psychoanalysis. But both these analysts – Lacan and Freud – held that the notion of the unconscious turned the spanning of this divide into a requirement. Unconscious structure is what forced their hand: from the beginning of Freud's work, structure was at play in the weaving of psychoanalytical procedures, and it is this structure that makes the movement possible, and that moreover compels it.

A human being is implicated in structures: this theme constitutes the center of the various research programs in psychoanalysis proposed by Lacan from the early 1930s to 1980. The particular formulations that he gave to his work over this period shifted almost every five years, but this central focus remained fixed. In the early years, he gave the appearance of inclining towards an informal analysis of images and language, and this implied an equally informal analysis of their structure. Later in his work he dispelled any illusions that such a reading of his work could be maintained: he claimed that a school of clinicians and researchers in psychoanalysis needs access to topologists – experts on the structure of space – in order to formulate and resolve its problems. So there is a direction, a trajectory, in Lacan's work, and this trajectory he referred to many times: a 1967 article by Lacan is a commentary on this movement from its beginning to its end.[3] Initially, Lacan had given a formulation of subjectivity that ascribed human bondage to the functioning of unconscious (complexes of) images. In this early version of human subjection, language is only implicit in human life, finding its place in structures that are determined by images. But Lacan revised this view of things soon after the end of the Second World War.[4]

Language, in his later view, provides the structure in which images make their home. The structure of language now acquires a determining role – this was the formulation that led Lacan to propose a structure to the unconscious determined by that of language – and such a structure raises the question of what apparatus will be used in its analysis. This step is what prepared the ground for the development of his notion of the Symbolic and the associated "registers" of the Imaginary and the Real, the three notions appearing as a trinity in Lacan's work by 1953. And it is this repositioning of his program that allowed Lacan to revisit Freud's clinical and theoretical work, and render explicit the functioning of threads of language as they determine the various connections and disconnections of the unconscious. It is in this sense that one can talk about the structure of language "in as far as the subject is implicated in it" – to use the formulation proposed by Philippe Lacoue-Labarthe and Jean-Luc Nancy in their famous commentary on Lacan.[5] There is a structure in the unconscious; it is determined by the networks of language; and a human being is given coordinates so as to be able to navigate his or her relations with others by means of this internal structure, by this structuring that they live within. People's judgments of the world – of their place in it, of the nature of their relations to others, and of who they are – are all structured by this apparatus of language. And just as a human subject is implicated in language, it seems that mathematics may also be implicated in this linguistic structuring. So to read the book of nature is no easy matter; it presupposes reading the texts in oneself.

This determination by language is what can be called the problem of the letter. Lacan in fact would often refer to his work throughout the 1950s in these terms. The two texts which centrally focus on this determination are the famous *Seminar on "The Purloined Letter"* from 1956 and "The agency of the letter in the unconscious" (*E/S*, pp. 146–78) from 1957.[6] The questions being raised in this way involve relations between psychoanalysis, linguistics, philosophy, and science – and they raise particularly the question of the place of mathematics in any proposed formulation of analysis. In the terms utilized by Lacoue-Labarthe and Nancy, Lacan's account of the "agency of the letter" raises the problem of giving a formulation to "the question of being" in such a way that it presupposes the philosophical problem of the determination of being by structure.[7] This is not a light problem that they propose. It is one thing to formulate a problem, and yet another to find a solution to it; ultimately, they choose to give a priority to philosophy, rather than to mathematics, in their formulation of it. The structure they are appealing to is the structure of the unconscious, and the question of interpretations of this structure they assume can be resolved by drawing on a number of domains. Lacan's two commentators invoke a range of supposedly affiliated fields: linguistics, "combinatorial" logic, "algorithmic" logic, "symbolic" logic (these last two of which they take to be "equivalent"), biology, psychology, and ethnology. These fields – these so-called fields – have at best a haphazard relationship to each other: Lacoue-Labarthe and Nancy assume that Lacan's aim is to order them through subordinating them to philosophy. Nothing could be wider of the mark. Lacan's strategy is very clear: he gives priority to psychoanalysis. It remains to analyze what that means.

The problem of the relations between psychoanalysis on the one hand and science and philosophy on the other was raised by Freud in 1933, in a recapitulation of issues that he had initially started to discuss with James Putnam in 1909. Putnam had originally wished to subordinate psychoanalysis to philosophy. He held that only the adoption by the psychoanalyst of the position of a moral philosopher could bring the clinical work to a conclusion that could be for "the good" of the patient. Philosophy, he said, should in this way serve as a guiding framework for the research and clinical practice of the psychoanalyst. Freud, from the start, took the opposite point of view. He held that psychoanalysis had no need of – and no use for – this dependency: psychoanalysis already had a guiding framework, he said, that provided by "the methods of the sciences." In claiming this, Freud took science to be made up of "critically tested" accounts of the world (*SE* 22, pp. 187–8). Methods of proposing such theories and of subjecting them to "relentless" criticism made up the framework supporting the sciences: a framework that Freud called the "Weltanschauung" of science. It is this "world-view" that Freud took to be shared by psychoanalysis, this orientation that gives direction to its research.

The methods of the sciences are still being built, claimed Freud, and just as science is incomplete – indeed the toleration of such incompleteness is one of its hallmarks – psychoanalysis has yet to formulate itself as a science. For Freud, two things followed from this. The first is that the inclusion of psychoanalysis in science would not in any way alter its methods; the second is that after this step the content of the sciences would change radically. Psychoanalysis changes classical assumptions about human nature; almost everything assumed by classical "pure and applied psychology" would be shifted by the introduction of structures discovered by psychoanalytical research into classical science. "The progress of scientific work is brought about in a very similar way to the furtherance of a psychoanalysis" said Freud. He did not give a reason for this; that the structure of the two fields is "very similar" remained tacit.

Not only does Freud give a priority to science, but he asserts that psychoanalysis is – or rather, can become – a science. In this way he is separating the future trajectories of psychoanalysis from the domain of philosophy. There are clearly many interrelations between philosophy and science, and to separate these two domains is not easy. Freud claims that philosophy, while using much of the methodology of the sciences – particularly deductive logic – has a tendency to gloss over incompleteness in its results, and that it does this usually by means of an idealization of its aims. It is the lack of this scientific ability to bear incompleteness of formulation and of results, according to Freud, that mainly distinguishes the philosophical enterprise from the traditions of the sciences. On the other hand, science needs philosophy: the overlap and difference between them is not such as to make philosophy alien to the sciences. And psychoanalysis, he insists, is orientated, not by philosophy but by "the methods of the sciences." What exactly do these methods consist of? Are the structures of the sciences related to the structures of mathematics? And is the structure involved in psychoanalysis in any way related to that of mathematics? Lacan was to find that such issues were pertinent to his work, and that some answers to these questions were available already in the 1930s.

Lacoue-Labarthe and Nancy formulate some things very well: for instance, that the subject enters into a discourse – into relations with others – already determined by the letter. However, they also propose that a science of such determinations can be constructed, and that its building will produce a range of philosophical problems for the psychoanalyst. There are a number of problems about this assumption, all of which produce more obscurity than clarity. Although this science is not yet constituted, they say, all that it requires is the definition of a concept, the concept of the letter. However, no science is ever constituted by a concept, but rather by the formulation that it gives to a series of problems. They also assume that the relations of science to psychoanalysis will be determined by the construction of this science, and all of this they put forward under the rubric of "the science of the letter." Now this – to take up a phrase dear to Lacan – is precisely the formulation to avoid. In the first place, it is precisely the incorporation into science of little letters (algebraic variables) that transformed science at the time of Descartes. Because of this, science is not something that "applies" to letters – it presupposes them. And finally, their proposed "science of the letter" is necessarily very different from any linguistic science on the one hand, and fails to grasp any entanglement of psychoanalysis with science on the other. Their choice of this term brings with it a confusion between science and philosophy, a confusion which they usually resolve by a subordination of science (and psychoanalysis) to philosophy, *pace* all the objections of Freud. And rather than such a science governing – or rather its philosophy governing – the letter, as they claim, science too remains subject to the structure of language (and this is nowhere more evident than in the foundations of mathematics and in formalized languages of logic). That this is so was clear from quite an early point in Lacan's work. How then did the formalization of structure become explicit in Lacan's work? How did Lacan's early statements on the psychopathology of love become resolved, at some intermediary point, into questions of formalization?

In the various versions of the *Seminar on 'The Purloined Letter*,' Lacan produced three different incorporations of mathematics: the rewriting of the 1955 seminar sessions in 1966, a mathematical appendix to this, and a mathematical appendix to this appendix. So by the time of the publication of Lacan's *Ecrits*, the relation of psychoanalysis to mathematics was already patent. In terms of the relations between psychoanalysis, mathematics, philosophy, and science, the way in which Lacan takes up Freud is fairly clear. Lacan gives priority to psychoanalysis over philosophy; Freud gives priority to science over philosophy; Lacan finds the structure of psychoanalysis in the structure of mathematics. Why?

The *Seminar on 'The Purloined Letter'* is very clearly buttressed by Lacan with mathematical architecture; in "The agency of the letter in the unconscious", the mathematical structure remains implicit. The agency of structure is Lacan's central theme in this text, an agency by means of which the human subject is rendered passive, mastered, reduced to being a "serf of language." The determination by this structure is fairly complete: "Of course, the letter killeth while the spirit giveth life . . . Even so, the pretentions of the spirit would remain unassailable if the letter had not shown us that it produces all the effects of truth in man, without involving the spirit at all" (E/S, p. 158). And it is something "already there," something that a human being is born into: "language and its structure exist prior to the moment at which each subject, at a certain point in his mental development, makes his entry into it" (E/S, p. 148).

The human subject questions the conditions of its existence, but "for there even to be a question . . . there must be language" (E/S, p. 172). Lacan cites Erasmus and the period of skeptical criticism of orthodoxies in science, criticisms that helped to construct the science of the modern world. Their outcome was a motif of "know yourself," but this Socratic adage, he says, needs to be taken in a somewhat novel way. Freud impels us, he says, to analyze and revise the paths that lead to it. And these pathways are linkages, connections in the (topological) spaces of the soul. They are to be considered, according to Lacan, à la lettre, and given such algebraic coordinates so that these pathways through the soul display a mathematical lineage. In such formulations the mathematical structuring is explicit. So at what point then did Lacan realize that his investigation of structure led to an analysis of problems of formalization and of its role in the sciences? In the seminar that he was presenting concurrently to the publication of "The agency of the letter in the unconscious," a seminar entitled The Object Relation, Lacan makes much use of formalization and of proofs of impossibility in relation to the structure of phobia in the case of Little Hans – who is mentioned in E/S, p. 168. But did Lacan's movement towards explicit mathematical formulation start earlier than this? This is a central problem, and a return to some of Lacan's early texts may provide us with guidelines to a way through it.

Already in the first decade of his work, Lacan was working with structure, both explicitly and implicitly: explicitly with the structures of psychoanalysis and psychoanalytical psychiatry, as well as explicitly with the structures of language, and implicitly with the structures of mathematics. Even in this period of Lacan's work, he was committed to the necessity of producing an analysis of the structures of language. "The lived experience of the paranoiac" he says, "and the conception of the world that it engenders, can be conceived of as an original syntax . . ." (PP, p. 387).[8] There are already present here, as in the rest of Lacan's work in this pre-war period, a range of terminologies that appeal for mathematical formulation: in this paper, for example, Lacan claims the symbolizations present in the structure of paranoia to be derivatives of what he calls "iterative identification of the object" (PP, p. 387). The scientific context of these terms – iteration, repetition, revolution – he would already have been quite familiar with by virtue of the use to which he put the work of Emile Meyerson, who is frequently cited in his doctoral thesis on paranoia. And when Lacan uses a phrase like "logical apparatus" in these texts, he is at the same time questioning what it is that constitutes a logic. Some of the answers to his questions he found later in the 1930s by having recourse to the works of C. S. Peirce.

The works of this period regularly contain formulations that implicitly appeal to mathematical structure. In "Beyond the 'reality principle' " (1936), he comments on the way in which clinical technique is founded on the topology of the signifying chains. Of course this is the terminology that Lacan would use later in his career; here, he talks of "the testimony of the subject" (E, p. 81) given in the analytical session, that is, within the structure of the analytical relation. He says that the analyst has to refuse to select from the symptoms or from the material presented in the session: an abstract reformulation of what the patient has to say would give priority to the "Imaginary" over the "Real". He calls this part of the protocol for the construction of the analytical contract the law of non-systematization. It is based on a previous rule, that of free association – or what he here calls the accompanying law of non-omission. It is an acute way of giving a protocol to the analytical situation, and he ascribes it to Pichon (E, p. 82). What is apparent in his description of this structure is its proto-mathematics. He calls the implementing of the law of non-systematization "respecting succession" – preserving, that is, the relations of order. He describes the "chaining" or connectivity between the elements of the material presented to the analyst, and the relation of the fragments of this material to the structure of which they are a part. The initial chaining of the narrative is different from the one that the analytical work is trying to construct. These are all notions that call on the terms of mathematics, and the question of formalization in these texts is already present.

The "identifying" function of the human mind is a central focus that Lacan gave to his work in the 1930s: more generally, the problem of identification can be seen as a central question throughout all of Lacan's psychoanalytical work, from beginning to end. Lacan used this main theme in the writings of the French philosopher of science Emile Meyerson as a way of relating his clinical and theoretical concerns at the start of the decade, and Meyerson's work functioned as an organizing principle for Lacan in succeeding years. The manifesto statements that Lacan placed at the end of his 1936 essay on the "Reality principle" are indicative of this: "Two questions arise here. How is . . . *reality* constituted . . . through images? How does the I – where the subject recognizes itself – become constituted through identifications that are typical of the subject?" (E, p. 92). So an inclination to locate problems of psychoanalysis within the problem-solving tradition of the sciences is present in this early period: even in this early work "problem" and "proposition" recur regularly as formulations of clinical or theoretical questions. Question/answer; problem/solution; mathematics and the methodology of the sciences: these themes can be described as the elements of Lacan's work in the 1930s.

After the end of the war, and with the re-settling of analytical work in France, Lacan moved to a reformulation of his earlier questions. Here the earlier priority given to image functioning over the structure of language is reversed. In "A few words on psychic causality," he uses the example of the word "curtain" (*rideau*) to show how it holds a place in a network constructed by metaphors and by play on words; *rideau* alludes in French to the laughter of water (*ris d'eau*), and in English, or in any translation, alludes to Hamlet's slaying of Polonius behind an arras (*E*, p. 166–7). It is in such a network that images make their nest. The Symbolic in this formulation is dominant over the Imaginary, and the aim of analysis is to give an articulation to its threads. In this text, Lacan re-addresses the question of language in terms of the "semantic system" which "forms the child" (*E*, p. 166). He looks to the work of linguists and philosophers to see what light they can throw on this problem – but not in order to base his science on theirs. He proposes even to construct a unit of semantics (a "semanteme," *E*, p. 167), but without wishing to take the notion from these allied fields. The formulations that he looks to in order to construct a solution to his problem are those of mathematics – a word, he says, "is not a sign, but a knot of signification" (*E*, p. 166).

The interest that Lacan maintained at this time in contemporary philosophy of science gave him reason to reflect on mathematics and on formalization. He would have found in Meyerson's work the idea that philosophy serves as a guiding framework for science. But this rich idea – that philosophical "research programs" orientate the direction of scientific research – was used by Meyerson to focus largely on this guiding philosophy, and its role in determining the choice of scientific problems, rather than on the internal structure of the science. Freud, however, had proposed a domain of differentiation between philosophy and science, and he had made use of this domain in determining the direction of psychoanalysis. Lacan needed some means of analyzing such a divide. None of the commentaries accessible at the start of this decade had focused on the programs of mathematics to be found within such programs of science. So a series of problems were leading Lacan in the direction of the study of the structure of mathematics, and he knew of one student of these themes whose work gave a priority to formalization and the foundations of mathematics: the Russian philosopher of science Alexandre Koyré.

Koyré was teaching in Paris from 1922; his first text on the foundations of science – on Copernicus – was published there in 1934. Whether Lacan's first encounter with Koyré's theses on science date from these years or from later is unclear. He had read Koyré's book on Jacob Boehme as early as 1929 and, by the time he attended Kojève's seminar in 1934, knew of the friendship and family relations between Koyré and Kojève. What is certain is that Koyré had an active involvement with Lacan from 1954: in the first session of Lacan's seminar in the winter of that year, Lacan referred to the seminar that Koyré had given on the previous day, 16 November 1954. Lacan refers to Koyré's contribution to a series of seminars organized by Lacan's part of the French psychoanalytic world, the Société française de psychanalyse, that ran throughout the winter and summer of 1954–5.[9] The bearing of Koyré's work on Lacan was by then long-standing; as he indicated himself: "it is well-known that everything I know about the 'Copernican revolution' has been taught to me by Koyré."[10]

Lacan chose as a title of a section of "Beyond the 'reality principle' " (1936) a phrase modeled on the language of the history of science. At the time when Koyré was describing "the revolution of the celestial orbits," Lacan chose the phrase, "The revolution of the Freudian method" (E, p. 81). Both terms are based on a equivocation: in Koyré's case between the Copernican revolution and the celestial paths of the planets, and in Lacan's between the Freudian revolution of the discovery of the unconscious, and the revolution brought about in a person's way of being in the world by this Freudian method. Here there is an immediate parallelism proposed between psychoanalytical method and the method of science – but there is no intention to reduce either of these to a fixed domain. The methods of the sciences – and the structures of mathematics which are at the heart of them – are subject to change, and Koyré was well aware that such changes applied also to mathematics. He had participated in controversial discussions with Bertrand Russell in 1912 on the foundations of mathematics, and he later remarked that "having ourselves lived through two or three profound crises in our manner of thinking – the 'crisis of foundations' and the 'eclipse of absolutes' in mathematics" he found himself as a result well positioned to "analyze the structure" of bodies of ideas belonging to the past.[11] These ideas about shifts in the domain of formal structure was not only current, but under discussion during the years of Lacan's early work.

In the late 1930s, Alonzo Church and others published in Paris a commentary on the foundations of mathematics.[12] In it, Church raised doubts about the adequacy of foundations that had been proposed for mathematics during the first four decades of the century: "questions in mathematics cannot be given a definite meaning, in fact do not have a definite *subject*," he claimed, unless they have been subjected to a process of formalization which has rendered the ideas concerned "precise and precisely communicable."[13] He commented in particular on systems which passed this test – the systems of Russell and Whitehead and those developed out of the axiomatization proposed by Zermelo. While Church developed what has later been called a metaphysical research program for the foundations of mathematics – one particular way of proposing how it is that the subject is implicated in structure – Koyré proposed a quite different program. He sought to describe how new mathematical structures, including structures of meaning, can be created out of the analysis of those of the past; in this way, he claimed, new "logical, axiomatic, and intuitive" foundations for structure come into being. Here is no fixed determination; it seems then that if the destiny of the letter lies in the structures of the mathematicians, the analysis of these structures had better include both psychoanalysts and experts in the foundations of mathematics. This inclusion – of mathematicians and foundationalists – became a central aim of Lacan's program.

Paul Valéry had tried, in his private notebooks, to develop a similar program. It aimed at a formalization of psychic structure, but without the "subject already determined by the letter." From very early on he had been determined to find in mathematics an instrument for charting the pathways within the soul. In his notebooks from 1894 he wrote: "What I posit is this: that mathematical science, disengaged from its applications . . . and reduced to algebra, that is to say, to the analysis of the transformations of a purely differential being . . . is the most faithful document of the properties of grouping, of disjunction, and of variation of the spirit."[14] Soon afterwards he had decided on topology as the favorite science: "Analysis situs seeks for the principles – the pure notations for all these relations that are expressed by – intus, extra, trans, circum, that's to say, the subdivision of a space . . . into regions."[15]

Valéry realized that a topology was necessary for his program, and on this basis he attempted to produce three registers: "The fundamental problem is a problem of analysis situs . . . The set of sensations – S; The set of representations – R; The set of 'acts' – A." This trinity he tried to relate to his intricate program for language; "language is more difficult than Chinese" he said, and more than "the most 'symbolical' algebra."[16] After investigating the possibility of formalizing "articulated" language algebraically, he proposed language as a fundamental, general, space – a heroic attempt to formulate within mathematical structure the condition of the human subject, but while taking the foundations of mathematics for granted. In devising this theory of the letter, he had drawn on his friendship with the French mathematician Emile Borel, as well as on the work of philosophers of science – including

Brunschvicg and Meyerson. A critical formulation of the foundations of structure had been available to Lacan, but Valéry in constructing his program had drawn on Meyerson, and did not have the benefit of Koyré's example.

II

The Archimedean inspiration of these methods stares you in the face.
Alexandre Koyré in "La Renaissance"[17]

Koyré gave three lectures on Descartes on the tercentenary of the publication of Descartes' *Method*, in Cairo in 1937. They were published almost immediately in French and Arabic, and republished again – in French – in New York during the Second World War. They thus form part of the intellectual culture shared and disseminated by Koyré, Jakobson, and Lévi-Strauss in their exile in New York. The theme of these lectures is that of a manifesto for formalization, almost a manifesto for the matheme. They thus give some insight into the way in which Lacan was caught up in the question of determining the place of mathematics in the modern sciences; moreover, this drive toward formalization is relevant to Freud's problem of the relation between psychoanalysis and science.

Koyré started his account with the early sixteenth century. He described some of the traditions of skepticism found in commentaries on the sciences from Agrippa to Montaigne. These and other criticisms had challenged assumptions about space and its relation to mathematics current in mediaeval science. These old world-views of the sciences had already been weakened when the pathways described by science were given literal and new coordinates by Descartes as he attempted to finally come to terms with this skeptical tradition. Koyré described the movement that was produced in terms of three shifts, and the organization of his lectures followed the theme of those three moments – a world rendered "uncertain"; the "disappearance" of a cosmos; and the consolatory "reappearance" of a universe. This formulation gives to the succession of these programs of science a "phallic" structure of loss and repossession. Freud had earlier determined such a structure to be at play – he called it then the *Fort-Da* principle – as his grandchild attempted to construct a world of relations to others.[18] The parallelism between the two – from Lacan's point of view – is to be expected.

Agrippa had described the variety of the sciences and their contradictions, speculations, and errors that could be found, he claimed, throughout the domain of the sciences and their techniques. "Some see the soul as a connectivity," others see it as a "point bound to the body," others as "a point with no anchoring in the body"; his survey of the sciences included moral as well as natural sciences, and, among other themes, detailed mathematics (geometry, arithmetic, and "mathesis" generally), astronomy, grammar, and the interpretation of dreams.[19] Koyré's version of the rise of the mathematical sciences revolves around his reading of these trajectories that started with Agrippa's text, *De incertitudine et vanitate scientiarum* (*On the Uncertainty and Vanity of the Sciences*). As the supposed unity of the world "fell into shreds" the questioning that had produced this effect itself became something that was put into question. The questioning of world-views became subject to analysis.

As Descartes took up the problems of what can be called a program of "critical skepticism," he found that the philosopher is constrained to adopt a position that had already been forced on Montaigne: he "interrogates the questioner." This Socratic questioning of the subject is engaged in the early parts of the psychoanalytic cure;[20] that it was a forced step in the Cartesian development of science is part of the presentation that Koyré gives of these developments. It was Descartes, according to Koyré, who pushed further the "analyses" initiated by Montaigne; the mathematization of the world introduced by Descartes appears simply, in this perspective, as a consequence of taking such an analysis "to its end."

Koyré stresses – contra the attempts of Bacon and Locke to move science towards "presuppositionless" foundations – that any experience of, or experiment on, the world "presupposes a previous theory." He is even more specific than this. Towards the end of his first lecture he says, "experience (of the world) implies a language within which one addresses it." It is "impossible," says Koyré, for any experience of the world not to draw on the language used to give a formulation to it.

Koyré sees the heart of Descartes' program in the formulation that he gives to a proposition known since the time of classical Greek science and philosophy, that nature speaks the language of mathematics. It is in this language, says Koyré, that nature will respond to the questions that a science puts to it. In this way the real conditions of our existence – questions of physics and questions of the nature of the human soul – can be formulated within a metaphysics of what Koyré calls "the real value of mathematicism."

In putting it thus, Koyré is taking informal descriptions of the world – and certainly "common sense" – to be clothed in what he calls the "imaginary"; the virtue of mathematical structure is that it allows such imaginary formulations to be left behind, as it opens up pathways that allow access to what is real.

Any such restitution of the sciences places mathematical relations at the center of its program. Koyré states that a science – in Descartes' view – needs a metaphysics: it is formulated and develops within a metaphysical orientation which both directs its researches and provides an apparatus for the solution to its problems. The "clear" ideas that Descartes seeks in order to constitute this basis of this science Koyré thinks can be characterized unequivocally: what is clear can only be mathematics, or more accurately, what is clear must be capable of being *mathematized*. Koyré cites Descartes' resolve "to seek no other science, than that which I could find in myself, or in the great book of the world." The result of this was a new logic and a new physics, together with a new metaphysics to guide its problems. Where Freud had started out his researches with a purification, a catharsis, Koyré sees Descartes as operating a revolution based on a *catharsis* of reason by doubt. In such a science the human soul is studying its own actions, analyzing its own operations.

It is only when a science has incorporated a mathematical apparatus, said Lacan, that it can become fruitful.[21] He stated this in the context of a discussion on the apparatus of science; he said the "drive is not a substance, but a vector," and if there were doubt as to how seriously he intended the mathematical reference, he immediately added a reference to the scalars that with this vector make up a vector field. In this text, Lacan described the start of his work clearly: "It's very simply language, absolutely nothing else". Even in this formulation, however, there are latent appeals to structure and to mathematics. The structure of language was of course always at play "from the beginning"; and as regards this structure, he states, "When Freud talks about this, it's always a question of a knot, of an associative net". A science unsupported by mathematics leads "strictly to nothing," and any such science is unable, he claimed, to "exit the field of the imaginary," and approach the real.

Lacan, in this text, finds the "real structure" of a scientific theory in its "logic, and not in its empirical face". With this logic in its turn, he wants to propose a parallelism between its domain, and that of the apparatus of the soul. The logic he talks of here is a "weak" logic, presumably an intuitionistic logic. He invokes not only this logic, but topology, calling on the notion of neighborhood in order to account for the position the human subject takes up within exchanges that determine the place of speech. In 1974, Lacan uses fragments of mathematics as guides for the investigation of the soul.

Late in 1971 Lacan had introduced his notion of the matheme. It can be found, for instance, in the session of 2 December 1971, of the seminar parallel to his public seminar, held that year at the Sainte-Anne psychiatric hospital in the south of Paris. The condition of the unconscious is that of being disconnected; it is by its very constitution submitted to the structuring of mathematics. While for Freud suffering takes up the forms given to it by the structure of the unconscious, for Lacan it is given form by the textures of language. Language is needed to give to suffering not only its formulation, but its expression. How does one approach any real determination of suffering in conditions such as these? Lacan, in his seminar, hoped to organize his response to this predicament by utilizing the proof procedures of the ancient Greeks. In his text "L'Etourdit", he attempted to formulate how the real can be formulated as an impasse within proofs of limitation or impossibility. In this, says Lacan, there is being grasped something of what in his account is the movement through the symbolic towards the real. This approach to the real presupposes the pathways in terms of which it is expressed: it cannot therefore be expressed independently of the apparatus of language. It is for this that Lacan devised his notion of matheme; with them, something is being encountered which it is impossible to fully formulate, but which when constrained within a formalization is susceptible both to proof and to its limitation.

Nathalie Charraud, in her account of the matheme, stresses the connection between clinical practice and this approach to the real. She indicates the effect of the matheme on psychoanalysis as a clinical activity, as well as a scientific research program: "If one takes Lacan's topology and mathemes seriously, the clinical scene changes too."[22] She cites Lacan's saying that "formalization is our goal, our ideal." The aim of psychoanalysis is to weaken ideals, and there is a certain irony here – intended, it seems, as a joke – as Lacan presents the apparatus for ensuring this as a replacement ideal. But the structure of the unconscious forces this application to mathematics: the construction of a program of formalization within psychoanalysis aims to give coordinates to what is real. Lacan, in 1971, had effectively been working on such a program for forty years. Today this work is carried on by many individual researchers, and within a number of series of seminars. If one were asked to formulate a (realistic) aim for a science in this field, it would be centered around suffering – around mathematical formulations of articulation, toleration, and connection. It is such an aim that informs Lacan's account of how the matheme can act for the good.

The formulation given to the good by M. F. Burnyeat includes the view that a central characteristic of mathematics is that it possesses the precision needed to focus on what is real. Once given a formulation in terms of mathematics, the soul is forced to find its access to what is real along such formal pathways.[23] Freud had organized his concept of the unconscious around this theme, and in this respect, Burnyeat, Freud, and Lacan are in agreement. Lacan and Burnyeat also agree on the special position of mathematics, in so far as it is, in Burnyeat's phrase, a "constitutive part of ethical understanding." For Lacan it is certainly a part of ethics, and the term that he introduced to indicate the intrication of the subject in such pathways is that of the matheme.

Koyré referred to the Archimedean method, and there is some connection between Archimedes and Lacan, between the geometer of Syracuse and the topologist and matheme-matician of Paris. Reviel Netz describes the method that made up Archimedes' revolutionary technique, saying that "in a remarkable *tour de force*" Archimedes "made a seminal contribution to the mathematization of the . . . world."[24] Here is the tradition of mathematical science. Jacob Klein, also commenting on Archimedes, says, "The systems of Archimedes . . . represent nothing but the consistent development of the Greek mode of thought and speech."[25] Here is the articulation of the field of speech. The relation between poetry and mathematics reappears again at this point, and Lacan worked in both these fields, of mathematics and language, as he attempted to bring reason to bear in a field defined from the beginning by its contrary.

In Descartes' time, it may have seemed that mathematics could rescue reason from doubt. After the crises of mathematics in the nineteenth and twentieth centuries, the situation of mathematics is more complex, and much less clear. Koyré commented on this in his Descartes text, and recapitulated this comment, with some vigor, in his retrospective formulations in 1951. But foundational complexity or not, mathematical formalization is the kernel of the program described by Koyré – it is at the heart of the version that he gave of Descartes. In a more modern form, it is at the heart of the program and strategies adopted by Lacan. Challenges are given to the proposed bases of mathematics from within mathematics itself, and far from being a fault, this augments the ability of such a program to approach what is real. Yes, admitted Koyré, "life is much more complex than an algebraic formula." But the option, he said, in these pre-war years, is either that of constructing an analysis of the human soul using the apparatus provided by mathematics, or alternatively, of giving ourselves up, of "submitting to deep and obscure forces" that, unanalyzed, would propel human beings to the abyss.

NOTES

1. Georg Kreisel, "Gödel's excursions into intuitionistic logic," *Gödel Remembered: Gödel-Symposium in Salzburg, 10–12 July 1983* (Naples: Bibliopolis, 1987) p. 132. The "as it were" is Kreisel's way of invoking a wide-ranging investigation of the foundations of mathematics that he takes to be necessary in order to resolve this question.

2. In "The question of lay analysis," Freud wrote: "We do not want after all to despise the word. It is certainly a powerful instrument; it is the means by which we convey our feelings to one another, our method of influencing other people.

Words can do unspeakable good, and cause terrible wounds" (*SE* 20, p. 187–8). For Freud's views of psychoanalysis in relation to science and philosophy, see also Chapter 25 of *New Introductory Lectures on Psychoanalysis* (*SE* 22). For a version of Lacan's reformulation of the same themes, see "L'Etourdit" (1973), *Autres écrits*, pp. 449–95. As will become clear, what Lacan means by analytical work is something that sometimes takes place in a consulting room, and sometimes takes place in a study. Finding the appropriate terms is demanded in both places.

3. Jacques Lacan, "Place, origine, et fin de mon enseignement" (1967), *Essaim: Revue de psychanalyse* 5 (Spring 2000), p. 5–31.

4. In terms of the series of Lacan's papers available in *Ecrits*, this shift is represented by the movement from the 1936 paper, "Au-delà du 'principe de réalité'" ("Beyond the 'reality principle'") to the 1948 paper, "Propos sur la causalité psychique".

5. Philippe Lacoue-Labarthe and Jean-Luc Nancy, *The Title of the Letter: A Reading of Lacan*, trans. François Raffoul and David Pettigrew (Albany: State University of New York Press, 1992).

6. Jacques Lacan, *Seminar on 'The Purloined Letter,'* trans. Jeffrey Mehlman, *The Purloined Poe*, eds. John P. Muller and William J. Richardson (Baltimore: Johns Hopkins University Press, 1988), pp. 28–54. At the start of his seminar of 25 March 1955, Lacan expressed a wish that Jacques Riguet, a leading French algebraicist who was working with Lacan at the time, be present to help them progress with their work.

7. This is a resumé of the content of their book in the introduction to its re-edition in 1990. The first publication, in 1973, had received a (respectful but ironical) response from Lacan in his seminar of 20 February 1973: "Read it," he effectively said to his audience, "they have read me very well."

8. Jacques Lacan, *Le Problème du style et la conception psychiatrique des formes paranoiaques de l'éxpérience* (1933), in *PP*, pp. 383–8.

9. Koyré's title of this series was "Problems of the Platonic dialogue." Koyré's book on Plato would later be published with his text on Descartes in Paris. The series had been opened the previous week by Jean Delay with a presentation on neurosis and creativity.

10. Jacques Lacan, "Radiophonie," *Autres écrits* (Paris: Seuil, 2001), p. 429. My translation.

11. Alexandre Koyré, "Orientation et projets de recherches," *Etudes d'histoire de la pensée scientifique* (Paris: Presses Universitaires de France, 1966), p. 4.

12. Alonzo Church, "The present situation in the foundations of mathematics," *Philosophie mathématique*, ed. Ferdinand Gonseth (Paris: Hermann, 1939).

13. Church, "The present situation in the foundations of mathematics," p. 67. Italics in original.

14. Paul Valéry, *Cahiers*, vol. I (Paris: Gallimard, 1973), p. 775.

15. *Ibid.*, p. 787.

16. *Ibid.*, p. 415.

17. Alexandre Koyré, "La Renaissance," *Histoire générale des sciences, II, La Science moderne (de 1450 à 1800)* (Paris: Presses Universitaires de France, 1958), p. 105.

18. Bernard Burgoyne, "Autism and topology," in *Drawing the Soul: Schemas and Models in Psychoanalysis*, ed. Bernard Burgoyne (London: Rebus Press, 2000).

19. Heinrich Cornelius Agrippa von Nettesheim, *Die Eitelkeit und Unsicherheit der Wissenschaften* (1530) (Munich: Georg Müller, 1913), preface and chapters 1 to LII, *passim*. See particularly Chapters XI, XXXIX, and LII.
20. See Bernard Burgoyne, "Freud's Socrates," *The European Journal of Psychotherapy, Counselling and Health*, vol. 4/1 (2000).
21. Jacques Lacan, "Le Phénomène lacanien" (1974), *Les Cahiers cliniques de Nice*, 1 (June 1998), p. 13.
22. Nathalie Charraud, "Matheme," *A Compendium of Lacanian Terms*, eds. Huguette Glowinski, Zita M. Marks, and Sara Murphy (London: Free Association Books, 2001). See also Charraud's *Lacan et les mathématiques* (Paris: Anthropos, 1997) and "A calculus of convergence," in *Drawing the Soul: Schemas and Models in Psychoanalysis*.
23. M. F. Burnyeat, "Plato on why mathematics is good for the soul," *Mathematics and Necessity: Essays in the History of Philosophy*, ed. Timothy Smiley (Oxford: Oxford University Press, 2000).
24. Reviel Netz, *The Shaping of Deduction in Greek Mathematics* (Cambridge: Cambridge University Press, 1999), p. 313.
25. Jacob Klein, *Greek Mathematical Thought and the Origin of Algebra* (Cambridge, Mass.: MIT Press, 1968), p. 131–2.

6

COLETTE SOLER

The paradoxes of the symptom in psychoanalysis

Lacan without paradox

Paradoxical formulas are not lacking in Lacan's texts and teachings. As far as the symptom is concerned, these paradoxes culminate in the idea that normative heterosexuality is itself a symptom, and that sexual partners are symptoms for each other. Is Lacan being facetious and indulging his notorious taste for paradox? Is he performing intellectual acrobatics? The questions can rebound endlessly, but I, for one, conclude from all my readings and my clinical experience that the Lacan we meet here is not paradoxical any more. In fact, with the symptom, each psychoanalyst should be prepared to be questioned, for what he or she has to say about symptoms provides a test for the consistency of his or her praxis and doctrine. No doubt Lacan has to be tested like all others on this point, and if he is, the verdict reached after we follow his successive elaborations will correspond to the rigor of a rationalism that is never canceled but always adjusted to the specificity of its field.

We just need to read Lacan closely. In some twenty years of teaching, his definitions of the symptom evolved. One can verify that, at each state, they were compatible with the overall theory, and in particular, with the successive definitions he gave of the unconscious. Thus, when he defined the unconscious as speech, which had been suggested by the technique of the talking cure, he treated the symptom as a kind of message, an encoded cipher for a gagged discourse containing a kernel of truth. When the unconscious was described not just as speech but as a language, the symptom became a signifier structured like a metaphorical chain concealing the primary signifier of the trauma. This thesis is understandable only if one admits that the signifier, by nature, is not necessarily verbal, even less phonetic. Hence, any discrete element of reality can be raised to the status of signifier, torn from the field of what we name things. One stage later, when the unconscious was defined as the "treasure of the drives" which implied a fusion, a wedding, as it were, between signifiers and living beings, the corresponding notion was the symptom as jouissance, a notion which Lacan never ceased to re-elaborate through the later years. The last stage sent us to the Real, whereas the symptom as message or as signifier sent us to the junction between the Imaginary and the Symbolic.

Thus Lacan came to the point where he recaptured the first as well as the last of Freud's theses on the symptom: the symptom is a mode of satisfaction. It can be deciphered like a message, but it is not only a way of speaking, it is also above all a form of jouissance, the key of its rebus being always the drive which is secretly satisfied. This is also why I have called Lacan's second step his "second return to Freud."[1] The first step emphasized the linguistic implications of the technique of deciphering and produced the famous thesis of an unconscious structured like a language. The second step, which is less visible, emphasized another aspect: the language of the symptom is, so to speak, incarnated, embodied; it organizes and regulates jouissance. Hence, the surprising formula one finds close to the end of *Encore*: "The real, I will say, is the mystery of the speaking body, the mystery of the unconscious" (*S XX*, p. 131).

The issue was always to make sense of possible therapeutic effects. In psychoanalysis, however, therapeutic effects testify to the grasp of language on what is most real in symptomatic disorders; one verifies that the least verbal manifestations (anxiety, somatic disorders, thought disturbances) can be transformed by the sole means of language. The curious docility of the symptom in an analytical setting supports this conception of the unconscious. On this point, Lacan went a step further, eventually reaching a concept of the symptom which accounted not only for therapeutic effects but for the very limits of these effects, as well as for those of the psychoanalytic operation. In this respect, he did far more than just question and reassert the rationality of the Freudian operation.

A reversal of perspective

Lacan's most paradoxical formulas are those which allow us to pinpoint his own contribution to psychoanalysis. Condensed in memorable statements, they circulate, are repeated, and generally remain misunderstood, until they turn into empty refrains – mere provocative enigmas defying good sense. "There is no such a thing as sexual relationship," "The woman does not exist," or the idea that a symptom is the way by which one "enjoys one's unconscious."[2] What is more, Lacan would claim that these were only "Freud's statements." It is true that one can make Freud say such things although he never worded his sayings in such a manner. Indeed, the deciphering of the unconscious, Freud's discovery, is intrinsically linked in his conception to the revelation of what he calls the *Triebe*, the drives, whose fragmented, multiple character is easily identifiable in the infantile "polymorphous perversion." As early as 1905, with his *Three Essays on the Theory of Sexuality*, Freud had pointed out the link between the unconscious and the characteristics of jouissance implied in the term of *Trieb*: the drives are fragmented, have a constant strength, a constant impulse. Freud stressed that the drive was unaware of the rhythms of biological life. He emphasized its partial and fragmented character, and also its insertion into the subject's body via erogenous zones, its indifference to the so-called objectal link. Hence the problem Freud faced, and whose evolution one can follow through the various footnotes added to the text through the years, was the following: how can a mode of jouissance that is so self-centered come to be reconciled with the relationship of desire and love for another body, which is obviously necessary for the constitution of the sexual couple, whatever it may be, but especially of the heterosexual couple? Thus, the discovery of the drive, far from leading to pansexualism, rather posed the question, from its very origin, of the libido that was apt to sustain the sexual link. And this is what crops up in Lacan's formula: "There is no such a thing as a sexual relationship." I shall come back to that point later.

If Freud opened this perspective, he did not carry it to its logical conclusion. To answer the question, finally, he has nothing to offer but his elaboration of the Oedipus complex, with the various identifications resulting from it. With this, he tried to explain one thing and its reverse, I mean the norm of heterosexual desire and what differs from it. And when he admitted that he did not know, it was the concept of "constitution" – that is, nature – so often referred to by him, that remained his last resort. After having clearly located the link between the symptom and sexuality – it is precisely on this point that he broke decisively with Jung – Freud turned the symptom into an anomaly of the sexual, more precisely a distorted substitute of the so-called normal sexual satisfaction. In doing this, he did not abandon the classical conception which more or less postulated that attraction between sexes was governed by nature. Hence, in this case, it was obvious that the symptom could only be conceived within the sphere of an individual pathology of jouissance.

It must be said that this point of view is strongly suggested by the most elementary clinical experience of hearing the complaint leading a subject to psychoanalysis: symptoms are presented to the analyst as those things which never stop from imposing themselves on one. It may take the form of not being able to refrain from thinking or feeling in the body or of experiencing certain troubling affects. Thus, symptoms are experienced as trouble, anomaly, deviation, and also as constraint. In this respect, the only difference between the patient and Freud is that the former does not immediately perceive the sexual implications although from the very beginning transference makes him aware of the incidence of the unconscious.

The primary affect created by the symptom as dysfunction is a fact that no clinician could deny, Lacan no more than any other. Feelings, however, are no sure guides to truth, and, moreover, psychoanalysis does not just aim at revealing what is not functioning properly. And what does it reveal when it deals with the "psychology of the love life," in its happy as well as unhappy forms, if not this – that it is the unconscious which is the master on board, presiding over what we call the mysteries of love, specifically over the choice of the object in so far as it causes desire and/or jouissance? To put it in another way, the love partner, in the sexual sense of the term, also partakes of the deciphering. Hence, this process is no less a "formation of unconscious," it is no less coded than an obsession or a somatization. Not only are the paradoxes of the drive at the core of the unconscious but they intervene as well between a man and a woman; more generally, it is between bodies that the unconscious is present, simultaneously separating and linking them. Freud perceived this fact at the level of our love life and of groups, but he did not draw its full consequences. This is why when Lacan drew the proper consequences, one could say that he extracted the truth-saying of Freud himself. And yet the reversal of perspective he introduced into the conception of symptom was so complete that it went far beyond Freud.

There is the symptom

The general formula could be as follows: if there is no such a thing as a sexual relationship, which suggests a basic flaw in human relationships, there is the symptom, or a substitute formation generated by the unconscious. Between the two formulas, a third one remains implicit, a concept at which Lacan hammered away for a whole seminar through the famous phrase: "There is (the) One." This formula is not as simple as it seems, whether it refers to the "One" of the signifier One as opposed to Two, or the "One" of the jouissance of the body beyond any reciprocal link. In each case, this formula underlines the primacy of a flow of jouissance in the subject which is incommensurable with his or her sexual partner's own jouissance. The symptom which achieves a union between the discrete elements of the unconscious and that other thing which is jouissance provides a replacement. Given that the appropriate partner for jouissance is lacking, symptoms put in place of it something else, a substitute. It contradicts the "there is no such thing . . . " of the impossible sexual relationship by erecting a "there is . . . " There is something, an element grasped from the unconscious that fixes the privileged jouissance in the subject.

Hence the symptom is no longer the problem but the solution, and, as I said, without any paradox. The solution is proper to everyone, the response to the "no relation" imposed on all, the universal illness for beings who are affected by the unconscious. This symptomatic solution can be more or less uncomfortable for the subject, more or less common, but in any case it responds to the lack which is at the core of language, the lack related to the impossibility of inscribing the other jouissance not connected with the unconscious. The spectrum of consequences is vast but the main one is this: there is no subject without a symptom, since the symptom signals an individual manner of confronting sexuality. It is through the symptom that everyone has access to his or her jouissance, supplying the lack proper to language via the forgeries of the unconscious. We can use the singular for this symptom, although of course there are many others, and we can even qualify it as a fundamental symptom. One should not dream of eliminating it: an analysis which starts with the symptom will also end with the symptom – hopefully transformed.

The Lacanian hypothesis

We must now return to what is specific to the Lacanian hypothesis. It concerns more than the function of speech in the field of language, it defines the function of speech and language in the field of living jouissance. The hypothesis does not correspond exactly to what Lacan demonstrated regarding the Freudian field, namely that it is structured like a language, since it asserts fundamentally that the unconscious and its effects on human beings are consequences of language. The seminar *Encore* formulates this hypothesis clearly, although it had been in the works before that date. To recognize an effect of language in the drive already meant assuming that language, far from being reduced to its function of communication, is an operator capable of transforming the Real.

With this hypothesis, Lacan differs from a linguist like Chomsky who assumes that language is an instrument and also from all those who cannot imagine that the drive is a consequence of speech in the body. If we ask, "Where does the drive come from?" we have only one answer: the drive is produced by the operation not of the Holy Ghost but of language. The drive derives from needs, the drive is a transformation of natural necessities produced by language, through the obligation of articulating demands. Such is the Lacanian thesis without which no one can be called a Lacanian: language is not an instrument that we can use as we want, is not just an organ allowing one to express oneself or to communicate with others, as it is often believed, but language is fundamentally inscribed in the real. The human being, in so far as he is speaking, loses the instinctual regulations of animality and is made a language-being or *parlêtre*. To use the vocabulary of Lacan's *Seminar VII, Ethics of Psychoanalysis*, one might say that language is the cause of *das Ding* (the Thing), which is something like a hole in the real, something that creates a will to jouissance, a constant pressing toward satisfaction. But language is not only the cause of human de-naturation, it is also the way, the only way perhaps, to obtain at least partially what *das Ding* demands.

Freud distinguished between two types of drive satisfaction: on the one hand, the symptom, which implies repression; on the other hand, sublimation, which does not suppose repression and which resolves conflicts. In both cases, we can say that language shows the way. In the first case, there is a fixation of jouissance produced by the first encounter with sexuality which returns metonymically or, in a more Freudian vocabulary, through displacement. The second case seems to be different. Of sublimation, we can say: where the void of *das Ding* was, something is produced, invented, an object providing a partial satisfaction. Except that this invention has nothing to do with the sublime: to keep trash in one's pockets is already a sublimation, and when the little child needs any small object as a transitional object, as Winnicot discovered, this is also a sublimation.

It seems that the last teachings of Lacan collapsed the Freudian distinction between symptom and sublimation. At the beginning, he approached Freud's terms through the distinction between signifier and object. But this was not Lacan's last word. When he started to consider more explicitly the jouissance contained in the symptom, he was obliged to recognize that any signifier by itself could be an object, that a letter is also "a litter" as Joyce suggested in *Finnegans Wake*. In the void of *das Ding* we can put any thing that will function as associate of jouissance, but it will always be an invention of the unconscious.

The letter as partner

It is not a mere accident if Lacan did not respect his own texts' chronology and began *Ecrits* with the *Seminar on "The Purloined Letter,"* a text which is itself a collage of fragments belonging to various periods. The fact is that this text already deals with language as disconnected from any meaning linked with the Imaginary. The psychoanalyst, no less than the "man of letters," often appears to be in thrall to meaning. This seminar demonstrates that the letter is not only a message but also an object: it cannot be reduced to its content since, in Poe's tale, it operates without ever being opened, thus without the intervention of its message. It is enough that the letter exists for one to know that the order – political as much as sexual – represented by the royal couple in the coupling of their two signifiers, is threatened. Here, the letter is the name of a dissident jouissance that Lacan, moreover, assimilates to that of woman. Lacan's commentary on Poe's tale is comparable to his other commentaries on literature: a series of symbols, once put in motion, always entails constraints that produce an ordering law independent of any meaning.

It is no accident that the text of 1955 which defines the symptom as a metaphor, that is, a function of the signifier as a chain, is called "The agency of the *letter* in the unconscious" and not the agency of the *signifier*. Lacan uses the term "letter" to designate that which in the field of language is characterized by the identity of self with self, which the signifier lacks. The text defines the letter as the "localized structure" of the signifier. The Freudian notion of fixation keeps all its relevance without, however, being able to compete with the notion of the letter, which more accurately designates what is at stake, and which Lacan clarified over the years. On the one hand, we can say that the letter is something like the mooring of living jouissance, something which fixes a memory of jouissance; on the other hand, in a deeper sense, the letter is enjoyed in and for itself, it becomes an object of jouissance. It is not so much that jouissance is the referent of the letter, it is rather that the letter is an element of language that is enjoyed. Hence, Lacan's very frequent recourse to writers and to literature, in which – and here he differs from Freud – he does not so much seek to recapture the message of the unconscious as its very materiality, that is to say, its letter.

To put it in different terms, the letter does not "represent" jouissance, it *is* jouissance. It has no referent, it is thus real. It is One, outside the chain, outside discourse, consequently it does not preside over any other link but that of the subject and his or her jouissance. The letter cancels the referential function of language: the letter imposes itself, within language, as an exception to the chain. And Lacan finally found in *Finnegans Wake* the supreme display of what Freud had perceived about schizophrenics: their tendency to treat words as things, outside meaning.

The very general definition of the symptom as a function of the letter in *R. S. I.* unified the different aspects of symptom previously distinguished by Lacan. He writes it as $f(x)$, with "f" representing the jouissance function and "x" as any element of unconscious which is, as it were, raised to the status of the letter. The formula states that the symptom is "the way every one may find jouissance in his or her unconscious." Not only is there no subject without a symptom, but there are no other partners than symptomatic

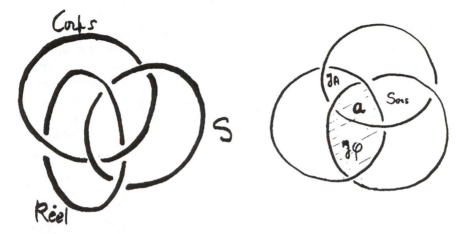

Figure 6.1 Lacan's rendition of the Borromean knot[3]

partners invented by the unconscious. When we speak about the "symptom-partner" we stress the idea that every partner, in so far as he, she or it is an object of jouissance, is determined by the unconscious, by an element of unconscious language. Thus Lacan could call both a woman and the literary use of letters a symptom. It is not that there is a sort of literature which is symptomatic, but that literature itself is a partner of jouissance.

If the symptom designates whatever participates in jouissance, it may or may not be in conformity with the norms of discourse; jouissance has more than one modality. We have to distinguish along with the jouissance of the pure letter (something symbolic transformed into something real) and the jouissance of meaning (a mixture between symbolic and imaginary elements), that which is neither of the letter nor of meaning. A jouissance that remains alien to any form of symbolization, that in no way reaches the unconscious but may haunt the imaginary form of the body, is what we may call the Real. There are thus not just one but three modes of jouissance, which leads to another question: are they linked or not? In fact, the Borromean knot provides an answer.

A new symptomatology

The Borromean knot, a formation of three linked rings in which each ring prevents the other two from drifting apart, was evoked for the first time by Lacan in his *Ou pire . . .* seminar. It was a means by which Lacan tried to extend his definition of the symptom; as a consequence of its introduction in his theory, a whole new program opened up. In Lacan's later seminars, one can witness his methodical effort, using the knot as an operator, to think differently about clinical issues previously formulated in terms of language and discourse. For instance, in the seminar of 18 December 1973, entitled *Les Non-dupes errent*, Lacan distinguished different types of love according to different modalities of knotting. A week earlier, Little Hans' phobia had been interpreted in a different light through the knot. It was as though all the terms of the clinic could be reconsidered in terms of knots: inhibition, symptom, anxiety, the broken sentences of psychosis, the Oedipus complex, and, of course, the function of the father.

Yet this Borromean clinic not only involves a reformulation of traditional clinical issues, it also introduces new categories of symptomatology. Lacan, like Freud, remained rather faithful to classical diagnoses, borrowing paranoia from Kraepelin, schizophrenia from Bleuler, and perversion from Krafft-Ebing. It is still to this clinic that he refers in his 1973 introduction to the German edition of *Ecrits*. The contrast is striking between Lacan and IPA psychoanalysts who try to avoid these classical formulations with categories such as "borderline" or "narcissistic personality." When Lacan innovated, he did so by following the rhythm of his elaborations on structures, and the peculiar structure of the Borromean knot led him to produce totally unheard-of diagnoses. These diagnoses relied not only on the three categories of the Imaginary, the Symbolic, and the Real that he already had at his disposal, but also crucially depended on the three modes of jouissance: the jouissance of the letter as One, the jouissance in the chain of meaning, and the jouissance which can be said to be Real because it exists as a subtraction from the two preceding ones. In light of these distinctions, it is not enough to say that the symptom is a mode of jouissance; one must define which mode, and thus produce a new declension or grammar of symptoms according to the jouissance that gives them consistency. Then one will be able to speak of Borromean symptoms in the cases where the three consistencies and the three jouissances are bound (neurosis and perversion), of symptoms that are not Borromean (psychosis) and others still that simply repair a flaw of the knot. For this last type of symptom, using the example of Joyce, Lacan produced the new category of the *sinthome*, which he used afterwards in a more general way.

The symptom and mentalities

When Lacan called Joyce "the symptom," he produced a new diagnosis, stating that with Joyce one would cover a whole new range of possibilities in symptomatology. In *Finnegans Wake*, Joyce illustrates the autistic jouissance of the pure letter, which is unmoored – cut off from the Imaginary, from exterior meaning, and thus from any social link.[4] In addition, the artist who uses his art as a means of self-promotion becomes thereby a *sinthome*, to quote the archaic spelling of symptom in French used by Lacan. What Lacan calls *sinthome* is "what allows the Imaginary, the Symbolic and the Real to be held together."[5] I might add: with or without the father. This possibility opens the field of radically new perspectives which modify classical distinctions between psychosis and neurosis.

The disease of "mentality" is another conceptual innovation generated from the Borromean knot; it designates an emancipation of the Imaginary unburdened of the Real. Although less explored, this path was introduced by Lacan on the occasion of a clinical presentation dealing with a young woman whose discourse, quite normal at first, could have been confused with hysterical ramblings. This woman, however, revealed through her testimony that nothing, no objective, and, above all, no object, not even her child whom she claimed to love, was of any importance or consequence. She was not at all delirious, but she testified that for her, the social link with the other had no consistency.

This unanchored imaginary is quite a different avatar of the Imaginary compared to what Lacan diagnosed with Joyce. We all have a mentality: with words, representations come into being in so far as language gives existence to what does not exist outside thought. Fabulation (whether normal or not), mythomania, dreams, delusion and the capacity for creative fiction all proceed from there. Yet, a mentality raised to the status of illness is another thing: it is a mentality which does not have the ballast of any Real. Let us say it is free "joui-sense" without a body, for it is neither linked with the jouissance of the living body or with the fixity of the letter. In this sense, mentality opposes the letter and its jouissance anchored in the One. This is why in the Borromean knot, Lacan inscribes the symptom as a letter outside the two circles of the symbolic and the imaginary. Of Joyce, at least Joyce-the-letter, one cannot say that he suffers from mentality, but rather that he abstracts himself from it.

This may be formulated differently so as to establish a link with classical nosography. Lacan asserted that the "pulverulent discourse,"[6] that is, a discourse without direction, was generally impossible. For a subject integrated in a social link, in a discourse, "it is impossible to just say whatever comes randomly." Conversely, in psychosis there is access to the pulverulence of discourse, since psychosis is less subject to the constraints of the discursive order. But this pulverulence has several aspects: *Finnegans Wake* illustrates that of the object-letter, while the disease of unanchored mentality illustrates the pulverulence of meaning.

Writing as symptom

We can ask if those distinctions that are so fecund in the field of the classical clinic give us new and specific points of view about symptomatic literary works. What could convince us more of the jouissance of language than literature? Other questions arise here: are poetry and novels part of literature in the same way? In the case of Joyce, how could he, as a writer, put an end to literature, to what Lacan called the dream of literature? Lacan's thesis about poetry is forceful: he puts the poet beside the prophet, which means that poetry belongs to the dimension of pure saying (*le dire*). It is the least stupid saying, since only poetry (or prophecy) manages to say something new, even unique, using old and worn-out signifiers. Poetry produces new meanings, and with this new meaning, new perspectives on reality.

Here we are able to highlight a semantic problem. Let me explain my use of *sense* and *signification*. There are two kinds of signifieds: *signification* is the signified as grammatically determined, produced and fixed by syntax. It is what we are looking for when we try to explain a text. *Sense* is that part of the signified which is not reducible to signification. It is a fact that, after we have explained the grammatical and semantic significations of a text, we can always wonder: but what does it mean? As saying, poetry belongs to this last register, thus to *sense*.

A novel is not *saying*. A novel is a mixture of little stories, a big soup of significations, a heap of metonymic significations, whether it is a realistic or a non-realistic novel. To explain what I mean, I will evoke the novel that made cultured Europe tremble in the eighteenth century, Jean-Jacques Rousseau's *La Nouvelle Héloïse*. It was an attempt at reinventing the signification of love, at producing a new figure for love which is today completely out of date, but had at that time a stunning effect.

We might then distinguish three aspects of the literary work: the literary symptom of signification, of meaning, and of the letter. They are respectively related to the signifier as producer of signification, the signifier as producer of meaning, and the signifier made letter. A specific type of writing becomes like the implied signature of any writer. I took Rousseau as an example of the first type, and thus I call him "Rousseau, the symbol" by analogy and difference with "Joyce, the symptom." Let me provide another example by setting beside Joyce's unreadable letters the polymorphous letters of Pessoa. These are two kinds of literary symptoms, each author being the best in his language at the beginning of the twentieth century.

Readable and unreadable letters

With Joyce, we have an example of unreadable letters. But what does "unreadable" mean? As Lacan said, "one cannot become mad by deciding it." No one can make himself crazy just because he wants to be so. In the same way, no one can make himself unreadable just because he wants to be so. There are true and false unreadables. Lacan for example. He has been called unreadable, because he was difficult to understand. But it was a false unreadability due to the fact that he was introducing a complete change in the vocabulary and theory of psychoanalysis. It is often the case with precursors. In twenty years, we have greatly reduced the unreadability of Lacan, except of course to people who do not want to read him.

An example of true unreadability would be the French writer Raymond Roussel. Even when he wrote *How I Wrote Some of My Texts*, in which he explained the artificial rules of his method, his texts remained unreadable: you can give neither signification nor meaning to this writing. You can just explain how it is done, and do the same thing, if you want.

Now to Joyce, or more precisely, *Finnegans Wake*. Joyce managed to fascinate in his time and today many readers buy his works; university students are still interested, even stimulated in their thinking by him. In what sense can a psychoanalyst say: "he is unreadable"? Most often, literature is a composite of the jouissance of the letter, the jouissance of meaning, and the jouissance of signification. Lacan diagnosed in *Finnegans Wake* a special multiplication of equivocation that reduces the signified to an enigma, short-circuiting usual meaning. This process concerns psychoanalysts because psychoanalysts, like the unconscious, operate with equivocation.

Joyce's puns, wordplay, and linguistic transformations have an affinity with unconscious mechanisms. It looks like slips of tongue, parapraxes, or jokes, but this is just an appearance. Jokes themselves play with language but they stop when the little meaning necessary to make you laugh is produced. Even the slip of the tongue which is a mistake in the signifier can be readable because its meaning is a limited one, linked with the unconscious of the subject. Joyce pushes the game further and goes methodically beyond limited meaning to a point when the play with signifying materials is no longer submitted to the message, which produces what I call a powderiness of meaning. Years ago, before Lacan, Jung was struck by this peculiarity of Joyce, and he hated it; he was infuriated by it. It is in that sense that *Finnegans Wake* awakens us, and puts an end to the great dream of meaning cultivated for centuries by literature.

We can see the difference with psychoanalysis. To read, in the psychoanalytic experience, means to interpret a subject listening to his or her speech as a spoken text. Thus to read and to interpret the subject's unconscious desire are equivalent. Obviously with literature, things are different. Despite what Freud thought, we do not apply psychoanalysis to literature, and we do not interpret authors through their works. Nevertheless we can grasp the subject presupposed by a text, the subject signified by a text. For instance, in *A Portrait of the Artist as a Young Man*, we cannot say that Stephen, the young artist, is James, the author, even if they are not without likeness. Nevertheless, this portrait, unlike *Finnegans Wake*, is readable, and we can get an idea of Stephen. On the contrary, in *Finnegans Wake*, the letter does not represent a subject, the letter is outside meaning, but not outside jouissance.

To summarize, the signifier is readable when it supposes a subject, that is, the meaning of a desire, and a jouissance in the text. In that case, we say that there is a meaning, a readable meaning. Freud said that the whole set of dreams and free associations of an analysand has only one meaning, the meaning that he calls unconscious desire. The friction between psychoanalysts and critics is understandable. The first group claims that *Finnegans Wake* is a work beyond meaning, and the second group sees meaning in every word. Both are right, but in a completely different way. The meaning which interests a psychoanalyst is the meaning limited and ordered by the jouissance of the subject, so that it allows us to interpret. When the letter becomes a signifier in the real, outside the chain, as it happens in psychotic phenomena, meaning flashes from everywhere, every word, every syllable, it is so powdery, that it is the reader who should decide about meaning. He or she has too many choices. This is why every interpretation of *Finnegans Wake* looks like a projective test that says a lot about the interpreter and nothing about the author. And it seems that Joyce wanted it this way and was very delighted with it.

Now, the literary symptom of unreadability is more than uncommon. It is something completely exceptional. To use language without saying anything is a performance. In the common case, with language we always say more than we want, more than we know. In others words, our speech is the vehicle, the medium of a saying which can be interpreted. In that sense, with the unconscious, everyone is not a poet, but poetry. Through unreadability, the mother tongue is made an object, the Symbolic is converted into the Real without the mediation of the Imaginary which is short-circuited. In *Finnegans Wake*, Joyce appears neither as a novelist nor as a poet: he does not subscribe to the unconscious any longer, he produces strange objects made up of words. Sometimes we can explain how he did it, with what words, what homophonies, what epiphanies, what languages, and so on, but we cannot listen to it, because he doesn't say anything: he is beyond the novel and even beyond poetry. Critics look into his life to find the sources of this material. But his work owes nothing to biography. On the contrary, his work inverts biography – that is, his work is an autography, a life of merely writing, a life of words.

The polymorphous letters

One can set Pessoa in contrast with Joyce. Pessoa, perhaps not as famous in English-speaking countries, is also a paradox, perhaps a greater paradox than Joyce. To be brief, I will say that far from having canceled his subscription to the unconscious, Pessoa has a multiplicity of unconsciouses. He is not a poet, he is a plurality of poets; he was also a critic, a philosopher, a theoretician of trade, a humorist. Obviously, I refer here to the strange phenomenon of heteronymy. We could say that Pessoa is not an author, but a multiplicity of authors. Four of them are well known, Alberto Caeiro, Alvaro de Campos, Ricardo Reis, and Bernardo Soares, but, when he died, more than fifty other authors were discovered in his unpublished papers. The case of Pessoa is like a Russellian paradox, a catalog of all catalogs that lists itself among its contents. In his work, when he signs "Fernando Pessoa," he is only one among many others authors and he is at the same time the one who wrote the complete set of works. The classical sentence asserts that "style is the man himself." With Pessoa, we have the paradox of a man who has a plurality of styles. Lacan has introduced another statement: "style is the object," meaning that only the remaining object explains the singularity and the unity of a writing. The object is a principle of consistency, and here, we guess that there may be a defect, a failure at this level, a strange lack of unity.

We can thus ask: what is the name of Pessoa, if we consider that the name gives away the true identity of a man, which is always the identity of jouissance? As we have seen, Lacan has called Joyce "Joyce le symptôme" and even "Joyce le sinthome," with the old spelling of the word introduced in a Joycean equivocation. We hear in it the English words *sin* and *home*, as well as the French words *saint* and *homme* which, translated, would mean "saintly man." Pessoa's patronymic means "no one" in Portuguese and he could speak about himself as "the man who never was." Nevertheless, the man who never was did a lot of things; we may wonder, where did they come from? I believe Pessoa when he says that his creations were produced by what he called "depersonalization." In this depersonalization, I see the equivalent of the failure of the ego in Joyce. But, if the artist as unique is a substitute for the lacking ego in Joyce, what can we say about this plurality of artists for Pessoa?

We shouldn't let ourselves be fascinated by the brilliance, the veneer of Pessoa's fictions. It is true that his plasticity, his polymorphism, and his ability to be a prophet of possible worlds are impressive. In his multicolored fictions, without the anchoring of a consistent ego, his free imaginary, and by consequence without the weight of flesh, the Word, capitalized, was not made flesh but image, an image in only two dimensions, as he says himself, without the ballast of the object. All of this could allow us to name him "Pessoa, the mentality." All his created beings are just evanescent worlds, multicolored and inconsistent fictions.

I have evoked the strange lack of the One, the One of unity, but I hope that I have managed to demonstrate that nevertheless there is a One. A deep voice, something like the *basso continuo* in music, which always asserts the same things: the suffering, the despair of being alive. Here we have the song of a melancholic man exiled from life, horrified not only by being alive, but as he said, by the fact of "having been alive." In Pessoa's work, the apocalyptic feeling of life, the weight of what he calls the real and impossible world, the presence of nonsense and the void, and the oppression of facticity are repetitively stressed. Here we have a Pessoa so immersed in the Real that we might call him: "Pessoa, the unnamable." It is from this primary and melancholic experience that the literary work is produced as a solution, not via the letter in the Real, but via the imaginary worlds which are as many possible solutions to the unnamable and unbearable existence. The Joycean writing of *Finnegans Wake* ties a knot between the Real and the Symbolic as a mother tongue. The solution elected by Pessoa was just a knot between the Real and inconsistent resemblances. Perhaps this is why he was not far from delusion.

The love letter

If the symptom is the partner of jouissance, which is the first thesis of Freud, and if any partner, in the common meaning of the word, is also a symptom, which is the thesis introduced by Lacan, what about the access to the big Other? If this partner is "unapproachable in language," and if we only have language to establish a link, then everyone enjoys only his or her own unconscious. As a result, love, true love becomes a problem, because when Lacan talks of the Real "capable only of lying to the partner" (*T*, p. 10), then we can understand: the Real of jouissance. And here we encounter a final paradox, the paradox of love letters.

Love letters belong with popular songs and poetry. Usually, love songs are a common way of talking about the loved partner, and are shared by all those who come from one community. To say it differently, songs, like love letters, are a signified of the Other, the Other specific to a language and a region. True love letters, on the contrary, are never like old common meanings. They invent the partner – that is to say, they belong to poetry: they produce a new meaning, a new saying about what you, my love partner, are for me.

Love letters are most paradoxical, Lacan says, because they seem to speak about the big Other and to be directed to the everyday other; but, in fact, they are made with the unconscious of the subject. Thus, they are symptoms which lie to the partner, because for the subject who writes they are only a way of enjoying his or her own unconscious. You see the paradox: the love letters are in fact a wall between subject and partner. So, we can conclude that the lover who writes too many love letters is just a lover of himself as unconscious. We also understand why it is so pleasant to receive love letters, in so far as love letters lend themselves to a confusion with the name. They seem to name what you are, unknown to yourself. But they fail obviously, and the sign of this failure is the fact that with love letters you have always to start again. We cannot imagine a lover who would pretend to write just one letter, once and for all. Finally we understand why Lacan, in *Encore*, can say that he writes a love letter when he produces the matheme of the signifier of the barred Other, that is the matheme of woman's jouissance or of woman as absolute Other. Perhaps it is the only possible love letter: a letter-matheme, the only one which does not belong to the unconscious, one which tries to make place for the unsayable, unpronounceable Other.

NOTES

1. Colette Soler, "Le Second Retour à Freud," *Boletín del círculo psicanalítico de Vigo* (Vigo, 1986).
2. Jacques Lacan, *RSI*, seminar of 18 February 1975.
3. The knots here come from "La Troisième," a talk given in Rome on 1 November 1974.
4. Colette Soler, *L'Aventure littéraire ou la psychose inspirée* (Paris: Editions du champ lacanien, 2001).
5. Jacques Lacan, *Joyce le symptôme*, seminar of 17 February 1976.
6. Jacques Lacan, "Compte-rendu du Séminaire 'L'Acte psychanalytique'" (1967–1968), in *Ornicar?* 29 (Paris: Navarin, 1984), p. 22.

7

NÉSTOR A. BRAUNSTEIN

Desire and jouissance in the teachings of Lacan

Jouissance, the opposite pole of desire

On 5 March 1958, the theory, the technique, and the history of psychoanalysis were substantially changed. This change came about almost unnoticed by anyone, perhaps even unnoticed by Lacan himself, who could not have predicted where the path he had undertaken would lead. On that day, the teacher told his students that he wanted to show them what was meant by "... a notion ... that has always been implied in our reflections on desire but that deserves to be distinguished from it, and which can only be articulated after one is sufficiently imbued in the complexity that constitutes desire. It is a notion that will be the other pole of today's discourse and it has a name: it is jouissance."[1] He ended this lecture by referring to "the essential question of desire and jouissance of which I gave you, today, a first gram."[2] When editing that fourteenth session of the seminar, *The Formations of the Unconscious*, Jacques-Alain Miller justifiably gave it the title *Desire and Jouissance*.

The following twenty years of Lacan's teaching (who would have guessed the kilo that followed that first gram?) revolved around this opposition. Until then, the word jouissance had appeared in the Lacanian vocabulary simply as a word whose meaning – the conventional one – required no further explanation. Yet from that day on it became a term rich in nuances, a term that would get progressively more complicated, multiplying and defining itself until it was transformed into the foundation of a new psychoanalysis: a "notion" without which all else becomes inconsistent. Together with the topological elaborations of the same epoch, the concept of jouissance became a fundamental cornerstone of Lacan's thought, allowing him to say in 1966 that "with jouissance we meet the only ontic to which we may confess."[3] Soon afterwards, he turned it into a "substance," the "substance" with which we work in psychoanalysis (*S XX*, pp. 23–4).

From that inaugural day, the notion of desire, central in Freud (*Wunsch*) as well as in Lacan ("desire is lack of being," "desire is its interpretation," "desire must be taken at the letter," "desire is the desire of the Other," "desire is the metonymy of being," etc.), would be displaced and repositioned in an antinomic polarity to this newcomer, jouissance. The French word, given its indissoluble relationship to all the rest of Lacan's teaching, including his mathemes or his logical and topological formulae, is difficult to translate into English. Lacan himself was aware of the problem and favored a combination of "enjoyment" and "lust"[4]; however, all translators have noted the conceptual loss that is sustained in the use of these terms, and therefore the great majority prefer to keep the French word, without italics, as a word already recognized by the *OED* and as a psychoanalytic contribution to the English language. In German, jouissance translates faithfully into *Genuss*, a term used with some frequency by Freud; but here we should point out that in Freud, *Lust* and, sometimes, *Libido* are equivalent to jouissance.

These problems, however, should not disturb our readers: no fundamental concept of any relevant writer can go through the ordeal of translation without sustaining a loss of some kind, and nothing can relieve the author's own discomfort when he is obliged to use words whose meaning has either been loaded down or worn out by so much previous use. However, new wine always starts in old casks. By giving words a new or modified meaning, we seek a precision which enriches both the concept and the language. Jouissance is an equivocal word in French as well as in English, and therefore, at the same time that we take advantage of this ambiguity, we must also free ourselves from it. Fortunately, difficulties in translation are almost always incentives to conceptual rigor. If we think about the loss in meaning that is sustained in going from jouissance to enjoyment, we will realize that jouissance is not a feeling of pleasure or an experience of joy. This difference becomes evident in Lacan's less known but very enlightening statement made in his 1966 lecture on "Psychoanalysis and medicine":

> What I call jouissance – in the sense in which the body experiences itself – is always in the nature of tension, in the nature of a forcing, of a spending, even of an exploit. Unquestionably, there is jouissance at the level at which pain begins to appear, and we know that it is only at this level of pain that a whole dimension of the organism, which would otherwise remain veiled, can be experienced.[5]

It is unthinkable that anyone could translate this notion, as it is defined here, into "enjoyment." Another problem that the translator faces is the absence of a much needed English equivalent to the verb *jouir*, of which Lacan makes frequent and legitimate use and which, once more, cannot be translated as "to enjoy."

Thus, with jouissance we have a double polarity; first in respect to desire, as advanced in 1958, and then in respect to pleasure, according to conventional use. Jouissance is the dimension discovered by the analytic experience that confronts desire as its opposite pole. If desire is fundamentally lack, lack in being, jouissance is positivity, it is a "something" lived by a body when pleasure stops being pleasure. It is a plus, a sensation that is beyond pleasure.

Having distinguished jouissance from desire and from pleasure, a further distinction is necessary. It is becoming increasingly frequent to find jouissance linked to "satisfaction," and then to see this "jouissatisfaction" proposed as a goal to the psychoanalytic process in lieu of the supposedly old-fashioned, Freudian, proto-Lacanian notion of desire. So it is not so strange (although in this case, strange enough) to see Bruce Fink, the author of informed Lacanian essays, introduce in the analytical index of his 1997 book the following cross-reference: "Satisfaction: as term, 225 n 15. See Jouissance." And the note says: "In this book, I employ the French term Jouissance more or less interchangeably with Freud's term 'satisfaction.'" We also find other examples of this indistinction in his book, such as, for instance: "Jouissance (or satisfaction)."[6]

It is crucial to remind ourselves of the origin of this confusion, given the fatal consequences it unleashed on the theory and practice of psychoanalysis. In *Seminar VII, The Ethics of Psychoanalysis*, Lacan said:

> The problem involved is that of *jouissance*, because *jouissance* presents itself as buried at the center of a field and has the characteristics of inaccessibility, obscurity, and opacity; moreover, the field is surrounded by a barrier which makes access to it difficult for the subject to the point of inaccessibility, because *jouissance* appears not purely and simply as the satisfaction of a need, but as the satisfaction of a drive – that term to be understood in the context of the complex theory I have developed on this subject in this seminar.
>
> As you were told last time, the drive as such is something extremely complex . . . It isn't to be reduced to the complexity of the instinct as understood in the broadest sense, in the sense that relates it to energy. It embodies a historical dimension whose true significance needs to be appreciated by us.
>
> This dimension is to be noted in the insistence that characterizes its appearances; it refers back to something memorable because it was remembered. Remembering, "historicizing," is coextensive with the functioning of the drive in the human psyche. It is there, too, that destruction is registered, that it enters into the register of experience.   (*S VII*, p. 209)

Having said that, Lacan elaborated on the drive as the death drive, whose effects could only be defined in relation to the chain of signifiers. The problem for the Lacanian doxa started when Jacques-Alain Miller gave this section of the seminar the subtitle of "Jouissance, the satisfaction of a drive" (*S VII*, p. 205); as a result, hundreds of well-intentioned commentators found a simple and economical definition of jouissance as "the satisfaction of a drive," without taking into account the more "complex theory" Lacan developed on this subject, where it is evident that the satisfaction proper to jouissance is neither the satisfaction of a need nor the satisfaction of a demand. It is also not the satisfaction of any bodily drive but one linked to the death drive and thus related to the signifier and to history, a satisfaction that consists of nothing that could be related to any kind of *Befriedigung*.

Let us be clear: the term "satisfaction" has a long Freudian lineage starting at the time when the founder spoke of the "experience of satisfaction" (*Befriedigungserlebnis*) (*SE* 1, p. 318) as the mythical moment that founded human psyche, and of desire (*Wunsch*, sometimes also *Begierde*) as the craving for the return to the jouissance inscribed in the newborn child as the passage from helplessness to satiety and whose model and object is his first contact with the nipple. But *Befriedigung* (whose root is *Friede*, peace, and which translates as appeasement or satisfaction) is a convenient term to use in reference to necessity as well as to demand. Satisfaction remits us to *satis*, a Latin term that means "enough," and is defined as a state of satiety, of completion, of glut.

The drive, the Freudian drive such as it is understood and taken up by Lacan in his *Seminar XI* is a *konstante Kraft* (*SE* 14, p. 118), a constant force, an unending requirement imposed on the psyche due to its link with the body, an instigation that, in Mephistopheles' words, "presses ever forward, unsubdued." It "presses" (*dringt*), which suggests a relationship with *Drang*, the force of the drive, and with *Verdrängung*, or "repression," a fundamental concept in psychoanalysis. In this text by Freud (*SE* 18, p. 42) on which Lacan comments extensively and to which he adheres without reserve, the drive is a factor that, on finding closed the regressive path to the encounter with the lost object – the object of desire – is left with no alternative but to press forward, "truly without perspectives of ever ending the march or of reaching the goal." In this sense, the drive is jouissance, not because it has a calming effect, not because it achieves satisfaction or satiety, but because it builds the historical, it establishes the memorable in an act that is inscribed, in relation to the order of the signifying chain, as a deviation or even a transgression; the drive signals the appearance of a dimension of surprise which is essential to the psychoanalytic act and to the ethical acts that define, in a different way, the place of the subject.

In the chapter "The deconstruction [*démontage*] of the drive" (*S XI*, pp. 161–73), Lacan reiterates again and again: the whole object of the drive is to stress the impossibility of satisfaction. This impossibility is found in neurotic patients and its name is the symptom, a paradoxical satisfaction, the jouissance of denying jouissance, an enjoyment in the complaint which is an accusation and a demand made to the Other. The drive is a constant force, not Freud's *momentane Stosskraft* (*S XI*, p. 164), not the force of a momentary impact that can go through cycles of tension and satisfactory relaxation. Jouissance is the dimension that opens beyond satisfaction precisely because the path of desire, which would lead back in search of the lost and impossible object, is closed and only "driving" is possible (here again we run into problems with language, since the English verb "to drive" sounds rather bizarre in this context).

In 1964, Lacan said that the drive does not reach its object in order to obtain satisfaction; rather, the drive traces the object's contour, and on the arch of the way back it accomplishes its task. Here again he is close to Freud: ". . . it is . . . the difference in amount between the pleasure of satisfaction [*Lustbefriedigung*] which is demanded and that which is actually achieved that provides the driving factor which will permit of no halting at any position attained" (*SE* 18, p. 42). Therefore, for Freud as well as Lacan, jouissance is what the drive "aims at" (in this instance it is Lacan himself who in his search for precision opts for the verb in English rather than in French). Lacan ridicules the idea that the aim of the drive is to reach a goal and be satisfied; he says almost dismissively, that such an image is "in harmony with the mythology of the drive" (*S XI*, p. 165). A week later, he states:

> When you entrust someone with a mission, the aim is not what he brings back, but the itinerary he must take. The aim is the way taken. The French word *but* may be translated by another word in English, goal. In archery, the goal is not the *but* either, it is not the bird you shoot, it is having scored a hit and thereby attained your *but*. (*S XI*, p. 179)

The example quoted shows that the *but* or "goal" is not on the side of the object and of gratification, but on the side of the signifier. Satisfaction, symptomatic or bodily, is linked to the displeasure-pleasure principle, while the jouissance of the drive "will permit of no halting at any position attained" (Freud), and this is precisely why it is memorable, transgressive, the forger of the historical. Jouissance is indeed the satisfaction of a drive – the death drive.

Such is the basis of the opposition between desire and jouissance. Desire points towards a lost and absent object; it is lack in being, and the craving for fulfillment in the encounter with the lost object. Its concrete expression is the phantasy. Jouissance, on the other hand, does not point to anything, nor does it serve any purpose whatsoever; it is an unpredictable experience, beyond the pleasure principle, different from any (mythical) encounter. The subject finds himself split by the polarity jouissance/desire. This is why desire, phantasy, and pleasure are barriers on the way to jouissance. As is satisfaction, the source of pleasure, inasmuch as it pacifies and blocks the way of the drive, which is closer to pain, and whose paradigm is found in those tensional states which allow the body to experience itself as such. In the sexual field, the orgasm, obedient to the pleasure principle, is the paragon of "satisfaction" and not so much of jouissance, since it represents its interruption; the orgasm demands the capitulation of jouissance to the commandments of a natural law. Never did psychoanalysis (with the exception of Wilhelm Reich) sing the praises of the orgasm. Freud could say, "I know that the maximum pleasure in the sexual encounter is nothing but the pleasure of an organ that depends on the activity of the genitals" (*SE* 16, p. 325), while Lacan later repeated that "The big secret of psychoanalysis is that the sexual act does not exist." He also considered copulation a "masturbatory concession."[7]

In one of his most suggestive remarks on the relationship between the two concepts, Lacan held that "desire comes from the Other, while jouissance is on the side of the Thing."[8] Without making an explicit reference to it, although using the same words, he falls back on the Hegelian opposition in the *Philosophical Propaedeutic* of 1810. For Hegel, mere pleasure – as the particular subjective experience – must be renounced in favor of *das Ding*, where the subject, through the exercise of his profession or art, transcends the experience of pleasure (*Lust*) and reaches beyond (*jenseits*) himself in *das Ding*: "Whosoever seeks pleasure merely seeks his own self according to its accidental side. Whosoever is busied with great works and interests strives only to bring about the realization of the object itself. He directs his attention to the *substantial and does not think of himself but forgets himself in the object*."[9] Hegelian jouissance, such as can be obtained through the dedication to art or to a profession, results in the creation of the transcendental and sublime. This is not far from Lacan's formula that "sublimation raises an object to the dignity of the Thing" in *Seminar VII*, which leads him to note: "The sublimation that provides the *Trieb* [drive] with a satisfaction different from its aim – an aim that is still defined as its natural aim – is precisely that which reveals the true nature of the *Trieb* insofar as it is not simply instinct, but has a relationship to *das Ding* as such, to the Thing insofar as it is distinct from the object" (*S VII*, p. 111).

Another prevalent confusion which ought to be clarified is the statement so often made about the dialectical nature of desire and the non-dialectical nature of jouissance. One is told that jouissance is solipsistic and untransferable, but it is evident in all of Lacan's teachings that jouissance can only be approached through language and that the Other is always involved. The jouissance of neurotic symptoms, the most common mode of encounter with jouissance in the psychoanalyst's experience, is a way of relating to the Other. Symptoms only exist insofar as they are actualized under transference. As Freud wrote, "Symptoms serve as a substitution for sexual satisfaction in the ill, they are a substitute for this satisfaction which is missing from their lives"; in short, they are "libidinal substitutive satisfactions" (*SE* 17, pp. 273, 404). Symptoms are not a mere subjective suffering as official psychiatry would like us to believe; they are a form of jouissance and are addressed by an other and to the Other. The jouissance to which the perverse subject dedicates his life is a will to jouissance that can only be understood in its relation with the Other, in fact, it could not even exist without the subjective division of the "victim." The psychotic feels engulfed by the jouissance of the Other who controls his thoughts and transforms his body. Lacan insists on the necessary presence of the other and the Other for the drive to manifest itself: "The subject will realize that his desire is merely a vain detour with the aim of catching the jouissance of the other – in so far as the other intervenes, he will realize that there is a jouissance beyond the pleasure principle" (*S VII*, pp. 183–4).

The jouissance involved in the utilization and the destruction of "goods" (for example in the institution of the potlatch as mentioned in *S VII*, p. 235) can be understood insofar as those goods are sundered from the use and exchange value they hold in society, and the prestige associated with their destruction passes through the value they hold for the Other. Jouissance is a sacrifice made at the altar of more or less obscure gods; it is the malefic jouissance of stripping the other of the goods he holds dear. Jouissance is linked to the law and so to its transgression. It is thanks to the law (and we must remember that the law is the other face of desire) that a certain act provokes the jouissance which the drive aims at. The drive does not aim at a visible, sensitive goal, but at the effect produced in its return, after having missed and gone around the target, after confronting the real, that is, the impossibility of full satisfaction. Thus we can say with Lacan that the real, the real of jouissance, is the impossible (see *S XI*, p. 167).

Jouissance appears in guilt, in remorse, in confession, in contrition, more in paying than in being paid, in destroying more than in conserving. Its essence is the suspension of the reflex act, of the pursuit of satisfaction, of service to the community, of the "good reasons" governing rational behavior. It carries within it its own reason. Being ineluctably linked to the Other, its existence has an ethical and not a physiological substance. This is why we must emphatically affirm the dialectic nature of jouissance. Jouissance is the substance of neurosis, of perversion, of psychosis, and of the *sinthome*. We know of it only by the way in which it manifests itself in transference and relation to others.

Twenty theses on jouissance

Since jouissance is not homogeneous, we must distinguish its different modalities. We can recognize modalities generated and preserved by language and thus linked to the signifier, but also those which do not depend on the articulation of speech. In order to explore this logic and its genealogy, I will sum up my argument in twenty theses:

1. In human beings, the satisfaction of necessities, of life itself, goes through a system of symbolic exchanges, thus trapping the subject in the net of language, through a discourse and a social bond that are induced and commanded by the Other.

2. The *infans*, even before acquiring the function of speech, is already submerged in a world of language in which the Other gives a name, signs of identity, a place in the division between masculine and feminine – ideals that will constitute his I when this I is established in the passage through the mirror stage. Through "deeds" he is given what is "properly" his, and so, indirectly, he is made aware of what belongs to others. He is introduced to the Law. This turns flesh into a body, an organism. The object becomes a subject.

3. In its state of helplessness (*Hilflosigkeit*) and out of sheer necessity, this proto- or archi-subject manifests itself with a desperate cry to which the maternal Other, interpreting the demand, responds by offering her breast. This act transforms a part of the body of the mother into the signifier of her desire.

4. The resulting state of extreme tension and release, characterized by Freud as the "experience of satisfaction," has as its sign the cry, which reveals the maximum closeness of the Thing and at the same time, the definite and irrevocable separation from it. From this moment on, life is lived in exile from the Thing.

5. The experience of despair and helplessness followed by an ideal, mythical satisfaction is inscribed, written, as a jouissance which is alien to speech, a bodily hieroglyphic that can only be deciphered after the incorporation of the subject in the world of language. We might call this initial state the "jouissance of being." The ineffable, primary jouissance of being corresponds with the unnamed and unnamable that Freud subsumed in the term *Urverdrängung* (primal or original repression) and which is the bedrock of the unconscious.

6. A human being is a subject with certain demands, mostly oral, and at the same time the object of demands made by the Other, especially linked to bowel training. He or she enters into a system of exchanges and must be included in the registry of the word, alienating his or her being in the paths offered by the Other, substituting the direct jouissance of the body by rules imposed by the Other. Jouissance becomes possible on the condition of being de-naturalized, filtered through language.

7. Demand is a demand for satisfaction. However, the agent of the demand goes beyond necessity, it is the desire for absolute and unshared signifiers of the desire of the Other, in other words, for his/her love. Thus "satisfaction" (of the need and of the demand) always leaves a trace of disappointment: there is something missing in the object that the other offers. It is never enough (*satis*). And it is this unsatisfied remainder of "satisfaction" that engenders an object: the object cause of desire, the object of a surplus of jouissance and, at the same time, a lost jouissance (*plus-de-jouir*) which Lacan calls *objet a*. The *objet a* has no representation, it lacks a specular image and will forever elude the efforts of the most determined photographer.

8. In the initial state which we have called "jouissance of being," a mutual fulfillment exists between the *infans* and the Other, the mother. This "moment" comes prior to lack and desire. The necessary absence of the mother throws the child back into a state of helplessness. The subject thus appears, already and from the beginning, as the subject of a lost jouissance. The subject discovers his or her incapacity to be the "all and only" of the Other and must go through the mourning of a previous mythical union with the mother. The question arises: "What does the Other lack that I am unable to fulfill?" The desire of the Other for something which cannot be provided is revealed in the castration of the maternal Other, which institutes the phallus as signifier of this desire. "It is what predestines the phallus to embody jouissance in the dialectic of desire" (*E/S*, p. 319).

9. The subject realizes the impossibility of satisfying either his/her drives or his/her demand for love with any object whatsoever. The lack results in this condition as an eternally desiring subject, and the sentence that he or she will be obliged to serve for life: jouissance has to be filtered through discourse. This lack sends us back to the fundamental signifier, the phallus. "Castration means that jouissance must be refused, so that it can be reached on the inverted ladder of the Law of desire" (*E/S*, p. 324). Jouissance in the being who speaks (*parlêtre*) is jouissance of the signifier; it is a semiotic and phallic jouissance. It goes without

saying that this is true for both subjects placed on the masculine side as well as on the feminine side of the sexual divide, as explained by the graph of sexuation (*S XX*, pp. 78–89).

10. The phallus is a signifier without equal: as a number, it is perpetually odd. It cannot be coupled, has no opposite in any other signifier. Such is the fundamental condition of speech; it is simply the signifier of the inherent lack in the being who speaks, the divided subject ($) , exiled from the real by the symbolic. Its representation falls upon the sup-posed bearer of the phallus, that other who would fulfill the maternal Other. It is here that a new signifier comes as substitute for the phal-lus: the Name-of-the-Father, which can function as Signifier one (S1) and will allow the subject to be represented by it before all the signi-fiers that together make up unconscious knowledge, the system of the Other as language, culture, and the Law (i. e. the Signifier two or S2).

11. The subject, having gone through castration, is incorporated into the world of humans. From now on he or she can be e-ducated, that is, led inside of a system of renounced drives, able to experience the jouissance of all who participate in "civilization and its discontents," producing and pursuing this surplus jouissance, which, emanating from him, nev-ertheless constantly escapes him (like the perfume in Süskind's novel), while pressing (*dringen*) him ever forward.

12. The subject recognizes himself or herself from the beginning as an object for the desire, the phantasy, the drives and the love of the Other. At the same time, the jouissance which a subject can experi-ence leaves him/her unable to know what is involved in the "jouissance of the Other." One cannot *jouir* (that is experience jouissance) of the "jouissance of the Other," which, in any case, is only a supposition, a phantasy, something imaginary and impossible to apprehend, and therefore, something which belongs to the Real. Let us be clear: the jouissance of the Other is not in the Other (who anyway does not exist) but in the subject himself. A good example of this structure could be found in President Schreber, Freud's paradigmatic case study of paranoia.

13. Jouissance, just as much as desire, is dialectical and at the same time is not bound by universals, in spite of Kant's claims (systematically parodied in the Marquis de Sade's texts). The Other's jouissance is an ineffable mystery, beyond words, outside the symbolic, beyond the phallus. Its model is surfeit, a surplus, the supplement to phal-lic jouissance of which many women speak without being able to say exactly what it consists of, like something felt but unexplainable. The jouissance of the Other is therefore assumed as the jouissance of the

Other sex, an other than phallic jouissance, in other words feminine jouissance.[10]

14. The function of speech permits us to separate the three modalities of jouissance: (a) Jouissance in the word, of the speaking being as such, phallic jouissance, subservient to castration, the Law, and the Name-of-the-Father; (b) Jouissance before the word, experienced in relation to the mother's jouissance, to the proximity of the Thing, a jouissance written on the body, but unnamable, mythical, a retroactive creation, impossible for the subject already immersed in speech to objectify and consequently, forever sundered from it, a jouissance of being; and (c) Jouissance beyond the word, beyond the regulation of the Law and of the phallus, jouissance of the Other, feminine jouissance, which for the very same reason – lying somewhere beyond speech – is equally impossible to objectify, impossible for the *parlêtre* to articulate. It is this jouissance which prompts Lacan to say, "Naturally, you are all going to be convinced that I believe in God. I believe in the jouissance of the woman, insofar as it is extra (*en plus*) . . . Doesn't this jouissance one experiences and yet knows nothing about put us on the path of ex-sistence? And why not interpret one face of the Other, the God face, as based on feminine jouissance?" (*S XX*, p. 76–7). It may be relevant to point out that after this remark in *Seminar XX, Encore*, Lacan never again referred to feminine jouissance. It is fair to ask: why?

15. We can now establish a logical sequence in the substitutions already noted. The Thing and jouissance of being are displaced by the phallic signifier. The symbolic phallus is uncoupled and leaves its place to the signifier as the Name-of-the-Father, which can be articulated with the set of signifiers, the Other; thus the subject can be included in the symbolic system. He/she speaks, we speak, but all our talk cannot bring back our lost jouissance, except through the path of castration offered by speech and discourse. Lacan wrote, "But we must insist that jouissance is forbidden to him who speaks as such" (*E/S*, p. 319). The object that escapes being caught in the chain of signifiers is the *objet a*. The remainder left by the inclusion of the subject into the world via castration and the Oedipus complex is phallic jouissance and its multiple fates – neurotic symptoms, perverse acts, psychotic engulfment, and the production of objects of sublimation that aim to have access to the place left empty by the Thing, objects Lacan termed *sinthomes*. Then we can think of the other jouissances: feminine, mystical, literary . . .

16. The passage from jouissance of being to phallic jouissance and, eventually, to the jouissance of the Other demands a progressive system of transcriptions that lead from one to the next. As Freud presented it

in letter 52 to Fliess,[11] these systems are at least three: first, perceptive signs (*Wahrnehmungszeichen*) that would correspond to the jouissance of being, not linked to the signifiers of the Other; secondly, the system of the unconscious (*das Unbewusste*) where jouissance is already subject to the phallic signifier but in which the primary processes still rule: there is no contradiction, no representation of death, and synchronicity reigns; and thirdly, the preconscious system (*das Vorbewusste*), the one of the "official" I, the secondary processes, and the logic of discourse.

17. These systems of inscriptions require a process of translation allowing the passage from one to the other. Since in the first of these systems there are no signifiers, I will call "deciphering" the passage from the jouissance of being (beyond the Imaginary, the Symbolic, and the Real) to the unconscious, and keep the term "interpretation" for the passage from the unconscious to the preconscious. As Lacan stated in *Television*: "Now, what Freud articulates as primary process in the unconscious . . . isn't something to be ciphered, but to be deciphered. I mean: jouissance itself" (*T*, p. 18–19; translation modified).

18. Allow me to read Freud's *Wo Es war, soll Ich werden*[12] as describing the place where the jouissance of the subject has been lying, buried and mute, locked up in symptomatic coffins; from here jouissance must find its way towards speech, as a key to the act that incurs the risk of transgression and that impels the subject to another jouissance. Through the analyst's acts, which includes the performative act of interpretation, psychoanalysis steers towards the deciphering and the putting into words of jouissance, transcending the barriers of meaning and satisfaction, beyond convention and the mere tending of one's possessions.

19. Clinical structures constitute organizations of barriers built against jouissance: repression, subjection to the Law and to the other's demand in neurotics; disavowal, as the foundation of the pervert's relation with the Law; foreclosure, as the invasion of the body and the apparatus of the soul of the psychotic by the ineffable jouissance of the Other. The diaphragm of jouissance closes intermittently in the neurotic, it is fixed and immutable in the pervert, and destroyed or non-existent in the psychotic. This metaphor – the word as diaphragm of jouissance – allows us to understand why the direction that the psychoanalytic cure must take has to be organized in radically distinct ways according to each of these different clinical structures.

20. Let us note the similarity among the statements made by Lacan in diverse moments of his teaching and which, in appearance only, differ drastically in the themes they deal with. "Castration means that

jouissance must be refused, so that it can be reached on the inverted ladder of the Law of desire" (*E/S*, p. 324). "One can dispense with the Name-of-the-Father on condition one makes use of it";[13] "The analytic act is determined according to jouissance and, at the same time, by what is needed to protect oneself from it."[14]

To end, I would like to frame the following two references taken from the crucial Seminar X on *Anxiety* (1962–3). In his graph of subjective causation, Lacan inscribes anxiety at the point of a passage from the jouissance of the subject – taken as point of departure – to the desire of the subject – seen as point of arrival. Just after this, as if he was asking forgiveness for the new pastoral tone of his discourse, Lacan provides this gnomic formula: "Only love can make jouissance condescend to desire."[15]

Few references are as decisive for the development of our theme (jouissance and desire) as these, in which the two terms are conjoined and presented not as mutually exclusive but intimately connected: two real keys for our reflection and for the practice and the ethics of psychoanalysis. Regrettably, after Lacan's death in 1981 and with the passage of time, Manichean formulations have arisen that tend to oppose the two terms, provoking a forced choice loaded with hidden agendas between the first Lacan (the Lacan of the signifier and of desire, allegedly a "primitive" or "archaic" Lacan), and the second Lacan (the Lacan of jouissance and the *objet a*, who would be the desired one, a point of arrival that only "advanced" Lacanians could reach). It is important, therefore, to emphasize the ethical basis of these two propositions taken together: between jouissance and desire there are two alternatives: anxiety or love. Both the subject and the psychoanalytic experience have to choose between the two modes of passage. Now, if jouissance has to be refused so that it can be reached on the inverted ladder of the Law of desire, then love is left as the only recourse capable of allowing "desire to condescend to jouissance."[16]

Translated from the Spanish by Tamara Francés

NOTES

1. Jacques Lacan, *Le Séminaire V. Les Formations de l'inconscient, 1957–8* (Paris: Seuil, 1998), p. 251.
2. Lacan, *Le Séminaire V. Les Formations de l'inconscient*, p. 268.
3. Jacques Lacan, "Compte-rendu du Séminaire 'La Logique du fantasme'" (1966–7), *Ornicar?* 29 (Paris: Navarin, 1984), p. 17.
4. Jacques Lacan, *Le Séminaire XIII. L'Objet de la psychanalyse, 1965–6*, seminar of 27 April 1966. Unpublished.

5. Jacques Lacan, "Psychanalyse et médecine" (1966), *Lettres de l'école freudienne* I (1967), p. 60.

6. Bruce Fink, *A Clinical Introduction to Lacanian Psychoanalysis* (Cambridge, Mass.: Harvard University Press, 1997), p. 226 and index.

7. Jacques Lacan, *Le Séminaire XIV. La Logique du fantasme, 1966–7*, seminar of 12 April 1967. Unpublished.

8. Jacques Lacan, "Du 'Trieb' de Freud et du désir du psychanalyste," *Ecrits* (Paris: Seuil, 1966), p. 853.

9. G. W. F. Hegel, *The Philosophical Propaedeutic*, trans. A. V. Miller (Oxford: Blackwell, 1986), p. 39. Italics in original.

10. Jacques Lacan, *Le Séminaire XIII*, seminar of 8 June 1966. Unpublished.

11. *The Complete Letters of Sigmund Freud to Wilhelm Fliess*, ed. Jeffrey Masson (Cambridge, Mass.: Harvard University Press, 1985), p. 207. This letter from 6 December 1896 was formerly known as Letter 52: see *SE* I, p. 317.

12. See *Ecrits* pp. 128, 136, 171, 279, and 299 for Lacan's various retranslations of Freud's famous sentence.

13. Jacques Lacan, *Le Séminaire XXIII. Le Sinthome, 1975–6*, seminar of 13 April 1976. Unpublished.

14. Jacques Lacan, "Compte-rendu du Séminaire 'L'Acte psychanalytique'" (1967–8), *Ornicar?* 29 (Paris: Navarin, 1984), p. 24.

15. Jacques Lacan, *Le Séminaire X. L'Angoisse, 1962–3*, seminar of 13 March 1963. Unpublished.

16. See Néstor A. Braunstein, *Goce* (México: Siglo 21, 1990), p. 244. French version: *La Jouissance: Un concept lacanien* (Paris: Point Hors Ligne, 1994), p. 328.

8

CHARLES SHEPHERDSON

Lacan and philosophy

No writer in the history of psychoanalysis has done more to bring Freudian theory into dialogue with the philosophical tradition than Jacques Lacan. His work engages with a dauntingly wide array of thinkers, including not only his near contemporaries (Saussure, Benvéniste, Jakobson, Bataille, Merleau-Ponty, Lévi-Strauss, Piaget, Sartre, Kojève, Hyppolite, Koyré, and Althusser), but also other figures reaching back to the Enlightenment (Nietzsche, Kierkegaard, Marx, Hegel, and Kant) and beyond, from Spinoza, Leibniz, and Descartes, to Pascal, Saint Augustine, Aristotle, Plato, and the pre-Socratics.[1] His references, moreover, are not limited to the familiar land-marks of the post-Structuralist tradition who have so often been used to interpret him (Kojève and Hegel, Saussure and Lévi-Strauss), but include nu-merous figures from the British tradition (Bertrand Russell, Jeremy Bentham, Isaac Newton, Jonathan Swift, and George Berkeley), as well as from the history of science and mathematics (Cantor, Frege, Poincaré, Bourbaki, Moebius, Huyghens, Copernicus, Kepler, and Euclid). While some of these references are no doubt merely grace notes, introduced to embellish a noto-riously labyrinthine and Gongoristic style, it is impossible to ignore the fact that his engagement with a large number of these figures is serious, focused, and sustained over many years.

The task of commentary is therefore enormous. Lacan's early seminars (1953–5) are marked by a prolonged encounter with Hegel, who had a sub-stantial and abiding effect not only on his account of the imaginary and the relation to the other (jealousy and love, intersubjective rivalry and narcis-sism), but also on his understanding of negation and desire while leading to the logic of the signifier.[2] His Seminar on *The Ethics of Psychoanalysis*, well-known for its extended reading of Sophocles' *Antigone*, also contains a treatment of Kantian ethics, Bentham's utilitarianism, and Aristotle's philos-ophy, including not only the *Nicomachean Ethics*, but also the *Poetics* and the *Rhetoric*, and especially their discussions of "catharsis" – a term which has an elaborate history both in esthetic theory and in psychoanalysis itself, where the "cathartic method" played an important role.[3] Here already, an enormous task is proposed, concerning the relations between art and psychoanalysis, as well as the transformation that separates modernity (Kant's esthetic theory) from the ancient world (Aristotle's *Poetics*) – a historical question that is repeatedly marked by Lacan, as if to suggest that psychoanalytic theory, in order to be truly responsible for its concepts, must account for its own historical emergence as it seeks to articulate its place in relation to the philosophical tradition which it inevitably inherits.

Every text is full of such challenges. His Seminar on *Transference* provides a sustained reading of Plato's *Symposium*, and his Seminar on *The Four Fundamental Concepts of Psychoanalysis* contains a well-known commentary on Merleau-Ponty's discussion of painting, which appeared in the philosopher's posthumously published book, *The Visible and the Invisible*, a work which had a significant impact on Lacan's concept of the gaze.[4] Each of these encounters, taken by itself, calls for a careful analysis, and there are many others, including influences that were not the subject of explicit commentary, beginning with his attendance at Kojève's lectures.[5]

Lacan spoke frequently of Heidegger, starting in 1935, in *Recherches philosophiques* and *Evolution psychiatrique*, where we find early book reviews of Henri Ey and Eugène Minkowski.[6] References to Heidegger continue in "Propos sur la causalité psychique," in *Seminar II*, in "Le Mythe individuel du névrosé," in the discussion of Heidegger's "Das Ding" in *Seminar VII*, in "L'Instance de la lettre," and elsewhere, including texts that are less well known to Anglo-American readers, such as "Allocutions sur les psychoses de l'enfant," and the "Rome discourse."[7] It would be a mistake, moreover, to suppose that all these references merely repeat the same idea or formula, for in one case he is concerned with the temporality of the subject and the text of *Being and Time*, while in another he is concerned with the distinction between the "thing" and the "object," and the text of *Poetry, Language, Thought*.[8] A cursory mention of "the famous being-towards-death" will simply not do justice to these complex relationships. Lacan's interest was sufficiently piqued that he translated Heidegger's essay "Logos" for the first issue of *La Psychanalyse*; and the most frequently cited of these references, taken from the final pages of the "Function and field of speech and language in psychoanalysis," reads almost like a manifesto: "Of all the undertakings that have been proposed in this century, that of psychoanalysis is perhaps the loftiest, because the undertaking of the psychoanalyst acts in our time as a mediator between the man of care and the subject of absolute knowledge" (*E/S*, p. 105). Such a proposal, placing Freud in relation to both Heidegger's account of *Dasein* (the "man of care") and Hegel's phenomenology ("the subject of absolute knowledge"), could occupy more than one doctoral thesis, as could any number of these engagements with the philosophical tradition.[9]

Canonical figures in continental philosophy, moreover, are not the only important names for Lacan. Readers who are accustomed to a reception governed by Hegel and Saussure may be surprised to know that Aristotle is one of the most frequent points of reference in the entire Lacanian oeuvre. In *Seminar XX: Encore*, for example – as we shall see more clearly in a moment – Aristotle provides a guiding thread for an argument that passes from Freud's account of masculinity and femininity, through symbolic logic (the famous quantifiers of sexual difference), and thence to the modal categories of existence (possibility, impossibility, contingency, and necessity) found in Aristotle but reconfigured through the semiotics of Greimas – all this being punctuated by references to angels (discussed thereafter by Irigaray), the concept of the "soul," and the *Nicomachean Ethics*, which is particularly interesting to Lacan for Aristotle's remarks on "courage" and "friendship." A heady mix, to be sure, but we shall see that these references are not simply thrown together in a careless manner.

In the face of these many references, we can hardly do more than sketch a few aspects of this vast territory. Even if we bracket the figures in anthropology, linguistics, and mathematics (though they have an unmistakable claim to philosophical significance), drawing a very narrow limit around the title of "philosophy," each of these relationships, taken by itself, would merit an extended commentary.[10] In addition to these many *names*, moreover, there are numerous *concepts* that Lacan develops as an explicit challenge to the philosophical tradition – from "doubt" and "certainty," or "belief" and "truth," to "representation" and "reality" – each of which has a basis in Freud (one has only to recall "The Loss of Reality in Neurosis and Psychosis," *SE* 19, pp. 181–7, or the important discussion of "doubt," "affirmation," and the "judgment of existence" in Freud's remarkable article on "Negation," *SE* 19, pp. 233–9).[11] (When I "believe" in the existence of the maternal phallus, even as I "know" that it does not "exist" in "reality," what exactly are the stakes of these terms, and how might the psychoanalytic elaboration of these terms challenge the philosophical use of this same vocabulary?) And there are countless *propositions* that Lacan puts forth which have a claim to philosophical significance. These pronouncements have often been used to encapsulate Lacan's general position, but they are not as simple as they appear. Consider his remark that "there is no such thing as pre-discursive reality." While such formulae have often been used to construe Lacan as a theorist of "discursive construction," here too a meticulous treatment is required, for one can hardly conclude from this remark that "everything is symbolic" for Lacan (given that the Real and Imaginary are irreducible to discourse), any more than one can suppose that Lacan's reasons for putting forth this proposition automatically coincide with the arguments of others (historicists, Structuralists, pragmatists, etc.) who might make the very same statement.[12]

In addition to all this, moreover, there are extended discussions of figures who have received far less attention in the Anglo-American literature on Lacan, due in part to the fact that many texts have yet to appear in English, or even in French. His discussion of Marx, for example – especially in *La Logique du fantasme* and *D'un autre à l'autre*, in both of which he discusses the notion of "surplus value" – remains unpublished. And in the case of Descartes, one would have to account not only for the well-known comments in *The Four Fundamental Concepts of Psychoanalysis* and "The agency of the letter" (comments taken up almost verbatim by Foucault in *The Order of Things*[13]), but also for Lacan's remarks in "Propos sur la causalité psychique" (1946), "La Science et la vérité" (1965); and two unpublished seminars, *Seminar XII: Problèmes cruciaux* (1964–5), and *Seminar XIV: La Logique du fantasme* (1966–7), where one finds an extended variation on the formula "cogito ergo sum."[14]

Nor can one dismiss these many excursions into philosophy as a digression from "properly psychoanalytic" concerns, as though readers with a clinical interest could somehow avoid them, for it is clear that Lacan turns to the philosophical tradition, not for philosophical reasons, but in order to clarify matters that lie at the very heart of Freudian theory.[15] In the case of Descartes, for example, the relation between "thinking" (the *cogito*) and "being" (*sum*) is explored, not for epistemological reasons, or in order to establish the truth of any beliefs ("What can I know with certainty? What object escapes the corrosive movement of doubt?"), but for the light it casts on the problem Freud raised by speaking of "representation" (*Vorstellung*), and more precisely the *limits* of representation. For, as Freud famously said, there is something of the unconscious that remains unavailable to interpretation. Recall the well-known formulation in *The Interpretation of Dreams*: "There is often a passage in even the most thoroughly interpreted dream which *has to be* left obscure; this is because we become aware during the work of interpretation that at that point there is a tangle of dream-thoughts which *cannot* be unravelled and which moreover *adds nothing to our knowledge* of the content of the dream. This is the dream's navel, the spot where it reaches down into the unknown" (*SE* 5, p. 525, emphasis added). This "nodal point" in the unconscious remains inaccessible not because interpretation has been deficient, but in principle and by its very nature, which means not only that it *has to be* left obscure, but also that it cannot be construed as an *object of knowledge*: like the navel of the dream, something of the unconscious thus falls outside the field of representation.

Lacan likewise remarks on the limits of representation, and this is what guides his remarks on the disjunction between "thinking" (the *ego* in *ego cogito*) and "being" (the register of the subject). As is often the case with Lacan, one has to be particularly careful not to impose a familiar Lacanian dogma on these philosophical references. For the distinction between the "I" of *ego cogito* and the "I" of *ego sum* is not the usual Lacanian distinction between the Imaginary and the Symbolic, whereby the "ego" that speaks at the level of consciousness is distinguished from the "subject" of the unconscious, which speaks through the symbolic material that intrudes upon the discourse of the ego. Lacan indeed stresses this distinction, not only in the often quoted "schema L" but in formulae such as the following: "the unconscious of the subject is the discourse of the Other" (*E/S*, p. 172), or "the unconscious is that part of the concrete discourse, insofar as it is transindividual, that is not at the disposal of the subject in re-establishing the continuity of his conscious discourse" (*E/S*, p. 49). But when it comes to this Cartesian meditation of his, played out as a disjunction between thinking and being, we are faced with a very different issue. And here again, we have a limit to the supposedly "linguistic" account of the unconscious in Lacan's thought. For while signifiers certainly play a formative role in organizing the life of the subject (mapping out various symbolic identifications, as "obedient," "unconventional," "masculine," etc.), functioning differently at the level of conscious and unconscious thought, they will never entirely capture the "being" of the subject, according to Lacan. *This* disjunction is what the notorious Lacanian "alienation" actually means – not simply the imaginary alienation in which the ego is formed through identification with an alter ego in the mirror stage (a thesis used to link Lacan to Kojève and Hegelian rivalry), nor even the symbolic alienation in which the subject is forced to accept the mediating role of language and its network of representations (a thesis used to link Lacan to Saussure, Lévi-Strauss, and Althusserian "interpellation"), but rather that alienation in which the subject, by virtue of entering the symbolic order, finds itself lacking, deprived of a measure of its "being" – a thesis which complicates the supposedly symbolic account of the subject, and also has effects on our understanding of the unconscious.

Thus, following Descartes, we are led to the conclusion that, while it may be correct to say the unconscious can be followed through various symbolic manifestations (the lapsus, the dream, free association, negation), there is also an aspect of the unconscious which belongs to the order of the real, understood as a dimension irreducible to representation. The "subject" of the unconscious in Lacan is therefore something other than a symbolic phenomenon, and constantly disappears with the "closing" of the unconscious. "The signifier," Lacan says, "makes manifest the subject . . . But it functions as a signifier only to reduce the subject in question to being no more than a signifier . . . There, strictly speaking, is the temporal pulsation . . . the departure of the unconscious as such – the closing," which Ernest Jones caught sight of when he spoke of the disappearance or "aphanisis" of the subject. Thus, we may indeed follow the position of the subject at the level of the signifier, where unconscious "thought" is revealed, but "aphanisis is to be situated in a more radical way at the level at which the subject manifests himself in this movement of disappearance that I have described as lethal" (*S XI*, pp. 207–8).[16] This means – contrary to Descartes – that thinking and being will never coincide, and that we are faced with a constitutive rupture between the symbolic and the real.[17] It also means – contrary to what many readers of Lacan may suppose – that the famous symbolic order will never be sufficient to grasp the "subject" of psychoanalysis, because the being of the subject is irreducible to any symbolic or imaginary representation. In short, Lacan's account of the Freudian theory of "representation" puts a limit to the famous "linguistic" interpretation of psychoanalysis that Lacan is so often said to have promulgated, and Descartes is the avenue through which this point is made.

This thesis is certainly of interest to the philosopher, and to anyone interested in the status of the "subject" in contemporary thought, but we must also attend to the clinical aspects of the argument. For as a result of this claim, analytic practice will require a technique that is able to follow not only the symbolic trail of the unconscious, but also its movement of disappearance or fading – as Freud suggested in his remarks on the death instinct, which concerned a movement of annihilation to which the subject as such is prone. Without developing the technical consequences of this step, we can nevertheless indicate its importance, in terms of the distinction between the symbolic dimension of the unconscious and the transference. For in fact, as Russell Grigg has shown, it is precisely this opening and closing of the unconscious that led Freud to discover the transference in the strict sense, as an aspect of the unconscious that is conceptually quite distinct from whatever is revealed through the signifying chain of the dream and free association.[18] As Freud himself remarked, there is often a point in the discourse of the analysand where the chain of associations runs dry. "Perhaps you are thinking of me?" he suggests, as if this impasse in discourse somehow appeared in conjunction with the presence of the analyst. Freud thereby marks a clear division between the signifier (the labor of free association and dream elaboration), and a new domain of the transference, wherein a certain lethal dimension of the subject is revealed. Lacan formulates this clearly in *Seminar XI*, in a chapter called "The transference and the drive": "What Freud shows us, from the outset, is that the transference is essentially resistant, *Übertragungswiderstand*. The transference is the means by which the communication of the unconscious is interrupted, by which the unconscious closes up again" (*S XI*, p. 130). This movement of disappearance or "closing," in which the "being" of the subject is excluded from the chain of signifiers, also leads Lacan to elaborate a distinction between the signifier and jouissance, understood as a dimension of lethal enjoyment in which the desire of the subject is compromised. Even without developing these points, we can already see that Lacan's ultimate concern is not with the texts of philosophy, and that his protracted engagement with Descartes has a bearing on Freudian theory. This is finally why Lacan argues that the "being" of the subject as such is irreducible to the symbolic order (the unconscious "I think").

This brings us to the central problem facing anyone who wishes to address the question of "Lacan and philosophy." On the one hand, Lacan's references to the philosophical tradition are intended to be serious, and require a rigorous and properly philosophical exposition – he cites particular texts, puzzles over problems of translation, and clearly expects his audience to follow individual passages; on the other hand, his reasons for turning to the philosophical tradition are not, finally, philosophical, but derive from the field of psychoanalysis itself, understood as a domain that, whatever it may stand to learn from philosophy, has its own theoretical specificity, and develops in relation to a clinical field that is simply not present in the philosophical arena. Any attempt to clarify Lacan's use of philosophical texts must attend to this double trajectory.

Our survey of names, however daunting in itself, thus only hints at the depth of the problem, for with every philosophical reference, Lacan is simultaneously concerned with matters that lie within psychoanalytic discourse itself. This means that the serious reader will be obliged not only to develop the philosophical background of the references Lacan makes (for it must be acknowledged that Lacan himself never provides a properly philosophical exposition of the concepts and texts on which he depends), but also to isolate the clinical issues that are at stake whenever Lacan engages with the philosophical tradition (identification, the object-relation, transference, the drive, and other concepts that are particular to psychoanalysis). A simple gesture towards "philosophy" or "Hegelian alienation" or "structural linguistics" will therefore do nothing to clarify his many allusions. In each case, the clinical stakes of his remarks must be isolated and defined, if we are to see how Lacan makes use of the philosophical tradition. And in each case, we must mark the disjunctions that arise whenever the interests of philosophy run up against the exigencies of the clinical domain.

Lacan's treatment of negation is an excellent case in point. For his remarkable analysis of the three types of negation in Freud's vocabulary, while it certainly relies on philosophical resources for its development, and leads him to a long immersion in Hegel's "dialectical" or "productive" negation, nevertheless has a diagnostic purpose that is entirely absent from Hegel's own work. For Lacan, *Verneinung, Verleugnung,* and *Verwerfung* (respectively "denial," "disavowal," and "foreclosure") in Freud's terminology designate three distinct forms of negation, not merely in a logical sense, but in the sense that they correspond to three distinct psychic mechanisms that can be correlated with the diagnostic categories of neurosis, perversion, and psychosis. Where "denial" indicates the neurotic repudiation of a thought which the unconscious is in the process of expressing ("You will say it's my mother in the dream, but I assure you it's not my mother," *SE* 19, p. 235), "disavowal" by contrast indicates a more profound refusal, which does not so much acknowledge the truth under the sign of negation ("it's not my mother"), but rather repudiates altogether what is negated. The standard clinical case of disavowal concerns castration, and more precisely maternal castration, and the subjective consequences include a *perceptual* aspect (an *imaginary distortion* of sexual difference, notably in fetishism) that is distinct from the symbolic mechanism of neurotic denial. Freud expressly underscores this point in "Fetishism" (*SE* 21, pp. 149–57). Noting, first of all, that the term "repression" can explain this phenomenon, in which an observation (the lack of a penis) has been registered and is nevertheless simultaneously refused, he specifies further. For in the case of denial – "it's not my mother" – are we not also dealing with a repression, which bears on an unconscious idea? To be precise, then, Freud observes that the *affect* associated with the perception of woman's lack of a penis is repressed, while the *idea*, by contrast, is "disavowed": "If we wanted to differentiate more sharply between the vicissitude of the *idea* as distinct from the *affect*, and reserve the word *Verdrängung* ['repression'] for the affect, then the correct German word for the vicissitude of the idea would be *Verleugnung* ['disavowal']" (p. 153). The affect – anxiety, for example (as in "castration anxiety") – is then no longer experienced as such, having been repressed, while the idea *remains present* under the form of disavowal. This "remaining present" suggests why Freud writes that, in the face of woman's castration, the fetishist "retains this belief [in the presence of the phallus] but also gives it up." One might think this formulation functions precisely as repression does, since we have a "no" and a "yes" simultaneously, such that the belief is both maintained and renounced ("it is/is not my mother"). But Freud insists that, in fetishism, "repression" characterizes what happens to the *affect*, whereas "disavowal" is what happens to the *idea* or "belief" – what Lacan would call the symbolic representation, the order of the signifier. What then distinguishes "disavowal" from repression, and why does Freud say that "repression" in this case only bears on the affect? Does not repression normally bear also on ideas, as when a repressed thought emerges under the sign of negation ("it's not my mother")?

The solution is that, in the case of "disavowal," the mode of rejection is stronger than in repression. What is disavowed is not "repressed" (and thus able to return), but is rather more profoundly refused; and in order to clarify this difference, Freud relies on the *perceptual dimension*. The "idea" (or signifier) of castration is indeed "retained" and "given up," but unlike repression, where the idea is normally retained only in the unconscious, in disavowal the affect is repressed, while the idea of maternal castration is not repressed, but remains present alongside its negation. This is why the fetishist requires another mechanism by which the negation of this idea can be maintained – not a mechanism of repression, by which the symbolic representation (the idea or signifier) would be lodged in the unconscious, but a mechanism of disavowal, by which the imaginary representation (the visual image) remains present in the field of perception, by means of the fetish. Accordingly, Freud immediately points out that Laforgue is wrong to suggest that in fetishism the perception is simply eliminated, "so that the result is the same as when a visual impression falls on the blind spot on the retina" (*SE* 21, p. 153). On the contrary: in disavowal, the mode of negation is different from mere absence or blindness, and Freud therefore says that in fetishism, "we see that the perception has persisted, and that a very energetic action has been exerted to keep up the denial of it" (*ibid.*). We thus see more clearly why Freud claims that the affect is "repressed" while the idea is "denied": if the subject denies the idea (the concept or signifier), and yet simultaneously retains it as a conscious belief, that retention takes place in the Imaginary, through the perceptual presence of the fetish. The logic of negation in Freud's work thus requires an account that will be sensitive to the mechanisms of psychic life, at the level of the symbolic, the imaginary, and the real. As for the final term, "foreclosure" by contrast indicates, for Lacan, a still more profound absence of lack, such that the subject has not even registered the difference, the symbolic differentiation, that the fetishist seeks to conceal. "Foreclosure" thus designates a mode of negation that is closer to psychosis than the other mechanisms, which remain inscribed within the system of representation more securely. Thus, even without elaborating these distinctions in any detail, we can already see that it is not enough to point to Lacan's supposed reliance on Hegel, or any other logic of negation, without also exploring the clinical dimension of Lacan's formulations.

This conceptual movement, whereby a meticulous attention to philosophical distinctions is sustained, but mobilized in the interest of the clinical domain, is evident throughout Lacan's work. In *Seminar VII*, for example, Lacan turns from Kant's ethics, which has been a central focus in his argument, and takes up *The Critique of Judgement*, citing particular passages and insisting that his audience look closely at the text: "I intend to have you go over the passages of Kant's *Critique of Judgment* that are concerned with the nature of beauty; they are extraordinarily precise" (*S VII*, p. 261). Two chapters later, he is still reading the text, focusing in particular on one of the most obscure passages in Kant's account, namely section 17, entitled "Ideal beauty" – a passage in which Kant argues somewhat strangely that an ideal of beauty cannot properly be considered as belonging to the experience of the beautiful. An "ideal" of beauty is not rejected by Kant because it has an abstract, cognitive component (for an "ideal" is not an "idea"). Nevertheless, the ideal introduces a standard that thwarts the free play of the imagination, and thus it cannot be considered to yield a pure judgment of taste. Without quoting, Lacan repeats Kant almost verbatim: "The beautiful has nothing to do with what is called ideal beauty" (*S VII*, p. 297). This brings us to the crucial point, for what Kant tells us in section 17 is that there is only one ideal of beauty, and that is the form of *the human body*. "Only man," Kant says, "among all objects in the world, admits, therefore, of an ideal of beauty, just as humanity in his person, as intelligence, alone admits of the ideal of perfection."[19] The human image is therefore not one image among others, but has a special character that disrupts the category of the beautiful in Kant's analysis, by bringing into play a dimension of infinity, a rupture with visibility, an "ideality" that in fact only genuinely finds its place in the second book of Kant's text, the analytic of the sublime (this is why Kant excludes the "ideal of beauty" from the category of the beautiful – a point Lacan does not follow, preferring to alter the conception of the beautiful as such, so that it will account for this rupture with the visible). This is the crucial point for Lacan: "Even in Kant's time," he says, "it is the form of the human body that is presented to us as the limit of the possibilities of the beautiful, as ideal *Erscheinen*. It once was, though it no longer is, a divine form. It is the cloak of all possible fantasms of human desire" (*S VII*, p. 298). Thus, even without following the details of this analysis with the care that they deserve, we can see that Lacan's reference to "Kant's theory of the beautiful" is hardly a passing fancy, thrown out to buttress his intellectual credentials, but a genuine and meticulous encounter with the philosophical tradition.

And more important still, for our present argument – and this is why a little detail has been necessary – is the fact that Lacan does not simply impose his well-worn doctrines about "the imaginary body" onto the philosophical text, but on the contrary, seems to be transforming his own conceptual apparatus under the influence of the philosophers he reads. For he claims here that the image of the human form, unlike other instances of the beautiful that may be apprehended in the perceptual image, has a sublime element to it, a rupture with visibility, an aspect that touches on the infinite and the "unpresentable," as Kant says, which means that it can no longer be understood in terms of the thesis on the imaginary body so dear to the early Lacan, in which the human form would be captured by the unified totality that is given through the *Gestalt*. The impasse that Kant's own analysis of the beautiful confronts when it reaches the human image ("the *limit* of the possibilities of the beautiful") thus provides a path for Lacan's own conceptual development, even if, as we have already stressed, that path swerves off in the direction of psychoanalysis, towards an account of the "fantasms of human desire."

Virtually every text presents us with difficulties of this order, which demand an enormous erudition on the part of the readers, and a careful attention to the details of the texts Lacan takes up, even if (it cannot be said enough) Lacan's own reasons for pursuing these details will lead him in another direction, not towards a philosophical discourse, but towards problems internal to psychoanalysis – as in the present case, where the stakes of his analysis are clearly focused, finally, on the question of the gaze, the human body, and the concept of "fantasy." This is indeed the fundamental challenge posed by the conjunction of "psychoanalysis and philosophy." And Lacan's major contribution to the analytic community was to push this confrontation to its limit, in order that it might yield genuine results. For psychoanalysis is clearly a discipline in its own right, with a technical vocabulary and a field of investigation that distinguish it from the domain of philosophy; and yet, at the same time, psychoanalysis itself cannot possibly flourish if it refuses to develop its concepts in a rigorous manner, shrouding itself in the private "enigma" of the clinical experience, or borrowing an inappropriate luster from its proximity to a "medical" or "scientific" model that obscures the specificity of the analytic process, and avoids the question of the "subject" in favor of vaguely psychological notions that distort the very arena in which psychoanalysis operates. "Concepts are being deadened by routine use," Lacan used to say, and analysts have taken refuge from the task of thinking: this has led to a "dispiriting formalism that discourages initiative by penalizing risk, and turns the reign of the opinion of the learned into a principle of docile prudence in which the authenticity of research is blunted before it finally dries up" (*E/S*, pp. 31–2). Such is the paradox that leads Lacan to this chiasmus of engagement with philosophy and other conceptual fields: it is only through contact with these *other domains* that psychoanalysis can find *its own way* in a more rigorous fashion.

When Lacan draws on philosophical texts, it is never simply to subject psychoanalysis to concepts extracted from another field; on the contrary, the very terms that he borrows from other domains are themselves invariably altered when they enter the clinical arena. If this is indeed the case, however, it should be possible to show precisely how considerations internal to psychoanalysis will affect whatever concepts Lacan may draw from the philosophical tradition. And in fact, Lacan is careful to mark these transformations as he proceeds. Thus, for example, his analysis of Descartes – from the method of radical doubt by which Descartes suspends the pieties of the tradition, interrogating any knowledge he has inherited from his ancestors, and bringing into question every certainty of the subject (in a procedure that is not without interest for the psychoanalyst), right down to the details of the "third party" who stands as a guarantee for the "I am" in the "Third meditation," when doubt threatens to swallow up every assertion – all this nevertheless leads Lacan to "oppose any philosophy directly issuing from the *Cogito*" (*E/S*, p. 1), not because he wishes to elaborate a philosophical position, but precisely because of the clinical orientation that makes Lacan's relation to the question of the "cogito" something other than a philosophical relation. Lacan says that the Freudian cogito is "desidero," and when the process of doubt reaches its end in analysis, it is not because an epistemological foundation has been reached, but because a "moment to conclude" has been fashioned for the subject.

The same point arises with respect to his notorious Hegelian influences. Hegel certainly had a powerful impact on Lacan's conceptual formation, but Lacan does not fail to mark out his difference from Hegel, which derives from a perspective that is clinically informed. Consider the relation between "truth" and "knowledge": just as, for dialectical thought, the movement of *truth* will always exceed and disrupt whatever has been established as conscious *knowledge*, such that knowledge will be exposed to a process of perpetual dislocation and productive negativity, so also for Freud, the *consciousness of the ego* remains in a state of permanent instability, perpetually disrupted by the alien *truth of the subject* that emerges at the level of the unconscious (the "discourse of the Other"). According to Lacan, Hegel saw clearly this discrepancy between "knowledge" and "truth," and gave it both a logical coherence and a temporal significance from which psychoanalysts could certainly profit. Indeed, this Hegelian framework went far towards establishing the crucial distinction between the "ego" and the "subject," and led Lacan to argue that the analyst should always stand on the side of truth, which implied a rigorous suspicion with respect to "knowledge" ("truth," Lacan says, "is nothing other than that which knowledge can apprehend as knowledge only by setting its ignorance to work"). In this sense, "Hegel's phenomenology . . . represents an ideal solution . . . a permanent revisionism, in which truth is in a state of constant reabsorption in its own disturbing element." This movement of reabsorption, however, is typical of the philosophical arena, devoted as it is to a *conceptual* exhaustion of the phenomena it discovers ("an ideal solution"). In this sense, for Hegel, according to Lacan, the disruptive power of the real finds a perpetual synthesis with the symbolic elaboration of knowledge: as Lacan says in "Subversion of the subject," "dialectic is convergent and attains the conjuncture defined as absolute knowledge," and as such "it can only be the conjunction of the symbolic and the real" (*E/S*, p. 296). But where Hegel regarded "truth" and "knowledge" as dialectically intertwined, such that the disruptive power of truth could eventually be formulated conceptually, and thus put in the service of knowledge ("reabsorbed" by the discourse of philosophy, such that negation is always "productive," always symbolically elaborated), Freud leads us in a very different direction, according to Lacan, insofar as repression – and above all sexuality – put truth and knowledge in a "skewed" relation that cannot be dialectically contained: "Who cannot see the distance that separates the unhappy consciousness . . . from the 'discontents of civilization' . . . the 'skew' relation that separates the subject from sexuality?" (*E/S*, p. 297).[20] For Lacan, then, "Freud reopens the junction between truth and knowledge to the mobility out of which revolutions come" (*E/S*, p. 301).

Again and again, he will make the same assertion, on the one hand urging psychoanalysts to take greater responsibility for their concepts by having recourse to other fields, but on the other hand insisting that Freud's discovery has produced a domain which must be grasped and developed as a field in its own right. In the case of Saussure, he insists that psychoanalysis stands in need of the conceptual resources that linguistics can provide, but this is not to turn psychoanalysis into a linguistic discipline. Psychoanalysis would therefore do well to consider the work of linguistics in more detail (and Lacan goes on to link substitution and displacement with metaphor and metonymy), and yet the conceptual task cannot end there, for Lacan immediately adds a twist: "Conversely, it is Freud's discovery that gives to the signifier/signified opposition the full extent of its implications: namely, that the signifier has an active function in determining certain effects" (*E/S*, p. 284) – effects which concern the clinical register. The most obvious of these effects, which linguistics would hardly be required to consider, is the bodily symptom, which has a symbolic dimension for Lacan, as Freud already suggested when he ascribed the hysterical symptom, not to organic dysfunction, but to the activity of unconscious representations, saying "hysterics suffer mainly from reminiscences" (*SE* 2, p. 7).

Following Freud, but also learning from Saussure, Lacan insists on the autonomy of the signifier, whose operation should not immediately be situated at the "psychological" level. For the "reminiscence" in this case is not a conscious or even merely an unconscious "memory," in the usual sense of the word, and cannot really be grasped as a "psychic" phenomenon at all, but is rather a signifier that (1) has been detached from its signified (since, as Freud argues, the patient generally does not remember the pathogenic event – the "signified" – which has undergone repression, or been emptied of meaning, or replaced by an apparently "innocent" or "nonsensical" substitute), but at the same time (2) remains present, inscribed at the level of the body, such that the symptom remembers in place of the memory. The symptom, Lacan says, is "the signifier of a signified repressed from the consciousness of the subject," and "written in the sand of the flesh" (*E/S*, p. 69). The broader philosophical consequence is immediately evident here, for this also means that the symptom in psychoanalysis, in spite of its concrete physiological manifestation, can never be confused with a biomedical phenomenon of the kind that would have a correlate in the animal world, since it only belongs to the being who speaks, and whose very life is reconfigured when it passes through the network of the symbolic order – "which makes of the illness the introduction of the living being to the existence of the subject" (*E/S*, p. 69).

If this characterization of Lacan's general stance is correct, it should not only guide us in reading his work, but also warn us against several interpretive shortcuts which have marked the secondary literature. For we can hardly be content with a cursory gesture that pretends Lacan produced a "Hegelian reading of Freud," or applied "structural linguistics" to the unconscious, as though clinical considerations played no part in the formation of his concepts.[21] Yet this very impression has been popularized by accounts which reduce Lacan to an amalgam of his sources, as though the "imaginary" relation and the question of narcissism could be translated back into the terms of intersubjective rivalry developed by Kojève, or as though Lacan's understanding of the "symbolic" were imported without the slightest change from the field of structural anthropology.[22] Such claims may satisfy our inclination to package and digest material that is notoriously difficult, and may even give us permission to avoid the challenge of his vocabulary, by recasting it in terms of a more familiar academic discourse; but such a translation will invariably obscure Lacan's terminology and avoid the clinical dimension of his work, and in return, the philosophical resources on which he draws will never be genuinely affected by the transformation they undergo when they are placed in the context of psychoanalysis.²³ The very challenge that is posed by the question of "psychoanalysis and philosophy" will have been eliminated altogether, in favor of a reception that makes Lacan's work recognizable, but at the cost of eliminating the specificity of the field in which he operates.

Consider the distinction between "need" and "desire." Lacan borrowed this distinction from Kojève, who insisted that human desire, which Kojève called "anthropogenetic desire," is essentially a "desire for recognition," and is therefore fundamentally different from "animal desire," which Lacan called "need," and which is modeled on an instinctual relation to the object and the requirements of biological survival (the classical example being the "need for food"). The animal's *relation to the object* of need is thus usefully distinguished from the human *relation to the other*, which is fundamentally a relation to the other's desire. Hence the famous formula Lacan absorbs from Kojève: "Man's desire is the desire of the other." This is all well and good, but Kojève's conceptual framework does nothing to clarify Lacan's distinction between "desire" and "demand" (as is evident from the fact that the secondary literature speaks indifferently of a "demand for recognition" and a "desire for recognition" as though there were no difference between the two). The appeal to Kojève's framework thus obliterates the distinction between demand and desire in the very gesture that offers to explain Lacan's work. Nor does the reference to Kojève help us to grasp the Freudian problematic of the "object-relation." Starting from the philosopher's distinction between the human and the animal, we can speak of the peculiar character of "recognition" and "intersubjectivity" in the human sphere, but when it comes to the object-relation and the question of bodily satisfaction, the Kojèvean framework leaves us at a loss, by presupposing that the bodily "relation to the object" is always a natural or "animal" relation (as with the "need for food"). To be sure, the commodity presents us with an "object-relation" that escapes from the order of need, but in this case, the fundamental function of the object is to mediate a relation to the other's desire (the commodity only rises above need to the extent that it has a symbolic function in relation to the other), and in this sense, the entire discourse of "recognition" and "intersubjectivity" short-circuits the clinical problem of the "object-relation."

This is especially important when it comes to the problem of embodiment. In the case of the satisfaction of the oral drive, for example (to stay with the Kojèvean example of food), the subject departs from the order of biological need, and may eat too much, or refuse to eat at all. Such a phenomenon, which Lacan would characterize as a *bodily demand* – an oral demand in which the desire of the subject is compromised – leaves the philosopher silent.

In short, from Kojève's perspective, the "human" or "anthropogenetic" relation is deftly explained at the level of intersubjectivity, but the "body" as such is prematurely relegated to nature and animality, in keeping with a long philosophical tradition. As a result, the question of sexuality, the symptom, and the libidinal organization of the body – all of these issues, which were so crucial to Freud's thinking, are simply cast aside, displaced in favor of a disembodied discourse on the "relation to the other." And in this way, the terminology of psychoanalysis ("the other" or "the symbolic") is devoured or incorporated by philosophy, integrated into a familiar discourse on "recognition" as though psychoanalysis made no intervention whatsoever in the vocabulary it borrows from other domains. A relation to the other, indeed. In place of a genuine encounter, the discourse of psychoanalysis is simply reabsorbed by the philosophical tradition, and the problems that animate Lacan's theoretical development are abandoned in favor of a conceptual arrangement that is already established in the academic discourse of post-modernism. Paradoxically, then, the popular demonstration of Lacan's debt to philosophy, while it promises to elucidate his work, has tended not only to avoid Lacan's most important conceptual innovations, but also to promote the erasure of the psychoanalytic domain as such.

Generally speaking, the central problem in the reception of Lacan in the English-speaking world has been the mobilization of an interpretive machinery on the part of readers who simply do not know enough about psychoanalysis, and for whom the erasure of the clinical domain takes place without even being noticed. But this difficulty is also something for which psychoanalysis itself is responsible. For the psychoanalytic community has often been all too reluctant to develop its conceptual apparatus in a way that would speak to other disciplines – though Freud himself obviously had such ambitions for his work. This is perhaps understandable, since the principle interest of psychoanalysis rightly rests with its own internal affairs, and not with an exposition of its consequences for another field. Thus, if the Lacanian concept of the gaze develops in dialogue with Merleau-Ponty, the task of the analyst is not to demonstrate the effects of this concept on the phenomenological account of perception, but simply to refine the theoretical framework of psychoanalysis itself, and to grasp what Lacan means when he characterizes the gaze as an "object of the drive." And yet, Lacan's work does have consequences for other fields which are worthy of greater exposition, as in the cases of Kojève and Saussure.

This same difficulty could be traced across an entire range of thinkers. We have seen how Lacan was "influenced" by Heidegger, and how he referred to the philosopher on many occasions. But we do not yet know how Lacan's discussion of anxiety, based as it is on a clinical problematic (the logic of the relations among anxiety, jouissance, and desire) and a reading of Freud's work, might challenge the philosopher's account of Being-in-the-World. Is anxiety, in the peculiar relation to death which it discloses, together with the ex-static temporality it reveals, the manifestation of our fundamental and authentic mode of being, as Heidegger suggests, or is it in fact a transformation of libido, or perhaps rather a disposition of the ego in the face of some danger, as Freud argues? Or is it still rather a particular moment in the relation to the Other, a mode of jouissance in which the desire of the subject is suspended, as Lacan claims in his analysis of Abraham and Isaac? In order to begin to answer such questions, the philosopher would have to read the texts of psychoanalysis with a view to grasping the clinical stakes of these issues. A simple documentation of the references Lacan makes in passing to the texts of Kierkegaard, Heidegger or Sartre will do nothing to clarify such questions, but will only perpetuate the vague idea that Lacan somehow borrows the idea of "being-towards-death" from his philosophical rival. In this way, the encounter between philosophy and psychoanalysis will once again be missed.

Even among Lacanians, who are generally more engaged with conceptual developments in other fields, a genuine encounter with philosophy has been largely circumvented, as is evident in the secondary literature, where a gesture of expertise among devotees has tended to dismiss the philosophical tradition as an arena of benighted confusion. This is, of course, the strict counterpart to the recuperative gesture of academic knowledge, which delights in demonstrating the absolute dependence of Lacan on the thinkers to whom he refers ("once again, the shadow of Hegel falls over the corpse of Lacan's terminology"). These gestures of authority and debunking ("Lacan alone can explain what all previous thinkers misunderstood," or "Lacan merely quotes and recapitulates an assemblage of sources") are the predictable signs that a disciplinary boundary is simply being protected, and has yet to be traversed in a mature fashion – which only indicates that important work remains to be done. But even this hasty survey suggests that Lacan's own procedure was more open, and that he read the texts of philosophy with a seriousness of purpose, and with a willingness to have his own concepts challenged, while at the time preserving the specificity of his task, and the difference between the clinical and philosophical domains.

By the same token, therefore, it would be a mistake to conclude that Lacan's own system is a self-contained apparatus, an interpretive juggernaut that can be mechanically applied to every other conceptual field – as though the categories of the Imaginary, Symbolic, and Real, having established themselves with dogmatic certainty, could now be unleashed on painting, cinema, Yanomamo culture, theories of democracy, or contemporary debates about ethnicity and national identity, without the theory itself developing in response to the fields with which it engages. If there is traffic between philosophy and psychoanalysis, it does not move in only one direction. When one follows the procedure of Lacan himself, and his often labyrinthine protocol of reading, it is clear that the self-sufficiency of the Lacanian system – however satisfying it may be for his followers to deploy – was never so secure, and that Lacan himself insisted on this long detour into foreign philosophical territory, not to demonstrate what he already knew, but to develop his own conceptual apparatus through the challenge of this other domain.

Lacan turned to other thinkers, then, neither to demonstrate their failure to arrive at properly psychoanalytic conclusions, nor to deploy his own categories, repeating on other terrain the conclusions he had already reached, but rather because the psychoanalytic community had not done enough to refine its own conceptual domain, and stood to gain from a sustained encounter with its neighbors. His turn to philosophy was therefore neither an abandonment of psychoanalysis in favor of Structuralism or anthropology or philosophical discourse (since he is not ultimately interested in solving philosophical problems), nor simply a matter of stealing from others (since the concepts he finds are invariably altered when they enter the domain of psychoanalysis); nor, finally, did he aim at the sort of self-enclosed system that could serve as the intellectual trump card in relation to other knowledge. This is the great gift bequeathed to us by Lacan's often infuriatingly difficult work: one can no more be content with a superficial glance at "the famous being-towards-death," tossed off on the way to a demonstration of Lacan's superiority to every other thinker, than one can retreat into the haven of familiar formulae drawn from Kojève and Saussure.

This double gesture is the fundamental mark of Lacan's relation to the philosophical arena – maintaining without compromise the theoretical specificity of the psychoanalytic field, which has its own complex and often technical vocabulary, and develops in response to a distinctive clinical field, and yet taking full responsibility for the articulation of its concepts, by a rigorous engagement with other relevant domains, as the earliest analysts themselves were always careful to do. The persistent exploration of this disciplinary border, and the double movement it entails, is the hallmark of Lacan's relation to other areas of knowledge: "In a discipline that owes its scientific value solely to the theoretical concepts that Freud forged . . . it would seem to me to be premature to break with the tradition of their terminology. But it seems to me that these terms can only become clear if one establishes their equivalence to the language of contemporary anthropology, or even to the latest problems in philosophy, fields in which psychoanalysis could well regain its health" (*E/S*, p. 32).

It is clearly not possible to cover such a complex set of issues in a short space, but having sketched out the general terrain, let us now narrow our inquiry quite sharply and take up an example in a bit more detail, in order to see more concretely how Lacan works across various borders as his thinking unfolds. We will see how a number of threads are woven together, linking Aristotle's *Ethics*, modal logic, and sexual difference in a strange but intriguing fabric. The complications of the argument are enormous, as will quickly become apparent, and we will do no more than outline a few of the pathways that are opened by this example – four paths, to be precise, before we conclude. But even this minimal sketch will be sufficient to give readers a more concrete sense of how Lacan's thought intersects with the philosophical tradition.

In 1972–3, Lacan gave a seminar entitled *Encore*, in which his thinking about sexual difference takes a dramatic step forward. The text of this seminar, recently translated as *On Feminine Sexuality*, has had an enormous influence, not only within the Lacanian tradition, but in French feminist theory and in broader debates about gender and sexual difference in the Anglo-American context, due largely to the translation of a portion of the work in Jacqueline Rose and Juliet Mitchell's anthology, *Feminine Sexuality*. In *Seminar XX: Encore*, Lacan famously develops an account of "feminine sexuality" – or more precisely of the "Other jouissance" – which seems to break with his earlier work. For in earlier years, Lacan had provocatively insisted upon maintaining Freud's thesis that "there is only one libido," and that this libido is "phallic," arguing that what Freud meant thereby – though obviously he did not use this terminology – was that human sexuality is not governed by the laws of nature, and does not culminate in a "normal genital sexuality" which aims at procreation, but is rather governed by the symbolic order and the law of the signifier. As Freud said in *Three Essays on the Theory of Sexuality*, there is no genital normalization leading to a proper biological object, but only a series of libidinal sites (usually located in relation to the bodily orifices) which are not mechanically situated in a natural development, but are shaped by psychic traces of memory and relations with others. Sexuality has a *history* in the human animal, rather than a simple *evolutionary unfolding*, precisely because it is not automatically bound to the mechanisms of natural development (so much for Steven Pinker). And this fact about sexuality holds for all speaking subjects as such, regardless of sex or gender: there is only one libido, and it is phallic, in the sense of being subject to the signifier. Where instinct provides animals with a biological grounding and a *telos* of reproduction, divided between two sexes, humans are faced instead with modes of libidinal satisfaction that are organized by representation. Without entering into the details of this discussion, we can nevertheless see why Lacan claims that "there is only one libido," meaning that the satisfaction of the drive in human beings is detached from the order of nature, and subjected to a symbolic organization, such that the satisfaction of the drive is always caught up in the relation to the other, and the symbolic codification of the body.

The peculiarity of this position is that there seems to be no clear way of distinguishing between the sexes. And indeed this is Lacan's position for many years: for psychoanalysis, sexuality is not divided into a "feminine" and "masculine" form, or structured according to the two biological "sexes" – as though biological difference might, after all, provide a foundation for this question, in spite of Freud's claims to the contrary. Nor can one take comfort in the culturalist notion that the social codification of "gender" will somehow establish what nature fails to provide. Historically speaking, of course, various cultures indeed organize sexuality in many ways, and Lacan hardly ignored this fact. But the social dimension of "gender identity," structured as it is at the general level of cultural practices and norms, is insufficient to tell us what psychoanalysis needs to know about the subject, whose *relation* to the symbolic order is always particular. Thus, while a given culture may well mobilize a host of images for femininity which offer an emaciated ideal of the body, we cannot conclude that every woman will automatically become anorexic in response, as if the subject were simply a social construction. Lacan's "advocacy of man's relation to the signifier has nothing to do with a 'culturalist' position in the ordinary sense of the term" (*E/S*, p. 284). "Gender" is thus a useful category for historical analysis, but from the standpoint of psychoanalysis, the subject's sexuality will be fashioned in every case according to a distinctive organization, with particular modes of satisfaction, and this is why psychoanalysis, as a matter of methodical procedure, cannot take place in a classroom, or be transmitted like other forms of knowledge, but rather requires that each subject explore the singular discourse that defines each one alone. This is the great mystery of psychoanalysis, but also its philosophical importance, when it comes to sexual difference: the question of "sexual difference" cannot be resolved by any appeal to the usual categories of biological "sex" and cultural "gender." And paradoxically, it is the thesis on "one libido" that helps to establish this claim.

In 1972, however, Lacan's thinking takes a new step forward. Where he had previously insisted that the libido, in humans, is governed by the symbolic order and the laws of language – a "relation to the Other" which structures every subject, regardless of biological sex – he now proposes that there is more than one way of relating to this Other. Lacan even stresses the apparent contradiction this presents, in relation to his earlier work: "I say that the unconscious is structured like a language. But I must dot the i's and cross the t's," and this means exploring not only the laws of the symbolic order, but also "their differential application to the two sexes" (*S XX*, p. 56). And he knows his audience will be stunned: "So, you've admitted it, there are two ways to make the sexual relationship fail" (*S XX*, pp. 56–7), he writes, two ways for the lack of genital normalization to be manifested. Such is the claim in 1972, and we can perhaps understand already why Lacan hesitates to designate this "second way" under the sign of "femininity," since the customary usage of such a term would imply that we are dealing either with biological sex or with the broadly social category of gender identity, while in fact it is a question of another jouissance that appears with some subjects, but cannot be attached to a social or biological group as a whole ("women"), or even restricted, necessarily, to one gender or one sex: "There is thus the male way of revolving around it [i.e. the phallic way], and then the other one, that I will not designate otherwise because it's what I'm in the process of elaborating this year" (*S XX*, p. 57). One understands the hesitation, then, but it is nevertheless clear that Lacan's aim is to intervene in the classical psychoanalytic debate on sexual difference, through this thesis on a mode of jouissance that is "not-all in the Other," or not wholly governed by the order of the "phallic" signifier: "it is on the basis of the elaboration of the not-whole that one must break new ground . . . to bring out something new regarding feminine sexuality" (*S XX*, p. 57).

This is our example, then, and in many respects, we can recognize it as an attempt to clarify some of Freud's most famous remarks on femininity: for Freud observes that women have a different relation to castration, and indeed a different relation to the "law," as his notorious claims about the lack of a super-ego in women (or, more precisely, the formation of a different super-ego in women) make clear. And Lacan elaborates these claims by suggesting that femininity entails the possibility (and I will already stress this word, *possibility*, in which sexual difference and modal logic come together – as though femininity were only a possible and not a necessary mode of being) of a different relation to the symbolic order, a relation that may have ethical as well as clinical consequences.

The debates about Freud's views on "femininity" are obviously enormous, and we can do no more than mark the issue in a general way. Let us then simply recall Freud's statement in "Some psychical consequences of the anatomical distinction between the sexes":

> I cannot evade the notion (though I hesitate to give it expression) that for women the level of what is ethically normal is different from what it is in men. Their super-ego is never so inexorable, so impersonal, so independent of its emotional origins as we require it to be in men. Character-traits which critics

of every epoch have brought up against women – that they show less sense of justice than men, that they are less ready to submit to the great exigencies of life, that they are more often influenced in their judgements by feelings of affection or hostility – all these would be amply accounted for by the modification in the formation of their super-ego which we have inferred above.

(SE 19, pp. 257–8)

Whether one dismisses this statement as a stereotypical expression of the prejudices of Freud's day, or celebrates it as an insight into the fact that sexual difference may have a bearing on ethical questions (such that femininity may make possible a "different voice" or an "ethics of care" – a sense of justice in which the rigidity of a masculine law is implicitly criticized), it is clear that Freud has opened a path that is at once clinical and philosophical, insofar as it points to a "modification" in the form of the super-ego (what Lacan would call a different relation to the law) that not only seeks to identify some aspects of psychic life, but also has implications for our understanding of what Freud calls "justice." In Freud, the question of sexual difference is thus explicitly linked to ethics, and here again we should stress the double trajectory that Lacan has done more than any other figure in the history of psychoanalysis to maintain. For the interpreter's task is complicated by the fact that the clinical field cannot be directly superimposed on the domain of philosophy: the "law" in psychoanalysis (and its "modification") does not immediately coincide with the "law" in the philosophical domain, and cannot automatically be translated into a generalized discourse on ethics and the good. Nevertheless, if we recall that Freud himself spoke of the super-ego as the foundation of the moral imperative in Kant, we begin to see how clinical issues, forged on the terrain of psychoanalysis, might nevertheless have a legitimate impact on the domain of philosophy. With this example in mind, let us follow Lacan's itinerary a little further.

First path: the sexuation graph. Having taken this step towards the "Other jouissance," in which the general law of symbolic castration is no longer the whole story, Lacan now develops Freud's claim by means of symbolic logic, in the "sexuation graph" which maps out two modes of relation to the Other, correlated with sexual difference.

On the "male" side, the "normal" or "phallic" position is defined through the proposition that all subjects, being unmoored from nature, are destined to find their way through the symbolic order. Lacan expresses this claim in symbolic notation, with the formula $\forall x\ \Phi x$ ("All subjects are submitted to the phallic signifier"). Now this position (the universal law of symbolic existence) is paradoxically held in place by an exception to the law, which Lacan elaborates in keeping with Freud's analysis of the primal horde in

Masculine		Feminine	
$\exists x$	$\overline{\Phi x}$	$\overline{\exists x}$	$\overline{\Phi x}$
$\forall x$	Φx	$\overline{\forall x}$	Φx

Figure 8.1 Lacan's sexuation graph

Totem and Taboo, where Freud explains that the sons all agree to abide by the law (to accept symbolic castration), precisely in contrast to the "primal father," who stands as the exception to the rule, in relation to which the law is to be secured. Thus, the "male" side of the sexuation graph includes another formula, $\exists x\,\overline{\Phi x}$ ("There is one subject who is not submitted to the phallic signifier"), and this second formula, which forms part of the law of castration on the male side, is cast as an excluded position, an exception to the law, as Freud also claims when he explains that the primal father must always be killed, since his expulsion from the community by murder insures that the symbolic community will be established. The two formulae thus appear to present a simple contradiction, logically speaking, but in a clinical sense they are intended to define the antinomy that structures masculine or phallic sexuality, in the sense that the exception to the law, where the possibility of an unlimited jouissance is maintained ($\forall x\,\overline{\Phi x}$), is precisely the jouissance that must be sacrificed, expelled, or given up for the field of desire and symbolic exchange to emerge. Such is the logic of symbolic castration. It would obviously be possible to play out this "logic of masculinity" in some detail, with reference to Arnold Schwarzenegger and others, whose films represent the masculine fantasy in which the law of the civilized community can only be upheld, paradoxically, by an exceptional figure who is able to command an absolute power of violence, which is itself used to expel the monstrous, mechanical, or demonic figure (the uncontrollable machine or corrupt corporate demagogue) whose absolute jouissance threatens the space of democracy and capitalistic exchange. In masculinity, democracy and totalitarianism are not simply contradictory, as though they could not exist together, but are on the contrary twins, logically defining and supporting one another. Such elaborations – always too quick in any case – are not our purpose here, but we can at least note Lacan's attempt to provide a rigorous theoretical account, through symbolic logic, of the "contradictions" of masculinity.

While the "masculine" side of the graph provides a relation to symbolic castration which is total ("All men are subject," etc.), the "feminine" side, by contrast, provides a second pair of formulae in which the subject is not altogether subjected to the law. The second of these formulae, $\overline{\forall x}\ \Phi x$, can be read as "Not all of a woman is subject to symbolic castration." The universal, which functions on the masculine side ("All men"), is thus negated on the side of femininity ("Not all"). Something of woman may thus escape symbolic castration, or does not entirely submit to the symbolic law ("they show less sense of justice than men" and "their super-ego is never so inexorable"). "Feminine jouissance" is thereby distinguished from "phallic jouissance" by falling partly outside the law of the signifier. Subjected to the symbolic order like all speaking beings, the "feminine" position is nevertheless "not-all" governed by its law. And as was the case on the masculine side, so here we find a second formula, but in this case it is not an exception to the law (as with the primal father). Instead, we find a formula that indicates an inevitable inscription within the law: $\overline{\exists x}\ \overline{\Phi x}$ ("There is no subject that is not subjected to the symbolic law"). These formulae have been much discussed, and there is no need to rehearse the literature here. But since we are exploring the way in which Lacan uses symbolic logic to sharpen some issues in the debate on sexual difference, and to account for its peculiar "paradoxes," it is worth noting that in this second formula, which articulates the feminine version of subjection to the law, we do not find a universal proposition, a statement that could be distributed across all subjects ("All men," etc.). Instead, we find a formulation that relies on the particular ("There is no woman who is not" etc.). The universal quantifier "all" ($\forall$) is thus replaced with a quasi-existential "there is" ($\exists$) which any reader of Heidegger or Derrida will recognize is immensely rich and complex – the il y a (or "there is") in French being also the translation of Heidegger's es gibt, in which a massively complex meditation on the "givenness" of Being can be found. With Lacan, then, there is a link between the mode of being of femininity – which does not appear or give itself in the universal, and is not entirely inscribed within the symbolic law – and the question of Being itself. And the form of symbolic logic brings these issues prominently to the surface.

An enormously tangled set of issues thus emerges, and one can see how Irigaray took up this challenge, linking femininity to questions of being and language. And angels.[24] For Lacan remarks on the "strangeness" of this feminine mode of being: it is étrange, Lacan says, playing on the word for "angel" (être ange means "to be an angel"), this mode of being which falls outside the grasp of the proposition ("it is . . ."). We cannot say that "it is" or "it exists," just like that, because it does not all belong to the domain of symbolic predication, and yet, this same impasse in symbolization means that we cannot say "it is not" or it "does not exist" (or indeed that "there is only one libido"). Beyond the "yes" and "no" of the signifier, beyond symbolic predication and knowledge (is/is not), this mode of being, presented through the Other jouissance, would thus be like God, or perhaps (*peut-être* – a possible-being) more like an angel. Thus, as Lacan suggests, and as Irigaray also notes, though in a very different way, the question of feminine sexuality may well entail a theology and an ontological challenge in which the law of the father is not the whole truth. "It is insofar as her jouissance is radically Other that woman has more of a relationship to God" (*S XX*, p. 83).

In these formulae for femininity, moreover, we again find a curious use of negation, for the strange "there is" of femininity, already detached from the simple assertion of existence, is also presented only under the sign of a certain negation ("Not all of a woman is . . ."). Even in the first formula, we are faced with a double negation ("There is no woman who is not"). This is very different from what we find on the masculine side ("All men are . . ."). "It is very difficult to understand what negation means," Lacan says. "If you look at it a bit closely, you realize in particular that there is a wide variety of negations" and that "the negation of existence, for example, is not at all the same as the negation of totality" (*S XX*, p. 34). Thus, we cannot regard the feminine formulation for symbolic inscription ("There is no woman who is not subject to the signifier") as the equivalent of its masculine counterpart ("All men are subject to the signifier"), even though *logically* these two may be the same. In fact, sometimes a thing can "appear" or "exist" only by means of a kind of negativity ("there is . . . none that is not . . ."), particularly if the "normal" symbolic discourse of propositions ("All men are") already presupposes a mode of being or existence that is itself inadequate. The vehicle of symbolic logic thus seems to force to the surface a variant in the mode of negation that ends up bearing on sexual difference. Woman does not "exist," then, and yet "there is" femininity. We cannot say, in the form of a symbolic assertion, that she "is" this or that (a subject with a predicate that would cover the field of "all women," and allow us to capture her essence as a social or biological totality), and yet it is "possible" that "there is" something of femininity, which has precisely the character of not being fully inscribed in the signifier – a being in the mode of "not-being-written," Lacan says. "The discordance between knowledge and being is my subject," Lacan says (*S XX*, p. 120). Lacan does not say that woman "exists," then, or indeed that she "is not," but rather that she ex-sists: "Doesn't this jouissance one experiences and yet knows nothing about put us on the path of ex-sistence?" (*S XX*, p. 77). All of this may seem far removed from the clinical field we have stressed, and yet it is clear that many experiences, from practices of meditation or ecstatic dance to the paralyzing encounter with absolute solitude into which no other can reach – a black hole of truth from which no words can escape – all testify to a place on the margin of language where enjoyment and exile await us all. Thus, while the I may belong to speech, not all of the subject is inscribed there. As Lacan says: on the one hand, "the I is not a being, but rather something attributed to that which speaks"; but on the other hand, "that which speaks deals only with solitude, regarding the aspect of the relationship I can only define by saying, as I have, that it cannot be written" (*S XX*, p. 120).

A parenthetical note of a methodological nature is worth making at this point. For one might think that these exotic formulae are intended to *describe* in a more or less logical way what has already been discovered in the clinical domain, so that these formulae would be nothing more than the dispensable and esoteric Lacanian translation of Freud's theses on the feminine super-ego or *Totem and Taboo*. These attempts at a logical formalization of Freud are not merely descriptive, however, but are used as a means of discovery. It is almost as if Lacan believes that the conceptual impasses which his logical formulations produce are themselves capable of revealing something about the real. That is to say, if our theories have developed to some extent, but remain inadequate in some respects, and incapable of reaching as far as one might wish, such formulations may produce a sort of impasse that bears fruit. "The real can only be inscribed on the basis of an impasse of formalization," Lacan says (*S XX*, p. 93). A similar wager is present in contemporary science, whereby mathematical accounts of cosmic phenomena, by virtue of their own internal consistency or instability, are somehow supposed to point to features of reality itself ("God does not play dice with the universe"). Mathematics is thus not merely a descriptive device, but an actual method of investigation and research (a curious border between the purely symbolic operations of mathematics and the real of the universe for which physics is intended to be responsible). Here again, we see that Lacan's appeal to other disciplines, however strange and exotic it may seem, is not a simple departure from psychoanalytic concerns but is rather an attempt to use what he finds in other domains to explore the terrain of psychoanalysis itself.

Second path: equivocation, conditional being. Leaving all these questions abruptly to one side, let us now take the next step, in order to see how Lacan immediately reformulates this entire presentation in terms of a certain "equivocation." For as we have already seen, "there is only one libido," and yet, perhaps... How, then, does this equivocation reformulate what we have just seen expressed in symbolic logic? We know that the sexual relationship fails, for Lacan, in the sense that there is no libidinal maturation that would secure masculine and feminine sexuality in a harmonious mutual destiny of natural reciprocity. In place of the sexual relationship, we have a passage through the signifier in which "sexuality" is produced as a phenomenon that is irreducible to any natural reproductive instinct. Accordingly, Lacan will go on to say that "what makes up for the sexual relationship is, quite precisely, love" (*S XX*, p. 45). This thesis on the symbolic displacement of sexuality, its lack of any natural foundation, guided Lacan for many years, and led him to claim that the sexual relation fails. Such is the consequence of life in the universe of discourse: "the universe is the place where, due to the fact of speaking, everything succeeds . . . Succeeds in what? . . . succeeds in making the sexual relationship fail" (*S XX*, p. 56).

Now in the sexuation graph, Lacan defines this failure on the masculine side in terms of a logical duality, such that inscription within the symbolic law is attended by an exception, and it is precisely this exception (an absolute jouissance) that must be excluded in order for the sons to enter the universe of symbolic exchange (just as the child, for Freud, must relinquish the oceanic feeling of infantile grandiosity or "primary narcissism" in order to communicate with the other). But this same duality in relation to the symbolic law can be formulated in another way, as a prohibition: "primal jouissance *must be renounced*, in order for the pleasure principle and the order of symbolic exchange to be established." This "it must" (or *il faut* – it is necessary) is the law of symbolic castration. And Lacan thus says of absolute jouissance that it "must not be" (*qu'il ne faut pas*), in the sense that it must be relinquished or cast off. And yet – for here is the equivocation – this very statement, the very enunciation of the law, carries an ambiguity within it which holds out the possibility of the very thing that has been prohibited. For as Lacan points out, "il ne faut pas" (it must not be) in French also suggests that "it never fails." Playing on the equivocation between two verbs, *falloir* ("to be necessary") and *faillir* ("to fail"), two verbs which share the same form in the third person (*il faut*), Lacan thereby points to an equivocation: the jouissance that *must be excluded* or prohibited *never fails to arrive* anyway (*S XX*, pp. 58–9). Phallic jouissance, which covers all speaking beings, all subjects who submit to symbolic castration, is thus a jouissance of the signifier (Freud's libido) which nevertheless retains an obscure relation to the primordial jouissance that was purportedly renounced. This might seem to hold true for all speaking subjects who are faced with "sexuality" as such, and yet, Lacan now marks this equivocation as a masculine phenomenon. This equivocation, given through the ambiguity of natural language, would thus reformulate what the sexuation graph provided through symbolic logic.

What, then, of femininity, in this new formulation? Particularly if the only jouissance we know, the only one of which we can speak, is phallic jouissance? How to designate, or approach, another jouissance, if such a thing exists (and we cannot say "it is")? Lacan continues, using the conditional tense: "were there another jouissance than phallic jouissance, it shouldn't be/couldn't fail to be *that one*" (*S XX*, p. 59, italics added). That is to say, if we were for a moment to entertain another jouissance, it would only be sustained through the conditional, in the grammatical form of a "contrary to fact" ("were there another one . . ."). And as soon as one sought to consolidate this possibility into an assertion of existence, it would have already been translated into phallic jouissance. "What does *that one* designate?" Lacan asks. "Does it designate the other [the Other jouissance] or the one on the basis of which we designated the other as other [namely, phallic jouissance]" (*S XX*, p. 60). Femininity is thus sustained in the conditional mode, for a time ("were there another . . ."), until it is designated as "existing" ("it couldn't fail to be"), at which point it disappears, having been replaced by the usual phallic jouissance ("that one").

We thus see, in this second version of the argument, where the notations of symbolic logic are replaced with an actual statement or sentence, the curious way in which femininity "haunts" the margin of language, emerging as a possibility, but refusing to be rendered in propositional form. Where masculinity can be formulated more directly, "presented" as it were in an equivocation (the one that is excluded/never fails), femininity by contrast emerges under the conditional, and remains possible for a time that the sentence suspends before us ("were there another . . ."), a time that is held open only until this possibility is designated "to be," at which point it disappears ("to be *that one*"). Note that, in this second formulation, Lacan stresses that the conditional tense ("were there another . . .") also functions like an "if . . . then" proposition. "If there were another jouissance . . . then . . ." Speaking of this conditional tense, Lacan says: "that suggests to me that to use it we could employ protasis and apodosis" (*S XX*, p. 59). As the annotations to the translation point out, "the protasis takes on the meaning of an 'if' clause in an if-then type proposition, and the apodosis takes on the meaning of the 'then' clause" (*S XX*, p. 59, note 23). What is gained through this formulation that the mathemes of the sexuation graph did not reveal is that we can designate – or better, begin to approach – the question of the "existence" of the Other jouissance only if we distinguish the propositions of the symbolic order ("All men are . . ."), not only from the conditionality he has outlined ("if there were . . ."), the "contrary to fact" statement in which no assertion is actually made, but also from the *mode of being* implied in the "if-then" proposition.

For in such propositions, as Russell and Whitehead argued, we are not asserting *that something exists*, but only that *if it exists, then it will have* such and such a mode of being – namely, the mode of being that does not consolidate itself into an entity of which one can say, "it is." Thus, "it is false that there is another one, but that doesn't stop what follows from being true"; or again, "the first part [of the sentence] designates something false – 'were there another one,' but there is no other than phallic jouissance [and the case seems to be closed, except . . .] – except the one concerning which woman doesn't breathe a word, perhaps . . ." (*S XX*, p. 60). These two formulations thus bring out another dimension of what we have seen presented through symbolic logic – an equivocation that reconfigures the "masculine" side of the sexuation graph, and a conditional possibility ("were there," and "if-then") that reworks the formulae for femininity, by stressing a conditional mode of being and a peculiar temporality sustained by a discourse that collapses as soon as it seeks the resolution of a judgment of existence.

Third path: modal logic. The *equivocation* we have just followed (*il ne faut pas* as "it must not be" and "it never fails") is thus a reworking of the "masculine" antinomy from the sexuation graph, while the *conditional* sentence, with its peculiar capacity to sustain another jouissance without asserting its existence, together with its logical formulation as an "if" that can be elaborated without requiring that the thing in question be actual – all this will now be reformulated once again, in a third version which will have much greater consequences for Lacan, but whose character we can only touch on briefly. This time, it is a question of modal logic, and once again, it will entail a treatment of the two formulae with which we began. Once again, moreover, it would seem that Lacan's emphasis falls on femininity, and that his reason for working and reworking this terrain has to do with an effort to formulate a jouissance that lies at the limit of symbolization.

Let us begin again with the "masculine" side. Phallic jouissance, which is characteristic of all speaking beings, is the jouissance that "never fails." It is the jouissance to which "all men" are subject, as all are subject to a libido that is distinct, according to Freud, from instinctual sexuality. In this sense, we can say that phallic libido is "inevitable" for all speaking beings. It has the mode of being of necessity. But the advantage of modal logic is that it allows us to formulate other modes of being. We may be able to say that something "is" or "is not," but this is not enough, for we may ask of something that "is" whether it is in fact, or only as a possibility, whether it is necessarily, or only in a contingent way. The modal forms allow us to be more precise than the simple judgment of existence. If Socrates tells us that "All men are mortal," this means that mortality attaches to "men" as an inescapable predicate, and that it is a necessary feature of their being. But if I am a man, I may not necessarily be living in New York. If I am in fact living in New York, this attaches to me, not by necessity, but in a contingent way. It is in fact the case, but it could be otherwise. Another mode of being, distinct

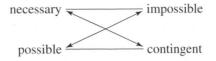

Figure 8.2 Standard version of the logical square showing relations between the four modes of being

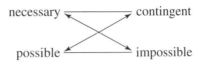

Figure 8.3 Lacan's modification of the logical square showing relations between the four modes of being

from the necessary, is the possible, for as Aristotle showed at great length, a thing can "be" in the mode of being-possible, without being actually the case. Contingent being is therefore distinct from possible being, and both of these are distinct from necessity. And there are beings which we must designate as "impossible," such as "round squares."

These categories – the necessary, impossible, contingent, and possible – which Lacan discusses in a chapter called "Aristotle and Freud," have been organized into a logical square, which gives rise to further relations that are quite complex. Without entering into those relations (though they are important to Lacan), let us simply recall the standard version presented by Algirdas Greimas.

The square not only designates each of the four modes of being, but maps out their relations to one another, as indicated by the connecting arrows. The necessary is thus opposed to the contingent, as the possible is opposed to the impossible. If we then return to the "contradiction" of masculinity, we can say that phallic jouissance, which is "necessary" as the law of the symbolic order, appears only when the unlawful jouissance of the primal father has been expelled – excluded or banished as "impossible." In the universe of discourse, phallic jouissance is necessary, it never fails to arrive, and it is predicated on the exclusion of the absolute jouissance of the primal father, henceforth designated as unlawful or "impossible." Lacan's earlier exposition thus leads him to modify the usual logical square, by opposing the "necessary" to the "impossible." He is explicit about this revision: "the necessary," he writes, "is a modal category," and its opposite "is not the one you might have expected to be opposed to the necessary, which would have been the contingent. Can you imagine? The necessary is linked to the impossible" (*S XX*, p. 59). Lacan's reconstruction is therefore as follows.

As we saw in the sexuation graph, then, phallic jouissance has the force of necessity (All men), and depends on the exclusion of an unlawful or "impossible" jouissance of the primal father. On this reworking, femininity will therefore be elaborated in terms of the "possible" and the "conditional." We have already approached this point in our previous remarks, which underscored Lacan's claim that, when it comes to feminine jouissance, we cannot say that "it is" (necessarily), or even that it "is not" (or that it is "impossible"), but only that it "may be" or "is possible." But there is a further distinction between the possible and the actual that femininity may require us to elaborate. For if we say that femininity, or the Other jouissance, cannot be excluded (since we can no longer say "there is only one libido"), this does not mean that the possibility will actually come to pass. If it were to be, it would not be in the mode of necessity, but only in the mode of a contingent being, but we do not know that this contingent being is actual. We only know thus far that it is a possibility. How then do we pass from the possible to the contingent? This is the crucial question raised by Lacan's reformulation of the logical square, where, once again, the curious operations of logic seem to yield unexpected fruit.

It is here, to conclude, that we must turn to Aristotle, who speaks of "friendship" and "recognition" under the sign of love: ". . . what Aristotle evokes with the term φιλία (*philia*), namely what represents the *possibility* of a bond of love between two of these beings, can also, manifesting the tension towards the Supreme Being, be *reversed* . . . it is in their courage in bearing the intolerable relationship to the Supreme Being that friends, φίλοι (*philoi*), recognize and choose each other" (*S XX*, p. 85). Such friendship, of course – "the eminently contingent encounter with the other" (p. 145) – is an approach to a relation (love) that would take the place of the sexual relation, that natural reciprocity which does not exist in the human sphere. As such, this friendship would not be evidence of "femininity." But it does show us the movement by which a "possibility" of love "can . . . be reversed," and *actualized* as the contingent being of friendship.

This same axis moving from the possible to the contingent reappears at several crucial moments in Lacan's text, in a movement of exposition that eventually binds the question of "the sexual relation" to that of femininity, as two modes of being which cannot be entirely inscribed in the symbolic law. For both of these, in Lacan's account, "do not exist." We have seen that "there is no sexual relation," for Lacan, and we have seen that, when it comes to femininity, we cannot simply say that "it exists." As his seminar progresses, however, we also see that, by the same token, we cannot simply say "there is no such thing" as the Other jouissance, and the logic of femininity thus holds open a possibility beyond the affirmation or negation of our normal discourse. Because of this possibility, phallic jouissance cannot be the whole truth. "Because of this," Lacan says, "the apparent necessity of the phallic function turns out to be mere contingency" (*S XX*, p. 94). Towards the very end of the seminar, Lacan returns to this issue, stressing the impossibility of the sexual relation, but also the other modes of being which proliferate around this impossibility: "Isn't it on the basis of the confrontation with this impasse, with this impossibility by which a real is defined, that love is put to the test? Regarding one's partner, love can only actualize what, in a sort of poetic flight, I called courage – courage with respect to this fatal destiny" (*S XX*, p. 144). Such "actualization" allows the possibility of a relation to take form, to emerge beyond mere possibility, in all its mortal and precarious being, for a time, however contingent. A curious mode of being, but "Isn't it in love's approach to being that something emerges that makes being into what is only sustained by the fact of missing each other?" (*S XX*, p. 145).

NOTES

1. For a biographical account and a useful bibliographical appendix on Lacan's published and unpublished work, see Elisabeth Roudinesco, *Jacques Lacan*, trans. Barbara Bray (New York: Columbia University Press, 1997). For a critical account including short text-by-text summaries of published and unpublished work, see Marcelle Marini, *Jacques Lacan: The French Context*, trans. Anne Tomiche (New Brunswick: Rutgers University Press, 1992). For more developed discussions of major influences, see Anthony Wilden, "Lacan and the discourse of the Other," *The Language of the Self* (Baltimore: Johns Hopkins University Press, 1968), pp. 159–311, and Jonathan Scott Lee, *Jacques Lacan* (Boston: Twayne, 1990), reissued by the University of Massachusetts Press. For a collection focusing on engagements with individual philosophers, including contributions by Derrida, Lacoue-Labarthe, Nancy, Balibar, Badiou, and others, see *Lacan avec les philosophes* (Paris: Albin Michel, 1991).

2. For a good introduction to the relation between Lacan and Hegel, see Edward S. Casey and J. Melvin Woody, "Hegel, Heidegger, Lacan: The dialectic of desire," *Interpreting Lacan*, Psychiatry and the Humanities, vol. 6, ed. Joseph H. Smith and William Kerrigan (New Haven: Yale University Press, 1983), pp. 75–112; see also, in the same volume, Wilfried Ver Eecke, "Hegel as Lacan's source for necessity in psychoanalytic theory," pp. 113–38. For a good account of the relation between Lacan's use of Hegel and his clinical observations, with extensive bibliographical references, see Dany Nobus, "Life and death in the glass: A new look at the mirror stage," *Key Concepts of Lacanian Psychoanalysis*, ed. Dany Nobus (New York: The Other Press, 1998), pp. 101–38. Lacan's own references to Hegel are too numerous to cite, but see his introduction and response to Jean Hyppolite's commentary on Freud's article on "Negation." A short version appears in *Seminar I*. A longer and revised version appeared as "Introduction et réponse au commentaire de Jean Hyppolite sur la 'Verneinung' de Freud," in *La Psychanalyse* 1 (1956), and was republished together with Hyppolite's own text in *Ecrits*.

3. For Lacan's remarks on catharsis, see *Seminar VII: The Ethics of Psychoanalysis*, pp. 48–56, 244–58, 312–15. His most extensive discussion of "affect" more broadly appears in the unpublished seminar on anxiety, *Seminar X: L'Angoisse*. An extended commentary is available in Roberto Harari, *Lacan's Seminar on Anxiety* (New York: The Other Press, 2001). See also André Green, *The Fabric of Affect in Psychoanalytic Discourse*, trans. Alan Sheridan (New York: Routledge, 1999). For an extended discussion of catharsis in the century prior to Freud, see Léon Chertok and Isabelle Stengers, *A Critique of Psychoanalytic Reason: Hypnosis as a Scientific Problem from Lavoisier to Lacan*, trans. Martha Noel Evans (Stanford: Stanford University Press, 1992).

4. For Lacan's account of Merleau-Ponty, see James Phillips, "Lacan and Merleau-Ponty: The confrontation of psychoanalysis and phenomenology," *Disseminating Lacan*, ed. David Pettigrew and François Raffoul (Albany: State University of New York Press, 1996), pp. 69–106. See also Charles Shepherdson, "A pound of flesh: Lacan's reading of *The Visible and the Invisible*," *Diacritics*, 27:4 (Winter 1997), pp. 70–86.

5. For Lacan's relation to Kojève and other figures in the 1930s, see Roudinesco, *Jacques Lacan*, pp. 88–106. Lacan's frequent remarks on Saint Augustine – concerning jealousy, envy, and imaginary identification – are heavily influenced by Kojève, and have been followed at length by Shuli Barzilai, in *Lacan and the Matter of Origins* (Stanford: Stanford University Press, 2000).

6. Lacan's review of Minkowski appeared in *Recherches philosophiques* 5 (1935–6), pp. 424–31. The journal was founded in 1933 by Alexandre Koyré and Henry Corbin, and ran for six issues until 1937, with contributions from Bataille, Caillois, Lévinas, Dumézil, Klossowski, Sartre, and others. Lacan's review of Henri Ey's *Hallucinations et délires* appeared in *Evolution psychiatrique* 1 (1935), 87–91. For a broader survey of Lacan's relation to the French engagement with Heidegger, see Roudinesco, *Jacques Lacan*, p. 98, p. 513, and chapter 10. For two short discussions of Heidegger and Lacan by William J. Richardson, see "Lacan and Non-Philosophy," *Philosophy and Non-Philosophy Since Merleau-Ponty*, ed. Hugh Silverman (New York: Routledge, 1988), pp. 120–35, and "Psychoanalysis and the Being-question," *Interpreting Lacan*, pp. 139–59.

7. "The neurotic's individual myth," trans. Martha Noel Evans, *Psychoanalytic Quarterly* 48 (1979). "Propos sur la causalité psychique" in *Ecrits*, 151–94. Readers have sometimes confused the "Rome discourse" with "The function and field of speech and language in psychoanalysis," because they originated in the same occasion, the Congress of Romance Language Psychoanalysts in Rome in 1953. The first text is published in *Autres écrits*, pp. 133–64; the second text, "Function and field," appears in *E*, pp. 229–322, and *E/S*, pp. 30–113. See Marcelle Marini, *Jacques Lacan: The French Context*, p. 153, and Roudinesco, p. 517. In the 1967 text, "Allocutions sur les psychoses de l'enfant," *Autres écrits*, pp. 361–71, Lacan poses the question of a relationship between being-towards-death and sexual difference – a difficult question that Derrida has raised in some detail in "*Geschlecht*: Sexual difference, ontological difference," *Research in Phenomenology* 13 (1983), pp. 65–83. See also my "*Adaequatio Sexualis*: Is there a measure of sexual difference?" *From Phenomenology to Thought, Errancy, and Desire*, ed. Babette Babich (Dordrecht: Kluwer, 1995), pp. 447–73.

8. Heidegger's *Being and Time* is the text behind Lacan's account of the temporality of the subject in the closing pages of "Function and field." His discussion of Heidegger's "Das Ding" appears in Chapters 4 and 5 of *The Ethics of Psychoanalysis*, and he refers several times to the *Introduction to Metaphysics* in his reading of the first choral ode (the "ode on man") in Sophocles' *Antigone*, citing the same "paradoxical" or "aporetic" moments in the Greek text as those Heidegger discusses. See Martin Heidegger, *Introduction to Metaphysics*, trans. Ralph Mannheim (New Haven: Yale University Press, 1959).

9. Although Lacan's debt to Heidegger has often been neglected or diminished by Lacanians, it remains crucial even when it is not explicit – for example in his treatment of Parmenides, in *Encore*, where his reliance on Heidegger is conspicuous. A discussion of this issue would require a serious treatment of Derrida as well. See Jacques Derrida, "Pour l'amour de Lacan," *Lacan avec les philosophes*, pp. 397–420, and essays by others on Heidegger in the same volume. Lacan's (incomplete) translation of Heidegger's "Logos" article appeared in *La Psychanalyse* 1 (1959), pp. 59–79.

10. For a book-length discussion of Lacan and Kant, see Alenka Zupančič, *Ethics of the Real: Kant, Lacan* (New York: Verso, 2000) and Joan Copjec, "Sex and the euthanasia of reason," *Read My Desire: Lacan Against the Historicists* (Cambridge: Massachusetts Institute of Technology Press, 1994), pp. 201–36.

11. I have discussed Lacan's treatment of "doubt" and "negation" in "Vital signs: The place of memory in psychoanalysis," *Research in Phenomenology*, vol. 23 (1993), pp. 22–72. For a longer discussion of Freud's "Negation" which includes material on Spitz and other analysts, see Wilfried Ver Eecke, *Saying "No"* (Pittsburgh: Duquesne University Press, 1984). See also Joan Copjec, "Cutting Up," *Between Feminism and Psychoanalysis*, ed. Teresa Brennan (New York, Routledge, 1989).

12. One of the major puzzles for Anglo-American interpreters has been to determine whether Lacan's work coincides with the arguments of "social construction" (by virtue of his emphasis on the "symbolic order"), or whether there is a dimension of his work ("sexual difference" or "the real" or indeed "the unconscious") that gives it an ahistorical dimension, or a biological foundation that conflicts with the arguments for social construction. This has been perhaps the central issue in the Anglo-American reception of Lacan, and yet, one might argue that the very question is misplaced. I have addressed this problem in "The intimate alterity of the real," *Postmodern Culture*, vol. 6, no. 3 (May 1996), focusing on the question of whether the concept of the "real" in Lacan is pre-discursive, as some commentators have claimed, or whether it is a non-discursive effect of the symbolic order, in which case, I argue, we are faced with a conceptual difficulty (one might call it the "limits of formalization") that Lacan shares with a number of contemporary philosophers, even if his response to the problem differs from theirs. On this issue, see also Joan Copjec, *Read My Desire: Lacan Against the Historicists* (Cambridge: Massachusetts Institute of Technology Press, 1994), Judith Butler, "Arguing with the Real," *Bodies That Matter* (New York: Routledge, 1993), and Tim Dean, *Beyond Sexuality* (Chicago: University of Chicago Press, 2000).

13. For Foucault's elaboration of Lacan's famous subversion of Descartes, "I think where I am not, therefore I am where I do not think" (*E/S*, p. 166), see *The Order of Things: An Archaeology of the Human Sciences*, trans. Alan Sheridan (New York: Random House, 1970), in the section called "The cogito and the unthought," pp. 322–28; see also "Discourse and man's being," pp. 335–40. For more on the relation between Foucault and Lacan, see John Rajchman, *Foucault, Lacan, and the Question of Ethics* (New York: Routledge, 1991). *Seminar XIII* contains a session devoted to Foucault's *The Order of Things* (New York: Random House, 1970), which focused on the opening chapter on *Las Meniñas*, at which Foucault was present (18 May 1966). Lacan also commented on Foucault's "What is an Author?", in a text published in the *Bulletin de la société française de philosophie* 3 (1969), p. 104. See also Roudinesco, *Jacques Lacan*, p. 295 and p. 312.

14. For Lacan's remarks on Descartes see *S XI*, pp. 35–7, and pp. 220–1. "Science and Truth" appears in *E*, pp. 855–77. It is the opening session of *Seminar XIII: L'Objet de la psychanalyse* (1965–6) and has been translated into English by Bruce Fink in *Newsletter of the Freudian Field* 3 (1989), pp. 4–29. Lacan's use of Descartes has been discussed by Slavoj Žižek in *Tarrying with the Negative: Kant, Hegel, and the Critique of Ideology* (Durham: Duke University Press, 1993). See also Mladan Dolar, "Cogito as the subject of the unconscious," *Cogito and the Unconscious*, ed. Slavoj Žižek (New York: Verso, 1998), pp. 11–40.

15. As William Richardson has said, "Jacques Lacan is first, last and always a psychoanalyst." He certainly "theorizes about his practice," and "this has led him to dip into the waters of the philosophical tradition more often and more deeply than any other interpreter of Freud," but his purpose, Richardson insists, is not guided by the internal affairs of philosophy. "Philosophers have the right . . . to probe the implications of these allusions according to the criteria of their own discipline," but the clinical dimension of Lacan's work should not be ignored. William J. Richardson, "Lacan and non-philosophy," *Philosophy and Non-Philosophy Since Merleau-Ponty*, p. 120.

16. Readers who wish to pursue a similar thread in Freud's own discourse may follow his remarks in the article on "Repression," in which "ideas" or "representations" ("signifiers" in Lacan), are distinguished from another dimension of the unconscious, which Lacan will develop through the concept of jouissance. Freud marks this distinction concerning the limits of representation as follows: "In our discussion so far, we have dealt with the repression of an instinctual representative, and by the latter we have understood an idea or group of ideas which is cathected with a definite quota of psychical energy (libido or interest) coming from an instinct. Clinical observation now obliges us to divide up what we have hitherto regarded as a single entity; for it shows us that besides the idea, some other element representing the instinct has to be taken into account, and that this other element undergoes vicissitudes of repression which may be quite different from those undergone by the idea. For this other element of the psychical representative the term *quota of affect* has generally been adopted. It corresponds to the instinct insofar as the latter has been detached from the idea and finds expression, proportionate to its quantity, in processes that are sensed as affects. From this point on, in describing a case of repression, we shall have to follow up separately what, as a result of repression, becomes of the *idea*, and

what becomes of the instinctual energy linked to it" (*SE* 14, p. 152, original italics). I have discussed this passage in "The elements of the drive," *Umbr(a)* 3 (Fall 1997), pp. 131–45. See also André Green, *The Fabric of Affect*, pp. 38–45.

17. The best-known account of the disjunction between "thinking" and "being" in Lacan appears in *S XI*, pp. 203–15. See Eric Laurent, "Alienation and separation," pp. 19–38, and Colette Soler, "The subject and the Other," pp. 39–53, in *Reading Seminar XI: Lacan's Four Fundamental Concepts of Psychoanalysis*, ed. Richard Feldstein, Bruce Fink, and Maire Jaanus (Albany: State University of New York Press, 1995).

18. See Russell Grigg, "Signifier, object, transference," *Lacan and the Subject of Language*, ed. Ellie Ragland-Sullivan and Mark Bracher (New York: Routledge, 1991), pp. 100–5.

19. Immanuel Kant, *The Critique of Judgment*, trans. James Creed Meredith (Oxford: Oxford University Press, 1952), p. 77.

20. For another treatment of the difference between Hegel and Freud, one could turn to the distinction between the "discourse of the master" (which takes Hegel as its model) and the "discourse of the analyst" – a distinction formulated at length in *Seminar XVII: The Other Side of Psychoanalysis*, ed. Jacques-Alain Miller, trans. Russell Grigg (New York: Norton, forthcoming). Lacan suggests here that the position maintained by the analyst is structurally different from that of the "agent" of a philosophical discourse, and that the "product" of each discursive structure is also distinct. In "Subversion of the subject" he also says that the "subject" of Hegelian dialectic (the *Selbstbewusstsein* or consciousness-of-self in which Hegel's thought culminates) is distinct from the subject of psychoanalysis.

21. Lacan's reliance on Kojève and a Kojèvean account of Hegel is the most conspicuous occasion for this temptation; it has been much discussed and overused by certain interpreters, who, in the course of exploring the *relation* between the two thinkers, end up *reducing* one to the other, thereby diminishing the specificity of Lacan's concepts, and ignoring their clinical dimension altogether, in favor of an interpretive schema of existential negativity that is more familiar to the continental tradition. See Mikkel Borch-Jacobsen, *Lacan: The Absolute Master*, trans. Douglas Brick (Stanford: Stanford University Press, 1991), Peter Dews, *Logics of Disintegration* (London: Verso, 1987), and David Macey, *Lacan in Contexts* (London: Verso, 1988). For a response to this overreliance on Kojève, and to the general tendency to reduce Lacan to his sources, see Tim Dean, *Beyond Sexuality*, pp. 22–60.

22. For two accounts of the imaginary that make its clinical basis clear, see Nobus (note 2) and Richard Boothby, *Death and Desire: Psychoanalytic Theory in Lacan's Return to Freud* (New York: Routledge, 1991), and "The psychical meaning of life and death: Reflections on the Lacanian Imaginary, Symbolic, and Real," *Disseminating Lacan*, pp. 337–63; for a more extended account of the development of the imaginary through various incarnations, see Philippe Julien, *Jacques Lacan's Return to Freud: The Real, the Symbolic, and the Imaginary*, trans. Devra Beck Simiu (New York: New York University Press, 1994).

23. If we consider, for example, Lacan's distinction between "demand" and "desire," it is clear that the accounts which rely on Kojève eliminate the problem of the unconscious, and avoid altogether the questions of embodiment and symptom-formation which Lacan's distinctions were intended to address. The

philosophical reception thus tends to eliminate the clinical dimension of Lacan's work altogether, in a process of reception that is not without interest, but would require a longer discussion to demonstrate. I have developed this claim in more detail in "The gift of love and the debt of desire," *Differences: A Journal of Feminist Cultural Studies*, 10:1 (Spring 1998), pp. 30–74.

24. See Gail M. Schwab, "Mother's body, Father's tongue: Mediation and the symbolic order," *Engaging with Irigaray*, ed. Carolyn Burke, Naomi Schor, Margaret Whitford (New York: Columbia, 1994), pp. 351–78.

9

JOSEPH VALENTE

Lacan's Marxism, Marxism's Lacan (from Žižek to Althusser)

The first question to be posed in an essay addressing Lacan's Marxism must be: can such a thing be said to exist? In the absence of any profession of socialist allegiance on Lacan's part, and given his notorious allergy to institutionalized political commitment, the relevance of Marxist doctrine or methodology to Lacan's theory cannot be presumed but must rather be interrogated and qualified. Do those elements of Marxist theory – individual concepts and broader paradigms alike – that are scattered in Lacan's discourse find their way back out again with all their force and defining political impetus?

Slavoj Žižek, the figure most often identified with a combined Marxist-Lacanian approach to cultural politics, has acknowledged the need to dispel some uncertainty on this point. It is worth exploring in some detail the roots of what may be called Žižek's "Lacano-Marxism," since one may safely assert that it is because of the strong impact and infectious charm of Žižek's many books that Lacan's name has remained so popular in English-speaking countries and has moreover weathered the anti-theoretical storm of the nineties. After having explored Žižek's unique visibility as a self-appointed Marxist Lacanian, I want to then go back in time and engage with Louis Althusser, whose unorthodox, not to say heterodox tendencies in the sixties were all but confirmed, in the eyes of the French Communist Party, by his dalliance with the "decadent" enterprise of psychoanalysis.

Žižek's sublime compromise

Three decades after Althusser and his disciples promoted "symptomal" readings of Marx, Žižek reopened the issue at the outset of his influential early book, *The Sublime Object of Ideology*. There Žižek wonders whether Lacan's oracular thesis, that "Marx invented the symptom," should be discounted as "just a . . . vague analogy."[1] To counter this possibility, so menacing to his own theoretical agenda, Žižek installs the concept of the "symptom" as nothing less than the fulcrum of a "fundamental homology" between psychoanalytic and Marxist procedures of interpretation. Marx and Lacan would concur on the means and aims of a "symptomal reading." Žižek undeniably succeeds in demonstrating that the Lacanian symptom and its anterior Marxist "invention," the materialist contradiction, follow a similar formal logic. In either case, the pathological secret resides not in some concealed, subterranean content, but in the desire-ridden signifying machinery whereby that content is articulated within the larger psychic or political economy. In either case, therefore, the pathological instance is not only anomalous to the system that it troubles, but uniquely characteristic of that system as well.

Žižek's central argument is that the psychoanalytic symptom amounts to a distorted expression or enactment of desire that is itself strictly consistent with the normative, Oedipal construction of that desire, its profoundly split and substitutive character. The task of the signifier in which hysterical and obsessive neuroses inextricably knot pleasure with suffering, action with paralysis, passion with debility, also happen to form the exclusive and necessary condition of the object-relation as such.

For all its ingenuity, Žižek's exposition of a "fundamental homology" (*SO*, p. 11) between the Marxist and the Lacanian symptom is belied by what appears as a stark opposition in their import and function. Marx's surplus value, the realization of labor-power, harbors a latent centrifugal force; it is symptomatic less in its everyday operation than in its potential for catalyzing the revolutionary disruption of its own systemic conditions. That is to say, the formation and expropriation of surplus value are "strictly internal" to fully developed commodity exchange, but are also creative of those excesses, of extremes of economic contradiction and class antagonism, that will, in Marx's view, destroy the capitalist system. Lacan's symptom, by contrast, bears a centripetal energy. It can disrupt and even disable the subject's everyday routine, family life, job performance, romantic and sexual involvements, etc., but it is also the mechanism that allows the subject to organize the enjoyment associated with such enterprises. In so doing, it lends the subject a consistency of being amid his or her discomposure. In Lacan's phrase, the symptom is "in you more than you." The symptom is that which sustains you even as it seems to destroy you. For Marx, conversely, the symptomatic contradiction, such as surplus value, works against capitalism more than capitalism can possibly know since it corrodes (even as it appears to crown) universal commodity exchange.

If we map these respective positions by the light of Marx's Eleventh Thesis on Feuerbach, we can appreciate how deep is the division that Žižek would have us elide. Marx famously wrote: "The philosophers have only *interpreted* the world, in various ways; the point is to *change* it."[2] Over the course of his long career, Lacan progressively favored the symptom as a means of interpreting the neurotic's persistence in his or her subjection to the socio-symbolic order. Throughout his long career, by contrast, Marx progressively enthroned his symptomatic construct, the materialist contradiction, as a means of theorizing the liability of any given socioeconomic order to revolutionary change.

Žižek concludes his chapter entitled "How Marx invented the symptom" much as he began it, reiterating the homology between Marxist and Lacanian constructs, especially the paired surplus value (*Mehrwert*) and surplus enjoyment (*plus-de-jouir*). But as if to confirm an unanswered need for a functional analysis, Žižek slants his closing comparison for the purpose of making the systemic effects of surplus value conformable not only with the economy of *plus-de-jouir*, but also, and perhaps primarily, with the workings of Lacan's symptom.

Žižek identifies surplus value with surplus enjoyment on the grounds that, in either case, the quality of excess does not add to or supervene upon an already consolidated substance, but is necessary to the existence of the substance in question. "It is this paradox which defines surplus enjoyment: it is not a surplus which simply attaches itself to some 'normal' fundamental enjoyment, because *enjoyment as such emerges only in this surplus*, because it is constitutively an excess" (*SO*, p. 52).

The "paradox" of constitutive overplus has a still more far-reaching purchase in Marx's political economy. If we subtract the surplus from surplus value, we do not simply return to the exchange value upon which it is allegedly based. We impair the very medium by which such value comes to predominate: the capitalist mode of production would necessarily grind to a halt. For this reason, Žižek argues, capitalism must be understood as living in a perpetual disequilibrium, driven by the structural contradictions between the forces of production (labor power) and the appropriative relations of production to be perpetually "revolutionizing its own material conditions" (*SO*, p. 52). There is no "accordance" in the process of capitalist production because this one economic system alone "ceases to exist if it stays the same, if it achieves an internal balance" (*SO*, p. 53).

To extend his own Marx-Lacan "accordance" beyond a merely formal symmetry, Žižek takes a further, deeply misleading step. For Marx, the structural possibility of the breakdown and collapse of capitalism resides in its need to transform itself relentlessly for the purpose of extracting surplus value on an ever-accelerating basis. But Žižek conflates the need for capitalist transformation with its prospective achievement, converting surplus value from a point of dangerous unpredictability to a guarantor of dialectical sublation or ideal resolution.

> Herein lies the paradox proper to capitalism, its last resort: capitalism is capable of transforming its limit, its very impotence, into the source of its power – the more it putrifies, the more its immanent contradiction is aggravated, the more it must revolutionize itself to survive. (*SO*, p. 52)

Thus, the real thrust of Žižek's argument builds not to his claim that surplus value as "a coincidence of limit and constraint" is identifiable with Lacan's *objet a*, the bearer of *jouissance*, in other words the embodiment of a "constitutive fundamental lack" (*SO*, p. 53). Rather it aims at the inference that surplus value is functionally analogous both to the Lacanian symptom *and* to *plus-de-jouir*. The *plus-de-jouir* is understood here as that which subtends the very signifying chain that it intermittently disrupts. The stakes of Žižek's argument involve adapting the notion of surplus value to a paradoxically conservative role in political economy that is far more compatible with the conservatism of Lacan's radical analytical formulations than with the revolutionary impetus of Marx's analysis of generalized commodity exchange.

Steeped as he is in the (late) Lacan against (early) Lacan school of psychoanalytic theory, it is no surprise to see Žižek disavowing his own misappropriation of the concept of surplus value. This is what he does when he pits Marx against Marx under the very rubric of Freudian disavowal.

> All this, of course, Marx 'knows very well . . . and yet'; and yet in the . . . Preface to the *Critique of Political Economy*, he proceeds as *if he does not know it*, by describing the very passage from capitalism to socialism in terms of . . . [a] vulgar evolutionist dialectic of productive forces and the relations of production. (*SO*, p. 53)

But Žižek's treatment of surplus value does not, in fact, contest this evolutionist model on behalf of a more sophisticated Marxist alternative that we might call the "revolutionist" program. On the contrary, in making surplus value the empowering rift in capitalist development, he not only disputes the economistic tenet that contradictions between the forces and relations of capitalism must inevitably usher in the socialist revolution, he also forecloses on the idea that those same contradictions can lay down favorable conditions for intervening in the capitalist order of production to effect its downfall. Put another way, Žižek theorizes surplus value as a force that brings about a perpetually "revolutionizing" overhauling *of* the system which in itself forestalls revolution *against* the system. This position seems closer to Marx's postmodern critics, such as Foucault and Baudrillard, than to Marx himself.

In providing an incisive Lacanian analysis of the capitalist economy, Žižek unwittingly reveals the subtle yet profound incompatibility of the Marxist and French psychoanalytic paradigms. Both Lacan and Marx conceive existing social economies or psychic systems as harboring sites of disruption that are internal and even essential to the operations of the systems themselves. However, the plane of operation upon which those agonistic sites appear differs importantly from one case to the other. Surplus value in Marx constitutes an a priori structural necessity of capitalism, and its disruptive effects, accordingly, function like a "poison pill" within the system, creating the conditions of its prospective demise. Lacan's symptom, by contrast, constitutes a contingent, retroactive necessity: contingent, because any signifying trace may do, but placed in a retrospective future: it *will have proven* how disruptive necessities in the system are altered by it. The symptom obeys and exemplifies the Freudian and Lacanian causal logic of retroversion, which unfolds in an anterior future. Whereas the logic of contradiction charts a cycle of dissolution and reconstruction, with visible enactments of historical instability and flux, the logic of retroversion charts a recuperative cycle in which change is what has already occurred.

There is, then, no such thing as Lacan's Marxism. Not because a Lacanian Marxism imbued with the agenda and spirit of broadly social, class-based revolution does not exist – though that may be reason enough – but because the causal logic deployed by Lacan does not delineate the mechanism of historical agency along Marxist lines, does not entertain a revolution (as insurgency) that will not also be a revolution (as repetition and return).

There is clearly, however, such a thing as Marxism's Lacan or, rather, there has always been, since the beginning of Lacan's career, attempts to assimilate his theories to the philosophy of dialectical materialism. As Lacan might have predicted, his own indifference to Marxism has been repaid in a certain Marxist fascination with him. The reason centers on the question of agency, despite and, to a certain extent, because of the specific irreconcilability of Lacan and Marx on this score. The revolutionary pragmatism of Marxism ultimately requires a robust version of agency, which the deterministic sociopolitical ontology of Marxism tends to preempt or undermine, particularly in its high liberal guise. In other words, Marxism requires an account of the insertion of subjectivity within the prevailing mechanism as something other than a free agent or a simple arm of the machine, in short, it requires a subjectivity seen as fully *intentionalized contingency*. Lacan's systematic construction of the signifier as symptomatizing, positing language in its material form as simultaneously motivating, stabilizing, and decentering, could easily look like a blueprint for squaring Marxism's vicious circle. However, Lacan's blueprint tends to point in the opposite direction from Marxism: instead of extracting revolutionary agency from the toils of determinism, it locates agency as a fading mediation in the auto-positioning of the signifier through which any social determination is apprehended.

As a result, the Marxist use of Lacan to theorize the question of agency has often been far more invested in exploring how subjects *forfeit* agency under the spell of some "ruling" ideology. In what might be called a "Lacanian" revolution, neo-Marxist theorists such as Althusser, Jameson, Laclau and, more self-consciously, Žižek treat the Lacanian subject as the site of potential political resistance to the reigning social and ideological order. However, they end up conceiving this subject as the site of resistance to the *disruption* of that order, a view more compatible with the Freudian model of resistance seen as the therapeutic counterpart of repression than with Marxism.

For a variety of reasons, Louis Althusser seems the best case study of what can be called Marxism's Lacan. Unlike Laclau or Žižek, he was a committed Marxist, as opposed to a left-leaning social democrat. He appears at the other end of the spectrum in the group of those who attempted to provide a Marxist version of Lacan. Unlike Jameson, Althusser did not just critically reflect upon Lacanian theory, but sought to make it an integral aspect of his own theoretical outlook. And unlike these other figures, Althusser corresponded with Lacan on the issue of establishing an intellectual and institutional alliance between Marxism and the latter's French brand of psychoanalysis. Finally, while Althusser's appropriation of Lacanian concepts joined an interest in agency and ideology from the beginning, his emphasis shifted from agency to ideology, a paradoxical move, since at the same time his interpretive focus moved from the Imaginary register to the Lacanian concept of the Symbolic. I want to explore the paradox of this double shift, since it will serve to highlight a term that has always proven compelling and yet indigestible to Marxism: the unconscious.

Althusser's mirror relations

Decades after Marxist intellectuals in Paris made their initial overtures to a young Jacques Lacan concerning his reputedly "materialist" brand of psychoanalysis,[3] the now celebrated analyst-heretic, recently exiled from the International Psychoanalytic Association, was drawn into an intellectual and professional alliance with the Marxist Althusser, who had become suspicious, as we have seen, in the eyes of a French Communist Party then caught in the throes of accelerated de-Stalinization, by his fascination with psychoanalysis. Beyond a common maverick status, a strong bond in itself, the men shared a commitment to the Structuralist method, which both sought to introduce into their respective critical discourses as a means of reversing the prevalent deviations, psychologism and economism, from the revolutionary principles of their eponymous founders.

Even so, the recently discovered correspondence between Lacan and Althusser indicates something of the old unevenness to the affiliation. Once again, the conceptual or theoretical attraction was entirely on the Marxist side. Althusser hailed Lacan's work as providing psychoanalysis with a scientific basis not unlike that enjoyed by Marxism. Lacan's interest seems to have been largely professional; having lost the Sainte-Anne venue for his lectures, Lacan needed not just alternative facilities, but a new infusion of audience support and excitement, which Althusser, from his post at the Ecole normale supérieure, was eager to rally (see *JL*, pp. 293–308).

In keeping with these divergent investments, the impression that Lacan and Althusser's work took from one another's discursive field was dramatically different in kind and saliency. In his pedagogy, Lacan periodically set his own theoretical discoveries in loose analogy to broadly Marxist principles, mainly for the purpose of familiarizing the younger and more politically minded intellectuals at the Ecole with his highly specialized conceptual vocabulary. By contrast, Althusser seized upon the most settled and influential aspect of Lacan's own theory, the Imaginary, as the provisional key to all social mythologies or, rather, to social mythology as such. It is at this moment, during the early 1960s, that the distinction between Lacan's incidental affectation of Marxism and Marxism's instrumental appropriation of Lacan comes into plain view.

Althusser found Lacan's account of the mirror stage as introducing the Imaginary register so compelling because it suggestively inflected Marx's canonical reflex-model of ideology. In *The German Ideology*, Marx and Engels craft their most famous rendition of the characteristic dynamics of ideology.

> Consciousness can never be anything else than conscious existence, and the existence of men is their actual life-process. If in all ideology, men and their circumstances appear upside down as in a camera obscura, this phenomenon arises just as much from their historical life-process as the inversion of objects on the retina does from their physical life-process . . . we demonstrate the ideological reflexes and echoes of this life process . . . All of the rest of ideology and their corresponding forms of consciousness thus no longer retain the semblance of independence. They have no history, no development; but men, developing their material production and their material intercourse, alter . . . their thinking and the products of their thinking. Life is not determined by consciousness, but consciousness by life. (*GI*, p. 47)

Althusser's major intervention on the topic, "Ideology and the State," reads this passage as relegating the ideological register to the status of epiphenomenon. "Ideology," Althusser writes, "is conceived as a pure illusion, a pure dream, i.e. a nothingness. All its reality is external to it . . . it is merely the pale, empty and inverted reflection of real history."[4] On his account, such a de-substantialized view of ideology entails the reification of mental content shorn from material practice and so betrays a latent idealism, the legacy of Hegelian legacy which Marx did not fully shake until the *Grundrisse*. Althusser's alternative construction tends to shift the tenor of ideology from the epistemic to the onto-pragmatic domain, from questions of false consciousness to questions of a "false position," all without losing the pejorative sense of mystification crucial to any Marxist treatment of the concept. To this end, he needs to theorize errancy or misapprehension as part of rather than a departure from the reality thus mistaken, to move from "pure illusion" to performative illusion. It is no coincidence that his first serious effort in this regard, the essay "Marxism and humanism," appeared in the year following his initial encounter with Lacan's work.

Upon first looking into Lacan's "The mirror stage as formative of the function of the I" (*E/S*, pp. 1–7), Althusser could not but have been struck by the overlap of Lacan's Imaginary register with Marx's characterization of ideology. Both serve to define consciousness not as a relatively autonomous vehicle of enlightenment but as a wholly reflexive, deeply heteronomous imposture. Of course, both represent consciousness as reflexive in the literal sense as well, since the inversion of the camera obscura image ("upside down") or the retinal image for Marx and the mirror image for Lacan each figures the alienation effected in the ideological and the Imaginary domains respectively. Both force the subject's understanding and self-awareness to take "a fictional direction" and an "alienating destination" as Lacan writes:

> . . . the total form of the body by which the subject anticipates in a mirage the maturation of his power is given to him only as *Gestalt* . . . it appears to him above all in a contrasting size (*un relief de stature*) that fixes it and in a symmetry that inverts it . . . Thus this *Gestalt* . . . by these two aspects of its appearance symbolizes the mental permanence of the *I*, at the same time as it prefigures its alienating destination. (*E/S*, p. 2)

Lacan's idea of a chimerical "identification" in the mirror also carries that performative impetus that Althusser misses in the Marxist conception of ideology. Still laboring under profound "motor uncoordination" (*E/S*, p. 4), the subject comes to be a (self-)recognizable whole through, and only through, the image of bodily form lent him in the mirror. Far from having "no history, no development," the Lacanian Imaginary is the very matrix of individual *Bildung*, where "a drama" with its own "internal thrust" takes the subject from the "insufficiency" of the "fragmented body image" through the integrated "form of its totality" to the "armour of an alienating identity"

(E/S, p. 4). The Imaginary function is thus factored into, and even constitutive of, man's living reality without being in any way coterminous with that reality or losing the connotation of illusion and error.

By the same token, the "alienating destination" of the mirror stage diverges from that of ideology in Marx, because the Imaginary preempts the very notion of a natural or proper condition of subjectivity, political or otherwise; the I is not alienated from its essence or truth but *in* its essence or truth. This vertiginous condition of being oneself *as another*, which Lacan calls *méconnaissance*, is in a sense still more estranging than classic Marxist alienation, for it implies a fundamental impossibility of self-coincidence. At the same time, it allows for a certain "agency of the ego" (E/S, p. 2), in which anticipatory misrecognition sutures the gap between the natural or biological support of the body and the social determination of the subject.

With its installation of the phantasmatic at the basis of lived experience, Lacan's mirror stage presented Althusser with an ontological role model for his revisionist theory. In his adaptation, ideology does not consist in an "imaginary construction" or "system of representations," but rather in "an imaginary, *lived* relation between men and their conditions of existence," i.e. the "real relations" of production that delimit their world. More succinctly, Althusser holds ideology to express the "overdetermined unity of the real relation and the imaginary relation between [men] and their real conditions" (FM, pp. 233–4), a formula no less descriptive of the infant's posture toward his *disjecta membra* as mediated by his imaginary assumption of a totalized body-form in the mirror.

In either case, the overdetermined unity of real and imaginary relations to the conditions of existence introduces a disarticulation into the determining conditions themselves, enabling actions to be taken, gestures to be made, and efforts produced that are not fully immanent in their circumstances or automatically dictated by their context. Althusser remarks, "It is in their overdetermination of the real by the imaginary and of the imaginary by the real that ideology is *active* in principle, that it reinforces or modifies the relation between men and their conditions of existence" (FM, p. 234).

With this logic, Althusser is able to reconceive ideology as a pragmatic rather than cognitive modality and as the ultimate locus of all social and political practice. That is to say, Lacan's model of specularity allegorized by the famous mirror stage enabled Althusser to find in ideology the source of agency as well as the site of its alienation. But of course the Imaginary has as its telos not subjectivity but self-objectification, and to the extent that ideology represents a public or collective form of Imaginary relation, it precludes any disentangling of the emergence and the alienation of agency. Althusser goes so far as to concede that the effectivity allowed by ideology can never be instrumentalized; whoever uses ideology is already ensnared by it. Indeed, ideology thus turns out to be the pragmatic modality par excellence precisely because, in this theory, men can only transform their conditions and make their own history through the detour of misrecognition. "Marxism and humanism" already embraces the substance of Lacan's Imaginary phenomenology, which is likewise not about self-knowledge but *the necessity of its failure* to the formation of the self, the ego, whose "agency" can accordingly never be exercised.

What Althusser does not fully grasp is that the Lacanian position on which he draws ultimately demands not just a revision in Marxist speculation about ideology, but a reconception of the problem of agency. By drawing the line at instrumentality rather than simple intentionality, Althusser disavows the most radical implications of his Lacanian prototype. His phrasing reflects the illusion that misrecognition is something of a compromise formation, in which, at any given synchronic moment, the possibility of purposiveness is preserved amid and even through its ideological displacements. But the Lacanian Imaginary more closely approximates another Freudian trope, the magic writing pad, in which, through a diachronic twist or loop, agency is produced as trace, as that which promises to have been already exercised. The logic of retroversion, Lacan makes clear, delimits not only the mirror specularity that is so crucial in the constitution of subjectivity but the ongoing function of the ego, and thus of the ideological subject.

Constituted "in a fictional direction" and via the "internal thrust" (*E/S*, p. 4) of imaginative self-projection, the Imaginary/Ideological self cannot have been submitted to any external forces of determination, social or otherwise, until it has been so constituted, until, that is, the "lure of spatial identification" (*E/S*, p. 4) or class identification has taken hold. In other words, it is neither determined elsewhere nor entirely alienated, but it *will have been both*. In that wrinkle of time, where future and past overlap and oust the present, is lodged what we might call the "virtual agency" of both theoretical models, their shared resistance to the totalization of sociohistorical conditions. In the temporal form as a whole, where the future outstrips the past moving backward, resides the impossibility of actualizing that virtual agency on an instrumental or even intentional basis. The assumption of mastery, whether "jubilant" (Lacan's infant, *E/S*, p. 1) or "cunning" (Althusser's ruling class, *FM*, p. 235), amounts to a betrayal of one's already captive status. In an inversion of the classic existential predicament, the Imaginary/Ideological self is not condemned to be free, but is free to be implicated, in advance.

This paradoxical ethico-political position is structurally consistent with Lacan's impasse described as the *vel* of subjectivity in *The Four Fundamental Concepts of Psychoanalysis* (*S XI*, pp. 209–15). There the subject can refuse to sacrifice its particularity, to "fade" under the weight of the symbolic order, but only at the considerable price of forfeiting subjectivity altogether in the manner of psychotic foreclosure. The homology of these developmental moments attests to what I have called the radical conservatism of Lacan's thought, radical in theorizing the constructedness of the subject *beyond* his or her positive sociohistorical determinations; conservative in delineating a symbolic machinery that perpetually converts this state of contingency into retroactive socio-historical determination.

The double bind that this logic poses for a Marxist critique of ideology should be evident: its aptness for articulating the problem of ideology is matched only by its inaptness for supplying a satisfactory dialectical solution. In Althusser, this double bind emerges at the point where ideology as the pragmatic dimension, that which enables concerted action, meets ideology as the site of constitutive misrecognition, that which severs action from conception, purpose, and strategy, thus vitiating the very agency it promised.

Althusser's silence on the implications of his practical register for revolutionary practice speaks volumes about the distance from traditional Marxism that he was taking in his intellectual affiliation with Lacan. That distance became much greater as Althusser continued his sociopolitical elaboration of the Imaginary, but did so in the context of an engagement with Lacan's Symbolic. Ironically, however, that distance brought him no closer to deploying or even understanding Lacan's own theory of subject formation during this period. To the contrary, Althusser's effort to establish the Symbolic as the ground of ideology only announces, with a megaphone, the underlying incommensurability of the Marxist and the psychoanalytic logic of causation. In fact, this undertaking brought his misapprehension of Lacan's "radical conservatism" to completion. Having underestimated the conservative tenor of the Imaginary, he proceeded to miss the radical import of the Symbolic.

The Imaginary Symbolic

Althusser has incurred criticism for isolating the Imaginary component of Lacan's complexly layered system in his rethinking of the ideological problematic.[5] But while that isolation involves an outright and disabling omission of the Real, it paradoxically comes to fruition *by way of* a solicitation of the Symbolic.

Shortly before he began borrowing from Lacan in earnest, Althusser wrote an article hailing Lacan's "return to Freud" as an occasion for his own Marxist audience to return to psychoanalysis. In the preface to "Freud and Lacan" and again in the introduction, Althusser takes care to segregate the revolutionary discovery and genuine critical object of psychoanalysis, the scene of unconscious representation, from the dominant ideological delusion of Freud, which Althusser designates as "psychologism."[6] This is an especially pregnant opening gambit, since Lacan himself, from whom Althusser undoubtedly took the term, identified psychologism with the American therapeutic philosophy of strengthening the patient's ego as a *socially adaptive* mechanism, hence with psychoanalytic conformism. Althusser explicitly reinforces this identification as a means of clearing Lacan in particular of the bourgeois stigma that psychoanalysis typically bore in Marxist eyes. He links psychologism, "in which all or a part of contemporary psychoanalysis, particularly in America, savours the advantages of surrender" (*FL*, pp. 200–1), with a similarly prudential "relapse" from core Marxist principles, "pragmatism" (*FL*, p. 201). His hedge on "all or part" has the effect of raising Lacan's exceptional status *within* "contemporary psychoanalysis" to the dignity of an exception *from* contemporary psychoanalysis, at least in its debased bourgeois profile, and to paradoxically realign him, by way of their commonly disposed enemies, with Marxism itself.

Indeed, one distinction that Althusser mounts between psychoanalysis proper, defined as an exclusively Freudo-Lacanian linkage, and psychologism, i.e. the rest of psychoanalysis, actually entails a subtler distinction between two points, each with its "socialist" as well as psychoanalytic variation. On one side is the endeavor to promote adherence to social normativity and compliance or cooperation with existing authority, whether for their own sake or for some ulterior motive; on the other is the effort to theorize the constitutive and therefore ineluctable heteronomy of men and women within the social order.

The former project is to be dissociated from Lacanianism and Marxism alike – under the headings of psychologism and pragmatism – as something they not only denounce but explain. The registers of this explanation are, alternatively, the Imaginary and the Ideological. Both psychologism and pragmatism foster the misrecognition of a unified, possessed, self-regarding consciousness, taking the imaginary function of the ego for the reality of a sovereign subject, but adopting, in the same motion, a conciliatory, if not complicitous, posture toward the dominant ideological concerns of bourgeois society. While those strategies would seem to underscore Althusser's contention that imaginary mastery is no sooner assumed than ideological captivity is sealed, they also attest to the distinctively bourgeois, hence historically relative character of the homology of imaginary and ideological *méconnaissance* (i.e. structurally necessary mis-recognition). It is exclusively the culture of liberal humanism, after all, that elevates individual *Bildung* or self-production into a broadly social injunction, thereby short-circuiting what Lacan calls "the jubilant assumption" of an integral self-image with the "armour of an alienating identity" (*E/S*, p. 2).

The latter project is identified with both Lacanianism and Marxism as what they respectively undertake, one focusing on the material conditions of socio-historical development (forces/relations of production) and the other on the material conditions of symbolic behavior (the dynamic chain of signifiers). For Althusser, the strategies or schools of thought find common ground in Lacan's conception of the Symbolic, reductively translated as the "law of culture," which nominally takes center stage from the Imaginary in this essay (*FL*, p. 209). Viewed as the repository for "codes of human assignment" (*FL*, p. 209), derived from concrete processes of material and social reproduction, the Symbolic offers an elaborate theoretical articulation of Marx's fundamental insight that "the human subject . . . is not the 'centre' of history" (*FL*, p. 218). Viewed as the theatrical machine of a desire constitutively inscribed in the texture of the unconscious (the discourse of the Other), the Symbolic gives elaborate theoretical expression to Freud's fundamental insight that the subject "has not the form of an ego, centered on 'ego,' on 'consciousness' . . . that the human subject is de-centered" (*FL*, p. 218). Whereas the Imaginary provides Althusser with a unified field theory of alienation, in which individual misrecognition and collective ideological mystification feed (into) one another, the Symbolic provides Althusser with a unified field theory of the still more radical estrangement involved in becoming human in the first place, whether *qua* sexed or fully social being.

There, once again, the itinerary of Marxism and psychoanalysis goes beyond tracing the origins and the complex lineaments of the particular species of radical heteronomy that they address. On vastly different scales and temporal rhythms, both seek to intervene in the mechanisms and counter the insupportable effects of that heteronomy. And if Althusser's concentration on the Symbolic register in "Freud and Lacan" succeeds in bolstering his case for the hermeneutical value of an alliance with "scientific" psychoanalysis, it aggravates the complications such an alliance poses for theorizing a powerful left-activist agenda, an agenda that requires a pragmatic dimension unenthralled to misrecognition. Far from establishing one, Althusser's version of the Symbolic as the "Law of Culture" grounds the Imaginary/Ideological in a domesticating, normalizing, finally quietistic matrix. That is to say, paired exclusively with the Imaginary register as it is in "Marxism and humanism," ideology serves as a necessary "relay" of resistance deflected by its more dominant or "ruling" variants. When it is later posited as embedded in the Symbolic order, ideology serves as the relay whereby the subject inexorably "finds its own place, its own anchor to its place" (*FL*, p. 213) precisely by assuming the intentionalized agency essential to any serious mobilization of resistance. Not coincidentally, the identification of the ideological with the pragmatic, so strenuously propounded in "Marxism and humanism," falls away altogether in the later piece, which makes no activist provisions whatever.

Part of the problem that Althusser encounters on this score arises from his unsophisticated understanding of the complex relationship of the Imaginary and the Symbolic in Lacan's system. Part arises from his related miscon-struction of the Symbolic itself. Both are the effects of a Marxist interpretive frame paradoxically militating against the promotion of Marxist political goals. Concerning the former problem, two basic postulates of Lacan seem pertinent: firstly, the registers (Imaginary, Symbolic, Real) are irrevocably knotted together; secondly, the Symbolic enjoys primacy, containing, in ef-fect, the other two. Taken together, these tenets yield a range of constructive possibilities. For example, the registers can be taken to align with distinct logical modalities: the Imaginary with a logic of identity, the Real with a logic of radical contingency, and the Symbolic with a logic of differential relation that not only articulates the others but potentializes them in the first place. Another option would be to see the social enactment of the Imaginary as a struggle, an *agon* of initiation and rivalry presupposing the Symbolic law in all its hierarchical articulation of differences, yet remaining irreducible to that law, capable even of having some impact upon its operations. Instead, Althusser treats the Imaginary as not simply inscribed within but subsumed by the Symbolic, a kind of wholly owned subsidiary.

> These two moments are dominated, governed and marked by a single law, the *Law of the Symbolic* . . . even the Imaginary . . . is marked and structured in its dialectic by the dialectic of the *Symbolic* order itself, i.e. by the dialectic of human order, of the human norm . . . in the form of the order of the signifier itself . . . The sexed child becomes a sexual human child by testing its phantasms against the Symbolic; and if all "goes well" finally becomes and asserts itself as what it is. (FL, p. 210–3)

Althusser merely adapts the eccentric curvature of Lacan's psychosocial to-pography to the vertical symmetries of classical Marxist thought: the Sym-bolic occupies the position of the material base, encompassing and deter-mining, while the Imaginary holds the place of the superstructure. But in the process, ideology, the public turn of the Imaginary, returns to the state that it had in the early Marx: an auxiliary, epiphenomenal, phantasmatic vapor, something to be demystified and dissolved.

From a Marxist perspective, the political implications of this reduction are all the more problematic owing to the equation of the Symbolic with "the human norm, of which the child's 'acceptance, rejection, yes or no' are merely the small change, the empirical modalities of this constitutive order" (*FL*, p. 210). In what amounts to an inversion of Lacan's political ontology, Althusser holds the "order of the signifier" to be the outward "form," the contingent vehicle, of a unitary species norm, instead of deeming contingent human norms, or normativity as such, as at once sustained by and subject to the law of the signifier. He thereby vitiates the distinctive character of Lacan's Symbolic, which is to be universal without being totalizing or totalitarian.

The key to Lacan's Symbolic, which Althusser misses, is that it does *not* constitute a law in the positive sense, i.e. a specifiable injunction or norm, however sweeping, but is a law in the transcendental sense, a constitutive negation which brings forth the very possibility of "acceptance, rejection, yes or no," of meaning and valuation: in short, all the diacritical features of social existence. The Symbolic establishes a fundamental limit which, in designating certain things taboo, paradoxically serves to canalize and elasticize desire at the same time, necessitating, but also facilitating, a battery of signifying substitutions, through which primordial affect might be channeled into the fabrication of a life-world. It is worth remembering in this regard that the primary signifier in Lacan's Symbolic, the phallus, not only denies the nascent subject the jouissance of the maternal dyad (the duet linking mother and child in a lethal embrace) but defends that subject against the dangerously claustrophobic demands of that primordial link.

> The mother is a big crocodile, and you find yourself in her mouth. You never know what may set her off suddenly, making those jaws clamp down. That is the mother's desire . . . There is a roller, made of stone . . . what we call the phallus. It is the roller which protects you, should the jaws suddenly close.[7]

In turn, the phallic substitute, the paternal metaphor, splits between the proscriptive "no" (*non*) and the authorizing name (*nom*), articulating a law whose formal obduracy (memorialized in the phrase "the rock of castration") is capable of tremendous variability in content. Through the self-same dynamic of figurative substitution, the Symbolic simultaneously admits a transference of authority from the Oedipal prohibition to more localized rules and codes defining positive law. The Symbolic also admits a transference of investment from the Oedipal taboo to new licensed objects and orientations. The Byzantine, agonistic intercrossings of these transferential vectors and intensities (as well as the blockages, incoherences, conflicts, disturbances, and ambivalences they engender) carve a network whose stability resides less in its powers of command than its powers of appropriation.

Famously represented by a signifier for another signifier, the subject of Lacan's Symbolic is not normalized thereby, as Althusser assumes. To the contrary, he is structured in errancy. His desire is not assigned a proper object or fixed path, but is mobilized in and through their irremediable loss or absence. It is precisely through this ongoing transaction that the Symbolic itself comes to cohere. Every subject redresses the absence in the Other by unconsciously referring his or her own "lack of being" to that Other as the only possible ground of fulfillment or validation. Two wrongs may not make a right, but for Lacan's sublimely recuperative machine, two voids make a plenum. It is a testament to the subtle yet significant differences between Lacanian dialectics, which traverse the curved space associated with quantum physics, and Marxist dialectics, which remain consonant with an Einsteinian, if not Newtonian framework, that Althusser manages to overestimate, on one side, the activist potential of Lacan's "practical" register, the Imaginary, while underestimating on the other, the deterministic function of Lacan's structural register, the Symbolic.

Another way of illuminating this issue is to recollect that the Symbolic is profoundly inconsistent, which also allows for its imbrication with the Real, which Althusser ignores. And this inconsistency is strictly correlative with the reality of the unconscious, the barred subject (or $). The former comprises a collective space requiring, as we have seen, the suture of subjectivity; the latter comprises a "private" reserve that is always already transindividual, the discourse of the Other. Out of this uneven and abrasive partnership comes both the production and the cooptation of political agency in Lacan, our capacity for interventions to ends not our own or that we would never "own." By contrast, Althusser envisions an utterly consistent symbolic, possessed of "absolute effectiveness" (*FL*, p. 209).

> Lacan demonstrates the effectiveness of the Order, the Law, that has been lying in wait for each infant born since before his birth. And seizes him before his first cry, assigning to him his place and role and hence his fixed destination. (*FL*, p. 211)

Lacan would say that the view of such a Symbolic characterizes the paranoid cast of mind, a hermeneutical perspective not unknown to conventional Marxism that insists upon finding everything to be densely and minutely interconnected in a closed, unbroken, and motivated whole. Under this dispensation, the Imaginary/Ideological can never be more than a reflex and a reinforcement of some integrated circuit of the unappealable "law of culture."

In an ironic twist, however, the Imaginary and, by extension, ideology can only be found determined by the Symbolic matrix insofar as the Symbolic is itself framed in the manner of the Imaginary, as an "orthopedic unity," a self-identical, unbarred Other, hence a kind of Imaginary-Symbolic. Not coincidentally, paranoia is itself a product of an arrested Imaginary phase, "a deflection of the specular *I* into the social *I*" as Lacan has it (*E/S*, p. 5). The turnabout surfaces clearly in Althusser's essay "Ideology and State,"[8] which makes explicit use of Lacanian conceits in the endeavor to synthesize the elements of his developing ideology theory. In the relevant subsection of the essay, "On Ideology," Althusser returns to his notion of an "imaginary lived relation" and explicates it via a separation of the elements. Ideology is "imaginary" in comprising an "illusory representation" of the conditions of existence (*I*, p. 162). But these imaginary distortions only have reality in being inserted into, and becoming an essential part of, material practices, the way in which subjects live their relation to the world. Because, following Lacan's specular logic, imaginary distortion proves enabling of the practices themselves, Althusser can reiterate his core innovation on Marxist ideology-critique: "There is no [material] practice except by and in ideology" (*I*, p. 170). But because material practices incorporate imaginary distortions as the vehicle of lived relations, Althusser must add a second thesis: "There is no ideology except by and for subjects" (*I*, p. 171). Our illusory "world outlooks" are always forms of *self*-misapprehension.

The latter thesis retains something of the "agency of the ego" and perhaps in order to dampen its voluntaristic thrust, Althusser proceeds to insist that "the category of the subject is only constitutive of all ideology insofar as all ideology has the function (which defines it) of constituting concrete individuals as subjects" (*I*, p. 171). On the one hand, this sentiment previews the framing of ideology as a far more *literal* approximation of the mirror-stage scenario than anything Althusser has yet attempted. Althusser's concept of interpellation describes the basic functioning of ideology: ideology works by calling my name. This new idea, introduced in this essay, envisages individuals assuming a social identity by (mis-)recognizing themselves in the image of one invoked by their social other. On the other hand, and still more importantly, the above sentiment portends a confusion of the "formative" register of the Imaginary with the register of inscribed subjectivity (the Symbolic). And that is exactly what ensues. Althusser's figure of interpellation is a policeman whose call, "Hey, you there!," fuses the role of social double with the law of the father.

In other words, the voice of authority functions as the formative agency of the Imaginary/Ideological self, rather than the "internal thrust" of the individual's self-projection. The subject is, accordingly, not just called to compliance with the normalizing designations of the "law of culture" but constituted as the (mis-)recognition of this call. Even the theoretical room for resistance, fleetingly opened in Lacan's mirror stage, is here shut in advance. Striking evidence of this foreclosure exists in the shift from the erring yet enabling "anticipation" of Lacan's Imaginary ego to the unerring yet reflexive acknowledgement of Althusser's ideological subject.

> The hailed individual will turn round . . . Why? Because he has recognized that the hail was 'really' addressed to him, and that it was *really him* who was hailed . . . verbal call or whistle, the one hailed always recognizes that it is really him who is being hailed. (*I*, p. 174)

The uncanny regularity with which the right passer-by answers the "call" is less empirical evidence than narrative emblem of the perfect efficiency of the ideological summons. Indeed, this perfection arises from the *non-empirical*, deep-structural, and transhistorical ("eternal") status of the Imaginary/Ideological. Althusser even invokes the classic example of symbolic inscription, "the unborn child . . . certain in advance that it will bear its father's name," as his means of illustrating the claim that "ideology has always already interpellated individuals as subjects" and "that individuals are always already subjects," i.e. subjects of ideology (*I*, p. 176).

Lest we mistake the operations of his Imaginary/Ideological register with the dynamics of the Symbolic order that it seems to be displacing, let me briefly contrast the way in which the summons always hits its mark in Althusser with the way in which a letter always arrives at its destination in Lacan. The summons always finds its way *directly* and seems to rely upon an assumed a priori circuit of social conditioning, in which the subject to be constituted is already present, as the preferred recipient of the call, in the individual addressed. In Lacan, the letter (in both senses) that always arrives at its destination is contingent and meaningless in itself and only possesses semiotic force in its articulation along a signifying chain exceeding the grasp of its recipient. As such, the letter is in no fashion designated for or particularly fitted to its recipient. To the contrary, it might well appear quite alien to him. But because this letter has been mediated in particular ways, by particular signifying clusters, and has acquired specific valences as a result, analysis of its figurative relationship to that exorbitant signifying network, the discourse of the Other, will always reveal a certain logic to its arrival and to the positioning of the subject that it affects. For Lacan, the letter always arrives at its destination precisely on account of the recuperative power of the signifier which, in preempting the very signified that it promises, perpetually turns arrival into destination, contingency into ratio.

Althusser's failure to grasp this logic tends to lock his own psychoanalytic thinking into an Imaginary frame. Although he rehearses the language of the Symbolic, he cannot speak to the discourse of the Other. Nowhere is this clearer than in his long concluding exemplification of the interpellative process. Combining the formative "mirror structure" of ideology with the paternal law, Althusser contrives to produce, in his words, a *"doubly specular"* structure (*I*, p. 177), a dual Imaginary, displacing the Symbolic altogether. On one side of the mirror, the ideological subject is constituted through a misrecognition confirmed, on the other side of the mirror, by a divine Father. It is easy to see how Althusser's interpellative scenario translates the elements of Lacan's Other into the elements of an imaginary other writ large. Instead of a network of signifiers that insistently decenter the subjects they position, Althusser hypothesizes a "Unique, Absolute Other Subject" – central to a phantasmatic theater of constitutive *"mirror reflections"* (*I*, p. 179). He grants the interpellated subjects an imaginary sense of secure self-identity in exchange for their willingness to "work by themselves" at their own subjection (*I*, p. 181). Thus at every stage of the ideological transaction, Althusser systematically elides the unconscious, replacing it with something akin to the old-fashioned notion of "false consciousness."

More than an individual vagary, Althusser's substitution is symptomatic of Marxism's long-standing propensity for thinking various forms of unconsciousness *without* the unconscious, a tendency which helps to explain both the persistent hope of a rapprochement with psychoanalysis and the persistent frustration of that hope. In *méconnaissance*, Althusser discovered a version of such unconsciousness with a Lacanian imprimatur to recommend it. But that also proved an all too tempting opportunity to engage the discourse of psychoanalysis without engaging the signature discovery of psychoanalysis. Althusser's promotion and adaptation of Lacanian conceptions thus tended to reproduce the failed encounter of Marxism and psychoanalysis under the guise of repairing it.

Lacan may have understood as much. The casual and perfunctory nature of his correspondence with Althusser certainly bespeaks a limited faith in the cooperative intellectual project that Althusser was proposing. What is more certain, and perhaps more surprising, is that at the end of the day, Althusser clearly understood as much. In a poignant letter to a friend, circa 1977, Althusser responds to an inquiry on "the 'relations' between ideology (or concrete ideological formations) and the unconscious" (*WP*, p. 4) by admitting that he had left this problem not just unsolved but untackled:

> I have said that there must be some relation there, but at the same time I forbade myself from inventing it – considering that it was for me a problem without solutions . . . in the final notes for Freud and Lacan, but there too, in the article on state ideological apparatuses, there is a limit that has not been crossed.　　　　　　　　　　　　　　　　　　　　　　　(*WP*, pp. 4–5)

Since Althusser had earlier declared the unconscious to be the defining object of psychoanalysis, his admission of having avoided applying it to the question of ideology is nothing less than extraordinary. Still more extraordinary is his confession of continuing, blank incomprehension of how and even whether such an application can be made.

> Thus, when you level at me "the question" "How do you see a conceptual elaboration between the unconscious and ideology?" I can only reply that I don't see it. (WP, p. 5)

Althusser goes on to say "Every question does not imply an answer" (WP, p. 5), and given the nature of the question, his reply may be translated, "Every protracted engagement – say between Marxism and psychoanalysis – does not imply a marriage."

To alter Lacan's famous motto, "There is no sexual relationship," there has been very little theoretical *relationship* between Marxism and Lacan. Just as the "masculine" and "feminine" partners in a sexual relationship are divided by differences of logical disposition so marked they can only be bridged with a mutually narcissistic imposition of each upon the other, so the logics defining either analytical formation have to date proven so importantly irreconcilable, despite their moments of affinity, that retroversion has either been reduced to contradiction (Althusser) or contradiction has been subsumed by retroversion (Žižek). Lacan's Marxism never existed, in recognition of this intractable discord; Marxism's Lacan did exist as the jubilant, but finally alienating misrecognition of a projected harmony.

NOTES

1. Slavoj Žižek, *The Sublime Object of Ideology* (London: Verso, 1989), p. 11. Hereafter cited in text as *SO*.
2. Karl Marx and Frederick Engels, *The German Ideology* (New York: International Publishers, 1981), p. 123. Hereafter cited in text as *GI*.
3. As mentioned by Elisabeth Roudinesco, *Jacques Lacan* (New York: Columbia University Press, 1997), pp. 58–60. Hereafter cited in text as *JL*. See also Louis Althusser, *Writings on Psychoanalysis* (New York: Columbia University Press, 1996). Hereafter cited in text as *WP*.
4. Louis Althusser, *For Marx* (New York: Pantheon, 1969), pp. 233–4. Hereafter cited in text as *FM*.
5. See Michele Barrett, "Althusser's Marx, Althusser's Lacan," in *The Althusserian Legacy*, eds. E. A. Kaplan and Michael Sprinker (London: Verso, 1993).
6. Louis Althusser, "Freud and Lacan," in *Lenin and Philosophy* (New York: Monthly Review, 1971), p. 201. Hereafter cited in text as *FL*.
7. Jacques Lacan, *Seminar XVII*, quoted in Bruce Fink, *The Lacanian Subject* (Princeton: Princeton University Press, 1995), pp. 56–7.
8. Louis Althusser, "Ideology and the State," in *Lenin and Philosophy*, pp. 159–60. Hereafter cited in text as *I*.

10

ALENKA ZUPANČIČ

Ethics and tragedy in Lacan

Lacan's discussion of the ethics of psychoanalysis is closely connected to his discussion of tragedy, yet one must not forget that this connection is not an immediate one. Ethics, as well as tragedy, is approached in relation to another central notion, that of desire. Whatever link there is between ethics and tragedy, it springs from this notion. One should also bear in mind that, in Lacanian theory, there is a very direct link between desire and comedy. Lacan introduces, develops, and illustrates his famous graph of desire through his reading of Freud's book on the *Witz* (*Jokes and their Relation to the Unconscious*), adding some of his own examples and bringing the discussion to its climax with a brief but poignant commentary on Aristophanes and Molière.[1] At the end of the *Ethics of Psychoanalysis*, the seminar in which the central question of the relationship between action and the desire that inhabits us is explored in its tragic dimension, Lacan reminds us again of this other, comic dimension:

> However little time I have thus far devoted to the comic here, you have been able to see that there, too, it is a question of the relationship between action and desire, and of the former's fundamental failure to catch up with the latter.
> (*SVII*, p. 313)

Indeed, the "relationship between action and desire" is what defines the field of ethics, and the exploration of tragedy as well as comedy offers a productive way to examine the different forms that this relationship can take. Although we will focus on the perspective of tragedy (the perspective that is largely identified with Lacan's discussion of ethics), the other, comical dimension should at least be mentioned as another possible entry into this topic.

Lacan's position on the ethics of psychoanalysis cannot be simply identified with his commentaries on different works of tragedy (and comedy). Hamlet is not here to illustrate some model of ethical conduct. Neither are Antigone or Sygne de Coûfontaine. They are here because they all give body to a certain impasse of desire, as well as to a certain way of dealing with this impasse. In other words, they are here because the impasse of desire is what psychoanalysis primarily deals with, brings forward, and bears witness to. They are here because this impasse is the stuff that dreams are made of – dreams that are none other than those that led Freud to the discovery of the unconscious.

The first remarkable feature that strikes the eye regarding Lacan's engagement with tragedy is the fact that everything happens within a precise and relatively short period of his teaching, between 1958 and 1961. While conducting his sixth seminar, *Desire and Its Interpretation*, he embarked on a long and elaborate commentary of Shakespeare's *Hamlet*. The following year, which is the year of *The Ethics of Psychoanalysis*, he presented his famous reading of Sophocles' *Antigone*. And the year after that, while focusing his seminar on the topic of transference, he proposed a stunning analysis of Paul Claudel's Coûfontaine trilogy (*The Hostage*, *Crusts*, and *The Humiliation of the Father*). In addition to that, there are abundant references to Oedipus (to both *Oedipus the King* and *Oedipus at Colonus*) in all of the above-mentioned *Seminars*.

It seems as if in these years Lacan wanted to explore and – one is tempted to say – to develop to its bitter end the fundamental conceptual frame that characterizes this period of his teaching, and that could be formulated in terms of an absolute antinomy between the signifying order and the realm of jouissance. Lacan situated jouissance on the side of the Thing (Freud's *das Ding*), and this schema constituted the pivotal notion of the seminar on *Ethics*. Absolutely isolated and separated from both the Symbolic and the Imaginary, *das Ding* appears as an inaccessible Real or, rather, as the Real the access to which can require the highest price. Insofar as it sets out to render this access, psychoanalysis itself constitutes a tragic experience. For Lacan, to state that "tragedy is in the forefront of our experiences as analysts" (S *VII*, p. 243), and to posit an equivalence between "the ethics of tragedy" and "that of psychoanalysis" (S *VII*, p. 258), refers precisely to the price the subject has to pay to get access to this Real. For the Real constitutes the very kernel of the subject's being, the kernel that is simultaneously created and extirpated by the advent of the signifying order. Lacan does not imply that the order of the signifier robs the subject of some previous (and full) possession of her being – this being is utterly coextensive with the symbolic order and yet it is separated from it by a gap that can be described as existential.

Oedipus: the risk of castration

The notion that articulates together the two sides of the dichotomy of the signifier and the Thing is that of desire. The structure of desire is the structure of the signifying order, of language and its inherent differentiation. Hence Lacan's insistence on the metonymical character of desire. However, what the desire ultimately aims at and what, at the same time, functions as its absolute condition, is situated on the side of the Thing. Desire incarnates the very split, or gap, between the signifying order and the Real, and one could be led to think that it is this split that accounts for the tragic nature of the experience of desire. Yet this is not exactly what Lacan has in mind. Not satisfied with simply pointing out this split at the very core of human existence, Lacan does not join in the lamentation of the tragic nature of the human condition. Rather to the contrary, he subtly reverses the very perspective that leads to such lamentations. For, according to him, the essence of tragedy does not lie in its displaying of this supposed tragic split of the human subject; instead, it lies in the fact that the tragic hero or heroine is precisely someone who (willingly or not) embarks on the path of abolishing the split in question. This is where the tragedy springs from: from what one has to do (experience or "pay") in order to gain access to the Real that the subject as such is by definition separated from. In other words, there is nothing "tragic" about the split itself that the signifier introduces into the subject. Recognizing this split is a common experience that can entail a certain amount of frustration and all kinds of neurosis, but does not in itself amount to what can be justly referred to as "tragic experience." The glorification of this split as "tragic," the positing of the pathetic *grandeur* of human existence as resulting from this wound at its core, is seen by Lacan as the ideological counterpart of every existing (political) order. Its message is simply the following: rather than pursue your desires, you should renounce them, accept the tragic impossibility that lies at their core, and join the path of the common good.

There is a very distinct political undertone to Lacan's developments in *The Ethics of Psychoanalysis* that has to do precisely with this critique of the tragic split. "There is absolutely no reason," he claims, "why we should make ourselves the guarantors of the bourgeois dream" (*S VII*, p. 303). What does this "bourgeois dream" consist of? It consists of the attempt to link individual comfort with the service of goods (private goods, family goods, domestic goods, the goods of our trade or our profession, the goods of the community, etc.). If what Lacan calls "the universal spread of the service of goods" implies "an amputation, sacrifices, indeed a kind of puritanism in the relationship to desire that has occurred historically" (*S VII*, p. 303), then the goal of analysis can not and should not be to make the subject as comfortable as possible with this "amputation." Analysis is not here to help us come to terms with the sacrifices that society inflicts upon us, nor to compensate for these sacrifices with the narcissistic satisfaction linked to our awareness of the "tragic split" that divides us and prevents us from ever being fully satisfied. Instead, it proposes a wholly different game, which reverses the perspective on the good, so that the latter is no longer seen as something that can be earned by certain sacrifices, but rather as something that we can use as a "payment" to get access to the one thing that really matters:

> We come finally to the field of the service of goods; it exists, of course, and there is no question of denying that. But turning things around, I propose the following . . . : There is no other good than that which may serve to pay the price for access to desire. (S VII, p. 321)

This reversal of the perspective on the good gets a very poignant illustration in the figure of Oedipus. Lacan focuses on the crucial period of time that passes between the moment when Oedipus is blinded and the moment when he dies (which roughly corresponds to the period covered by *Oedipus at Colonus*): a period of time that Lacan compares with what takes place at the end of analysis.

First of all, Lacan emphasizes that Oedipus has been duped precisely by his access to happiness, "both conjugal happiness and that of his job as a king, of being the guide to the happiness of the state" (S VII, p. 304), that is, the happiness related to the "service of goods." In his act of blinding himself, Lacan recognizes an act of giving up the very thing that captivated him (namely, this "happiness"). At the same time, Lacan insists on the fact that this giving up the good that captivated him doesn't prevent him from demanding everything, all the honors due to his rank. Although he has renounced the service of goods, none of the preeminence of his dignity in relation to these same goods is ever abandoned. Moreover, Oedipus continues to pursue the very desire that led him beyond the limit, namely, the desire to know. According to Lacan, "He has learned and still wants to learn something more" (S VII, p. 305). This zone that Oedipus enters by renouncing the service of goods is thus not some kind of nirvanic state where one is no longer driven by any desire or aspiration, completely detached from "worldly matters." It is not that the renunciation of goods and of power prevents or stops us from formulating any demands. On the contrary, it is precisely this renunciation that puts us in the position to make demands, as well as in the position to act in conformity with the desire that exists in us. But what exactly is this renunciation about? As said above, it is not about renouncing the "pleasures of life." Psychoanalytical experience rather shows that the true opposition is not between pursuing pleasure or happiness and renouncing them, say, in the name of some duty. Duties that we impose on ourselves and experience as "sacrifices" are, as often as not, a response to the fear of the risks involved in the case if we did not impose these duties. In other words, they are precisely the way we hang on to something that we fear most of all to lose. And it is this fear (or this "possession") that enslaves us and makes us accept all kinds of sacrifices. Lacan's point is that this possession is not some empirical good that we have and don't want to lose. It is of symbolic nature, which is precisely what makes it so hard to give up. To renounce this "good" is not so much to renounce something that we have, as it is to renounce something that we don't have but which is nevertheless holding our universe together. In other words, "psychoanalysis teaches that in the end it is easier to accept interdiction than to run the risk of castration" (S VII, p. 307). This formula is, in fact, crucial for the "ethics of psychoanalysis," which could be defined as that which liberates us by making us accept the risk of castration. In a certain sense, it puts us in the position where we have nothing to lose. However, while not false, this way of putting things can be misleading, since it suggests some kind of ultimate loss beyond which we no longer can desire or get attached to anything, which is precisely not the point. The loss in question is rather supposed to liberate the field of the desire – liberate it in the sense that the desire no longer depends upon the interdiction (of the Law) but is led to find and articulate its own law.

However, this is far from being obvious. The relation between desire and law is a complex one. One the one hand, it is too simplistic to maintain that interdictions and prohibitions suppress our desire and prevent its full realization. On the other hand, it is also not quite precise enough to say that they are constitutive of desire, that it is the very act of interdiction that constitutes the desire. The occurrence of desire is correlative with the occurrence of the signifying order, which is broader than the realm of laws and prohibitions. Desire occurs when a need is articulated in the signifier, thus becoming a demand. Desire is the something in the demand that can never be satisfied – that is, reduced back to a need. The very fact that I address my demand to the Other introduces something in this demand that eludes satisfaction; for example, a child who demands food from her parents will not be satisfied simply by the food that she receives. This is what accounts for the metonymy of desire:

> The man, a new Achilles in pursuit of another tortoise, is doomed, on account of his desire being caught in the mechanism of speech, to this infinite and never satisfied approach, linked to the very mechanism of desire which we simply call discursivity.[2]

What we are dealing with is an inherent impossibility for desire ever to be (fully) satisfied, and this configuration is at the same time the motor and the impasse of desire. The intervention of the law, far from simply "repressing" our desire, helps us deal with the impasse or impossibility involved in the mechanism of the desire as such. To put it simply: the law gives a signifying form to the impossibility involved in the very phenomenon of desire. The fundamental operation of the law is always to forbid something that is in itself impossible. The fact that the law links this impossible to some particular object should not prevent us from seeing this. By designating a certain object as forbidden, the law does two things: it isolates the impossible Thing that the desire aims at but never attains, and it provides an image of this Thing. This image (my neighbor's wife, for instance) has to be distinguished from what, on the level of the symbolic, is nothing else but the signifier of the impossible as such. The law condenses the impossible involved in desire into one exceptional "place." Via this logic of exception, it liberates the field of the possible. This is why the intervention of the law can have a liberating effect on the subject. It makes it possible for Achilles not to spend every minute of his life trying to figure out why he cannot catch up with the tortoise, or trying obstinately to do so. It can make him a productive member of the community. This is the reason why Lacan, although he refuses to put analysis into the service of producing happy members of the community, also refuses to subscribe to the discourse advocating the liberation of desire from the repression and the spoils of law. His point is that the law supplements the impossibility involved in the very nature of desire by a symbolic interdiction, and that it is thus erroneous to assume that by eliminating this interdiction, we will also eliminate the impossibility involved in the desire. What he warned against, for instance, in the turmoil of 1968, was not some chaotic state that could result from the abolition of certain laws and prohibitions. He didn't warn against human desire running crazy. On the contrary, he warned against the fact that desire, tired of dealing with its own impossibility, will give up and resign to anything rather than try to find its own law.

We have already quoted Lacan's thesis according to which "it is easier to accept interdiction than to run the risk of castration." However, as should be clear from what we just developed, this does not mean that interdiction keeps us safe from being exposed to castration (that is, from undergoing a loss of something that we have). The "fear of castration" is the fear of losing that which constitutes a signifying support for the lack involved in the experience of the desire as such. Interdiction is what provides that support; it is what gives a signifying form to the lack (or to the experience of "castration") which is already there.

Psychoanalysis, as Lacan conceived it, is not something that will restitute the good old law where it is lacking. Although many clinical problems can indeed be traced to the failure of the law to function for the subject as a stabilizing factor, the job of psychoanalysis is in no way to make sure that the subject will finally subscribe to the ideal of this or that authority. One should rather say that once things have gone so far (as to produce a neurosis, for instance), they can only go further. In principle, it is easier to go by the law than to find one's own way around desire. But all the malfunctions and dysfunctions that appear in the clinic (as well as in the psychopathology of everyday life) remind us not only that this doesn't always work, but also that it never works perfectly. Psychoanalysis is not here to repair the damage, to help the social machine to function more smoothly and to reconstruct whatever was ill-constructed. It is there to take us further along the path that our "problems" have put us on, it is there as the "guardian" of the other way, the one that consists in finding our own way around our desire. Emblematic of this "other way" is the story of Oedipus who, although unknowingly, steps out of the shelter of interdiction, is led to give up the thing that captivated him, and enters the realm where "the absolute reign of his desire is played out . . . something that is sufficiently brought out by the fact that he is shown to be unyielding right to the end, demanding everything, giving up nothing, absolutely unreconciled" (S VII, p. 310). This is what makes it possible for Lacan to insist upon the fact that the renunciation of goods and of power that is supposed to be a punishment, "is not, in fact, one" (S VII, p. 310). Consequently, tragedy, at least in the perspective of what Lacan calls the tragic dimension of analytical experience, is not necessarily all that "tragic," but can produce the kind of liberation that takes place in the case of Oedipus.

Hamlet: the desire lost

Laurence Olivier decided to accompany his film version of *Hamlet* with these words: This is a tragedy of a man who could not make up his mind. The comic ring of these words, the fact that the whole tragedy of *Hamlet* can indeed be expressed in this kind of *Witz*, should remind us of the central ambiguity at work in the impossible involved in desire, ambiguity that can take the path of comedy as well as tragedy. Shakespeare explores its tragic dimension, and Lacan follows him on this path:

> The fundamental structure of the eternal Saga, which is there since the origin of time, was modified by Shakespeare in the way that brought to light how man is not simply possessed by desire, but has to find it – find it at his cost and with greatest pain.[3]

Indeed, the story of *Hamlet* is not about giving up or not giving up on one's desire. Hamlet is a man who has lost the way of his desire, and the question "What to do?," so central to the play, points to this fact. One of the features that has always preoccupied interpreters of *Hamlet* is precisely the hero's incapacity to act, his doubts and hesitations that make him postpone the act of killing Claudius. Two readings of this incapacity that became the most famous are the romantic and the (early) psychoanalytic reading. The first one, based on Goethe's interpretation, emphasizes the antinomy of thought and action: the hero is an "intellectual," and this attitude of knowledge and reflection makes, to use Hamlet's own words, the currents of his enterprises turn awry and lose the name of action. The early analytical interpretation, based on some remarks of Freud, but developed extensively by several analysts of the "first generation," is also quite well known. In killing Hamlet's father and marrying his mother, Claudius realizes Hamlet's unconscious desire, the child's desire for his mother, the Oedipal desire to eliminate the one who seems to stand in the way of this desire. Faced with Claudius' actions, Hamlet finds himself in the position of an accomplice, and cannot strike against the usurper without simultaneously striking at himself.

Although preserving the two pivotal notions of these readings (knowledge and desire), Lacan's interpretation subverts them at the very core. As to the Oedipal reading, Lacan points out that if we accept its perspective, then Hamlet is driven by two tendencies: the one that is commended by the authority of his father and the one that corresponds to his will to defend his mother, to keep her for himself. Both these tendencies should lead him in the same direction: to kill Claudius. Moreover, had he immediately gone for his stepfather, wouldn't this be because he had found a perfect opportunity to get rid of his own guilt? Thus, everything drives Hamlet in this one direction, but still he does not act. Why? A genuine tour de force that Lacan performs in relation to this question is to point out that although desire is in fact something that Hamlet tussles with all along, this desire has to be considered at the exact place where it is situated in the play. And this kind of consideration leads Lacan to conclude that the desire at stake is far from being Hamlet's desire: it is not his desire for his mother, rather, it is *his mother's desire*.[4] It is not only in the famous climactic "closet scene" that Hamlet is literally driven mad by the question of his mother's desire: Why and how can she desire this spiteful, inadequate, unworthy object, this "king of shreds and patches"? How could she abandon so quickly the splendid object that was Hamlet's father, and go for this wretch that can give her but some fleeting satisfaction? This question of his mother's desire also plays an important part in the other question, the one that concerns the role of knowledge in *Hamlet*.

Concerning the portrait of Hamlet as that of a "modern intellectual" whose absorption in thought and meditation weakens his ability to act, Lacan insists upon a fact that already caught Freud's attention: on several occasions, Hamlet has no problem whatsoever with "acting." He kills Polonius without a twitch; he sends Rosencrantz and Guildenstern to death with no remorse. For Lacan, this clearly points to the fact that the difficulty Hamlet has with this one act lies in the nature of this particular act. Although it is true that the "rub" that makes this act so troublesome is the rub of knowledge, what is at stake is not simply Hamlet's knowledge, but his knowledge about the knowledge of his father. It often happens that most obvious things are the hardest to notice, and Lacan was the first to point out this most striking feature of *Hamlet*. What distinguishes Hamlet's drama from that of Oedipus and what, in the first place, sets off the whole drama of Hamlet, is the fact that the father knows. Father knows – what? He knows that he is dead, which does not only refer to the empirical fact that he passed away. It refers above all to the fact that he was betrayed, that he was cheated out of his symbolic function, and that, also as love object, he was immediately abandoned by the queen (and it is at this point that the question of the desire of Hamlet's mother is included in this question of his father's knowledge).

However, what is at stake is not simply the fact the Other knows, but the fact that the *subject* knows that the Other knows. Lacan points out that there is a direct correlation between what, on the side of the subject, can be expressed in terms of "the Other doesn't know," and the constitution of the unconscious: one is the reverse side of the other. To put it very simply, the presupposition that the Other doesn't know is what helps to maintain the bar that separates the unconscious from the conscious. An amusing illustration of this can be found in the joke in which a man believes himself to be a grain of seed. He is taken to the mental institution where the doctors finally convince him that he is not a grain but a man. As soon as he leaves the hospital, he comes back very scared, claiming that there is a chicken outside the door and that he is afraid that it will eat him. "Dear fellow," says his doctor, "you know very well that you are not a grain of seed but a man." "Of course *I* know that," replies the patient, "but does the chicken know it?" Here we can grasp very well the correlation between the Other who doesn't know and the unconscious.

Another interesting thing that is not unrelated to this question of the co-dependence between the "not knowing" of the Other and the unconscious, is one very peculiar feature of Hamlet, namely that fact that he feigns madness. Lacan stated,

> [Shakespeare] chose the story of a hero who is forced to feign madness in order to follow the winding paths that lead him to the completion of his act . . . [H]e is led to feign madness, and even, as Pascal says, to be mad along with everyone else. Feigning madness is thus one of the dimensions of what we might call the strategy of the modern hero.[5]

In relation to the joke that we recalled before, we could say that Hamlet is pretending to be scared of being eaten by a chicken, which is the only way he can keep the others from guessing what he knows about the knowledge of the Other, but also the only way he can himself deal with this unbearable knowledge.

In *Hamlet*, the Other knows and makes this known to the subject. What inaugurates the story of *Hamlet* is the fact that "something is lifted here – the veil that pushes down on the unconscious line. This is precisely the veil that we try to lift in analysis, not without getting, as you know, some resistance."[6] The veil in question is, of course, the veil of castration. Yet this does not mean simply that Hamlet is confronted with the fact that the Other is himself subject to castration, which is what occurs in any "normal" course of the subject's history. What is at stake with Hamlet's knowing about *his* father's knowledge is the difference between the fact that "the Other doesn't exist" (which is another way of saying that the Other is subject to castration) and the fact the Other nevertheless *functions* – that is, has a palpable symbolic role and efficacy. It is this difference that gets abolished in *Hamlet*, leading to the breakdown of the symbolic Other. This breakdown of the symbolic Other is thus related neither to the fact that the subject knows about the lack in the Other nor to the fact that the Other himself knows about it, but to the fact that the subject knows that the Other knows. It is only at this point that the knowledge in question can no longer remain unconscious. For Lacan, the unconscious is not simply about the subject not knowing this or that. A thing can remain unconscious although the subject knows perfectly well about it (as in the joke that we used as example). As far as the subject can pretend or believe that the Other doesn't know that he "doesn't exist," the (symbolic) Other can function perfectly well and constitute the support of the subject's desire. What provokes its breakdown is the fact that the subject's knowledge coincides with the knowledge of the Other.

Hamlet's famous words about the time being "out of joint" could be understood to refer precisely to this breakdown of the symbolic order. Hamlet's destiny is sealed by the fact that he is called upon "to set it right." This appeal could be considered the very opposite of what happens in analysis. By lifting the same veil that is so brutally lifted for Hamlet, analysis leads the subject to a relative autonomy vis-à-vis the Other, whereas what happens in *Hamlet* is that the hero's destiny gets enclosed in the destiny of the Other in a most definite and conclusive way. The debt that he has to pay, or settle, the debt that triggers this infernal machine, is the debt of the Other (his father). When he finally finds his desire and with it his ability to act, it is in relation to the Other (Laertes). He carries out his act during an event arranged by the Other (Claudius and Laertes); he kills Claudius with the weapon of the Other (Laertes); and he does it at the "hour of the Other" (the hour of death, when he is already mortally wounded). Lacan draws our attention to the fact that what prompts Hamlet into action and, although indirectly, to the carrying out of his act, is what takes place in the scene of Ophelia's burial. It is the image of Laertes who, in a violent expression of his grief for Ophelia, leaps into her grave. It is this representation of a passionate relationship of the subject to an object, that makes Hamlet (re)discover some of this passion and zeal. Seeing Laertes in grief, he utters some very emphatic words,

> What is he whose grief
> Bears such an emphasis, whose phrase of sorrow
> Conjures the wand'ring stars, and makes them stand
> Like wonder-wounded hearers? This is I,
> Hamlet the Dane.[7]

– and leaps into the grave himself. All of a sudden, we have this peculiar affirmation of what Hamlet is (implying also what he is here to do). He seems to have found his desire, "doubtlessly only for a brief moment, but a moment long enough for the play to end,"[8] and he has found it via what remains an imaginary identification with the Other (his once friend and now rival, Laertes). But still, even after this "metamorphosis" Hamlet does not simply go on and kill Claudius. Instead, he engages in what is supposed to be a friendly duel with Laertes. He engages in what could be called yet another metonymy, during which he gets mortally wounded by the poisonous rapier, the rapiers get accidentally switched, he finds himself in the possession of the deadly weapon, learns about the treachery, and only then, already dying, does he kill Claudius.

One could say that in *Hamlet* the problem is not that of an action failing to catch up with desire. It is rather that action has nothing to catch up with, since it is precisely desire that is lacking in *Hamlet*. The tragedy of Hamlet is the tragedy of desire that has lost its support in the unconscious (in the Other) and cannot find its own way, but can only try to hang onto what remains of the Other in the form of "empirical others" that surround the hero. Hamlet's relationship to desire never gets a resolution. His act is conclusive only on account of being, most literally, his final act. There seems to be no inherent necessity for Hamlet to accomplish his act. He does it by "catching the last train"; he accomplishes it by attaching it to something that is already being accomplished, or being drawn to a close, namely, his life.

We will now turn to two other tragedies which deal explicitly with the question of an inherent link that exists between desire and perspective of the *end*. Precisely insofar as desire is by definition inconclusive, involved in the potentially infinite metonymy of signifiers and objects, the question of the "realization of desire" (Lacan's terms) is closely connected to the question of putting an end to this possibly endless metonymy.

Antigone and Sygne: the realization of desire

Although Antigone and Sygne de Coûfontaine, the heroine of Claudel's play *The Hostage*, find themselves in very different positions and give body to two somewhat opposing ethical configurations, they nevertheless have one essential thing in common. This essential thing is the "realization of desire."

What exactly does the realization of desire mean in the context of Lacanian theory? As we have shown elsewhere,[9] it is clear that it does not mean the fulfillment of desire. It does not mean the realization of that which the subject desires. In Lacanian theory, there is no such thing as the desired object. There is the demanded object and then there is the object-cause of desire which, having no positive content, refers to what we get if we subtract the satisfaction that we find in a given object from the demand (we have) for this object. Essentially linked to this logic of subtraction which gives rise to a (possibly) endless metonymy, desire is nothing but that which introduces into the subject's universe an "incommensurable or infinite measure," as Lacan puts it. Desire is nothing but this "infinite measure," or, to borrow Kant's term, a "negative magnitude." In this perspective, to realize one's desire means to realize, to "measure" the infinite, and to give body to this negative magnitude. We said before that the realization of desire does not mean the realization of that which the subject desires; it does not mean the realization of a previously existing object of desire. The only existing object of desire is the lack that sustains its metonymy. In this perspective, the realization of desire can only mean one thing: to make an "independent," "self-standing" object out of this very lack. It means, strictly speaking, the production or "creation" of the object of desire. The object of desire, as object, is the result of this act (of realizing the desire). Producing the object of desire means making an object out of the infinite measure that is at work in desire in the form of lack or void.

In the sliding of signifiers, in the movement from one signifier to another, something is constantly eluded, or perceived as being eluded, as being under- or overshot. There is thus a lack of signifier that is present in every (signifying) representation, inducing its metonymic movement. Desire is formed as something supporting this metonymy. In this context, the "realization of desire" refers to the operation in which this void, which is only perceptible through the failure of signifiers to represent the Thing, gets its own representation. That is not to say that the Thing finally finds its signifier: there is no signifier of the Thing but there is a possibility of an object coming to represent this very lack of the signifier. And it is precisely such an object that can function as the incarnation of the Thing. (Later on in his teaching, Lacan conceived of this kind of object also in terms of a signifier: a unique signifier which represents the very lack of the signifier, the "signifier without signified.") The difference between the metonymy of desire and the realization of desire is the difference between the void present in every representation without being itself represented, and the void that gets its own representation. Lacan's topological example of an object that can represent the Thing is the example of a vase. A vase is "a hole with something around it." A vase is what gives body to the emptiness or void in its center. It makes this emptiness appear as something. A vase can be considered "as an object made to represent the existence of the emptiness at the center of the real that is called the Thing, this emptiness as represented in the representation presents itself as a *nihil*, as nothing" (*S VII*, p. 121). The "realization of desire" is to be situated precisely in the perspective of this nothing coming to be represented as something. That is to say, the lack which is involved in the endless metonymy of desire is, so to speak, isolated as such and presented in a unique representation, in a privileged and separate object, an object like no other object.

If one defines the realization of desire in terms of a creation of a unique object that incarnates the very void involved in the metonymical movement of desire, one can see better how it relates to the story of Antigone. *Antigone* is, in fact, one of the most splendid "vases" produced in the history of literature. For Antigone, one particular act comes to represent the Thing. This, of course, is not to say that the act in question *is* the Thing or that the burial of Polynices is the "realization of Antigone's desire." The Thing is nothing but the void that Antigone's actions give body to, and the realization of desire is nothing but what makes this void appear as such. In *Antigone*, the Thing is represented in this Other thing which is Polynices' burial or, more precisely, it is represented in what Antigone is subjected to because of her insistence on this Other thing. The Thing is represented in the very figure of Antigone who gives body to the emptiness or void at the core of desire.

The fact that she is to die because of her insistence has, of course, a crucial role in this particular "realization of desire." For what is the function of death in this configuration? Because of what is introduced by the advent of the symbolic order, death is not simply something that happens to us sooner or later (thus detaching us "empirically" from the symbolic order which has its own autonomous life), but can itself become a stake or a wager in the symbolic order. Whenever someone says, "I would rather die than . . . " this is precisely what happens. Cutting oneself off from the symbolic order becomes a possibility within the symbolic order, something that can be (symbolically) represented as such. It is the breakdown of the symbolic order as represented within the symbolic order. In *Antigone*, we are dealing precisely with this: the representation of the very break with the realm of the representation.

Death can enter the symbolic order as a kind of an absolute signifier, as a "negative" signifier of everything that the subject *is*. "Negative," because instead of endlessly enumerating all that can constitute a subject's being, it condenses this "all" in the form of the "loss of all." We have a perfect example of that in Antigone's famous lamentation that takes place after she is sentenced to death. In her long speech she mourns the fact that, among other things, she will never know the conjugal bed, the bond of marriage, or have children. The list of things that she will be deprived of by her early death (not only the things that she has and will lose, but also the things that she does not have but could have had, had she continued to live) does not have the function of expressing a regret. It has a very precise function of making a "whole" out of the inconclusive metonymy of her existence and of her desire. By accepting the death and speaking of it in the above-mentioned terms, Antigone puts an end to the metonymy of desire by realizing, in one go, the in(de)finite potential of this metonymy. Precisely because of its being in(de)finite, this potential can only be realized (constituted as an accomplished, "whole" entity) *as lost*, that is, cast in the negative form. Here, the realization equals representation of the subject's being that is by definition non-representable. This is what Lacan refers to when, in relation to Antigone, he speaks about the "point where the false metaphors of being [*l'étant*] can be distinguished from the position of Being [*l'être*] itself" (*S VII*, p. 248), locating this point in the circumstance that Antigone is to be buried alive in a tomb. The realization of desire thus implies the realization of the Thing, in the sense of introducing the Thing in the symbolic order at the expense of the symbolic order which is replaced, so to speak, by one privileged object that represents the very void at its center.

Yet this is not the only path that the realization of desire can take. In the year following his seminar on ethics, Lacan discussed a very different configuration while commenting on Paul Claudel's play, *The Hostage*. The heroine of this play, Sygne de Coûfontaine, is, no less than Antigone, under the ethical imperative to realize the Thing. However, the crucial difference resides in the fact that for Sygne, the path that leads to its realization in a privileged object or signifier that could represent it, is closed from the outset. More precisely even, the first thing that Sygne is asked to do in the name of the Thing, is to discard its signifier. She is asked to realize her Thing by discarding that which is already there to represent it. She is asked to realize it outside any signifying support, in the very denial (*Versagung*) of the signifier. She cannot even rely on the signifying support in a negative way, as in the case of "representing the non-representable" which is so crucial in *Antigone*.

This accounts for what is, from an aesthetic point of view, the most striking difference between Antigone and Sygne de Coûfontaine. In the case of Antigone, Lacan insists a lot on the effect of a "sublime splendor" or "sublime beauty" produced by the figure of Antigone. This effect, of course, has nothing to do with what Antigone looks like, but has everything to do with the place she occupies in the structure of the play. In the case of Sygne, on the other hand, Lacan points out that in spite of the martyrdom that she goes through and which could have produced the same effect, it is quite the opposite that happens. During the final scene of the play, Sygne is presented to us as being agitated by a nervous tic of her face. Lacan emphasizes that

> This grimace of life that suffers is no doubt more detrimental to the status of beauty than the grimace of death and of the tongue hanging out that we can evoke in relation to the figure of Antigone when Creon finds her hanged.[10]

We thus have the grimace of life as opposed to the grimace of death, and the destiny of the beautiful seems to be decided between the two. Yet, upon a closer look, one notices that the difference between the positions of the two heroines cannot be formulated simply as the difference between life and death, but rather concerns the possibility of death functioning as the absolute (albeit negative) signifier of the subject's being. What is at stake in *Antigone* is not simply the limit between life and death, but rather the limit between life in the biological sense of the word and life as a capacity of the subject to be the support of a certain truth of desire. Death is precisely the name of this limit between two lives, it is what underlines the fact that they do not coincide, and that one of the two lives can suffer and cease to exist because of the other. Death is what marks, crystallizes, and localizes this difference.

In the case of Sygne de Coûfontaine, the situation is very different.[11] In Sygne's story, death doesn't have this value of the limit. Death (which Sygne would gladly embrace were the opportunity to present itself) is not an option or at stake. One could even say that Sygne is already dead when the play begins: she continues to exist, but having lost all reason to live or, more precisely, having lost the possibility of being the support of a certain truth. Her cause in life is dead. She is waiting for death to come; she has nothing to lose. And yet, it turns out that she has nonetheless something to lose: precisely, death. What she is asked to do (in the name of the cause that is already lost but that has been her only cause), is to live in the most emphatic sense of the term: to marry, to make love, to procreate. We are really at the opposite of Antigone and her lamentation in which she recognizes that she will never marry, enjoy the conjugal bed, or have children. All that Antigone is being deprived of constitutes the martyrdom of Sygne, the crucial detail residing in the fact that she is supposed to live this "resurrection" with the one who has murdered her cause and her parents.

In the case of Antigone, the other life (life as support of the "Other thing" involved in the desire) becomes visible and is "realized" in the scene of death as the something of life that death cannot get to. It is thus visible *per negativum*, it is visible via the bedazzlement, the sublime splendor that is the very image of something that does not have an image. In the case of Sygne, this presupposition changes and the situation is reversed: she cannot die for her cause, she cannot realize it through the sacrifice of all that she has. She can only realize it by giving up what she *is* – through the rejection of the very signifier that represents her Being. The result is that in her case, the realization of desire produces something which is not a representation of the void, but rather its most material presence in the form of the heroine's flesh, which is brought into the foreground by the tic that animates it.

Lacan introduces his discussion of the representation of the Thing with the example taken from, as he puts it, "the most primitive of artistic activities," that of the potter. If, to a large extent, his commentary on *Antigone* can be related to the fundamental topology of the vase as emblematic representation of Nothing, then his commentary on *The Hostage* could be, topologically, related to another "artistic activity." What we have in mind is the work of Rachel Whiteread, which would doubtlessly have drawn Lacan's attention, had he lived to see it, if for no other reason than that hers is also a work of the potter, of "sculpting the Nothing," but in a way and with a result that are rather the opposite of that of the traditional potter. In the case of the vase, we have "nothing" with something around it. The material form of the vase gives body to the nothing at its center. This nothing is created with the creation of the vase and represented by it. This also means that the void or emptiness owes its objectivity to the something that surrounds it. Now, the question is how to make this emptiness "stand for itself"? How to render this emptiness without interposing the surface of representation? Rachel Whiteread exhibits the emptiness in the most literal meaning of the word. She takes a created object, for instance, a closet, a room, or a house, all of these belonging to those objects that give body to the emptiness in their center; one could say that what she starts with is nothing else but different representations of the Thing which, because of their incorporation in our daily life and routine, have somehow lost the power to fascinate us as such. What she then does is to fill up the empty space and then remove the something that has previously delimited and "given body" to this empty space. Her first work of this kind is "Closet" (1988), a plaster cast of the inside of a wardrobe. What was previously a void constituted in the reference to its material frame now becomes itself a solid object, standing for itself. She does the same in the case of the room. We get a big plaster cube: the void has been made solid and the walls have disappeared. Closet, room, table, chair, bed, house – all these things that we are very familiar with once again become Things. However, this time, the Thing is no longer simply "present as absent"; the very absence now becomes the most material presence (one could almost say that the Thing is now "absent as present"). And it is precisely this full presence which allows for no void or empty space that is the very body of absence; it is, so to speak, the thickest absence or void.

Whiteread's sculptures offer a very suggestive topological illustration of what the "realization of desire" means when it cannot take the path of the representation – when the void (as the real object of desire) cannot even be represented in a "negative form." In the case of Sygne de Coûfontaine, as well as in the case of Whiteread's work, the void of the Thing is realized in a material way: as twitching flesh, or as a massive block of matter. This is not to say that the tic of Sygne's face is equivalent to Whiteread's block of matter, it is rather that the tic makes us aware of the presence of her entire body as a "block of matter" that remains there after its symbolic support is taken away. In both of these cases, the Thing no longer appears as something existing beyond symbolic reality, something that can only be represented in the reality in a negative form. It has been "condescended" to reality, without simply merging with it: the Thing is now part of the reality as a "stumbling block" of reality itself. The Thing is the thing on account of which the reality never fully coincides with itself.

Let us conclude with what, here, cannot take any other form than that of a hint. This presence of the Thing as a "stumbling block" of reality already borders on what we mentioned at the beginning as the other possible approach to the question of "desire and ethics": the perspective of comedy. If comedy also deals with the relationship between action and desire, and with the former's fundamental failure to catch up with the latter, then one should stress the following difference between tragedy and comedy. Whereas in tragedy, the failure in question is essentially linked to the figure of the lack (which originates in the fact that the action always "undershoots" the Thing that desire aims at), in comedy, the failure rather materializes in the form of a surplus (resulting from the fact that the action goes too far or "overshoots" the desire). One could say that in the case of comedy, if Achilles cannot catch up with the tortoise, it is because he passes it with his first step. An example of this would be a situation (very much in line with Marx Brothers comedies) when you say to someone, "give me a break," upon which your interlocutor pulls a brake out of his pocket and gives it to you, thus, so to speak, putting an end to the possibly endless metonymy of desire.

NOTES

1. See Jacques Lacan, *Le Séminaire V. Les Formations de l'inconscient* (Paris: Seuil, 1998).
2. Lacan, *Le Séminaire V. Les Formations de l'inconscient*, p. 122.
3. Jacques Lacan, "Hamlet," *Ornicar?* 24 (1981), p. 24.
4. Jacques Lacan, "Hamlet," *Ornicar?* 25 (1982), p. 20.
5. Jacques Lacan, "Desire and the interpretation of desire in *Hamlet*," *Literature and Psychoanalysis*, ed. Shoshana Felman (Baltimore: The Johns Hopkins University Press, 1982), p. 20.
6. Lacan, "Hamlet," *Ornicar?* 25 (1982), p. 30.
7. William Shakespeare, *Hamlet*, *The Complete Works of Shakespeare*, 3rd edn., ed. David Bevington (Glenview: Scott, Foresman, 1980) 5.1.254–58.
8. Lacan, "Hamlet," *Ornicar?* 25 (1982), p. 24.
9. See Alenka Zupančič, *Ethics of the Real* (London: Verso, 2000), p. 251.
10. Jacques Lacan, *Le Séminaire VI. Le Transfert* (Paris: Seuil, 1991), p. 324.
11. For a more detailed Lacanian analysis of the play, see Slavoj Žižek, *The Indivisible Remainder* (London: Verso, 1996), pp. 115–19, and Alenka Zupančič, *Ethics of the Real*, pp. 211–59.

11

JUDITH FEHER-GUREWICH

A Lacanian approach to the logic
of perversion

Few are those who willingly confess that among their shortcomings they lack a sense of humor. Likewise, I have not yet encountered the rare specimen who would admit to being a pervert. This unfortunate state of affairs is due, among other things, to the fact that perversion, even in the Lacanian era, has always remained an outsider. Perversion is not a structure of desire that evokes sympathy or kinship. Moreover, Lacan did not describe perversion with the same plethora of clinical insights that he provided for hysteria, obsessional neurosis, and phobia. He was able to extract from Freud's cases – Dora, the Rat Man, and Little Hans – those strategies that underlie all of psychic life and that therefore no longer need to be perceived in pathological terms: it is inevitable that the human subject will "choose" a neurosis (*SE* 1, p. 220) enabling him or her to negotiate the thin line between the need to attain erotic gratification and the fear of losing the ability to want. Hence neurotic compromises are deeply ingrained in the fabric of daily life and are therefore no less respectable than any other creative productions. What psychoanalysis can offer, to those who seek its services, are merely alternative pathways that can potentially disrupt the deadly routine of the repetition compulsion.

Thus the clinical material provided by Freud offered Lacan the tools he needed to show how neurosis implicitly reveals that human beings are deeply invested in a research plan that places sexuality at its center. Probably because Freud himself did not provide a detailed clinical case of the mechanism of perversions but insisted on the radically perverse nature of infantile sexuality, Lacan's legacy on the question of perversion remains ambiguous. Lacan "enjoys" praising its modus operandi as the ultimate model of ethical life, as he does in his famous essay "Kant avec Sade."[1] By the same token, he does not explicitly detach the structure of perversion either from homosexuality or from what have been commonly described as perverse practices.

In Lacan's view, perversion is akin to desire per se. For him, as for Freud, human desire itself is perverse, insofar as it defies the laws of adaptation and survival found in the animal world. In that sense, the logic of perversion can only serve as a model of what is operative in all of us. Such a perspective, however, does not offer specific guidance on how to approach perversion clinically. Therefore I see my task as trying to extract from Lacan's corpus a theory of perversion that can do justice to the ways he approached neurosis. By this I mean a conceptualization of perversion without the pejorative definition that continues to be ubiquitous in medical and legal treatises as well as in most psychoanalytic writings.

What is perversion, then? Perversion is a way of thinking or desiring, of attempting to stay psychically alive. Like hysteria, obsessional neurosis, and phobia, perversion has a logic that organizes the psychic position of a subject in relation to others. Unlike the neurotic, however, the pervert can access psychic gratification only by becoming the agent of the other's fantasy (his target and/or partner), in order to expose the fundamental anxiety that such a fantasy camouflages. This no doubt explains why perverse desire produces horror, fear, and dismay in those who witness its mode of operation.

Perversion does not have the psychic tools to fabricate the Oedipal fantasy that can sustain the workings of desire. Instead, perverts excel in exposing the fantasy of the other and the various social lies that such fantasy necessarily enforces. This peculiar situation explains, on some level, why perversion has been perceived as a threat to the social bond. The mission of perverts, strangely, does not involve a wish to be happy. What they want at all costs is to discover a law, beyond the mask of the social order, that can bring solace to their torment. The drama of the pervert is that he or she succeeds where the neurotic fails: while the neurotic keeps desire alive by devising strategies to avoid its realization, the pervert succeeds in living out the desire of the neurotic at the cost of sacrificing himself or herself in the process. While perverts see more clearly than neurotics the architectonics of social life, they have less space to fool themselves, and without an other underfoot their capacity to foment dreams and expectations is seriously undermined.

I believe that Lacan's return to Freud has allowed the structure of perversion to emerge not as a form of sexual aberration – because, as Freud has amply demonstrated, all sexuality is aberrant[2] – but as a form of psychic functioning that can be traced back to the vicissitudes of the Oedipus complex. For Lacan, therefore, perversion is not a symptomatology like voyeurism, sadism, exhibitionism, bondage, and the like, but rather a specific mode of desiring and making sense of the world.

In order to grasp the distinction Lacan makes between the logic of perversion and the logic of neurosis, it may be helpful to think about the way one's own structure of desire has taken shape. This process may enhance one's understanding of the proximity of perversion and neurosis as one discovers that one's own mode of relating to the world may at times resemble what the pervert himself experiences. This exercise requires that we first turn to the main tenets of Lacanian theory.

It is well known that Lacan's most important contribution to psychoanalysis consists in having applied the insights of Structuralism to Freud's definition of the Oedipus complex. Yet it is impossible, in my view, to understand the dialectic at work in neurosis and perversion without describing how the Freudian psychic protagonists – id, ego, and super-ego – are rearticulated in the Lacanian model. Therefore, to make sense of Lacan's highly counterintuitive treatment of Freud's definition of the incest taboo, it is important to elucidate the Structuralist spin that Lacan applies to Freud's topological model.

Let us note first that Lacan breaks down Freud's stages of development by introducing at the outset the dimension of the Other at every crossroads of Oedipal dynamics. Like Freud, Lacan places narcissism at the heart of human sexuality. But, unlike Freud, he does not perceive narcissism as a stage that can be overcome through the introduction of the incest taboo. In a sense, the incest taboo is already present on the margins of the child's life even before she has had a chance to experience herself as having an ego identity. Because for Lacan self-love is always mediated and reverberated by the desire of the primordial others, there is no need, in his account, to make a radical distinction between the ego as the agent of the reality principle and the ego as an object narcissistically invested by the subject. The subject's vision of the world and of herself is necessarily mediated not only by the way the Other sees the child and the world, but also through messages and clues that the Other unwittingly transmits and that, for the child, form the landmarks of his or her reality. In that sense, Lacan introduces a primordial intersubjective dimension to Freud's theory of the ego. For Lacan, there is no other reality for the subject than the one that jeopardizes or reinforces his or her psychic survival.

The mirror stage

What is the ego? How do we constitute this apparatus that gives us the apparent certitude that we are who we are, and that we see what we see? Lacan traces the origin of the ego to what he calls the mirror stage. The mirror stage is a structural moment in psychic development, when the child encounters in the mother's gaze the image that will shape his or her self-perception. The mirror stage inaugurates for the child the moment of experiencing that he or she is the object of the mother's desire and love. One cannot recognize oneself as a desirable object unless the Other has signified that one is the apple of her eye, the exclusive object of her desire. This condition presupposes, of course, that the mother is a desiring being, in other words, that she wants something that she does not have. The experience of being the object of the Other's desire, moreover, implies that the subject registers that she or he could also fail to be recognized as such. Yet such a recognition depends on a mother who conveys to her child the sense that her desire goes beyond the pleasure she derives from the sight of her baby. In other words, the child must "work" to capture his or her mother's attention. Yet such a seductive strategy requires that the child has figured out to a certain extent what it is that the mother lacks. What is the nature of her desire? Where does she go to get what she wants?

As Freud noted in his last essay on femininity, the mother lacks the phallus (*SE* 22, p. 126), which means, according to Lacan, that she lacks that which could bring her fulfillment. Lacan reads Freud differently from other schools that continue to insist that Freud equates penis and phallus. For Lacan, the phallus represents for the child the signifier of the mother's desire with which the child attempts to identify. The phallus is therefore not an object but a "slot" that can be filled by any sign or signifier that conveys to the girl or the boy something related to what the mother wants.

The place of jouissance in Oedipal dynamics

If the mother's desire cannot situate her child as a separate being whom she can admire, love, and desire, the child will instead encounter the mother's jouissance. Jouissance is a legal term referring to the right to enjoy the use of a thing, as opposed to owning it. The jouissance of the Other, therefore, refers to the subject's experience of being for the Other an object of enjoyment, of use or abuse, in contrast to being the object of the Other's desire. It is only when the child comes to realize that the mother wants something the child does not have (and moreover does not understand) that the threat of her jouissance will become real and the child will be forced to change position.

It is at this juncture that the child's status as an object of desire will be jeopardized, and the sense of unity that he derived from his mother's gaze will give way to a fear of being devoured by the Other's incomprehensible demand. This fundamental anguish will force the child to find some way out of the frightening situation. If he is not the exclusive object of his mother's desire, he may risk becoming the object of the (m)Other's jouissance. The child will be led to wonder, "What does she want from me?" "What can

I do or be to satisfy her desire?" "Is there something or someone else that can answer her enigmatic demand?" In other words, the anxiety created in the child by the jouissance of the mother triggers the need to find an escape from what feels like a threat to the child's psychic existence. The solution to this frightening riddle is precisely where Lacan situates Freud's concept of castration, that is, the moment when the child is able to give a "translation" of the mother's incomprehensible demand.

If the mother indicates to her child that she desires something belonging to a realm situated beyond the gratification provided by the child, the child will be led to shift the nature of the query. Instead of wondering what it takes to be or not to be the phallus of the mother, the child will abandon the position of being the rival of the one who steals away the mother's attention (the sibling, the father, the telephone) and will come to question what it is that the Other has that he himself lacks.

At this point two different orders of reality present themselves. On the one hand, there is the discovery that the child cannot be all that can satisfy the mother; on the other hand there is the fact that, precisely because she cannot be the exclusive object of the mother's desire, she must be permanently lacking, so that her self-representation no longer matches the signifier of her mother's desire. In other words, the child (as object) experiences the difference between what the mother wants and the role she herself can play in that desire. The signal of desire (the signifier) becomes detached from the signified (the thing that the signal points to).

The birth of the unconscious

On the whole, Lacan's theory reverses our intuitive assumption about the relation between the word and the thing. The thing is not waiting for a word to represent it; rather it is the word that creates the thing. Language always precedes the world it represents. Lacan calls upon the insights of structural linguistics in order to demonstrate that the words we use have a function that transcends the need to communicate.

The term "signifier", coined by Ferdinand de Saussure, takes on a specific valence in Lacan's reading of Freud, because it provides us with a way of understanding how a specifically charged experience can leave behind a trace that is not directly related to the content of this experience as such. Thus, when Lacan says that the unconscious "is structured like a language" (S III, p. 167), this means that the unconscious is not the repository of the drives, or the storage room for "thing-representations" (SE 4, pp. 295–6). The unconscious does not have a fixed content. The moment the child encounters the signifier of his mother's desire, therefore, Imaginary, Symbolic, and Real break down into different qualitative categories. The child as a thing/object of jouissance (the Real), the child as a desired image (the Imaginary), and the child as failing to incarnate the signifier of the Other's desire (the Symbolic) are no longer fused by the pleasure principle. This disarticulation causes a shift that inaugurates primary repression and the birth of the unconscious.

Lacan transforms Freud's understanding of primary repression. What is being repressed is not the forbidden Oedipal yearning, but rather the charged signifiers that mark the psychic separation from the maternal realm. The unconscious thus evokes through a process of chain reaction the very experiences that allowed the subject to be cut off from the jouissance of the Other. The subject's unconscious, then, is born at the moment when the jouissance of the Other becomes translated into the desire of the Other. As Lacan says, "Castration means that jouissance must be refused, so that it can be reached on the inverted ladder (or inverse scale) of the Law of desire" (*E/S*, p. 324, modified). It is here that Lacan's concept of symbolic castration and Freud's super-ego part company. This transformation from jouissance to desire does not involve, as it does for Freud, a paternal injunction that forces underground the incestuous or Oedipal fantasy ("You may not marry your mommy, and your mommy may not spoil you to her heart's content"). Instead, as we shall see, castration is the operation that promotes the formation of the Oedipal fantasy.

For Lacan, therefore, the prohibition of incest, or the Name-of-the-Father, can be called a law only because the signifier detached from the child who is its signified operates as a psychic protection against the jouissance of the Other. Incest, in that sense, has a sexual connection only insofar as it refers to the "mix" between the child's erotic drives and the mother's enjoyment of her baby, that is, the mother's enjoyment of her baby as thing/signified. Lacan theorizes the prohibition of incest as the child's ability to identify with the clues, the signifiers, the signposts of the mother's desire for something that the mother's Other – the father, for example – seems to possess, something that can lead the child to a safer harbor provided by the desire and interests of this Other. We can see here how Lacan rejoins Freud's Oedipal dynamics by another route: the child is not forced to leave the mother and her jouissance; rather, he or she is led towards the paternal realm thanks to the hints suggested by the mother. The signifiers of the mother's desire save the child from her jouissance. Thus the law of the prohibition of incest is the operation through which, thanks to the desire of the mother for what lies beyond the child, the child will be propelled towards new poles of identifications in which the ego ideal will be constituted.

"Ego ideal" (*SE* 22, p. 65) is a termed coined by Freud to define certain parental traits that the child will appropriate to fortify his sense of identity. The process of identifying with these traits involves mimesis, but it also mobilizes the child's energy to be and to do things that, in turn, will bring narcissistic gratification (pitching the ball like dad, wanting to be a doctor, "being a good girl" according to parental directives, etc.). In this sense the ego ideal is the recipient both of the dynamics of the mirror stage (the source of narcissism) and also of the most elusive signifiers of the desire of the parents. This is why children are not clones of their parents; parental unconscious messages intervene in shaping the ways the child will attempt to be or to have what the Other wants.

Gender is not sexual difference

This question of what the Other wants involves the child in the crucial problematics of the enigma of sexual difference, which is the cornerstone of Freud's discovery of the unconscious. Here we must exercise caution, because when we say "sexual difference," we usually mean the difference between boy and girl. What Lacan shows, however, is that, although in the social world sexual difference seems to refer to anatomical differences between male and female, this is not what is meant in psychoanalysis. While it is true that, with the help of social discourse, the ego will eventually define sexual difference as something concrete, at the level of the unconscious sexual difference is not primarily related to biological difference but to something else.

The discrepancy between what the child is (as real) and what he represents (as imaginary) or fails to represent (the signifier of the desire of the other) opens up for him or her the possibility of discovering a new order, a new realm of investigation. The psychic energy awakened in the child through the signifiers of the mother's desire produces the enigma of sexual difference. By following the arrows of the mother's desire toward the signs usually provided by the paternal realm (i.e. the ego ideal), the child will be able to situate herself or himself as a girl or a boy in the social world. In this way the ego ideal contains, and to a certain extent resolves, the competition dictated by the dynamics of the mirror stage. The child is now given a path that will enable him or her to set a limit to the mother's jouissance and, by the same token, to push away the burning and unresolved question of sexual difference. To put it yet another way, the process of identification with the masculine and feminine traits of the parent, which seems to evoke qualities in tune with the desire of the mother, will provide the child with the ready-made answers that will define for her or him a place in the social fabric. Gender and its cultural expectations, obligations, and rituals are therefore one of the outcomes of Oedipal dynamics.

The division of the subject

But this solution does not take care of business all around, because the real of sexual difference is not at all addressed by the social ideals involved in the dissolution of the Oedipus complex. In that sense, as Lacan points out, the Oedipus complex is a ploy, a welcome distraction from the plodding work of research into a mystery that continues to haunt the child. It is not because the child is now identified with traits of her parents or grandparents that she can make substantial progress in figuring out this ineffable bond between what she feels from within (autoerotic yearnings) and that part of the jouissance of the Other that cannot be entirely translated through the signifiers of the desire of the Other. The erotic gratification that the child experiences in her body, and that she links to her experience of being the object of desire of the mother, cannot be separated from the fact that she is to a certain extent at the service of her mother's enjoyment ("Is she doing this for her benefit or for mine?"), which is an experience that is not devoid of anxiety.

In that sense, fending off the threat of the jouissance of the Other that is at work both at the level of the drives and at the level of the Other is precisely what produces the division in the subject between the unconscious and the ego. Therefore the formation of gender merely displaces the enigma of sexual difference; it does not solve it.

Thus these enigmatic signifiers of the Other's desire, which evoke the real of sexual difference, do not vanish out of existence. Precisely because they retain something of the experience of separation from the mother's jouissance and are charged with a feeling of exclusion from this mysterious order of reality in which the father is situated (Freud's primal scene), they contradict the order of fixed meanings that the process of identification provides. This explains why the ego "chooses" to ignore the explosive question of the real of sexual difference. Yet behind the ego's back, at the level of the unconscious, those very signifiers of the desire of the Other, calling up those moments of cuts from the jouissance of the other, continue to circulate. They attract into their web traces, words, smells, tastes, homophonic connections, metaphors, metonymies: anything related to similar ambiguous experiences evoking this strange mix of erotic pleasure and painful rejection.

Because these signifiers connote separation rather than fusion, our psychic economy at work at the level of consciousness – dependent on the rewards of the mirror stage, in which we were the exclusive object of the Other's desire – will repress them and concentrate instead on constructing a narrative that wards off the enigmatic nature of sexual difference. There is a solution to the enigma of love and desire, as fairy tales amply demonstrate: "One day my prince will come." Of course, such a narrative must to a certain extent conform to the rules set forth by the social contract. Hence for Lacan, as it is implicitly for Freud, the birth of the subject's ego in the realm of symbols, of language, of social signification is concomitant with the birth of unconscious desire.

The Oedipal fantasy revisited

It is here that we see how Lacan flips around Freud's Oedipal fantasy. At the level of the repressed, the signifiers of the desire of the Other, unfettered by the limitations of negation, gender, and death (this being Freud's characterization of the grammar of the unconscious) will connect in order to form a more potent answer to the enigma. In that sense, the fantasy of incest is not the cause of primary repression. On the contrary, this fantasy is produced after the formation of the unconscious. The signifiers of the desire of the Other that constitute the chain reaction at work in the unconscious represent the desire of the Other for something that remains beyond reach. Ultimately it is with the help of these signifiers that the child will fabricate a fantasy that appears to resolve the enigma of sexual difference. Yet because these signifiers condense the paradoxical experience of being saved through a separation that entails a mixture of pleasure and anxiety, they retain the "knowledge" that jouissance works against psychic survival.

It is no surprise, therefore, that the subject will attempt to maintain a distance between unconscious desire and the fantasy it has created. Both at the level of the ego and at the level of the unconscious, what Freud has called the super-ego comes to the rescue, punishing any attempt to transgress the barrier of incest. We can now better understand what Freud meant by his theory of infantile sexuality, according to which the boy fears castration and the girl envies the boy's penis.[3] Such a theory is merely a fantasy produced after the fact of castration.

From fantasy to neurosis

Such a theory/fantasy is at the heart of all neurotic constructions, from phobia to hysteria to obsessional neurosis. It is a montage based on the necessary psychic limitation of the individual, who is not equipped to accept, in the process of his or her development, that there is ultimately no answer to the riddle. The reason why human desire has been given a chance to operate is precisely because a slot must remain open in the system. Yet because the psychic economy perceives this open slot to be that which can threaten its search for satisfaction, which from the onset of life is bound up with the Other, the subject will be led to plug this lack with a fantasy that attempts to make sense of nonsense.

Freud's theory of infantile sexuality is indeed based on his patients' reconstructions of how they explain the difference between boys and girls. Yet such a theory is not a closed system. If boys imagine that the little girl must have lost her penis along the way, they will still wonder what crime she committed to endure such a fate, and they will fear that the same punishment will be inflicted upon them. Inversely, the little girl, appalled by such injustice, will not cease trying to figure out what it takes to obtain such a precious object. Thus the enigma persists, despite the false solutions that the ego continually attempts to provide.

The goal of psychoanalysis

What Lacan offers psychoanalysis, therefore, is an understanding of how the subject has been misled into believing that the access to his fantasy is bound up with an all-powerful Other who will punish any form of transgression. This is why the subject will devise the most elaborate neurotic scenarios to lure this Other, to defend against it, or even to claim responsibility and guilt so that the fantasy can remain intact. The process of psychoanalysis consists in coming to realize that the fantasy that plugs the lack in the Other is only an artifact meant to produce a wrong answer to a question that must remain open-ended.

The structure of perversion

We are now equipped to turn to perversion. At which moment of the Oedipal dialectic does the perverse structure come about?

While the neurotic invests all his psychic energy in creating barriers to protect his Oedipal fantasy and prevent its realization, the pervert cannot discover in the desire of the other the arguments that can justify the elaboration of such a fantasy. The lack that he will undoubtedly encounter in the mother, and that will enable him to constitute himself as her phallus, cannot in turn be reliably translated into a desire directed towards the paternal pole. The child is then stopped in his tracks. While he is confronted with the enigma of sexual difference formulated in the question "What does she want?" the child remains trapped between the mother's desire for the phallus that the child represents and her jouissance that she derives from that imaginary object. The possibility of inventing a fantasmatic solution that would bring the child over to the other side of symbolic castration is frozen, because the mother's signifiers of desire fall short in giving the child a sense that the enigma of sexual difference can find such a fantasmatic solution.

While the future neurotic is given a chance both to acknowledge the lack in the Other and to find a strategy that can cover over that lack through a division between the gendered ego and the pursuit of an unconscious fantasy, the pervert is confronted with a different problematic. Whereas her psychic development leads her to the point where the lack in the Other forces an encounter with jouissance, both at the level of the drive and at the level of the jouissance of the Other, the signifiers – the clues that permit the translation from jouissance to desire – are not available. The safe harbor of identifications through which she could find a gendered position in society is jeopardized, because the mother's desire is not directed toward the paternal pole and its cultural attributes. The pervert is forced to discover other alternatives to fend off the threat of the jouissance of the Other. What the pervert must deal with is the fact that the lack in the Other cannot find signifiers to symbolize its meaning, even if these symbols are purely imaginary.

The "real" lack in the mother

The mother's lack, in other words, is real. It truly stands for a force that destabilizes the already fragile anchoring point of her subjectivity. And so the pervert does not have a choice: he must disavow the mother's castration. But let us be clear. The pervert knows very well that there is a discrepancy between the phallus and himself, though he does not have the wherewithal to symbolize the discrepancy. Yet it is through the unveiling of this discrepancy that the question of the real of sexual difference is opened up. Perverts, however, do not have at their disposal the hints that will allow them to "accept" that symbolic castration is the condition for exploring the meanderings of the desire of the Other. They have no choice other than to devote their psychic energy either to making sure that the mother remains phallic, with the child identified as her object of desire, or to figuring out a solution to the "real" lack in the mother. In this process, of course, their yearning to make sense of the erotic enjoyment that surges from their drives forces them to bear the disastrous realization that the mother's "real" concerns them to the extent that they may or may not be the object of her desire.

Thus perverts' desire does not have the opportunity to be organized around finding a fantasmatic solution to the real of sexual difference. The classical scenario of Oedipal dynamics, with its share of lies, make-believe, and sexual theories, is not accessible to them. This is why they will search desperately to access the symbolic castration that could bring solace to their misery. Their only recourse will be to defy whatever law presents itself to them, transgressing this law in the hope of finally discovering an order of reality stronger and more stable than the lies and deceptions that organized the psychic reality of their childhood. Perverts will therefore need to enact a scenario that will enable them to expose such deceptions, in order to impose a law thanks to which the Other can remain all-powerful. However, because this law cannot be dictated by the signifiers of the desire of the Other, perverts are forced to create a law of their own making, a law that appears to them to represent an order superior to the one accepted by the common run of mortals.

The survival strategies of perversion

Yet in order to maintain the illusion that such a law exists, perverts are not afraid to offer themselves up to the Other's jouissance. In other words, they choose to expose the very place where the neurotic struggles with accepting the loss that symbolic castration entails. The pervert feeds on the anxiety of the neurotic in order to derive libidinal gratification.

One of my very first patients, whose perverse structure became readily apparent in the treatment, soon became suspicious of my status as an analyst. I was at the time trying to find my bearings as a research candidate in an American psychoanalytic institute, while simultaneously thinking of getting extra training from a Lacanian school. I had of course no idea of the signals that I was sending off, clearly a mixture of anxiety, arrogance, and hesitation, unaware as I was then that such a shift of theoretical allegiance was affecting the way I was listening to her. Shortly after I started seeing this patient, she sent me a letter describing in detail a murder she was planning to commit that same day. She completed the blow by recommending that I seek supervision for her case. I was trapped and terrified: which law should I submit to, the police, the psychoanalytic institute, or the law of my desire? What was my responsibility in this acting out? Clearly my patient's unconscious intent was to challenge my legitimacy as an analyst, and she had succeeded by exposing in me the place where I had refused to surrender to the law of castration.

Thus perverts strive to get to the point where the enigma can be formulated, yet they do not have the clues, the signifiers, with which to produce a theory/fantasy that could make sense of it. They are therefore forced to repeat over and over again a scenario that protects them against the terror of the jouissance of the other that is equated with the "real" reality of the mother's lack. Yet they experience this lack not as being related to the desire of the Other (e.g. desire for the father), but as a degraded state that must be refused at all costs by maintaining the conditions through which the Other remains phallic. For the pervert, the lack in the Other is experienced as something so disgusting that it cannot even begin to be formulated through language. In other words, this lack can under no circumstances be compared to the symbolic open slot that can be unveiled at the end of analysis, once the Oedipal fantasy has been reduced to some obsolete traces of childhood experiences. The lack is literally related to the impossibility of giving to feminine desire a status other than a phallic one.

Because of these psychic hurdles, the problems posed for the pervert in the formation of identity are not the same as those faced by the neurotic. Indeed, this identity is not organized by the principle according to which the neurotic is divided between the delusions of gender formations and the unconscious pursuit of the real of sexual difference. Despite appearances, the pervert's gender is not so stable and so defended as that of the neurotic; she or he is not so invested in defending a place as a girl or a boy in the social fabric. In this case, gender is a conscious construction or montage that is not directly meant to obliterate the slippery enigma of sexual difference. Such an enigma is not a question for the pervert. What preoccupies the pervert is the need to satisfy the erotic drive and at the same time to find a strategy that can obliterate the "real" lack in the Other.

Cultural representations of perverse strategies

We can easily find around us examples of what constitutes the perverse logic in cultural productions. The icon of the drag queen shows how gender is a social object that can be constructed or deconstructed at will. In the academic world, queer theory borrows from the logic of perversion the discursive act that exposes, in the other, precisely the ways in which gender does not correspond to the destiny of anatomy. Queer theory, in that sense, cannot function without a "victim" and for that reason refutes identity politics, gay solidarity, and a false sense of complicity among marginals. The essentialist bent of feminist theory is another target for queer theory, because, far from helping the cause of women, it instead obscures the fluidity of gender and its subversive potential.

Queer theory equally enjoys exposing the so-called neutrality of psychoanalysis as a sheer cover for its latent heteronormative intent. Yet if the effects of queer theory are highly instructive for its victims (if the latter only bothered to recognize its profound acumen, as some feminists and psychoanalysts have done), queer theory itself cannot function without the jouissance of a protagonist. This leaves little room for the elaboration of ideas, unless such ideas are directly part of the project of debunking neurotic compromises, whether these be theoretical, cultural, or personal.

An example of the perverse strategy at work

For the pervert, there is no comfort in the success of his operation. The fun is in the process, not in the result. A neurotic can derive a sustained pleasure in calling upon a fantasy to keep him company; a pervert does not have that luxury. He must work all the time on behalf of his drives, with a limited amount of outlets. One of the most powerful examples of this very process can be found in many passages of Nabokov. Nabokov, in my view, represents the best example of the art of perversion in action.

Let us consider a famous passage from *Lolita*. Humbert has unwittingly precipitated the death of his wife, Charlotte, after she discovered his diary, in which he calls her "the Haze woman, the big bitch, the old cat, the obnoxious mamma."[4] Charlotte runs out of the house and is killed by a car. Humbert's monologue triggers in the reader an unacceptable feeling of marvel:

> Had I not been such a fool – or such an intuitive genius – to preserve that journal, fluids produced by vindictive anger and hot shame would have not blinded Charlotte in her dash to the mailbox. But even had they blinded her, still nothing might have happened, had not precise fate, that synchronizing phantom, mixed within its alembic the car and the dog and the sun and the shade and the wet and the weak and the strong and the stone. Adieu Marlene! . . . And I wept. Ladies and gentlemen of the jury – I wept.[5]

So here we are, unable to get furious at Humbert, tempted to agree that Charlotte is "a cow," yet knowing only too well that Lo has just lost her mother and that she will now, with no escape in sight, be the prey of Humbert's lust. And yet we marvel, caught in our own jouissance, exposed at the very place where we – cultivated, moral, highly socialized readers – we almost weep because fate has been so aesthetically kind to Humbert. And if by chance we choose to be horrified, how come we keep on reading? Can we really convince ourselves that literature exonerates us from our own pedophilic voyeuristic tendencies? But what about Humbert himself? Once he has overcome this hurdle, can he enjoy himself for more than a few moments through his tears of bliss? No; the next page tells us as much: "One might suppose that with all blocks removed and a prospect of delirious and unlimited delights before me, I would have mentally sunk back, heaving a sigh of delicious relief. *Eh bien pas du tout*!"[6] Poor Humbert is back at the drawing board. The fantasy is not in the mind but in the making. More anguish, more plotting, more scenarios . . .

When perversion flirts with sublimation

It is very difficult to imagine the order of perfect bliss that the pervert seeks beyond his contempt for social life, social lies, cultural comforts, and agreeable received notions. In his *Lectures on Literature*, Nabokov remains our neighbor because we can follow him almost to the end. And yet there is something in his approach and his beliefs that gives us a sense of the strange world of perverse logic.

We could almost suggest that Nabokov gets as close as possible to giving perversion a quasi-sublimatory quality. His talent lies in our impression that he has attained a certain level of contentment because he has found, in the world of nature, the very law that can transgress social conventions. For him, nature almost replaces the enigma of the real of sexual difference.

"Literature is invention. Fiction is fiction. To call a story a true story is an insult to both art and truth."[7] Nabokov claims to find through fiction an alternative to truth: art informed by neurotic desire is never sure of anything. "Every great writer is a great deceiver, but so is that arch-cheat Nature" (p. 5). Here Nabokov finds a pole of identification that defeats the paternal metaphor and its unbearable division: Nature is truly the phallic mother who has elected Vladimir as an exclusive member of her constituency. Nature always deceives, and so does the phallic mother; isn't the pervert aware that she also lacks? "From the simple deception of propagation to the prodigiously sophisticated illusion of protective colors in butterflies or birds, there is in Nature [written with an upper-case N, of course] a marvelous system of spells and wiles. The writer of fiction only follows Nature's lead" (p. 5).

He can, this fortunate individual, believe in the wiles and spells of the phallic mother without risk of being swallowed by a wave or falling into a ravine. But Nabokov pushes his logic further. He finds in nature – that is, in the magic of literature – the space that permits him to elude the mystery of sex.

There are three points of view from which a writer can be considered: he may be considered as a storyteller, as a teacher, and as an enchanter . . . To the story teller we turn for entertainment, for mental excitement of the simplest kind, for emotional participation, for the pleasure of traveling in some remote region in space and time. We may go to the teacher not only for moral education but also for direct knowledge, for simple facts. Alas I have known people whose purpose in reading the French and Russian novelists was to learn something about life in gay Paree or in sad Russia . . . Finally and above all, a great writer is always a great enchanter and it is here that we come to the really exciting part when we try to grasp the individual magic of his genius.   (pp. 5–6)

This may be related to my own moronic French patriarchal education, but I confess that Nabokov has thrown a dart in my jouissance! I can only feel ashamed for having loved the tale of *The Three Musketeers*, for having been "morally" brainwashed by Sartre, for trying to learn about sex with *Madame Bovary* or, even worse, with Maupassant. With Mr. Nabokov as my teacher, I would not have fared very well, but his "perverse" intent may have saved me many years of psychoanalysis. "It seems to me," Nabokov writes, "that a good formula to test the quality of a novel is, in the long run, a merging of the precision of poetry and the intuition of science" (p. 6). This is a beautiful perverse twist that tells a truth that we often resist.

"In order to bask in that magic a wise reader reads the book of genius not with his heart, not so much with his brain, but with his spine. It is there that occurs the telltale tingle, even though we must keep a little aloof, a little detached, when reading" (p. 6). This is the place, of course, where the neurotic may choose passionate curiosity over aloofness and catch in his net not butterflies but rather those very sexually charged signifiers that in turn would lead him where Nabokov refuses to venture. He continues: "Then with a pleasure which is both sensual" – the purity of a drive detached from the horror of castration – "and intellectual" – unadulterated for him by the pressure of the enigma of the desire of the Other – "we shall watch the artist build his castle of cards and watch the castle of cards become a castle of beautiful steel and glass" (p. 6).

Here we have it: an order that is both nonenigmatic and solid, an order that has transcended the pathetic reality of history and of human beings' neurotic, debased aspirations. There is, then, such a thing as a perfect perverse montage. But let us not be lured by perfection, because once the page is written the work starts all over, with no respite and, worse, with no reliable starting point.

My essay is not an apology for perversion. It is simply an attempt to demonstrate that, thanks to both Freud and Lacan, we have been given the tools not only to demystify the distinction between the normal and the pathological, but also to understand how the mystery of sex is at the heart of human intelligence. The avenues leading to the forever unknown land of sexuality are obstructed by unexpected hurdles. Even if they cannot be overcome, the struggle to get over them requires that one develop those qualities of determination and creativity that are writ large in analytical – and indeed human – history.

NOTES

1. Jacques Lacan, "Kant avec Sade," trans. James B. Swenson Jr., *October* 51 (Winter 1989), pp. 55–75.
2. "[W]e were driven to the conclusion that a disposition to perversions is an original and universal disposition of the human sexual instinct" (*SE VII*, p. 231).
3. *SE IX*, pp. 207–26.
4. Vladimir Nabokov, *Lolita* (New York: Vintage, 1991), p. 95.
5. Nabokov, *Lolita*, p. 103.
6. *Ibid.*, p. 105.
7. Vladimir Nabokov, *Lectures on Literature* (San Diego: Harvest, 1982), p. 5. Further references will be made parenthetically in the text.

12

DIANA RABINOVICH

What is a Lacanian clinic?

Is there a Lacanian clinic? Undoubtedly. It is based on fidelity to the Freudian psychoanalytic method, a fidelity that, paradoxically, demands innovation. If Freudian psychoanalysis is a method of research and treatment of the psyche, it continues to be so in Lacan, although transformed. The psychoanalytic clinic employs the "talking cure," and Lacan, like no one else, revolutionized the relationship between language and psychoanalysis. Free association is still the thread running through psychoanalytic practice, enriched thanks to a subverted linguistics. Its rationality is formalized and determined by the rule of free association, a process in which chance is rigorously harnessed. This program results in a freedom from any a priori determinism, whether biological or sociological, which would undermine the very exercise of psychoanalysis. The psyche to be cured is regarded as a subject-effect caused by the interplay of signifiers in the unconscious, a process that dissolves its supposed ego-like solidity, and, in a word, de-substantializes it. Therefore, the Lacanian clinic requires a complex conceptual battery, which may be discouraging for those who expect comfortable technical recipes. If there is one thing the apprentice psychoanalyst will not find, it is a recipe. Not only because a recipe would not be appropriate to the specificity of each unconscious, but because the unconscious and the subject it generates are deeply marked by the historicity which affects the exercise of psychoanalysis in each period, and which retroactively affects the unconscious itself.

Lacan has been called a Structuralist, and this is of course partly true, but for him any structure – with a lack or hole in its center – is marked by the vicissitudes of history, precisely through the symbolic order it organizes. There is no better example than how childish babble, which Lacan termed *lalangue*, bears on the constitution of the subject on the one hand, and how, on the other hand, the products of science and technology affect subjectivity. Over time, the Freudian method has reached theoretical depths which give it new brilliance and increased efficacy. The parameters allowing for this conceptual and practical extension are the three orders of the Imaginary, the Symbolic, and the Real.

Lacan rethinks transference, and he does it through an unprecedented exploration of the triad guiding his work: love, desire, and jouissance. He starts with the redefinition of the psychoanalyst's role as one who occupies the symbolic locus of the listener, and whose "discretional" power consists in deciding the meaning of the subject's message. He can, however, only interpret this meaning as it is produced by specific signifiers provided by the analysand's free association. This privileged listener is one who is supposed to have some knowledge about the specific unconscious at stake; that is, as the "subject-supposed-to-know," he or she will form the structural basis of transference. But this transference is not merely the reproduction of what has already happened; at its center is a factor ignored by Freud but already described by Melanie Klein: the partial object, the latent referent that is revealed when the analysand's construction of the subject-supposed-to-know collapses. I will focus on one of the least developed aspects of the Lacanian clinic – its articulation of the neuroses, a theoretical endeavor that emphasized their logical dimension. In particular, I will examine the concept of the *objet a* (which, according to Lacan himself, was his only contribution to psychoanalysis), and the development of the formulae of sexuation. These concepts open a new dimension in our thinking about sexuality (particularly female sexuality), the position of the psychoanalyst, and the relationship between language and the unconscious.

The nucleus structuring the Lacanian clinic is the non-existence of the sexual relationship. This proposition can be rephrased in three different ways: there is no knowledge of sexuality in the unconscious; there is an unconscious because there is no complementarity in the sexes; and there is no sexual "act." The lack, a failure proper to the structure in Lacan, consists in the absence of sexual relationship. In the face of such a lack, several supplements are produced so as to suture it. At the center of the unconscious, there is a hole, the gap of the sexual rapport, a hole which is the Lacanian name for the castration complex. There are two forms of logical non-existence, i.e. of lack, which are central to praxis, insofar as they are the corollary of the non-existent sexual relationship: the non-existence of truth as a whole and the non-existence of jouissance as a whole.

The sexual law arises where sexual instinct is lacking. This law, this interdiction, is coherent with unconscious desire, and even implies the identity of desire and law. For the speaking being, it institutes the dimension of truth in a fictional structure. Thus, psychoanalysis "socially has a consistency that is different from that of other discourses. It is a bond of two. That is why it replaces and substitutes the lack of sexual relationship."[1] This lack establishes that real point by providing an "impossible" entirely specific to psychoanalysis. An opposition between truth and the Real runs through the Lacanian clinic in a dialectic which has neither been synthesized nor surpassed. The Real is that which always returns, and it is indissociable from the logical modality of the impossible, a logic that is incompatible with representation and a correlate of the not-all, that is, of an ineluctably open set. Truth in psychoanalysis is contingent and particular, a conception that was already expressed in Stoic theories of logic.

As to the clinic, the moments when Lacan stresses the relationship between what is true and the analytic interpretation are when the subject's historicization achieves primacy in the analytic work. When he gives priority to the real in its relationship with the psychoanalytic task, he stresses logic and structure. If interpretation is renewed by resorting to equivocation within language, this is also done, even scandalously, by modifying the orthodox length of sessions through scansion. We should remember that Freud fixed the length of a session at forty-five minutes in terms of the attention span that worked best for him, never in relationship to the temporality of the unconscious. Brief sessions became the center of a scandal, and because of the scandal, people forgot that sessions must be of variable length in response to how the analysand's work unfolds. The duration varies according to the opening and closing of the unconscious, which uses standard time to favor resistance so as to counteract the closure which results from fixed time sessions.

Chronological time and the temporality of the unconscious are different. Doubtlessly this change increases the psychoanalyst's responsibility, his "discretional power," but it also disrupts routine action; it awakens him or her from comfortable naps. Although Lacan pointed out that the analysand is perfectly capable of handling a 45-minute session, nothing changes in the ultra-short session. Cutting the session short emphasizes the simultaneity of several lines in the signifiers of the analysand's free association. Whether or not the cut is timely can only be known afterwards, *après-coup*, because the effect of an interpretation can only be read in its consequences. This involves a risk, which should be as calculated as possible, although this calculation is no guarantee against erring. Psychoanalysis is an atheistic practice, and the analytic act lacks an Other to guarantee it. No God, and no proper name can act as God for psychoanalysts; not even Lacan's name guarantees the efficacy and correctness of our work.

The same can be said of the calculated vacillation of analytic neutrality, in which the psychoanalyst intervenes by intentionally stepping back from his neutrality, levying sanctions or granting approval based on signifiers and the desire of the historical Others of the analysand, not as a function of her or his personal feelings. This vacillation has always been practiced, even though never publicly admitted, and it relies on the use of counter-transference. Thus the calculated vacillation entails the psychoanalyst's desire, a concept which corrects distortions of counter-transference, appropriately situating it as a dual imaginary reaction, which the psychoanalyst should approach as one plays the role of the dummy at a game of bridge – that is, by no longer participating in the specular game.

These kinds of interventions occur in the framework of a repetition that is not understood as a mere reproduction of the past, a concept which led to an interpretation of all free association relating to the psychoanalyst, in the "here, now, and with me" of transference, to the point of boredom. Calculated vacillation of neutrality is not a "technical" norm. It is employed because the psychoanalyst should preserve for the analysand the imaginary dimension of non-mastery, imperfection, ignorance (hopefully *docta*) facing each new case.

Transference love is instituted from the beginning since it is based on the structural formation of the subject-supposed-to-know, which produces a juncture between an undivided subject and unconscious knowledge. This construction makes possible the elision of the subject's division, a division which must never be lost sight of in psychoanalysis. When the psychoanalyst assumes that structural position, he must never forget that he too is a divided subject. When the analysand agrees to submit to the free association rule, she removes all supposition of knowledge from her sayings, accepting that she does not know what she says, although she does not know that she knows. The subject-effect produced by free association – the divided subject – comes into being insofar as it abandons its ego knowledge.

For Lacan, the psychoanalyst should play the role of subject-supposed-to-know but be situated in a skeptical position, rejecting all knowledge except for that gathered from the analysand's sayings. This is a skeptical version of Freud's rule of a floating attention according to which the psychoanalyst listens isotonically (assigning the same value to everything that is said) and does not offer any agreement. The psychoanalyst should even "pretend" to forget that his act (agreeing to listen to the analysand's words and accepting the cloak of the subject-supposed-to-know) causes the psychoanalytic process. This strategy leads to the position of the psychoanalyst as object, which subtends his or her position as a subject-supposed-to-know who accepts being the cause of this process.

We must now be more precise as to the function of the object *a*, a function which underpins the role of subject-supposed-to-know and is also the latent referent of transference. The *objet a* is the object which causes desire; it is "behind" desire in so far as it provokes it and should not be confused with the object that functions as target for the desire.

The first lack to which Lacan untiringly sends us is the lack of a subject. There is no given natural subject. Lacan criticizes all and every naturalistic concept of the subject. This lack sets in at the very moment when the human organism is captured by language, by the symbolic which deprives it of any possible subjective unity. But in the structure, that subject, which is not, has a locus as an object relative to the Other, whether relative to its desire or its jouissance. In other words, we are first an object. As an object, we can be a cause of desire for the Other or a condenser of jouissance, the point of recovery of jouissance for the Other. But for the human infant to find its place, whether as cause or as *plus-de-jouir*, a loss has to occur first. That loss operates in relation to its inscription in the Other. We are the remainder of the hole we make in the Other when we fall as objects, a remainder which cannot be assimilated by the signifier.

Thus the emerging subject tests his place in the Other by playing with disappearance; for example, he hides and waits for someone to look for him. This situation takes on dramatic overtones when this disappearance is not noticed. He seeks to create a hole in the Other, to be lacking for him. The Other, probably the mother initially, will mourn his loss. The child actively seeks to separate himself, in a *separtition*, as Lacan says in the *Seminar on Anxiety*, because when he creates a hole in the Other by turning himself into a loss, he goes out to seek something else.

Mourning after weaning is the mother's mourning, not the baby's. For that loss to start operating, the subject first has to discover lack, and the only place where he or she can discover it is in the Other, in other words, by finding the Other incomplete, or barred. That loss locates the subject in two ways. In one, the subject is that object taken as cause for the Other and that, in as much as it is an embodied cause linked with gut-emotions is the truth of a specific relation with the desire that determines the subject's position. Such a part- or partial truth uncovers both the subject's lack and the lack of the Other. On the other hand, it is a premium of jouissance which the Other recovers in the face of the absence of an absolute, whole, sexual jouissance. In this way, Lacan retrieves two main dimensions of the Freudian object: the object is first the "cause" as lost object of desire and trace of the mythical experience of satisfaction; the object is also a libidinal *plus-de-jouir* as in Lacan's translation of *Lustgewinn*, the distinctive pleasure gain provided by primary processes, a surplus in the energy of jouissance resulting from the circulation of cathexis; this second concept underpins the political economy of jouissance in the Lacanian clinic. Lacan shows how the nucleus of the preconscious, which provides the unity of what is usually called self, is the *objet a*, which provides the subject with a consolation in face of the absence of the whole jouissance.

A simple example can serve as illustration. A woman in her thirties comes to see me because she is going through periods of inertia during which she stops caring for her family, her work and her personal appearance. At these times she suffers from bouts of bulimia which she refers to as *comiditis* or "overeating," she eats mainly sweets, lies in bed reading romantic novels and sleeps. She has a slip of the tongue – she says "comoditis" (overcomfortable) instead of "comiditis" – which makes it possible to start formulating her basic fantasy whose axiom would be something like: "someone gives candies to a little girl." The comfort and the passiveness, both of which appear as character traits of women in the family, relate to the desire of a paternal grandfather, a professional baker, who fed all "his women." Passiveness, carelessness, wanting others to take care of her, are linked to being this object fed by the historical Other. In other words, she was an object allowing itself to be fed sweets. This provided her at the same time with a sweet premium of jouissance while allowing her to continue being the "cause" of the grandfather, whose role in the family had displaced her father. The analysis of her position as object relative to the desire of that Other altered her fixation to it and opened the possibility for her to decide whether she wanted what she desired.

The logical modalities of love

The *objet a* likewise latently organizes transference love. Psychoanalysis reveals that the main logical modality of love is contingency: psychoanalysis shows love to function as an interminable love letter underpinned by *objet a* as a remainder, its cause and its surplus-enjoyment. Lacanian psychoanalysis distinguishes thus two privileged, contingent forms of supplements to the sexual relationship which does not exist – the phallus and the *objet a*. Their conjunction produces that curious object, Plato's *agalma*, the miraculous detail that plays the part of object of desire. It is the lure which unleashes transference love and presents itself as the aim of the desire, not as its cause. The formula is precise: *objet a* is inhabited by the lacking phallus or "minus phi" and thus sends us on the trail of the imaginary phallus of castration. The subject imagines he will come to possess that object he lacks. But unconscious desire, understood as desire of the Other's desire, is not about possession. The Other's desire is always reduced to desiring *a*, the object which is its cause. He who gets lost on the road of possessing the object is the neurotic, who does not want to know either about his own position as object causing the Other's desire or that the Other's desire exists because the Other is incomplete – lacking – as well.

Sexuation	Type of love	Logical mode
∀x. φx	Neighborly love	Possibility
Not ∃x. *Not* φx	Courtly love	Impossibility
∃x. *Not* φx	Love letter	Necessity
Not ∀x. φx	*Lettre d'amur*	Contingency

Figure 12.1. Matrix of the four logical modes of love

Insofar as transference love is modulated through the analysand's demand, the latter likewise takes on different logical modalities. Each of these logical modalities develops Lacan's sexuation formulae from *Seminar XX*, and provides a new insight into the subject's sexuated position in love. From the seminars given in 1973–4 entitled *Les Non-dupes errent* one can deduce figure 12.1 that articulates the four logical modes of love following the sexuation formulae. Since Lacan's tables are underpinned by a pun linking *nécessité* (necessity) and *ne cesse de s'écrire* (does not stop being written), they are hard if not impossible to translate into English. Thus I will just reproduce the essential matrix.

Let me say briefly something about the last two types of loves. The modality of the "love letter" imagines love as necessary, and assumes that sexual love has to replace an always possible neighborly or brotherly love. This is the mechanism by which an illusion of sexual relationship is reintroduced: a logical necessity is substituted for the absent biological need or instinct. At the other end of the spectrum, the commandment "love thy neighbor" tends to expel the body and desire from their proper places.

On the female side of sexuation, no one can say "No" to the phallic function; impossibility arises with the non-existence of Woman as Woman. Courtly love appears at this point, it is love in its proper place in relation to desire, insofar as the imaginary of the body is the medium which gathers the Symbolic of jouissance and the Real of death. There the logical mode is the impossibility of sexual relationships. On the side of the feminine universal, the not-whole-woman, we find Woman who sustains herself as a sexual value by the modality of the love letter, since it is a mode through which love reveals its truth. The last modality is that of radical contingency and takes the form of what Lacan has called *lettre d'amur* (instead of *lettre d'amour*). There love reveals its truth, namely that for the speaking being sexual union is subject to chance encounters. In Lacan's special writing, *amur* – a neologism in French – is homophonically close to *amour*, love, but implies the privative particle *a-*, while suggesting the wall, *mur*, which sends us back to the wall of castration. Although love in its contingency does not reinforce that wall of castration, it accepts the gap opened by the absence of sexual relationship in the unconscious. Since *mur* is also homophonous with *mûre* (mature or ripe), *amur* ironically calls up the impossibility of mature love. However, love's movement aims at establishing it as necessary, thus hiding the bodily contingency of the *objet a* which underlies and triggers the encounter. Perhaps an adequate English version would be "love ladder," if perchance such a wall could be scaled. This entire movement from necessity to contingency and back is sketched in *Encore*: "The displacement of the negation from the 'stops not being written' to the 'doesn't stop being written,' in other words, from contingency to necessity – there lies the point of suspension to which all love is attached" (*S XX*, p. 145).

This trajectory resembles the progression that often appears at the end of an analysis, when the subject-supposed-to-know evaporates in loops and spirals. On the analysand's side, this marks the destitution of the subject; then, however, love for unconscious knowledge persists, without being sutured by a subject. The *objet a* also emerges in its incommensurability and radical contingency, which differentiates it from an object of exchange and its common measure, and marks the inassimilable remainder of the subjective constitution. Such remainder can be called *désêtre* or "lack in being" since it is no more than a false being whose emptiness is revealed on the psychoanalyst's side. The psychoanalyst then, far from being a listener endowed with discretionary powers, becomes the mere semblance of the *objet a*.

The unconscious structured as *a* language, that is to say, as *lalangue*, falls outside language as a universal, and its science, linguistics, is replaced by *linguisterie* (pseudo-linguistics) in conjunction with a clinic of the not-whole, of particularity, a clinic governed by a modal logic and a nodal topology. We need to underline that if the analysand's sayings adhere to a modal logic, analytic interpretation must in turn adhere to an apophantic logic, following Aristotle's notion (*apophanisis* means revelation in Greek), a logic of affirmation and assertion. Interpretation stands in relation to the saying of non-existence (of the sexual relationship, of the truth in its entirety and of the jouissance in its entirety). The apophantic saying places a limit, and is thus sense and goes against meaning. It will never place itself on the side of universal quantifiers because it is always a particular saying.

An example can illustrate how interpretation finds its bearings in this logical dimension. The patient was a womanizer, what we call a Don Juan, whose life was constantly beset by the many affairs he carried on. Throughout his analysis he would tell me: "You know doctor, all women want the same thing." When I asked: "What?" he would reply: "Oh, you know . . ." This would be repeated often until one day he fell in love with a woman. He told me he had doubts about her, and had concluded that this woman must be like all the others. I repeated my question, and finally he replied: "Well, you know, they are all whores." I replied immediately: "Thank you for the compliment," in a highly ironic tone calculated as a vacillation of neutrality, for I was neither angry nor offended. In fact, I had implied: "Thank you, I am also included in the all women, I am no exception." On this intervention, I interrupted the session. The important point had been that I had abandoned the position of exception in which the analysand had placed me. I was in the same position as *the* other exception, the master, his mother in the first place – the only woman to whom he was faithful – and in the second place his wife as a mother surrogate. By simply including myself in the series "all women are whores," I opened the closed set of the universal Woman, by refusing to take the place of the exception that would assure that the ensemble of Woman was a closed universal set. Here, what was signified was not the central issue. This interpretation produced an intense reaction in the analysand. It opened for him a space that was not limited exclusively by his mother's desire and stopped his compulsive womanizing.

When we are on the side of the not-whole linked with femininity, the unconscious remains an open structure; on the phallic side, the unconscious is a closed set. Signifiers, insofar as they are an open set, are not organized as a chain which implies a linear series. Instead, we are dealing with an articulation governed by the logic of proximity. This approach to unconscious knowledge is not contradictory with how it works as a closed set. Two ways of focusing on truth in its relationship with the unconscious are thus sketched out. Both are always half-truths. In relation to the closed set, truth involves the existence of a limit that makes it a half-saying. In the open set, we only find particular truths, one by one. The psychoanalyst, as though he were a Don Juan, is to take on each unconscious, one by one, because he knows there is no "unconscious as a whole," that the universal proposition will be denied to him. Every psychoanalyst will have to make a list, one by one, of the several unconsciouses he has had to analyze. Deciphering unconscious knowledge thus has two dimensions: the half-saying or *midire* of the closed set and the true saying of the maximum particularity of the open set.

The ethics appropriate to this set, both closed and open at the same time, which is the unconscious, is an ethics of "saying well" (*bien dire*). To be faithful to it involves being a dupe of the unconscious knowledge precisely because "non-dupes err" (Lacan's pun on *noms du père* – the names of the father – and *les non-dupes errent*, the non-dupes err). We are to be docile dupes of that unconscious knowledge because the Well Said we are dealing with is not that of literary creation, even though a rhetoric, which varies depending on the *lalangue*, is inherent in it. We are dealing with that Well Said which responds to the unconscious knowledge of each analysand. This is the deep reason why there is no psychoanalytic technique.

Neurosis and sexuation formulae

The sexual relationship which does not exist torments us, works on us, and ultimately leads us to psychoanalysis. Due to this impossibility which makes a hole in unconscious knowledge, psychoanalysis provides us with "truth cases," points out how real lives are tormented by this Real. The neurotic shows a truth which, since it is not said, is suffered and endured. This is his or her letter of introduction. Suffering is to be considered an event insofar as it covers for and is the effect of a saying, an enunciation. This suffering can be a symptom but also an *objet a* as cause. Then we can start working.

When the neurotic seeks knowledge, this search is on an ethical level, and, according to Lacan, he is the one who traces out new paths in the relationship between psychoanalysis and ethics. The search for the *père-vers* (Lacan's pun on "perverse" and "vers le père" – that is, "toward the father") is a search for jouissance. The neurotic questions himself about how to manage the impasses of the law. He knows, in his way, that everything related to jouissance unfolds around the truth of knowledge. The horizon of his search is absolute jouissance. Nevertheless, the central issue for him is that his truth is always on the side of desire, not of jouissance, precisely because he situates himself as a divided subject ($\$$). He situates himself relative to that which he believes in, those hidden truths which he represents in his own flesh. For him, as for the pervert, that which is foreclosed is absolute jouissance, not the Name-of-the-father.

When auto-eroticism is discovered, the subject's link to the desire of the Other (mainly the mother as Other) is often questioned, which risks unleashing a neurosis. This questioning puts the drama of the significance of the Other at stake, insofar as the latter has had a hole made in it by the *objet a*. Where the Other has had a hole made in it, the *a* will fall. The phallic signifier (ϕ) places itself in this same hole. That hole indicates the point where the Other is emptied of jouissance.

Each neurosis has its own way of coming to terms with this point of castration in the Other which indicates the non-existence of jouissance as whole or absolute. The two main neuroses – obsessional neurosis and hysteria – can be located on both sides of the sexuation formulae, insofar as the particular on each side shows us a different form of providing a basis for the primordial law.

On the side of the exception is the mythical father of *Totem and Taboo* – the figure Freud placed at the center of obsessive neurosis, who denies the phallic function and enjoys women "as a whole" – that is, all women. The mythical father is greedy for jouissance and drives his sons to a rebellion which culminates in his murder and totemic devouring. This ends with the communion of the brothers, each of whom can now take a woman, and the establishment of a mythical social contract, based on the interdiction of the "whole" of women. Let us underline that what is forbidden is the "whole" of women, and not the mother. In this case, jouissance as "whole" comes first, and is later forbidden by the contract among the brothers. The law which halts the absolute jouissance of the mythical father appears second. This law is an accomplice of the writing of love letters, which on the universal level is the basis for neighborly love or a sense of religious community.

On the side of the "there is not one" of the female particular, we find the Oedipal law, with the interdiction of the desire of the mother, which Freud discovered in his hysterical patients. The Oedipal law establishes a genealogy of desire in which the mother is declared to be forbidden. The subject is guilty without knowing it, because the law is there first and refers to the desire of the mother, not to jouissance. In *The Reverse of Psychoanalysis* we read: "The role of the mother is the desire of the mother . . . This is not something one can stand like that, indifferently. It always causes disaster. A big crocodile in whose mouth you are – this is the mother. One never knows whether she will suddenly decide to snap her trap shut."[2] The risk is to be devoured by that mother-crocodile, a risk from which the subject defends himself with the phallus. Lacan holds that Jocasta knew something about what happened at the crossroads where Oedipus kills Laius, and that Freud did not question her desire, which led to the self-absorption of the son/phallus that Oedipus was for her. Here we have first of all the forbidden desire of/for the mother, and secondly, their transgression. Observe that what is forbidden manifestly is the desire for the mother, but that behind this, the desire of the mother herself comes to the fore, to which the son's desire for her responds. Here the law points out the object of desire and at the same time forbids it. This law is a correlate of courtly love, the impossible, and shows an appropriate positioning of desire.

Let us start with obsessive neurosis and its desire that shows up as an impossible desire to possess the "whole" of women. The obsessive neurotic, faced with the impasses of the law, aspires to a knowledge which would allow him to become the master, a knowledge in which he is interested because of its relationship to jouissance. He also knows that faced with a loss of jouissance, the only available recovery of jouissance is provided by the *objet a*. That loss constitutes the center around which debt, which plays a crucial function for him, is structured. Jouissance must be authorized when it is based on a payment forever renewed: the obsessional neurotic is, therefore, untiringly committed to production, to unceasing activity. Different forms of debt are included in his rituals, in which he finds jouissance through displacement. The master is the exception for him, that Other prior to castration, to being emptied of jouissance, to the law after the murder of the father. He thinks about death to avoid jouissance and sustains the master with his own body, which acts as a cadaver, obeying, we might say, Ignatius Loyola's motto of *perinde ad cadaver*, to obey until the end as a cadaver. In the face of the exception which denies castration, his answer is to not exist, which gives rise to that peculiar feeling, which makes him feel always as though he were outside of himself, that he is never where he is. He thus sustains that exception which is the mythical father, that master whose cadaverized slave he becomes.

On the other hand, the hysterical patient both represses and promotes that point towards the infinite which is an absolute jouissance impossible to obtain. Since it is impossible to obtain, she refuses any other jouissance; none would suffice by comparison with that impossible jouissance. She supposes that Woman – the Woman that Lacan would call the "other" woman – has the knowledge of how to make a man enjoy, an impossible place she yearns to reach. In the face of this impasse, she sustains her desire as unsatisfied; if absolute jouissance is unreachable, everything she is offered is "not that." This situation drives her to question the master so that he will produce some knowledge, that knowledge Woman would have if she existed. This is why any weakness of the father is so important for her, like his illness or his death. She hurries to sustain him, it does not matter how, because she does not want to know anything of an impotence which would make absolute jouissance even more unreachable.

Her tragedy is that she loves truth as the non-existence of jouissance as a whole. If loving is to give what you do not have, she unfolds the charitable theater of hysteria in this respect, her own version of love thy neighbor, a counterpoint of everything for the other of the obsessive oblation. In this charitable theater she stages the sacrifice, not the debt, where she offers herself as guarantor of the castration, even unto her own life. In the face of the non-existence of Woman, she chooses to *faire l'homme* like the hysteric (to play the part of a man, but also "make" a man) with all the ambiguity of this formula, which can be understood either as her assuming the man's role or that she constitutes the man, although not any man, that man who would know what "the" woman, should she exist, would know. She identifies with the man relative to the woman. Therefore she pretends to have that semblance which the phallus is so as to relate to that "at least one man" who has knowledge about "the" woman. That woman as a whole who does not exist, impossible to register logically in the unconscious, is the basis of the unsatisfied desire of the hysterical patient.

What then is a woman? It is she who can see the light in psychoanalysis, who is open to a dual jouissance as not contradictory, who can place herself on both sides of the sexuation formulae. On the side of "not as a whole," a jouissance opens for her under the sign of mysticism; on the other side, there is phallic jouissance. That "one woman" registers on the male side as "one" woman, but not always the same one. Thus in this structure we have recorded the matrix of a misunderstanding between the sexes. Such a logical grid shows that neuroses are the truth of a failure, the failure of the structure of the signifier relative to the inscription of the sexual relationship.

How can we think of the relationship between structure and history in this clinic? For Lacan, a child's biography is always secondary in psycho-analysis, because it is told afterwards. How is this biography, this family novel, organized? It depends on how unconscious desire has appeared for the father and the mother. Therefore we not only need to explore history, but also how each of the following terms was effectively present for each subject: knowledge, jouissance, desire, and the *objet a*. Thus, the child's biography can be thought of as the way in which the structure became a living drama for each subject. The key to how that structure became drama is the desire of the Other in its articulation with jouissance. The central point is the link between absolute jouissance as lost and the desire of the barred Other. This link comes together in the *objet a*, the cause of desire and *plus-de-jouir*. The subject must place herself as the cause of desire that she was for the other, and decide whether she wants what she desires – whether she wants to be the cause of that desire. Likewise, the subject must abandon the fixation on the *plus-de-jouir* that supplements the loss of jouissance that also inhab-its the Other, thus opening up the space for other ways to recover jouissance. Our contingent biographies, which become necessary a posteriori, provide the possibility of a choice, and psychoanalysis takes us to this threshold. Lacan's clinic does not engage in absolute determinism, since it foregrounds the central role of contingency, which allows the analysand the small margin of freedom that makes psychoanalysis neither an imposture nor a mystifica-tion. In conclusion, I would like to stress that a Lacanian clinic aims above all at "speaking well" (*bien dire*). It should make a virtue of modesty without forgetting the psychoanalyst's own desire, with all the weight of the added responsibility this entails.

NOTES

1. Jacques Lacan, "La troisième," *Lettres de l'E.C.F.* 16 (Paris, 1974), p. 187.
2. Jacques Lacan, *Le Séminaire XVII. L'envers de la psychanalyse, 1969–1970* (Paris: Seuil, 1991), p. 129. See also p. 167 for another version of this passage.

13

DEBORAH LUEPNITZ

Beyond the phallus: Lacan and feminism

Above all, spare us any father educators, rather let them be in retreat on any position as master.[1]

In 1970s America, at the crest of second-wave feminism, Sigmund Freud was the man women loved to hate. They were not without reason. The medical specialty practiced in Freud's name by American analysts (mostly men) devoted itself not to helping patients (mostly women) discover their desire, but to enforcing ideas about "normal" femininity.[2] To those beginning to question the conventions of domesticity and heterosexuality, psychoanalysis, with its talk of "female masochism" and "penis envy," seemed the enemy of women's liberation. Freud's words were plucked out of context to prove it.

But in 1974, the British feminist Juliet Mitchell published *Psychoanalysis and Feminism*, which would have enormous impact on a generation of women, both academic and activist. Mitchell wrote: "[a] rejection of psychoanalysis and of Freud's works is fatal for feminism. However it may have been used, psychoanalysis is not a recommendation *for* a patriarchal society, but an analysis *of* one. If we are interested in understanding and challenging the oppression of women, we cannot afford to neglect it."[3]

Mitchell's work permitted those on the political left to go beyond the materialism of the "nature *vs* nurture debates" in social science. Neither biology nor culture could exhaust the meaning of individual fantasy, of subjectivity. Freud took the desiring subject as his main topic of investigation, and the reading of Freud that was most compatible with feminist politics, according to Mitchell, was that of Jacques Lacan. She even defended Lacan's recondite style by referring to the unfortunate consequences of Freud's accessible, easily bowdlerized style.

Mitchell continued such pathbreaking work with the publication in 1982 of *Feminine Sexuality: Jacques Lacan and the école freudienne*, co-edited with Jacqueline Rose – a book that marked a turning point in the encounter of English-speaking feminists with Lacan. Readers' reactions to their translated excerpts from the *Ecrits* and *Seminar XX* tended to divide sharply along discipline lines. Lacan developed a feminist following in the academy – mostly in the humanities – where his notions of "the gaze" and of the contested, troubled nature of gender inspired brilliant commentary. By 1992, just eighteen years after psychoanalysis had made its entrée into feminist theory, there was material enough to compile a five-hundred-page *Dictionary of Psychoanalytic Feminism*.[4]

Unlike their academic counterparts, most Anglophone feminist clinicians found in their encounter with Lacan's writing no reason to go further. Less accustomed to dealing with difficult philosophical texts, they viewed Lacan's style as obscurantist and elitist, and complained with some justification that his ideas could not be evaluated without access to the lengthy clinical illustrations offered by Freud, Klein, and Winnicott. Rumors had spread that Lacan was abusive with patients, and that he used the short analytic session to see huge numbers of people, charging astronomical fees.[5] Finally, most practitioners felt that Lacan's reliance on the concept of the phallus and the "paternal metaphor" returned them to all the wrong aspects of Freud. Freud, by his own admission, had underestimated the role of the mother in children's development. And unlike Melanie Klein and the object relations analysts in England, Lacan seemed to be carrying on the Freudian tradition of ignoring mothers and the pre-Oedipal. Most English-speaking feminist practitioners thus gravitated towards either Klein or object relations theory. Mitchell herself left Lacan behind and became a Kleinian psychoanalyst; her later work ignores him almost completely.

That Lacan would be rejected by practitioners, and keenly promoted in the academy is rather ironic. More than any other analyst, Lacan insisted that psychoanalysis was defined exclusively through a discursive exchange between analyst and analysand. Indeed, the psychoanalytic scene in France differed radically from that in North America: clinicians as well as academics – feminists and non-feminists alike – became "Lacanian." Even Simone de Beauvoir, ever wary of psychoanalysis, incorporated Lacan's mirror stage into her account of female development.[6]

Some Anglophone writers relying mainly on the *Ecrits* still appear to believe that Lacanian theory can be reduced to a few concepts, all glorifying the phallus. Thus it may be necessary to take the phallus off center stage to understand what else Lacan offers feminists, particularly those committed to psychoanalytic practice, whether as analysts or analysands.

The family complexes

An often neglected work is "The family complexes," which Lacan wrote in 1938 as an encyclopedia article.[7] According to Jacques-Alain Miller, it was excluded from the *Ecrits* only because of its length. Despite certain condescending references to "primitive peoples," "The family complexes" is in some ways ahead of its time, as it argues how little of what is considered "natural" about families, and about human development in general, can be ascribed to nature. This marks a significant motif in Lacanian theory. Later references to the "paternal metaphor" and the "name of the father" do not reflect a belief that families must consist of a male and female parent, joined in marriage. The "third term" needed to signal a limit to the child's jouissance with the mother can be provided by a flesh-and-blood father, by another adult who cares for the child, or simply through the mother's own speech.[8] Lacan argues further that the term "complex" should replace "instinct" in theorizing human beings, as human instincts are so much weaker than those of other species, and, moreover, are voiced as a demand through speech. A "complex" is neither organic nor learned, but situated "in between" the two. Freud, of course, had already formulated the Oedipus complex, and to this Lacan added two more: the "weaning" (*sèvrage*) and "intrusion" complexes.

In Lacan's discussion of the weaning complex, what is striking is the absence of a sentimental bond between mother and baby. He is even clearer than Freud on the point that having to *separate* from the breast – rather than being at the breast – creates the enduring desire for connection. Lacan acknowledges that weaning can become "traumatic," in ways associated with various neurotic symptoms. But nowhere does he suggest that it is the mother's behavior *per se* – her failure to adapt almost perfectly like the Winnicottian mother – that causes problems.[9] According to Lacan, it is the image of the maternal *sein* (in French both "breast" and "womb") that dominates human life. Our having to leave it, he asserts, is a reality inseparable from all human nostalgia, religion, and the belief in political utopias.

If the mother is not the dominant figure she is in object relations theory, then neither is she absent from Lacan's theory. Feminist Shuli Barzilai, in *Lacan and the Matter of Origins*, compares her to a "Cheshire cat" appearing and disappearing at crucial moments in his work.[10] Lacan does not offer helpful advice on mothering techniques, nor does he indulge in the facile mother-blaming for which British object relations and American ego-psychology are notorious. In those more conventional views of development, the mother becomes a precious commodity: we develop a True Self if we get ourselves a good one or, rather, one who is "good enough."

In Lacan's view, the most important thing a mother can do is to be *not* in a state of "primary maternal preoccupation" with her infant, but instead a subject in her own right, who does not look to the child to complete her. Who or what else she desires – husband, lover, or work – is not as important as the *fact* of her desiring something beyond the child. One might expect this notion of motherhood to appeal to feminists, who have struggled against the charge that "working mothers" are responsible for all human ills, and that it is "natural" for woman to be locked into a love affair with her offspring.

The ambiguity of the French word *sein* underscores a fundamental point: even the baby's separation from the breast, which some might consider the "original" separation, harks back to a prior event – the infant's leaving the womb. Lacan will always complicate our efforts to build a linear theory by making it difficult to think of a first stage. For him, there are only "firsts."

Some twenty years after "The family complexes," Lacan returns to the weaning complex in his seventh seminar, when he introduces the term *das Ding* ("the thing") (*S VII*, pp. 43–71). While an older child may relate to the mother as a subject in her own right, and the infant relates to her as an object or part-object, there is, according to Lacan, an anterior moment in which the child experiences the mother without any capacity for representation whatsoever. At this point, the mother exists not in the imaginary register, but only in the domain of the Real. It is to *das Ding* that we refer in our nostalgias. When, as adults, we long for what has been lost, we refer psychically to something unknown and prior to symbolization, though what eludes representation also has an abominable aspect. Thus, as much as we have unidentifiable longings for "what was," so are we also terrified by images of *das Ding*. (Slavoj Žižek has used this Lacanian concept to reflect on the placental images in horror movies such as *Alien*.)[11]

The slightly bizarre concept of *das Ding* has important clinical relevance. It is no accident that Lacan devotes two chapters to it in his *Ethics of Psychoanalysis*. There he explains why analysis must have nothing to do with helping the patient "adjust" better to society. For Lacan, the domain of analysis is desire; psychoanalysis can do nothing more than enable the subject to come to grips with his or her relationship to it. Desire, as we know, does not really have an object; it cannot be said to be *for* something. Or rather, to the extent that it is for something, it is also necessarily for something else. Needs and demands can be satisfied, but desire cannot, and substitution is its most reliable rule. Thus, if the analysand is in the process of discovering what we might call "the truth" of her or his own desire, this process will involve investigating the substitutions as they exist in that subject's history. The chain of displacements will always move in the direction of childhood and certainly to encounters with the mother – encounters that can never exclude *das Ding*. It is in analysis that we may come to realize that our first desires were inexpressible, our first object unknowable, and that every "refinding" of the object of our desire throughout life will never be entirely separable from illusion.

The "intrusion complex" refers to the young child's encounters with siblings and other rivals for parental attention, and it includes what Lacan calls "the mirror stage." The latter occurs when the baby is around 18 months of age, and recognizes its image in the mirror for the first time. The child at this point is relatively uncoordinated, and if ambulatory, is still striving to improve its sense of balance and muscular control. Having never seen itself from the outside, the infant has not had the opportunity to know that its body has a certain consistent form and size, easily locatable in space. Endlessly curious, the infant leans away from the mother or guardian, looks into the mirror and begins "the jubilant assumption of his specular image" (*E/S*, p. 2). This euphoric developmental moment has its melancholic side. Having recognized ourselves in the mirror, we are bound to go through life looking outward for evidence of who we are. We will seek out ordinary mirrors (which deceive if only by reversing left and right) and we will look into the mirroring gaze of others which will just as surely distort, diminish, aggrandize. Identity, for Lacan, is necessarily an alienated state – something crucial for functioning in the world, but also radically unstable. The analysand will look to the analyst as the ultimate mirror, believing that there might finally be an answer to the question, "Who am I?" The work of analysis prepares the patient to realize that there is no "thou art that" – no truth that can be given by an agency outside the subject.

On the question of the Oedipus complex, there are important differences between Freud and Lacan. Freud's boy and girl pass through their oral and anal stages in parallel fashion; in the "genital phase," they compare bodies, and conclude that since only the boy has a penis, the girl must have lost hers, or be awaiting one. This knowledge ends the boy's Oedipus complex and begins the girl's. What Lacan emphasizes is that these observations, fears, and fantasies about the body cannot be understood except in terms of antecedent moments – to the weaning complex, for example, in which the loss of a body part (the nipple) was already at stake. Toilet training presents another moment in which the child is forced to come to grips with something falling off or out of the body; the feces are lost or "given up." Lacan also reminds us that long after the mirror phase, we remain subject to the effects of the "fragmented body" with which it begins. Thus, he asserts in "The family complexes":

> This fantasy [of castration] is preceded by a whole series of dismemberment fantasies which go back in a regressive sequence beginning with dislocation and dismemberment, through deprivation of sexual organs to disemboweling and even to the fantasy of being swallowed up or entombed.[12]

Castration fear is thus an imaginary localization of a more pervasive, unnamable fear. When we return to the Freudian boy and girl in the sandbox comparing bodies, we see not a sudden fall from security to the terror of Adam and Eve in the garden, but instead children whose lives are coextensive with worries about the body. Somewhat later, children use their theories about sexual difference as a way of answering a question that they have lacked the ability to formulate in language until this important moment: "What is missing from this body of mine?" Something has always been experienced as lost, but the development of speech at this age means that it is the *Oedipal* body that is offered up as a means of addressing it. Lacan observed that many human beings use the penis to cover their pervasive sense of bodily lack, and so he chose the term "phallus" to refer to our wish for completeness. The phallus therefore signifies, paradoxically, the opposite of completion – that is, lack. Whereas the penis is an organ that some individuals possess and some don't, the phallus is what no one can have but everyone wants: a belief in bodily unity, wholeness, perfect autonomy. The phallus, as Lacan explains in his 1958 "The meaning of the phallus," is not an object like the breast, penis or clitoris. It is a signifier, eventually designating all binary difference.

Lacan would always speak of the phallus not as a thing but as a position through which different objects circulate. Adults can use wealth, accomplishments, or their own children as phallic objects. In this way, the "objects" are desired for their representative value, their capacity to make the subject feel complete. The "phallic function," in other words, is not gender-specific; it relates to being and having, to lack and the denial of lack – for all subjects. If biology does enter this crucial set of issues, it is mainly at the level of describing the "original" state of incompleteness. That is, according to Lacan, the experience of something lacking or lost may be conditioned by the "specific prematurity of birth" in our species, in contrast to others whose offspring are born much readier to fend for themselves (*E/S*, p. 4). In *The Project*, Freud had claimed that "the initial helplessness of human beings is the *primal source of all moral motives*" (*SE* 1, p. 318; emphasis in original). Diana Rabinovich maintains that this Freudian idea of helplessness is one that Lacan is constantly reworking.[13]

Castration

Given Lacan's unique formulation of the phallus, it is not surprising that his concept of "castration" is quite different from Freud's. Put most simply, castration is the ability of the subject to recognize, "I am lacking." Far from being something to avoid, castration is a necessity, and an absolute precondition for the ability to love. With respect to the two sexes, Lacan specifies that "[the] woman must undergo no more or less castration than the man."[14]

Lacan is by no means doing away with the difference between women and men; on the contrary he insists on it. Perhaps only psychotics such as Dr. Schreber (in Freud's famous case study) can live as man and woman at once – refusing the sacrifice that the rest of us (neurotics) make in giving up either an ongoing masculine or feminine identity. When Freud described the little girl's "discovery" of the inferiority of her genitals, many feminists asked if he was describing *children's* fantasies or his own. For Lacan, there can be nothing missing from the real of the female body. Lack is something that exists in the imaginary register; it is operative (although in different ways) for everyone. And so the phallus is not what men have and women lack; we might say that it is what men believe they have and what women are considered to lack.

A frequently asked question is: If Lacan wants us not to confuse the penis with the phallus, then why didn't he call the phallus something less penile – perhaps the "all" or the "omega"? Lacan, aiming to present his theory as a rereading of Freud, cites the overwhelming importance of the image of the phallus to the ancients. In a different context however, in a section on Aristotle and Freud, he wrote: ". . . we must use things like that, old words, as stupid as anything, but really use them, work them to the bone" (*S XX*, p. 60). In *The Daughter's Seduction*, Jane Gallop suggests that this passage describes what Lacan is doing with the words "phallus" and "castration." She writes: "Maybe he's using them up, running the risk of essence, running dangerously close to patriarchal positions, so as to wear 'phallus' and 'castration' out, until they're thoroughly hackneyed." And: "What a way of ruining exchange value by use!"[15]

Feminine jouissance

Freud had maintained that there was but one kind of libido, and that it was masculine. Throughout the 1950s, Lacan seemed to agree with him. In subsequent decades, however, the questions that Lacan's feminist interlocutors raised seemed to have an impact. Many observers believe that he was responding directly to them when he chose to devote his seminar of 1971–2 to questions of feminine sexuality. Indeed, that seminar is sprinkled with comments about the "MLF" – the *mouvement de libération des femmes* – comments that seem at turns playful and patronizing.

In one of his rare departures from Freud, Lacan asserts: "Freud claims that there is only masculine libido. What does that mean if not that a field that certainly is not negligible is thus ignored? That field is the one of all beings that take on the status of woman – assuming that being takes on anything whatsoever of her destiny" (*S XX*, p. 80).

Lacan proceeded to elaborate a theory of feminine sexuality in terms of a jouissance that was "beyond" phallic jouissance. The latter is a jouissance of the organ (women, of course, also have access to it). About this feminine or "supplementary" jouissance, Lacan was perhaps more than characteristically oblique. He compared it to the experience of the mystic, explaining:

> Mysticism isn't everything that isn't politics. It is something serious, about which several people inform us – most often women, or bright people like Saint John of the Cross, because one is not obliged, when one is male, to situate oneself on the side of [the phallic function]. One can also situate oneself on the side of the not-whole. There are men who are just as good as women. It happens. And who also feel just fine about it.   (*S XX*, p. 76)

Lacan held that feminine jouissance was, however, difficult for ordinary men to comprehend, despite their fascination: ". . . in all the time people have been begging them, begging them on their hands and knees – I spoke last time of women psychoanalysts – to try to tell us, not a word! We've never been able to get anything out of them" (*S XX*, p. 75). Was Lacan admitting to ignorance of women's experience in order to clear a space for their own accounts? Or was he actually spinning an old yarn about woman as the "dark continent?" Considering the "women psychoanalysts" and the other writers he chose to ignore, we may well ask if Lacan truly desired the knowledge for which he was apparently so willing to grovel.[16]

He was disingenuous, in any case, to maintain that he got nothing "out of them." In fact, there is reason to believe that Lacan, an inveterate borrower, drew primary inspiration for his model of feminine jouissance from "The mystic" – the penultimate chapter of *The Second Sex*.[17] De Beauvoir writes, for example, "St. Theresa's writings hardly leave room for doubt, and they justify Bernini's statue which shows us the saint swooning in an excess of voluptuousness."[18] Here is Lacan, writing twenty years later: ". . . it's like for Saint Teresa – you need but go to Rome and see the statue by Bernini to immediately understand that she's coming. There's no doubt about it" (*S XX*, p. 76).

Unlike Lacan, de Beauvoir described at least two types of mystics: "the narcissistic" (e.g. Mme Guyon), who simply craves the personal attention of all heaven, and "the virile" (e.g. Saints Theresa and John of the Cross), whose ecstatic visions form part of a theological project and a life of action. Intriguing is the fact that both Lacan and de Beauvoir privileged the sexed position of the other: he favored feminine over phallic jouissance, while she valued virile over non-virile mysticism. In neither case did these positions correspond literally to biological sex.

No sexual relation

One of Lacan's most important formulations concerns the "nonexistence" of the sexual relation. First mentioned in *Seminar XIV* and expanded in *Seminar XX*, this claim amplifies Freud's famous remark: "We must reckon with the possibility that something in the nature of the sexual instinct itself is unfavorable to the realisation of complete satisfaction." (*SE* 11, pp. 188–9).

Lacan did not mean that love doesn't exist or that people don't revel in sexual pleasure. What does not exist is a romantic love that allows individuals to complete each other, making one of two, like the fabled creatures in Plato's *Symposium*. It would seem that Lacan shared with feminist social critics a sense of the overvaluation of "true love" in the contemporary West. But whereas feminists have seen the problem as socially constructed, Lacan saw the impossibility of the sexual relation as largely structural – our fate as subjects divided by the unconscious.

French feminisms

In the years following Lacan's *Seminar XX*, a number of "French feminists" were using his reading of Freud to move on in their own theoretical directions. And somewhat ironically, many feminists working in English began enthusiastically promoting the ideas of Julia Kristeva, Luce Irigaray, and others, although it is not clear that they would call themselves "feminist" without significant qualification.

Kristeva, a Bulgarian-born philosopher of language and contributor to the avant-garde journal *Tel Quel*, is known for her interest in the limits of language – particularly in what she calls the "semiotic." This is the realm in which children, not yet able to speak, experience the "raw material" of speech – its sounds and gestures as they permeate the relationship of child and mother. Kristeva added to the pre-Oedipal mother-baby paradigm the concept of the "imaginary father," also called the "father of personal pre-history."

On the question of feminism, she said famously, "A feminist practice can only be . . . at odds with what already exists so that we may say 'that's not it' and 'that's still not it.' By 'woman' I mean that which cannot be represented, what is not said, what remains above and beyond nomenclature and ideologies. There are certain 'men' who are familiar with this phenomenon."[19] Some readers appreciate Kristeva's refusal of a liberal, co-optable feminism. Others see her as a "dutiful daughter" of Lacan, because she seems to adopt his somewhat ethereal vision of femininity.

Irigaray is perhaps best known for appropriating Lacan's structural reading of Freud, while refusing everything she sees as masculinist in psychoanalysis. In 1974, she published *Speculum of the Other Woman*, in which she repudiates the Freudian view of woman as defective man, tying his misogyny to that of Western philosophy. Her target is Freud, not Lacan, but clearly some of her fulminations against phallocentrism and the mystification of woman apply to him as well. Three weeks after the publication of *Speculum*, Irigaray was fired from her teaching position at the University of Paris at Vincennes.[20]

Irigaray does not settle for a feminist practice that simply insists "that's not it"; on the contrary, she argues for the formulation of new theories and practices – even a new language – that is not phallocentric but based on women's bodies and pleasures. She writes: "If we keep on speaking the same language together, we're going to reproduce the same history . . . If we keep on speaking sameness, if we speak to each other as men have been doing for centuries . . . we'll miss each other, fail ourselves."[21]

Against a feminism that would promote androgyny, or the erasure of gender, Irigaray advocates "an ethics of sexual difference." In describing the difference, she has written: "*But woman has sex organs more or less everywhere*. She experiences pleasure almost everywhere . . . The geography of her pleasure is much more diversified, more multiple in its differences, more complex, more subtle than is imagined."[22] Moreover, she argues that psychoanalysis has failed to represent lesbians except according to pre-existing models of male homosexuality. And she insists also on the importance of finding ways to represent the mother-daughter relationship in psychoanalysis.

While appreciating the boldness and vitality of Irigaray's writing, feminist Ann Rosalind Jones notes that Irigaray has little, if anything, to say about class, race, or women's history in particular, and is thus vulnerable to the charge of essentializing women's experience.[23] Margaret Whitford, in contrast, claims that such charges underestimate Irigaray's project, which she sees as nothing less than an attempt "to dismantle from within the foundations of Western metaphysics."[24]

Sexuation

The challenge to both feminism and psychoanalysis is to create theory and practice that neither deny sexual difference nor generate new, coercive antinomies. How can we describe difference without inscribing essential difference? Some believe that this is exactly what Lacan attempted to do with his diagram of sexuation, presented most fully in *Seminar XX*. The symbols and syntax of formal logic might seem the least likely idiom for something as alogical as sex, but it is precisely the diagram's minimalism that limits a proclivity towards misleading content.

On the "masculine" side of the diagram, Lacan wrote a formula generally read as "All men are subjected to the phallic function." On the "feminine" side, he wrote a formula generally read as: "Not all of a woman is subject to the phallic function." The difference is that whereas men can be discussed as a class, there is no set of "all women." Lacan believed that while women were a part of the phallic or symbolic order, they were not in it "all together." Thus, he would describe woman as *pas tout* [not all]. We know that women historically have been kept out of the symbolic order. We could also say that there is something about woman that resists it.

The lower half of the sexuation diagram shows the "feminine" side having access to two libidinal positions, while the "masculine" side has access to one only. Thus any given "woman" can choose to associate with the phallic function, or with the "signifier of the barred Other" – a way of describing the jouissance that is beyond the phallus.[25]

Again, if these distinctions appear outrageously subtle and abstract, they at least have the virtue of not trapping us into neo-Confucian paradigms according to which man is rational; woman, emotional – paradigms that surface endlessly in popular psychology.[26] Lacan also made it clear in explicating the diagram of sexuation that he was not simply placing biological males on one side and biological females on the other. As he explained, referring to the "feminine" side: "Any speaking being whatsoever, as is expressly formulated in Freudian theory, whether provided with the attributes of masculinity – attributes that remain to be determined – or not, is allowed to inscribe itself in this part" (*S XX*, p. 80).

How do the two sides relate to each other? How does desire move within and across the divide of sexuation? Ellie Ragland has suggested beautifully:

"Heterosexual or homosexual, we are drawn to each other sexually because we are not whole and because we are not the same."[27]

Lacan and the talking cure

Lacan always maintained that the only purpose of his teaching was to train analysts. As mentioned earlier, his clinical practice was non-normative in its aims. Whereas analysts of other schools want patients to identify with the analyst's ego, Lacan felt that analysis had failed if this occurred. Feminists might be interested in this and other aspects of Lacanian practice as well – aspects which have scarcely been mentioned in the literature.

Toward the goal of sketching foundations for a feminist articulation of Lacan's work that would go beyond theory to clinical practice, I offer the following questions: (1) What is the position of the analyst? (2) Where does neurotic suffering come from? (3) How can we understand the Oedipus complex? (4) Who may analyze?

(1) What is the position of the analyst?

In the Anglophone world, it has been common since Freud to speak of the "maternalization of the analyst." Rejecting Freud's metaphors of the analyst as picklock or surgeon, clinicians such as Winnicott represent the analytic relationship in terms of mother and infant. The analytic mother's job is not necessarily to love, but to recognize the patient and thus to make up for bad mirroring in childhood. A feminist critique of object relations might ask if the maternalization of the analyst and the corresponding infantilization of the patient make sense in an encounter meant to help women discover their desires as women.

The good enough mother is not Lacan's model of the analyst. Rather, he placed the analyst in the role of the Other, a position he also identified with death. The goal of analysis for Lacan is not to provide reparation for bad mothering, nor even to improve communication with the living, but to change the subject's relationship to the dead, and to help him or her examine the meaning of mortality.

(2) Where does neurotic suffering come from?

Freud stated after his analysis of Dora that he had never completely given up his "seduction theory," according to which actual sexual abuse causes neurosis. He came to believe, however, that unresolved Oedipal fantasies, even in the absence of trauma, could create the same kinds of symptoms.

Since Freud, much controversy has focused on the question of which aspect of his theory (seduction or Oedipus) is "truer."

There are people who spend years of their lives asking, "Was I sexually molested as a child or have I only imagined it?" The fact that there are no indications of reality in the unconscious does not mean that human beings are (or ought to be) indifferent to questions surrounding the occurrence of sexual abuse.

Lacan's formulation of the three registers can be helpful in mitigating the binarism: real or imagined? Consider a patient with phobias and gynecological symptoms so disabling that she wonders if she was abused in childhood, despite having no memories of such an event or events. During analysis, she learns that her mother at age thirteen had been raped by a male relative. Her mother had kept the secret with the benign intention of "not burdening" her child. Nonetheless, the same mother could not help but communicate unconsciously to her growing daughter a representation of the female body as shameful and prone to violation. Because the story of the wounding of the mother's body was repressed, it was bound to return somewhere in the next generation. The failure, thus, was not in the patient's Imaginary (a missing memory of an event) but in the Symbolic (a story withheld) resulting in a return in the Real (of the patient's bodily symptoms). It can also be said that every instance of sexual abuse needs to be considered in all three registers.

(3) How can we understand the Oedipus complex?

For decades, feminists have noted that the Oedipus complex takes its structure from a story whose protagonist is male. Moreover, the story has often been used to create a pat developmental narrative confined to: "Mommy, Daddy, and me." Lacan believed that Sophocles' *Oedipus at Colonus* – the story of Oedipus in exile – held more for psychoanalysis than *Oedipus Rex* for it is only in exile that Oedipus comes to ask the important questions, and to assume his castration. His tragedy, like ours, says Lacan, does not turn simply on the famous family triangle, but on a more fundamental case of mistaken identity.

Feminist psychologist Carol Gilligan who, like Luce Irigaray, has protested the absence of mother-daughter representations in psychoanalysis, recommends reviving the myth of Psyche and Eros. In this myth, which begins with a daughter's resistance to conventional love, the struggle for truth leads not to exile and suicide, but to marriage and the birth of a daughter named "Pleasure."[28]

In his *Seminar on Transference*, Lacan similarly introduced a trilogy of plays featuring female protagonists – the trilogy of the Coûfontaine family – by Paul Claudel. This work, which has yet to catch the attention of feminists, tells the story of three generations of women, beginning in the early nineteenth century, culminating in the figure of Pensée. Pensée may be a more subversive feminist figure than Psyche, whose story reinstates the nuclear family. Pensée refuses traditional marriage, loves her child, embraces the future. Moreover, unlike Antigone, Pensée – because she is able to ask questions about her mother and grandmother, and because she brings the family history to light – is not condemned to reproduce their tragedies. An eloquent spokesperson for desire, she asks: "Am I not mistress of myself and of my soul and of my body? And of this which I have made from myself?"[29] The editor of *Seminar VIII* labeled the section on the Claudel trilogy, "The Myth of Oedipus Today."

(4) Who may analyze?

Like Freud, Lacan believed strongly in the importance of training lay (non-physician) analysts. Lacan is said to have resigned from the Société psychanalytique de Paris partly over this issue.[30] Less well known is the story of Freud's refusal to exclude candidates based on sexual preference. In 1920 the Dutch Psychoanalytic Association asked the advice of Ernest Jones about whether or not to accept a known homosexual for membership. Jones was opposed, and wrote to Freud, who replied:

> Your query, dear Ernest, concerning the prospective membership of homosexuals has been considered by us and we disagree with you. In effect, we cannot exclude such persons without other sufficient reasons, as we cannot agree with their legal prosecution. We feel that a decision in such cases should depend upon a thorough examination of the other qualities of the candidate.[31]

While the British Psychoanalytic Society excluded gay and lesbian candidates until very recently, Lacanians apparently follow Freud in this matter.[32]

Lacan, who spent a career warning against "father educators" and other masters, continues to attract acolytes, including some feminists. Among the feminists who have engaged Lacan's work, more than a few have turned their back on it. Jane Gallop, for example, who defended Lacan's formulation of the phallus in her early work, changed her mind a few years later, declaring: "Phallus/penis: same difference."[33] Others have sustained a more balanced perspective.[34]

Today, at the crest of third-wave feminism, Lacan has ironically become the man many women hate to love. Residual resentment has not prevented their coming to understand that respect, if not love, is the wave of the present. For without psychoanalysis, feminism risks capitulating to a purely materialist understanding of women, or settling for a very reduced account of fantasy, sexuality, and subjectivity. Without feminism, psychoanalysis risks being used to enforce what Freud himself called "normal" misogyny. We have reason to hope that provocative contact between them will continue to enhance the powers of feminism and psychoanalysis both to liberate, and to question.

NOTES

1. Jacques Lacan, "Seminar of 21 January 1975," *Ornicar?* 3 (1975), pp. 104–10. In *Feminine Sexuality: Jacques Lacan and the école freudienne*, eds. Juliet Mitchell and Jacqueline Rose (New York: Norton, 1982), p. 167.
2. For a critical history of the Americanization of psychoanalysis, see Russell Jacoby, *The Repression of Psychoanalysis* (New York: Basic Books, 1983). For an early feminist critique of Freud and psychiatry, see Kate Millet, *Sexual Politics* (New York: Ballantine Books, 1969). See also Deborah Luepnitz, "'I want you to be a woman': Reading desire in Stoller's case of 'Mrs. G.'" *Clinical Studies: International Journal of Psychoanalysis* 2 (1996), pp. 49–58.
3. Juliet Mitchell, *Psychoanalysis and Feminism* (New York: Vintage Books, 1974), p. xiii.
4. *Feminism and Psychoanalysis: A Critical Dictionary*, ed. Elizabeth Wright (Oxford: Blackwell, 1992). Although the dictionary contains entries related to object relations theory, Klein, and Jung, the majority are related to Lacan. Several contributors are psychoanalysts, the majority academics.
5. See Pierre Rey, *Une saison chez Lacan* (Paris: Robert Laffont, 1989). See also Elisabeth Roudinesco, *Jacques Lacan & Co.: A History of Psychoanalysis in France 1925–1985*, trans. Jeffrey Mehlman (Chicago: University of Chicago Press, 1990).
6. Simone de Beauvoir, *The Second Sex* (New York: Vintage Paperback, 1952), p. 313.
7. The full text of Lacan's *Les Complexes familiaux dans la formation de l'individu* (Paris: Navarin, 1984) has not been translated into English. But see the abridged form translated by Carolyn Asp under the title "The family complexes," *Critical Texts* 5 (1988), pp. 12–29. Also in *Autres écrits*, pp. 23–84.
8. Charles Shepherdson has affirmed this point in his rigorous *Vital Signs: Nature, Culture, Psychoanalysis* (New York: Routledge, 2000).
9. See D. W. Winnicott, *Through Pediatrics to Psychoanalysis* (New York: Basic Books, 1975).
10. Shuli Barzilai, *Lacan and the Matter of Origins* (Stanford: Stanford University Press, 1999).
11. Slavoj Žižek, *The Sublime Object of Ideology* (New York: Verso, 1989).
12. Jacques Lacan, "The family complexes," p. 20.
13. Diana Rabinovich, *El concepto de objeto en la teoria psicoanalitica: Sus incidencias en la dirección de la cura* (Buenos Aires: Manantial, 1988), p. 122.
14. Jacques Lacan, Seminar of 21 January, 1975, p. 168.

15. Jane Gallop, *The Daughter's Seduction* (Ithaca, NY: Cornell University Press, 1982).

16. Lacan never commented directly on the work of Luce Irigaray, Hélène Cixous, or on writers such as Woolf, Colette, or H.D., whom many read for their insights on feminine sexuality. He turned down an invitation for a set of interviews with Simone de Beauvoir. Marguerite Duras, one of the few whom Lacan openly admired, found his praise to be both condescending and self-serving. See his "Hommage fait à Marguerite Duras du *Ravissement de Lol V. Stein.*" Duras' interview with Suzanne Lamy is quoted in Roudinesco, *Jacques Lacan & Co.*, p. 522.

17. See Françoise Collin's fascinating "La Liberté inhumaine: Ou le marriage mystique de Jacques Lacan et Simone de Beauvoir," *Les Temps modernes*, no. 605, août–oct. 1999, 90–114.

18. De Beauvoir, *The Second Sex*, p. 743.

19. Julia Kristeva, "La Femme, ce n'est jamais ça," an interview in *Tel Quel* 59 (Fall 1974), translated in *New French Feminisms: An Anthology*, eds. Elaine Marks and Isabelle de Courtivron (Amherst: University of Massachusetts Press, 1980), pp. 134–8.

20. See Ann Rosalind Jones, "Writing the Body: Toward an Understanding of *l'écriture féminine*," *Feminist Studies* 7 (Summer 1981), pp. 247–63.

21. Luce Irigaray, "When our lips speak together," *This Sex Which Is Not One*, trans. Catherine Porter (Ithaca: Cornell University Press, 1985), p. 205.

22. Irigaray, "This sex which is not one," *This Sex Which Is Not One*, p. 28.

23. Jones, "Writing the Body: Toward an Understanding of *l'écriture féminine*," p. 96.

24. Margaret Whitford, "Rereading Irigaray," *Between Feminism and Psychoanalysis*, ed. Teresa Brennan (London: Routledge, 1989), p. 108.

25. See Elizabeth Wright, *Lacan and Post-Feminism* (Cambridge: Icon Books, 2000), as well as Bruce Fink, *The Lacanian Subject* (Princeton: Princeton University Press, 1995), for helpful explanations of the sexuation graph. See also pp. 137–46 and pp. 219–20.

26. For an example of a popular work on sexual difference which avoids the usual traps, see Darian Leader, *Why Do Women Write More Letters Than They Post?* (London: Faber & Faber, 1996), published in the United States as *Why Do Women Write More Letters Than They Send? A Meditation on the Loneliness of the Sexes* (New York: Basic Books, 1996).

27. Ellie Ragland, *Feminism and Psychoanalysis: A Critical Dictionary*, p. 206.

28. Carol Gilligan, *The Birth of Pleasure* (New York: Knopf, 2002).

29. The trilogy consists of: *L'Otage*, *Le Pain dur*, and *Le Père humilié*. In Paul Claudel, *Théâtre, II* (Paris: Gallimard, 1965), p. 567. See Lacan, *Le Séminaire VIII* (Paris: Seuil, 1991).

30. See Roudinesco, *Jacques Lacan & Co.*

31. Quoted in Kenneth Lewes, *The Psychoanalytic Theory of Male Homosexuality* (New York: Simon & Schuster, 1988), p. 33.

32. Noreen O'Connor and Joanna Ryan, *Wild Desires and Mistaken Identities: Lesbianism & Psychoanalysis* (New York: Columbia University Press, 1993).

33. Jane Gallop, *Thinking Through the Body* (New York: Columbia University Press, 1988), p. 124.
34. For balanced feminist perspectives on Lacan, see, for example, Elizabeth Grosz, *Jacques Lacan: A Feminist Introduction* (London: Routledge, 1990) and Sherry Turkle, *Psychoanalytic Politics: Freud's French Revolution* (New York: Guilford, 1992), as well as Tim Dean and Christopher Lane, *Homosexuality and Psychoanalysis* (Chicago: University of Chicago Press, 2001), and Claude-Noëlle Pickmann, "Féminisme et féminité: Vers une hystérie sans maître?" *La Clinique lacanienne* 2 (1997), pp. 65–84.

14

TIM DEAN

Lacan and queer theory

Lacan died before queer theory came into existence, though he surely would have engaged this new discourse – as he engaged so many others – had he lived to know about it. His psychoanalytic critique of ego psychology and of adaptation to social norms shares much in common with queer theory's political critique of social processes of normalization. Indeed, while queer theory traces its intellectual genealogy to Michel Foucault, it can be argued that queer theory actually begins with Freud, specifically, with his theories of polymorphous perversity, infantile sexuality, and the unconscious. Lacan's "return to Freud" involves rediscovering all that is most strange and refractory – all that remains foreign to our normal, commonsensical ways of thinking – about human subjectivity. Thus from an Anglo-American perspective, Lacan makes psychoanalysis look rather queer. By virtue of its flouting norms of all kinds (including norms of intelligibility), Lacanian psychoanalysis may provide handy ammunition for queer theory's critique of what has come to be known as heteronormativity.

The term "heteronormativity" designates all those ways in which the world makes sense from a heterosexual point of view. It assumes that a complementary relation between the sexes is both a natural arrangement (the way things are) and a cultural ideal (the way things should be). Queer theory analyses how heteronormativity structures the meaningfulness of the social world, thereby enforcing a hierarchy between the normal and the deviant or queer. In its understanding of how the categories of normal and pathological emerge in a mutually constitutive relation, queer theory draws on Foucault's revisionary account of modern power and, more specifically, on Georges Canguilhem's critical histories of nosology.[1] Foucault argues that power in the modern era can be distinguished by its operating productively (to proliferate categories of subjective being), rather than merely negatively (by prohibiting or suppressing types of behavior). Instead of a centralized, top-down model of power (which he calls juridical power), the nineteenth century witnessed the birth of what Foucault calls biopower, a more diffuse form of power that actively brings into existence modes of being through techniques of classification and normalization. Unlike juridical power, biopower is not invested in an individual (such as the king) or a group (such as landowners), but operates transindividually through discourse and institutions. Although Foucault's conception of discourse differs significantly from Lacan's, his transindividual notion of power nevertheless is somewhat homologous with Lacan's theory of the symbolic order: both represent transindividual structures that produce subjective effects independently of any particular individual's agency or volition.

One of Foucault's prime examples of biopower's operation is the late-nineteenth-century invention of the homosexual as a discrete identity, a form of selfhood. Before roughly 1870, Foucault contends, it was not really possible to think of oneself as a homosexual, no matter what kind of sex one had or with whom, because the category of homosexuality didn't yet exist. Once the homosexual had been named as a type of person characterized by a distinct psychology, however, sexual activity with a member of the same sex could be understood as not only a sin or a crime, but also a sickness and a deviation from the norm.[2] Through transformations such as this, modern power relies less on laws and taboos than on the force of social norms to regulate behavior. And, as the example of homosexuality suggests, processes of normalization depend heavily on forms of identity to ensure social control. The greater the diversification of subjective identities, the more securely power maintains its hold on us.

From Foucault's account of power it follows that one does not resist the forces of normalization by inventing new kinds of social or sexual identity, as many sex radicals in the United States still seem to believe. In the 1960s and 70s, political movements such as civil rights, women's liberation, and gay liberation developed around identity categories (Black, woman, gay, lesbian) to resist the status quo. Central to these movements was the work of consciousness raising, in which one learned how to actively identify as a member of an oppressed minority group. These forms of identity politics proved remarkably effective in generating large-scale social changes; yet their limitations stemmed from their faith in identity as the basis of political action. The critique of identity politics that emerged in the 1980s and 90s came from feminism (particularly psychoanalytic feminism) and from the grassroots response to the AIDS crisis. Public discourse early in the epidemic aggressively stigmatized the groups of people that first manifested AIDS mortalities, primarily injection-drug users and gay men. Right-wing politicians and the media characterized AIDS as a disease of identity – something you would catch because of the kind of person you were. AIDS was represented as a "gay disease" and even explained as divine punishment for unnatural sex, though lesbians weren't falling sick.

In response to this reactionary discourse, gay activists insisted that HIV (the virus that causes AIDS) was transmitted via particular acts, not via types of people, and that the notion of AIDS as a "gay disease" was dangerously misleading because it promulgated the idea that one remained immune to HIV-infection as long as he or she identified as a normal heterosexual. Gay activists started to see how the discourse of identity that had proven so enabling in the 1970s had its drawbacks, as the hard-won political gains of gay liberation were eroded by the new rationale that AIDS seemed to provide for disenfranchising gay men. Rather than gradually being accepted into mainstream society, gays abruptly were recast as plague-spreading sex deviates, along with junkies and non-white immigrant groups (such as Haitians) that showed a demographically high incidence of AIDS. Public discourse showed less concern for helping those ill with the disease than for protecting the "general population" that they might contaminate. As Simon Watney has shown in his analysis of media discourse about AIDS in Britain and the United States, the idea of a general population implies a notion of *disposable populations* in much the same way that the category of the normal defines itself in relation to the pathological, on which it necessarily depends.[3] Hence the "general population" can be understood as another term for heteronormative society. Those excluded from the general population – whether by virtue of their sexuality, race, class, or nationality – are by definition queer.

In this way, "queer" came to stand less for a particular sexual orientation or a stigmatized erotic identity than for a critical distance from the white, middle-class, heterosexual norm. Newly demonized gay men in the AIDS epidemic took up the pejorative epithet "queer" and embraced it as the label for a new style of political organization that focused more on building alliances and coalitions than on maintaining identity boundaries: an activism that ceded mainstream political campaigning in favour of shorter-term, more spectacular guerrilla tactics. Whereas gay liberation had placed its trust in identity politics, queer activism entailed a critique of identity and an acknowledgment that different social groups could transcend their identity-based particularisms in the interest of resisting heteronormative society. Thus while gay opposes straight, queer sets itself more broadly in opposition to the forces of normalization that regulate social conformity. Following Foucault's understanding of the disciplinary function of social and psychological identities, queer is anti-identitarian and is defined relationally rather than substantively. Queer has no essence, and its radical force evaporates – or is normalized – as soon as queer coalesces into a psychological identity. The term "queer" is not simply a newer, hipper word for being gay; instead it alters how we think about gayness and homosexuality. Its anti-identitarianism gives rise to both the promise and the risk that queer offers for progressive politics – the promise that we may think and act beyond the confines of identity, including group identity, and the risk that in doing so the specificities of race, gender, class, sexuality, and ethnicity might be overlooked or lost. Queer theory is the discourse that explores those promises and risks.

Having its political origins in the AIDS crisis, queer theory found its intellectual inspiration in the first volume of Foucault's *History of Sexuality* (1976), a treatise that concerns power more than it does sex. How we understand the relation between Lacan and queer theory depends to a significant extent on how we interpret Foucault's treatment of psychoanalysis in *The History of Sexuality*. Received academic opinion maintains that Foucault's work provides a thoroughgoing critique of psychoanalysis, and many queer theorists have been quick to dismiss Lacanian thought as unremittingly heteronormative. Conversely, from a Lacanian vantage point, Joan Copjec has shown very persuasively the basic incompatibility between Lacan's methodology and forms of historicism derived from Foucault.[4] Yet in spite of its disparaging remarks about psychoanalysis, *The History of Sexuality* presents an argument that in certain respects is cognate with a radical Lacanian perspective on sexuality. Without diluting the specificity of either Foucault or Lacan, it might be possible to read them together in a new way, to rearticulate their bodies of work for the purposes of queer critique.

Composed in a Lacanian milieu (though without ever mentioning Lacan's name), *The History of Sexuality* launches a polemic against what Foucault calls the repressive hypothesis. This hypothesis states that human desire is distorted by cultural constraints, which, once lifted, would liberate desire and permit its natural, harmonious fulfillment, thereby eliminating the various neuroses that beset our civilization. Picturing desire and the law in an antagonistic relation, the repressive hypothesis infers a precultural or prediscursive condition of desire in its "raw" state. Foucault – like Lacan – maintains that no such prediscursive state exists. Instead, desire is positively produced rather than repressed by discourse; desire follows the law, it does not oppose it. In 1963, more than a decade before *The History of Sexuality*, Lacan argued that "Freud finds a singular balance, a kind of co-conformity – if I may be allowed to thus double my prefixes – of Law and desire, stemming from the fact that both are born together" (*T*, p. 89). This affirmation comports well with Foucault's critique of the repressive hypothesis.

Hence although it is accurate to characterize *The History of Sexuality* as a critical historicization of psychoanalysis, it is important to distinguish which version of psychoanalysis Foucault's critique assails. This distinction is trickier than one might imagine, because Foucault rarely attributes proper names to the positions against which he is arguing. The liberationist strand of psychoanalysis whose reading of Freud recommended freeing desire from social repression stems primarily from the work of Wilhelm Reich and Herbert Marcuse – thinkers of whom Lacan was equally (though differently) critical. Reich and Marcuse were the psychoanalytic architects of the sexual revolution of the 1960s and 70s, a project whose claims provoked both Foucault's and Lacan's skepticism.[5] Foucault objects most strenuously to the way in which the idea of repression encourages us to think of desire as something that culture negates; and certainly Freud's account of the incest taboo's function in the Oedipus complex represents cultural imperatives as negating primordial desire. However, Foucault's critique of a naive conception of repression – repression considered as a purely external force – prompts him to argue against all formulae of negation where desire is concerned, and thus his polemic leaves little conceptual room for any consideration of negativity.

Despite Lacan's affirmation of the consubstantiality of law and desire, he and Foucault part ways on the question of negativity. This fundamental difference becomes evident when one recalls that the French title of Foucault's introductory volume is *La Volonté de savoir* (the will to know), a phrase his English translator deliberately elided in titling that book simply *The History of Sexuality: An Introduction*. Foucault's preoccupation with charting epistemophilia – the project to elicit the truth of our being by "forcing sex to speak," as he puts it – directly contrasts with Lacan's emphasis on "the will *not* to know," a formulation he uses to characterize the unconscious. While Lacan wants to reconceptualize the unconscious in de-individualized terms, Foucault wishes to rethink that which structures subjectivity in purely positive terms, without recourse to notions of repression, negation, or the unconscious.

Nevertheless, Foucault's descriptions of power often sound remarkably cognate with a Lacanian conception of the unconscious. For example, in an interview conducted in France shortly after the publication of *La Volonté de savoir*, Foucault explained, "What I want to show is how power relations can materially penetrate the body in depth, without depending even on the mediation of the subject's own representations. If power takes hold on the body, this isn't through its having first to be interiorized in people's consciousnesses."[6] Speaking here of a force that affects the human body without the mediation of consciousness, Foucault makes clear that by "power" he does not mean ideology. In this schema, power achieves its effects via routes distinct from those of identification, interpellation, or internalization. Foucault thus distances himself from the Marxist-Lacanian theory of power associated with Louis Althusser. Yet by marking the inadequacy of interpellation as an explanatory category, Foucault implies that power should not be apprehended in imaginary terms – that is, in terms of the ego and its dialectic of recognition/misrecognition. Instead, power operates similarly to a de-psychologized conception of the unconscious, insofar as it compromises the autonomy of the individual will and thereby undermines the humanist notion of the constituent subject. Indeed, as Arnold I. Davidson recently observed, "the existence of the unconscious was a decisive component in Foucault's *antipsychologism.*"[7]

This commitment to antipsychologism betokens what Lacan and Foucault share most fundamentally in common; it is what makes them both in their own ways suspicious of subjective identity. For Lacan identity represents an ego-defense, a ruse of the Imaginary designed to eschew unconscious desire. Thus from his perspective – and here he parts company with Foucault – the category of desire is not wedded to identity, but, on the contrary, threatens identity's closely regulated coherence. For Lacan desire is no longer a psychological category, since it is conceptualized as an effect of language – that is, as unconscious. Lacan depsychologizes the unconscious by considering it linguistic: "The unconscious is that part of the concrete discourse, in so far as it is transindividual, that is not at the disposal of the subject in re-establishing the continuity of his conscious discourse" (*E/S*, p. 49). In Lacanian thought, the unconscious does not exist *inside* individuals: it composes a crucial dimension of one's subjectivity without being part of one's mind. Hence the psychoanalytic theory of the unconscious introduces a constitutive division into human subjectivity that thwarts the possibility of any unified identity, sexual or otherwise.

By theorizing subjectivity in terms of language and culture, Lacan also denaturalizes sex. There is no natural or normal relation between the sexes, he insists: "*il n'y a pas de rapport sexuel.*" The axiomatic status in Lacanian doctrine of the impossibility of the sexual relation aligns this brand of psychoanalysis with queer theory's critique of heteronormativity. As do queer theorists, Lacan maintains that no natural complementarity between man and woman exists – and that, furthermore, such complementarity is not a desirable ideal either. Indeed, Lacan warned his fellow psychoanalysts about using the power of transference in the clinical setting to inculcate cultural ideals such as harmonious heterosexuality. He launched his sternest polemic against viewing the goal of analysis as "adaptation to reality," because this goal reduces clinical work to little more than the imposition of social norms. Lacan was aware of how misbegotten the social ideal of genital heterosexuality is, how readily it functions as a normative requirement of adaptive therapies. As he scoffed in the *Ethics of Psychoanalysis*, "Goodness only knows how obscure such a pretension as the achievement of genital objecthood [*l'objectalité génitale*] remains, along with what is so imprudently linked to it, namely, adjustment to reality" (*S VII*, p. 293). Adaptation to reality and achieving genital heterosexuality go hand in hand as aspirations because, Lacan recognises, social reality is heteronormative. Since the purpose of Lacanian psychoanalysis is not "adjustment to reality," clinical work must take care to resist promoting heteronormativity. Earlier in the same seminar, Lacan is quite explicit about this danger, noting that "strengthening the categories of affective normativity produces disturbing results" (*S VII*, pp. 133–4). It is significant that Lacan emphasizes the potential dangers of abusing therapeutic power in his Seminar on *Ethics*, because he thus makes clear that far from operating as an agent of social normalization, psychoanalysis should consider its work as resisting normalization. Lacan's ethical critique of subjective adaptation marks his theory's distance from Foucault's representation of psychoanalysis as a normalizing institution.

But in denaturalizing sex and sexuality, Lacan suggests more than the comparatively familiar idea that sex is a social construct. Psychoanalytic antinaturalism does not boil down to mere culturalism. Rather, his account of how discourse generates desire specifies more precisely the function of negativity in creating human subjectivity. Lacan locates the cause of desire in an object (*l'objet petit a*) that comes into being as a result of language's impact on the body, but that is not itself discursive. The *objet petit a* is what remains after culture's symbolic networks have carved up the body, and hence the object reminds us of the imperfect fit between language and corporeality. Refusing the category of the prediscursive as a misleading fiction, Lacan argues that the object-cause of desire is *extradiscursive* – something that cannot be contained within or mastered by language, and therefore cannot be understood as a cultural construct. This distinction between the prediscursive and the extradiscursive is crucial for grasping the difference between Lacan and Foucault, since Foucauldian epistemology has no conceptual equivalent of the category of extradiscursivity. Foucault's theory of discourse, which so effectively accounts for the operations of power, fails to distinguish the prediscursive from what exceeds language's grasp.

By elaborating this distinction, Lacan provides a novel anti-identitarian account of desire. His concept of the object remains central to his demonstration that in its origins desire is not heterosexual: desire is determined not by the opposite sex but by *l'objet petit a*, which necessarily precedes gender. Lacan's theory of the object revises both the Freudian notion of sexual object-choice (in which the object is assumed to be gendered) and object relations theories that succeeded Freud (principally in the work of Melanie Klein and D. W. Winnicott). Lacan develops his theory of the object from Freud's ideas about polymorphously perverse sexuality and component instincts – that is, he develops Freudian theory beyond Freud's own conceptual impasses. In his *Three Essays on the Theory of Sexuality*, Freud claimed that the peculiar temporality of human sexual life compelled him to conclude that the instinct has no predetermined object or aim: "It seems probable that the sexual instinct is in the first instance independent of its object; nor is its origin likely to be due to its object's attractions" (*SE* 7, p. 148). By invalidating the popular notion that erotic desire is congenitally oriented toward the opposite sex, this psychoanalytic insight poses a fundamental challenge to heteronormativity. And it is thanks to ideas such as this one – the instinct's original independence of its object – that Freud rather than Foucault may be credited as the intellectual founder of queer theory.

In order to grasp Lacan's theory of *l'objet petit a* and how it deheterosexualizes desire, we need to consider further Freud's account of the sexual instinct and its contingent object. As his severing of the natural link between instinct and object implies, Freud disassembles the instinct into its components, arguing that the notion of a unified instinct in which the parts function together harmoniously on the model of animal instinct is a seductive fiction; it does not describe accurately how human instinctual life operates. There is no single, unified sexual instinct in humans, Freud maintains, but only partial drives, component instincts. Instinct is an evolutionary concept, a way of thinking about an organism's adaptation to its environment. For Freud, however, the human subject is constitutively maladapted to its environment, and the unconscious stands as the sign of this maladaption. Psychoanalytic thinkers after Freud have formalized the distinction between instinct and drive that remains somewhat inchoate in Freud's own work.[8] The distinction is particularly important in terms of the epistemological status of psychoanalysis, since drive theory tends to be taken as one of the most retrograde aspects of Freudianism, a mark of its essentialism. But in fact the instinct/drive distinction confirms Freud's departure from biologistic conceptions of sexuality. If instinct can be situated at the level of biological necessity, then drive is the result of instinct's capture in the nets of language, its having to be articulated into a signifying chain in any attempt to find satisfaction. Lacan spells out this distinction: "the instinct is the effect of the mark of the signifier on needs, their transformation as an effect of the signifier into something fragmented and panic-stricken that we call the drive" (*S VII*, p. 301).

Fragmented or partialized by symbolic networks, the drive is thereby *dis*oriented ("panic-stricken") in a manner that gives the lie to conventional notions of sexual orientation. The very idea of sexual orientation assumes that desire can be coordinated in a single direction, that it can be streamlined and stabilised. Another way of putting this would be to say that the idea of sexual orientation *disciplines* desire by regulating its *telos*. The notion of orientation – including same-sex orientation – can be viewed as normalizing in that it attempts to totalize uncoordinated fragments into a coherent unity. The conceptual correlate of orientation is sexual identity, a psychological category that conforms to the instinctual understanding of sex. Instinct, orientation, and identity are psychological concepts, not psychoanalytic ones. These concepts normalize the weirder psychoanalytic theory of partial drives and unconscious desire by unifying the latter's discontinuities into recognizable identity formations. The impulse to coordinate and synthesize is a function of the ego and betrays an imaginary view of sex. This is as true of the notions of homosexual orientation and gay identity as it is of heterosexual identity. Both straight and gay identities elide the dimension of the unconscious. As an orientation or identity, homosexuality is normalizing though not socially normative. In other words, while homosexuality is far from representing the social norm, as a minority identity it does conform to the processes of normalization that regulate desire into social categories for disciplinary purposes.

With this distinction in mind, we can begin to appreciate how Freud's radical claim that psychoanalysis "has found that all human beings are capable of making a homosexual object-choice and have in fact made one in their unconscious" does not go far enough in dismantling an identitarian view of sex.[9] The contention that everyone has made a homosexual object-choice in his or her unconscious undermines the notion of a seamless sexual identity, but without challenging the assumption that object-choice is determined by gender. For an object-choice to qualify as homosexual, it must represent a selection based on the similarity of the object's gender to that of the subject making the selection. This implies that the gender of objects still is discernible at the level of the unconscious, and that sexuality concerns recognizably "whole" objects, such as men and women (or at least masculine and feminine forms). But such assumptions are invalidated by Freud's own theory of partial drives, as well as by the concept of *objet petit a*, a kind of partialized object that Lacan derives from Freudian drive theory. In developing his concept of *objet petit a*, Lacan invokes the oral, anal, and scopic drives that Freud discusses in "Instincts and their vicissitudes" (1915), adding to Freud's incomplete list the vocatory drive (in which the voice is taken as an object). From the partial drives Lacan emphasises, one sees immediately that the gender of an object remains irrelevant to the drives' basic functioning. Indeed, throughout his work Lacan remained dubious about the idea of a genital drive, and he was less optimistic than Freud sometimes seemed concerning the possibility of subordinating the partial drives to genitality at puberty. Lacan never was prepared to concede unequivocally the existence of a genital drive. As he concluded late in his career, "[a] drive, insofar as it represents sexuality in the unconscious, is never anything but a partial drive. That is the essential failing [*carence*], namely the absence [*carence*] of anything that could represent in the subject the mode of what is male and female in his being."[10] The drives' partiality revokes heterosexuality at the level of the unconscious.

If, as far as the unconscious is concerned, it makes no sense to speak of heterosexual or homosexual object-choices, then a theory of subjectivity that takes the unconscious into account could be extremely useful from a queer perspective. Yet while Foucault's project to rethink power as intentional but nonsubjective introduces formulations that are homologous with a de-individualized understanding of the unconscious, queer theory generally has been reluctant to take on board any psychoanalytic categories except those of imaginary ego formation. Queer theorists have developed subtle analyses of heterosexual ego defenses, unpacking the various strategies that heterosexual identity employs to maintain its integrity. But the full potential of Lacan's radicalization of Freud has not yet been exploited by queer critique, which, in spite of its postmodernism, has tended to remain at a psychoanalytic level equivalent to that of Anna Freudianism. This disinclination to utilize Lacan may be explained in several ways, one of which has to do with the emphasis on psychic negativity that follows from understanding sexuality in terms of the unconscious and partial drives. Queer theory's social utopianism – its desire to create a better world – often carries over into a misplaced utopianism of the psyche, as if improved social and political conditions could eliminate psychic conflict.

Freud's partializing of the drive discredits not only the viability of sexual complementarity, but also the possibility of subjective harmony. In contrast to the functionality of sexual instinct, drive discloses the dysfunctionality of a subject at odds with itself as a result of symbolic existence. Characterized by repetition rather than by development, the drive does not necessarily work toward the subject's well-being. In fact, its distance from organic rhythms means that the drive insists at the level of the unconscious even to the point of jeopardizing the subject's life. For this reason, Lacan aligns the drive with death rather than life, claiming that "the drive, the partial drive, is profoundly a death drive and represents in itself the portion of death in the sexed living being" (*S XI*, p. 205). It bears repeating that the death drive is not an essentialist or organicist concept, since it derives from an inference about the effect of language on bodily matter; it is as *cultural* subjects that humans are afflicted with the death drive. There is no essential, inborn death drive; rather, the dysfunctional, antinaturalistic way in which partial drives fail to conduce toward life lends every drive an uncanny, death-like quality.

By conceptualizing human subjectivity in linguistic terms, Lacan divests Freud of the residual traces of biologism that persist in classical psychoanalysis. As part of this larger project, he develops psychic negativity – particularly the theory of the death drive – in terms of jouissance, a category technically absent in Freud's oeuvre. Primary among the many meanings that this strictly untranslatable French term may be said to evoke is that which lies "beyond the pleasure principle." Jouissance positivizes psychic negativity, revealing the paradoxical form of pleasure that may be found in suffering – for instance, the suffering caused by neurotic symptoms. As the death drive was for Freud, jouissance is an absolutely central concept for Lacan, though it too has been neglected in queer appropriations of French psychoanalysis. Queer theory, which has such an elaborate discourse of pleasure, shows little regard for what exceeds the pleasure principle. Although it emerged as a response to the AIDS crisis, queer theory has not shown itself especially adept at thinking about death as anything other than a terminus.[11]

This conceptual lacuna results in part from Foucault's extensive work on the meaning and role of pleasure in Greek culture. The second volume of his *History of Sexuality*, *The Use of Pleasure* (1984), examines how erotic and other pleasures became objects of Greek ethical thought – that is, how pleasure (specifically, *aphrodisia*) became a matter for debate and reflection centuries before it became a question of law or prohibition.[12] Part of what fascinates Foucault about Greek ethical discourse on pleasure is its difference from modern ideas about pleasure; in particular, he argues that although one's handling of pleasure in Greek culture was subject to discussion, pleasures were not understood as indices of one's identity. Greek ethical practice did not entail what Foucault calls a "hermeneutics of the self," that is, a process of self-decipherment based on one's erotic behavior. Skeptical about the deployment of theories of desire in understanding the self, Foucault counterposes to modern techniques of self-identification the elaborate Greek discourse on *aphrodisia*, in which self-fashioning didn't depend on uncovering the self's true desire. He thus develops an historical rationale for his introductory volume's polemic, which famously concludes that "the rallying point for the counterattack against the deployment of sexuality ought not to be sex-desire, but bodies and pleasures."[13]

By arguing against the potentiality of any theory of desire, Foucault is attempting to situate his account of sexuality firmly outside a psychoanalytic framework. In order to do so, he positions desire as an irremediably psychological category and, more improbably, implies that pleasure is a category somehow exterior to psychoanalysis. Foucault wants to suggest that pleasure remains epistemologically distinct from desire – that, as Arnold I. Davidson puts it, "although we have no difficulty talking about and understanding the

distinction between true and false desires, the idea of true and false pleasures . . . is conceptually misplaced. Pleasure is, as it were, exhausted by its
surface; it can be intensified, increased, its qualities modified, but it does not
have the psychological depth of desire."[14] From a psychoanalytic perspective, however, the distinction between true and false pleasures is precisely
what the concept of jouissance addresses. The elementary idea of subjective
division entails recognizing that one psychic agency may experience pleasure
at the expense of another – that pleasure or satisfaction at the level of the
unconscious may be registered as unpleasure by the ego.

Now the Freudian category of unpleasure is not exactly what Lacan means
by jouissance; neither should we understand it simply as an especially intense form of *aphrodisia*, since jouissance is not a subset of pleasure. Rather,
pleasure functions prophylactically in relation to jouissance, establishing a
barrier or limit that protects the subject from what Lacan calls jouissance's
"infinitude" – a limitlessness that can overwhelm the subject to the point
of extinction. Hence jouissance is not to be equated with the *petite mort* of
orgasm, since the latter confers a pleasure and a limit that helps regulate
jouissance. The existence of jouissance as infinitude – like the concept of the
death drive – remains an inference that Lacan draws from subjectivity's dependence on symbolic life: in the symbolic order, one's jouissance is always
already mostly evaporated. Thus Lacan develops Freud's notion of subjective
division in terms less of different parts of the mind (conscious, preconscious,
unconscious; ego, id, super-ego) than of a subject constitutively alienated
in the Other, where *Other* is understood not as another person or a social
differential, but as an impersonal zone of alterity created by language. For
Lacan there is no subject without an Other; and hence his theory of subjectivity de-individualizes our understanding of the subject, showing how
subject is far more than a synonym for *person*.

The significance of this reconception of subjectivity lies in how the jouissance of the Other complicates individual pleasure. Our existence as subjects
of language entails a self-division and loss of plenitude from which the Other
is believed to be exempt. Having lost something, I imagine the Other as enjoying it; or, to put this another way, correlative to any sense of subjective
incompleteness is the feeling that somebody somewhere has it better than
me. This is what Lacan means by his phrase "the jouissance of the Other" –
the suspicion that somebody else is having more fun than I am, and perhaps
that whole classes of people are better off than me. Elsewhere jouissance
appears unlimited, in contrast to the constrained pleasures that I am permitted to enjoy. Hence any experience of pleasure is intertwined with some
supposition about jouissance, specifically, the Other's jouissance. From this
it follows that a commitment to the individual "pursuit of happiness" (as the

US *Declaration of Independence* puts it) overlooks pleasure's dependence on the jouissance of the Other – and thus misconstrues the pursuit of pleasure as an issue of self-determination, rather than of one's relation to the Other.

Lacan's formulations concerning "the jouissance of the Other" are also useful for thinking about mechanisms of social exclusion, such as racism and homophobia. Slavoj Žižek has devoted many volumes to showing how ethnic intolerance, including its recent manifestations in eastern Europe, can be understood as a reaction to the Other's jouissance.[15] He argues that organizations of social and cultural life different from one's own, such as those maintained by other racial and ethnic groups, can provoke the fantasy that these groups of people are enjoying themselves at his or her expense. For example, the anti-Semite imagines that Jews have "stolen" his jouissance, while the white supremacist fantasizes that immigrants are overrunning his national borders, sponging off the government and enjoying entitlements that are rightfully his. This preoccupation with how the Other organizes his or her enjoyment helps explain the obsession with reviled social groups' sexual behavior, since although jouissance remains irreducible to sex it tends to be construed in erotic terms. The jouissance of different sexual groups – for instance, gays and lesbians – plays a significant role in how certain heterosexual fantasies are organized and can account for the violent reactions some straight people have to the very idea of homosexuality. Parents who believe that their child would be better off dead than gay may be caught in the fantasy of homosexuality as an infinitude of jouissance, a form of sexual excess incompatible with not only decency and normalcy but even life itself. Indeed, this is how AIDS often has been understood: death brought on by too much jouissance. As a reaction formation to jouissance, homophobia thus involves more than ignorance about different sexualities; it is unlikely to be eradicated via consciousness-raising or sensitivity-training.

I have suggested that the emphasis on pleasure in Foucault's genealogy of sexuality remains compromised by his neglecting its negative dimension, a negligence that follows as a consequence of his methodological insistence on thinking of power productively, in purely positive terms. But Foucault does come close to conceptualizing jouissance at one crucial moment in his first volume of *The History of Sexuality*. Less than five pages from the end of the book, Foucault claims that sexuality is imbricated with the death drive in as much as the deployment of sexuality has succeeded in persuading us that sex is so important as to be worth sacrificing one's life for the revelations it can impart: "The Faustian pact, whose temptation has been instilled in us by the deployment of sexuality, is now as follows: to exchange life in its entirety for sex itself, for the truth and the sovereignty of sex. Sex is worth dying for. It is in this (strictly historical) sense that sex is indeed imbued with the death instinct."[16] This remarkable passage provides another way to grasp the fundamentally psychoanalytic idea that for historical reasons we aim at jouissance through sex, even though jouissance comprehends more than what is meant by eros. Jouissance has as much to do with Thanatos as with Eros. Freud's separation of sexuality from genitality – a separation that decisively loosens the grip of heteronormativity on our thinking – was reconceived by Lacan in terms of jouissance and *l'objet petit a*. As the cause not the aim of desire, *objet a* deheterosexualizes desire by revealing its origin in the effects of language, rather than the effects of the opposite sex. His insistence that jouissance is not reducible to sex – like Foucault's demonstration of the historically contingent relation that sex bears to identity – represents another way of pointing to the comparatively incidental place of genitalia in sexuality.

Hence the Lacanian category of jouissance could be extremely useful to the kinds of analysis that interest queer theory. Unfortunately, however, Foucault's strategic account of pleasure has misled many US queer theorists into viewing pleasure optimistically, as if it weren't complicated by jouissance and could be extended without encountering anything but ideological barriers. In other words, queer theory's utopianism often pictures the obstacles to sexual happiness as wholly external, as if there were no *internal* limit to pleasure. (By "internal," I mean in the sense not of psychologically inside a person, but inside the mechanism of pleasure itself – the mechanism whereby pleasure is understood as inseparable from the Other's jouissance.) Developing a discourse about sex that focuses primarily on pleasure rather than on either biological reproduction or the reproduction of social norms remains a vital political enterprise. But it is awfully naive to imagine that sex could be a matter only of pleasure and self-affirmation, rather than a matter also of jouissance and negativity. If sex is to be understood in more than naturalistic terms, we will need to think about those forms of negativity that Freud named the unconscious and the death drive. To render political and cultural discourses on sex less naive would involve the considerable effort of reshaping those discourses according to psychoanalytic rather than psychological principles. This implies not a project of translating Anglo-American debates into Lacanian vocabulary, but the far more challenging enterprise of thinking about sex in terms of the queer logics that psychoanalysis makes available.

NOTES

1. See Georges Canguilhem, *The Normal and the Pathological* (1966) (New York: Zone Books, 1989).

2. Michel Foucault, *The History of Sexuality*, Volume 1: *An Introduction*, trans. Robert Hurley (New York: Random House, 1978), pp. 42–3.

3. Simon Watney, *Policing Desire: Pornography, AIDS, and the Media* (Minneapolis: University of Minnesota Press, 1987).

4. Joan Copjec, *Read My Desire: Lacan against the Historicists* (Cambridge, Mass.: MIT Press, 1994).

5. See Herbert Marcuse, *Eros and Civilization: A Philosophical Inquiry into Freud* (New York: Random House, 1955) and Wilhelm Reich, *The Function of the Orgasm: Sex-Economic Problems of Biological Energy*, trans. Theodore P. Wolfe (New York: Noonday Press, 1961).

6. Michel Foucault, "The history of sexuality" (interview with Lucette Finas), *Power/Knowledge: Selected Interviews and Other Writings, 1972–1977*, ed. Colin Gordon, trans. Colin Gordon, Leo Marshall, John Mepham, and Kate Soper (New York: Pantheon, 1980), p. 186.

7. Arnold I. Davidson, "Foucault, psychoanalysis, and pleasure," *Homosexuality and Psychoanalysis*, ed. Tim Dean and Christopher Lane (Chicago: University of Chicago Press, 2001), p. 44; original emphasis.

8. See *S XI*, esp. pp. 161–86; and Jean Laplanche, *Life and Death in Psychoanalysis*, trans. Jeffrey Mehlman (Baltimore: Johns Hopkins University Press, 1976).

9. Freud makes this claim in a 1915 addition to a famous footnote in his *Three Essays on the Theory of Sexuality* (*SE* 7, p. 145).

10. Jacques Lacan, "Position of the unconscious," trans. Bruce Fink, *Reading Seminar XI: Lacan's Four Fundamental Concepts of Psychoanalysis*, eds. Richard Feldstein, Bruce Fink, and Maire Jaanus (Albany: State University of New York Press, 1995), p. 276.

11. The principal exception to this general problem is Leo Bersani's work; see especially Bersani, "Is the rectum a grave?" *AIDS: Cultural Analysis/Cultural Activism*, ed. Douglas Crimp (Cambridge, Mass.: MIT Press, 1988), pp. 197–222.

12. Michel Foucault, *The History of Sexuality*, Volume 2: *The Use of Pleasure*, trans. Robert Hurley (New York: Random House, 1985).

13. Michel Foucault, *The History of Sexuality*, Volume 1: *An Introduction*, p. 157.

14. Davidson, "Foucault, psychoanalysis, and pleasure," p. 46.

15. See, for example, Slavoj Žižek, *For They Know Not What They Do: Enjoyment as a Political Factor* (New York: Verso, 1991).

16. Michel Foucault, *The History of Sexuality*, Volume 1: *An Introduction*, p. 156.

15

CATHERINE LIU

Lacan's afterlife: Jacques Lacan meets Andy Warhol

Jacques Lacan is a thinker and clinician whose apprehension of recording and broadcast media allows him to live on posthumously with the pop star status he gained in post-war Parisian intellectual life. He is not only a serious rival to the official heirs of Freud, but has emerged as a rival of that other superstar, Jean-Paul Sartre. The history of his exclusion (or excommunication)[1] from the International Psychoanalytic Association, and his subsequent notoriety is crucial for the theorization of his reception in Anglophone academia: there is an aura of transgression, or the smell of sulfur surrounding the sovereignty of his actions and thinking. His insistence on the signifier is key to an undoing of a humanist hermeneutics that swaddled more orthodox receptions of Freud. In addition, Lacan's interest in cybernetics seems to anticipate the plague of questions raised by technological progress. The reactions to his deviation from psychoanalytic orthodoxies revealed the religious fervor with which the guardians of Freudianism tried to protect their territory. Today, Lacan's work continues to teach us lessons, not only about psychoanalysis, but about media and history as well.

Playing the master on the airwaves allowed for Lacan to perform as both charlatan and master – consider his performance in *Télévision*: his analytic attitude seemed like a posture of pure provocation of his more conservative colleagues. In his pedagogical performances, Lacan demonstrated that all forms of inter-subjectivity, whether mediated by transference or other forms of telecommunication, are based upon a bewitching mirage of reciprocity or mutual understanding. Using the insights of Structuralist linguistics and anthropology as the conditions for thinking through the question of "la pa-role," Lacan often stated the obvious: "To speak is first of all to speak to oth-ers" (*S III*, p. 36). In so doing, however, he emphasized the primary status of linguistic material and revealed the limitations of approaches that neglect it.

How can we "explain" or "unpack" Lacan? Laurence Rickels has taught us that the process of explanation involves the melancholic incorporation of a sovereign discourse that ends up digesting and doing violence to the unassimilable text by pre-chewing it for easier consumption. Moreover, Lacan's mapping of the four discourses (of the master, university, hysteric, and analyst) invites the work of explanation to take up the discourse of the university. This discourse is the place where all forms of complexity and ambiguity are mapped onto the field of knowledge. The discourse of the university reproduces as a pale, domesticated double the uncanniness of the heterogeneous and the radically diverse. Michel de Certeau pointed the way out of this impasse and towards a historiography that, in its attentiveness to writing and history, demonstrates that it is possible to deal psychoanalytically with unruly subjects of study without wrestling them into submission in order to fulfill the institutional order of the day: it is his work that opened the path for what follows.

Warhol's Lacan

Putting Jacques Lacan and Andy Warhol together requires an explanation: even if it seems that their paths never crossed, the empirical non-encounter might give way to a conceptual intimacy that has yet to be excavated. While Lacan emerged as an intellectual apostate in the field of psychoanalysis who struggled against truisms of ego-psychology after being banished from the psychoanalytic bureaucracy, Warhol gained notoriety through his photo-silk screen works, which functioned as a seductive polemic against the notion of authenticity in the trace of the artist's hand and gesture. Both Lacan and Warhol were masters of image control, and they affirmed, albeit in very different ways, the radically mediated quality of intersubjectivity while refusing to concede a space of positive political activity, initiating a negative dialectics with regard to critical thinking that was both the subversion of and the radicalization of the Frankfurt School's engagement with mass culture. They attacked a modernist Utopia that was based in Lacan's case on the therapeutic, ego-psychological readings of Freud, and in Warhol's case on the institutionalization of Abstract Expressionism as high art. Is it mere coincidence that for both Jacques Lacan and Andy Warhol, 1964 proved to be an enormously significant year? In 1964, Lacan gave his first seminar after his official "excommunication" from the Société française de la psychanalyse, the SPF, and, by proxy, the International Psychoanalytic Association (IPA); this seminar redefined fundamental issues of Lacan's teaching, and was called *The Four Fundamental Concepts of Psychoanalysis*.[2] The year 1964 was also the one in which Andy Warhol had his first one-person show in New York City at the Leo Castelli Gallery, launching a career as an artist who brought popular culture into the making of "fine art" by affirming the saturation of the visual field with "lapidary iconography" of the commodity and imitating the techniques of mass production. Marcel Duchamp with his ready-mades had hailed the importance of the mass-produced object for contemporary art production, but he was mostly ignored by the painters of the New York School: Warhol took Duchamp's lessons further.

Lacan took issue with the International Psychoanalytic Association's emphasis on adaptation to the conditions of post-war existence that were increasingly streamlined according to a society of consumption – or life, American Style. It would seem as if Lacan and Warhol should be at loggerheads then, for one seems to refuse the happiness promised by American, consumerist versions of therapeutic psychoanalysis while the latter seems to produce an art that was ready-made for consumer culture. Benjamin Buchloh argues for the rigor of Warhol's polemical position against the elitism of high modernist Abstraction. Buchloh demonstrates that Warhol was able to overcome the compromise formations in the work of Robert Rauschenberg and Jasper Johns whose collage technique and citations of commodity culture appear coy and precious next to Warhol's all-out affirmation of the mass produced image's invasion of the picture field.[3] We cannot separate Warhol's productivity from the Factory, which provided unique working conditions that he fully exploited. He told collectors outright that he did not make many of his paintings. He is supposed to have "bought" the idea of the Campbell's soup paintings from a willing seller. He testifies enthusiastically to his admiration for the creativity and energy of others, and speaks of himself as someone barely able to keep up with his dynamic cohorts: "I suppose I have a really loose interpretation of 'work' because I think that just being alive is so much work at something you don't always want to do. Being born is like being kidnapped."[4] But where others found a magical process of art-making in action, Warhol saw himself as being on the job, "Why do people think artists are special? It's just another job."[5]

The Factory was comprised of a group of ardent fans and followers who understood on some level that in attacking the foundations of high art, Andy was going to give the motley crew of aspiring rock stars from Long Island, the drug-addled heiresses, the petit bourgeois drag queens and frustrated butch dykes access to an enclave of artistic production that had hitherto included only straight, white, and sometimes closeted males. The notion of alternative access that Lacan promised was somewhat different: he offered his followers a reading of Freud that was punctuated by the advent of the signifier, and in so doing liberated psychoanalysis from the burden of an ossified orthodoxy based upon the normative constrictions of ego-psychology and its emphasis on connectedness, healthy relationships, etc.[6] Lacan and Warhol both affirm a subject whose submission to the laws of repetition renders its relationship to the sign (as both letter and icon) inexorable. Under the aegis of the commodity, the barred subjects of Lacanian psychoanalysis and contemporary art face down the conditions of desire in the field of the signifier.

An alternative psychoanalytic movement crystallized around Lacan's person and work, which bore the indelible imprint of his defiance and charisma. Before Sherry Turkle studied forms of life on-line, she undertook an investigation of the culture of French psychoanalysis during the seventies and eighties.[7] Turkle concludes that Lacan's emergence as the cult hero of a dissident movement spurred the dissemination of a culture of psychoanalysis in French culture in general. Turkle's definition of popular culture may be a bit vague (interviews with people from all walks of life seem to suffice as her raw material, and a sampling of newspaper coverage stands in for her work on mass media); she was nevertheless an important witness to the passionate conflicts and intense debates that raged in the Lacanian movement. Her account of the psychoanalytic civil war is corroborated by Elisabeth Roudinesco's work on the history of psychoanalysis in France. Under the star of Lacan, an enormous amount of work was accomplished, scandals ignited, passions inflamed, careers made and destroyed, people turned on and off. A transferential space of productivity crystallized around his person and this ambience inspired both madness and work.

Critical resistors

Benjamin Buchloh concludes that the political significance of Warhol's work must be grasped in an allegorically negative manner: before the work of the Pop master, the viewer of contemporary art can no longer deceive herself about the flimsy firewall between art and commerce. Warhol consigns the viewer to the tragic fate of the consumer:

> Warhol has unified within his constructs both the entrepreneurial world-view of the late twentieth-century and the phlegmatic vision of the victims of that world view, that of the consumers. The ruthless diffidence and strategically calculated air of detachment of the first, allowed to continue without ever being challenged in terms of its responsibility, combines with that of its opposites, the consumers, who can celebrate in Warhol's work their proper status of having been erased as subjects. Regulated as they are by the eternally repetitive gestures of alienated production and consumption, they are barred – as are Warhol's paintings – from access to a dimension of critical resistance.[8]

Warhol understood the conditions of contemporary art to be barred from critical resistance, and in affirming such a limit, he confronts the situation rather than shrinking from the contemporary conditions of art production. To understand Warhol's political importance as an artist, we must grasp his asceticism with regard to the possibility of critical resistance. The uncannily affirmative attitude he had toward mass culture on the one hand, and repetition and chance on the other allowed him to vacate artistic intentionality with the rigor of Cage, while going beyond him at the same time. In his mobilization of indifference and contingency, Warhol's hypnotized gaze was directed at the firmament of the mass-produced and degraded images whose tarnished aura he reproduced and celebrated. In Liz Kotz's reading of his *a: a novel*, she emphasizes that the publication of a transcription of conversations with Factory Superstar Ondine deploys the "ready-made" principle of art-making that Duchamp put into place earlier in the twentieth-century. According to Kotz, *a: a novel* captures the "continuous streaming of language" and the consistency of babble, ambiguity, and nonsense that characterizes oral communication.[9] The literary establishment rejected Warhol's novel as gibberish, refusing to acknowledge that the conceptual mechanisms of a Duchamp, a Cage, or an On Kawara might have an effect on the ideal of literary production as a heroic enterprise. Therefore, Warhol's work in general, but especially his literary work, is not apolitical in a simple way. By focusing exclusively on a process of painting that attacked the notions of creativity and originality, Warhol undermined the *popular* idealization of artistic production: therefore, his work and the way in which it is made launches a campaign of destruction against any idealization of creativity or intentionality. By refusing to edit the transcriptions of endless conversations he had with the speed-addled Ondine, he allowed the tape recorder and the transcriber to leave their mark on a work of literature whose radical openness to the accident, the slip-up, the typo, and the lapse of attention is predicated upon the indifference of a time-based medium: electro-magnetic tape. He allowed tape recording and its translation or transcription into text to have the final word in a process he did not hesitate to call "writing." *a: a novel* is therefore an anti-novel: it is a novel that aims at destroying lyricism by using low-tech gadgets to take James Joyce's "stream of consciousness" aesthetic literally.

Lacan and his lessons can be understood as political precisely because he too maintained a dandy's indifference (not unlike Warhol's "phlegmatic vision") and imperturbability before the events of May 1968. In "Radiophonie" Lacan elaborates upon his refusal of academic notions of pedagogy and his contempt for the idealization of political activism by recounting the following anecdote:

> I remember the uneasiness of a young man who wanted to be Marxist and had gotten mixed up with quite a few members of the (one and only) Party, the French Communist Party, who had showed up in strength (God knows why) as I was reading my paper on 'Dialectics of Desire and the Subversion of the Subject' . . .

He asked: 'Do you believe that you will have any sort of effect just by writing a few letters on the blackboard?' Such an exercise, however, had its effects: and I have the proof – my book, *Ecrits*, was turned down by the Ford Foundation . . . The Ford Foundation found that its pockets were not deep enough to help the publication and in fact thought that it was quite unthinkable to publish me. It is just that the effect I produce has nothing to do with communication of speech, but everything to do with a displacement of discourse.[10]

The Ford Foundation refused to fund the translation of *Ecrits* into English; in contrast, it had provided the funds for the translation of Heinz Hartmann's *Ego Psychology and the Problem of Adaptation*,[11] written by Hartmann in Vienna in the thirties and published in English in 1958. In this work, Hartmann asserts that the ego should not be seen as the site of conflict between super-ego and id, but rather as a function that allows compromise and accommodation of an unquestioned *reality* to take place. Lacan had nothing but contempt for Hartmann, who was president of the IPA during the years of his own marginalization, and so this rejection by the American foundation must have been doubly insulting. That he related this anecdote in a radio interview is all the more significant: wired as he was, he understood radio's function as a super-egoic voice. Radio transforms the voice into aural material that shakes us up because it seems to be audible everywhere, all at once. Lacan is chiding the leftist movement for its naïveté: the demand for "an immediate effect" is part of a fantasy of political efficacy and critical resistance. He is warning his interlocutors that American institutions have an invisible political effect on post-war intellectual life, censoring and policing the translation of texts and that Lacan himself is hardly on the side of power here. With the publication of Frances Stonor Saunders' *Cultural Cold War: The CIA and the World of Arts and Letters*,[12] we can no longer view the activities of these American philanthropic organizations as innocent: the Ford Foundation was engaged institutionally and ideologically with the Central Intelligence Agency in the dissemination of an imperialist vision of post-war Europe, re-formed and re-structured under American domination.[13] Lacan's position was one predicated on a double refusal: the first resists the Marxist call to immediate and effective action; the second resists reworking his writing to suit the standards of the Ford Foundation.

October revolutions

Rosalind Krauss has condemned the Lacanian account of subjectivity for its complicity in celebrating and affirming the febrile pleasures of visual and popular culture. Mobilizing Lacan's theorization of identification in relationship to the image, Joan Copjec and Slavoj Žižek inverted critical theory's relationship to popular culture.[14] Krauss charges that in this version of Cultural and Visual Studies, there is no possibility of arriving at critical resistance against a consumerist reception of the products of mass media. From Krauss' arguments, what critical resistance might be is unclear, but it is perhaps related to a distaste for the popular that is reflected in the magazine *October*, which became the materialist standard against which the work of Lacanians fell short. In a sense, she echoes Lacan's angry student, and her critique can be paraphrased very roughly as, "Do you think you can have a political effect by describing subjectivity as constituted by an identificatory relationship with the image?" Her mode of critique deploys the negativity of the Frankfurt School without, however, mention of Horkheimer or Adorno. She points out that often Cultural Studies offers nothing more than "a mythical recoding of popular culture." When she tries to offer an alternative to the infernal repetition of consumerism, however, her lessons become less compelling. She finds Cultural and Visual Studies to be neglectful of historical materialism: she offers critical resistance as a strategy that will put an end to the madness of repetition, mirroring, and mimesis that shapes the relationship between the academic discipline and consumer culture. Like "fetishism," the term "resistance" does double duty in the line of fire for Marxist and psychoanalytic discourses, playing the uncanny double agent of two entirely different accounts of determinism. Lacan's *Four Fundamental Concepts (S XI)* offers an account of the repetition (*automaton*) that occurs in language as chance (*tuché*). This affirmation of repetition is first and foremost a way in which the Lacanian analyst refuses to promise the attainment of the cure as the end of the repetition.

In Krauss' critique of Cultural Studies, the history of this academic discipline is all but ignored. Visual Studies shaped by Lacanian theory is the stand-in for a discipline that originated in Birmingham, England, shaped by the work of Raymond Williams and Stuart Hall. For Krauss, Lacanian theory and its reception in the United States has no history either. We shall discuss the consequence of neglecting the latter: the question of the former is outside the scope of this paper, but should be kept in mind when considering the broad strokes with which Krauss sketches her argument.

On one side of a certain political spectrum, it is considered an aberration that the university thinks about psychoanalysis or popular culture at all because the objects of academic knowledge should be consecrated by a tradition that seems nevertheless increasingly contingent. From the other side, popular culture's accessibility is opposed to the elitism of academic objects of study, objects of enigmatic aesthetic value, which the traditional critic serves as a kind of guardian and vestal virgin. Žižek, however, mines American popular culture for illustrations of the master's thinking. A method is at work here, and one that demands reflection. Is popular culture the mirror of psychoanalytic theory? For Rickels, California's specificity as a philosopheme and hieroglyph of modernity can only be read through psychoanalytic theory. For Žižek, there is no historical marker in place and even the rather obvious relationship between Hitchcock's Cold War sensibility and Lacan's relationship to Marshall-planned French academia are abjured in the name of pure theory.

Krauss concludes that the Lacanians have been conspiring with Cultural Studies and modernist aesthetics to produce global capitalism's most faithful minions, initiated into the pleasures of the dematerialized image, ready to take their full upright positions as competent and depoliticized consumers. It was never quite clear that psychoanalysis aspired to or was capable of offering a critique of capitalism: certainly the very status of critique and criticism should be slightly disturbed by the most radical aspects of the Freudian adventure. Lacan certainly acted more as a Baudelairean *agent provocateur* during the events of May 1968, but the radicality of his insistence upon a linguistic and Structuralist reading of the analytic relationship was often more performed than communicated. And the foment of those years certainly contributed to the risks he took in his pedagogical and analytical experiments.

When Lacanian lessons are idealized as lapidary aphorisms, we are doomed, like Žižek, to endless explanations. His are more brilliant than others, but no less symptomatic. It is no accident of course that explanation is the follower's lot, for under the star of Lacan and in the net of his transferential field, his most difficult, off-the-cuff, improvised statements are received as if they were comprehensible. This apprehension of Lacan forecloses on the material support of his lessons and the role that the tape recorder and transcriber have played in preserving his lessons. Krauss pays lip service to the importance of material supports and alludes to cultural changes that are related to "electronic media [that] are now reorganizing vast segments of the global economy,"[15] but she ignores the problem of electromagnetic tape. For Krauss, Cultural Studies suffers from a fundamental misunderstanding of visual material, and she sees the emphasis on identification and the mirror stage in psychoanalytically-based cultural theory as being continuous with the modernist refusal of textuality in the visual field. This visual turn and the cultural revolution it promises are symptoms for Krauss of the Academy's participation in the production of "freshly wrought, imaginary spaces in which subjects of the new cultural and social order might narratively (and phantasmatically) project themselves."[16] Krauss implicitly accuses Žižek, Copjec, and Norman Bryson of misreading Lacan because they privilege the realm of the imaginary over the realm of the symbolic, and in doing so, neglect the signifier, which Krauss describes as "foundational" for the constitution of the subject. *The Four Fundamental Concepts* is the place from which most academic Lacanians have derived a theory of subjectivity based upon a specific reading of the gaze, and this work has shaped much of the Anglophone reception of Lacan.[17]

It is impossible to decide who is right and who is wrong here: it is more important to grasp that in accusing the "Foucauldian and Althusserian Lacanians" of misunderstanding "material supports" Krauss ignores the omnipresent tape recorder and the transcription as the material support on which Lacan's teaching is based. For fear of belaboring the obvious, I must insist that the *Seminars* are no more and no less than the reconstitution of taped transcripts and lecture notes. Thus, what is important here is a continued displacement of the question of material support itself – the pseudo-contradiction between image and the signifier defers the very question of transmissibility and comprehensibility. Just as Warhol's novel was apprehended by the literary establishment as nothing more than gibberish, so have the enigmatic transcriptions of Lacan's seminars been received by his most fervent followers as enigmatic koans of a psychoanalytic Zen master. It is not my goal here to decide whether or not transcriptions transmit merely nonsense or surplus wisdom: what I would like to point out is that "blah blah blah" and a sage's parables may not be that far apart, when they persist as the residue of tape recording.

The other condition of material support is the emergence of an "underground" or alternative psychoanalytic milieu with a charismatic master at its center whose work and personality represent a certain relation of absolute openness to recording media. As the influential media theorist Friedrich Kittler has shown, the tape recorder was on all the time. Warhol's Factory offers us good lessons in understanding repetition, transferential space/time warping and acting out; Lacan's teaching also created an alternative space for psychoanalysis. In founding his own school, he too saw talented people gravitate into his sphere of influence, ready to work under his tutelage, inspired by his teaching. In Warhol's case, the Factory's denizens were inspired by Warhol's negative charisma and his uncanny ability to aid and abet them in making of themselves the very material of his work. Lacan's inspiration functioned in the same way because of an ethical position that he took with regard to the International Psychoanalytic Association on the one hand, and the language of psychoanalysis on the other. Warhol's ethical position with regard to originality and repetition implies, as we have shown, a certain asceticism that was inspiring in its own right. His ethical position is certainly at odds with a moral one – he was not interested in being *good* or even in being a good artist, and it often seemed at the end of his life that he was much more interested in success, fame, and money. He was ethically consistent: he espoused an admiration for Business Art, and never allowed himself to pretend that he was not just "working." His refusal of the "magic" originality of the artist and the aura of artistic production was both frightening and liberating.

For Gérard Pommier, Lacan's ethical position also allowed for an explosion of productivity:

> After the war, and the Berlin association's blindness towards or compromises with Nazism, psychoanalysis gained the ground lost in Germany only with great difficulty. On the other hand, Lacan's ethical position was enough to produce a significant expansion [of psychoanalysis] in France. Ethics . . . evokes Socratic courage, and more simply the strength that certain men have always had to stand up to imposture.[18]

Pommier is referring to Lacan's confrontation with the ego-psychological impostors who coveted Freud's position in the International Psychoanalytic Association after his death. Instead of mourning Freud, Hartmann and company filled in the void with the image of his daughter, Anna Freud, whose ego-syntonic take on psychotherapy shaped the agenda of Freudian associations that wanted her support. In the context of the anecdote from "Radiophonie," we can also apprehend Lacan's ethics as having something to do with his refusal to idealize immediacy in the political sphere.

The "live" performance of Lacan's seminars was captured and preserved obsessively. Friedrich Kittler has identified sound as the medium of the Real: portable technology of sound recording is what made possible the very dissemination of the Lacanian lessons. Kittler reminds us that the seminar was formed by Lacan's relation to the amplification and recording of his voice:

> Only tape heads are capable of inscribing into the real a speech that passes over understanding heads, and all of Lacan's seminars were spoken via microphone onto tape. Lowlier hands need then only play it back and listen, in order to be able to create a media link between tape recorder, headphones, and typewriter, reporting to the master what he has already said. His words, barely spoken, lay before him in typescript, punctually before the beginning of the next seminar.[19]

Lacan's feedback loop was plugged into the various low-tech media: the spontaneity and obscurity of his speech was guaranteed by the transcription that was made for his eyes only. His audience had to be all ears, or else smuggle in tape recorders of their own, which was more and more possible as reel-to-reel gave way to the portable cassette deck favored by Warhol in 1964[20] as the instrument with which he would write a novel, which he celebrated as his attempt at writing:

I did my first tape recording in 1964 . . . I think it all started because I was trying to do a book. A friend had written me a note saying that everybody we knew was writing a book, so that made me want to keep up and do one too. So I bought that tape recorder and I taped the most interesting person I knew at the time, Ondine, for a whole day.[21]

Gadget-lovers both,[22] Warhol and Lacan understood that writing and speaking had been permanently transformed by technological advances in recording media.

It seemed as if for a while, that Rosalind Krauss and *October* magazine accepted that a Žižekian version of Lacanian theory would overcome certain impasses reached by the neo-Marxist Ideologiekritik they had promoted. But in her 1996 critique, she concludes,

Cultural Studies has always proclaimed itself as revolutionary, the avant-garde operating within the Academy – as an insurgency – in the wake of the events of May 1968. Visual Studies has very little to do to map itself onto the model of its (Cultural Studies) model, since, as I have tried to suggest, that earlier model was already thoroughly dependent upon a certain nonmaterialist conception of the image: the image as fundamentally disembodied and phantasmatic. But whether this revolution is indeed an insurgency, or whether it – as an unexceptional case of 'cultural revolution' – serves an ever more technologized structure and helps acclimate subjects of that knowledge to increasingly alienated conditions of experience (both of them requirements of global capital) is a question we must continue to ask . . .[23]

Contemporary subjects need very little help from Cultural Studies to "acclimate" themselves to the strange weather of increasing alienation: in addition, "technologized structure" remains an unexamined evil in this version of the political situation. If Krauss' argument seems to fall apart here, it is precisely because it falls into a non-dialectical dogmatism that Žižek along with Fredric Jameson has identified as the constitutive limit of Theodor Adorno's work, where in trying to break through the "Hegelian self-transparency of notion, he remains thoroughly Hegelian . . ."[24] In her recourse to "social conditions" and "materialism," Krauss invokes these terms like a magical incantation and implies that there is a form of resistant critique that can work against the adaptation of subjects to technology, and in so doing struggle against global capitalism itself. It is self-evident in her argument that technology is a handmaiden of alienation and global capitalism. Thinkers such as Kittler and Žižek are able to address and play with vulgar materialism and its limits. It is no coincidence that both were educated in the former

Soviet bloc and that their disillusionment with materialist accounts of critical resistance and social conditions acted as inspiration to overcome the impasses reached by orthodox leftist notions of critique. It is one of the ironies of the end of the Cold War and certainly a sign of American victory that it is the American who serves up a lesson in Marxism and revolution to the former citizens of the Soviet bloc.[25]

Žižek performs a compelling analysis of representational democracy by demonstrating the unbearable abstraction of equality for subjects of such a state. He insists that the persistence of an irrational desire for a strong patriarchal figure in certain emerging nation states cannot be conjured away by the Enlightenment's magic wand, and criticizes the generalized application of a Western European political model for countries that could not bear the weakness of the Executive branch. Borrowing a page from Carl Schmitt and emphasizing Lacan's reading of Hegel's master/slave dialectic, Žižek is able to advocate a therapeutically correct form of constitutional monarchy for the emerging democracies of Eastern Europe and beyond.

For Kittler, the states of emergency and states of exception evoked by war-time produce the greatest leaps in technological innovation while technical media are mapped onto the Lacanian schema of Symbolic, Imaginary, Real: the typewriter is the medium of the Symbolic, film the medium of the Imaginary and sound recording the medium of the Real.[26] Great leaps forward in technological progress are based upon a war-time psychology of shortages and extreme measures. From telegraph to radar, sonar, rocket technologies, and the Internet (a by-product of the Cold War), Kittler shows that innovation always takes place under duress. He underlines what Žižek, Krauss, and Cultural and Visual Studies miss when they intellectualize mass media and popular culture by making it the bone of academic contention:

> Technical media have neither to do with intellectuals nor with mass culture. They are strategies of the Real. Storage media were built for the trenches of World War I, transmission media for the lightning strikes of World War II, universal computing media for the SDI: *chu d'un désastre obscur*, as Mallarmé would have it, fallen from an obscure disaster. Or, as General Curtis D. Schleher put it in his Introduction to Electronic Warfare: 'It is a universally accepted military principle that the victory in every future war will be on the side which can best control the electro-magnetic spectrum.'[27]

Star quality

The very possibility of teaching critical resistance seems to rest upon a notion of communication that Lacan seeks to undermine. Lacan has formulated most forcefully the ways in which "disinterested communication is ultimately only failed testimony, that is, something upon which everybody is agreed" (*S III*, p. 38). The difficulty of Lacanian formulations lends itself to a certain kind of obsessional explication, whether it be through endless "introductions" or brilliant demonstrations that scan the multifarious narratives and images of popular culture for the example and the illustration that will unlock the enigmatic formulations of the master. Slavoj Žižek has overcome the difficulty of Lacan's lessons by making the material of the Lacanian example the very stuff of popular culture itself. After reading enough Žižek, it might appear that academic Lacanianism was the very addressee of popular culture itself. If one does not recognize the Lacanian aphorism that Žižek is putting to the test, one recognizes more easily the examples that he chooses to cite – and identifies with the jubilation of his powers of interpretation. Ranging from film noir to science fiction, from Hitchcock to Stephen King to the advertising jingle, Žižek has made popular culture the material of the Lacanian lesson and offered a certain kind of initiation into the master's teaching. He is not only involved with the smuggling of contraband or the degraded objects of popular culture into the halls of academia, his approach aspires to free us of a certain mode of leftist or materialist critique that has proven radically incapable of accounting for the pleasures and complexities of mass-media constructions of the gaze and the contingency of subject formation.

Žižek's account of transference and intersubjectivity is derived from Hitchcock's films and the logic of how "we effectively become something by pretending that we already are that. To grasp the dialectic of this movement, we have to take into account the crucial fact that this 'outside' is never simply a 'mask' we wear in public but is rather the symbolic order itself."[28] The affirmation of masks and superficiality in all its forms is a direct attack on high modernist notions of esthetic sublimity in both gesture and representation. In an interview with Gretchen Berg, Warhol said: "If you want to know all about Andy Warhol, just look at the surface of my paintings and films and me, and there I am. There's nothing behind it."[29] Lacan launched an attack on the notion of authenticity in intersubjectivity: the beginnings of work on the gaze would lead him to theorize the superficiality of the subject in terms of topography. The surface, skin, or inscriptional support for the signifier became a liminal space of difference and differentiation upon which the signifier would make itself legible. Topography and the matheme become the enigmatic formulae of a kind of subjectivity without depth. He, like Warhol, attracted to his person, because of his personal charisma, a group of ardent followers who would represent the Lacanian movement, a dissident form of psychoanalysis that would be called the Ecole freudienne de Paris. In Žižekian terms, the by-product of Warhol's flatness would be the transferential field of magical attraction, or *objet petit a*.

Both Krauss and Žižek seem to understand Lacan, albeit for very different purposes. Krauss' rehearsal of Lacanian gaze theory goes off without a hitch. If one re-reads the actual seminars on the gaze, things become much more ambiguous. Žižek's famous rhetorical move often begins, "Is it not obvious that . . .?" seducing us with an example taken from everyday life in juxtaposition with some Lacanian paradox. For Lacan himself, ambiguity is a condition of language: Jean-Michel Rabaté has shown that this is one of the reasons why Lacan favored literature as a way of thinking through and resolving difficult problems.[30] We can also recognize that transcription captures the spontaneity of the improvised and the extemporaneous in a pedagogical performance: often, the process of decontextualization itself provides Lacan's pronouncements with an aura of enigmatic complexity. Of course, the process of editing a transcription adds another layer of complexity to the attempts to reconstitute the unpredictability of the pronouncement. Warhol was correct to try to "write" by tape recorder.

The confusion of words, the unaccountability of certain turns of phrase make understanding what Lacan says very difficult. Lacan shows, in *Seminar III*, *The Psychoses*, that the *précieuses* of the seventeenth century tried to refine a language of the salons that would be a mark of their elite status, but certain expressions that they innovated, such as "le mot me manque,"[31] have passed into everyday, contemporary French. He then goes on to talk about how much confusion there is about words and their meanings. This takes place in the context of a discussion of Schreber's memoirs and Freud's reading of them. The psychotic's slippery relationship to meaning and complexity is shown to be on a continuum with confusions of everyday usage:

> The state of a language can be characterized as much by what is absent as by what is present. In the dialogue with the famous miracled birds you find funny things . . . – who among you has not heard *amnesty* and *armistice* commonly confused in language that is not especially uneducated? If I asked each of you in turn what you understand by *superstition*, for example, I'm sure that we would get a fair idea of the confusion that is possible in your minds on the subject of a word in current usage – after a while, *superstructure* would end up appearing.
> (*S III*, pp. 115)

Kristin Ross has pointed to the French denial of complicity with colonial conflict after the Algerian War and has added a new dimension to our understanding of the post-war French situation; however, her condemnation of certain intellectual positions does not take into account the fact that responding to a historical situation often takes place in a deferred manner.[32] In 1957, the year of the *Seminar on Psychoses*, the year of the Battle of Algiers, Lacan was working on Schreber's account of his psychotic break with reality. After weeks of being unable to sleep, he gave in to the fantasy that he was being transformed into a woman so that he could have sex with God and thereby prevent the destruction of the world. If Lacan was talking about war in the *Seminar on Psychoses*, it was the intra-subjective conflict of the psychotic however and it had everything to do with securing the boundaries of one's identity. Lacan was indeed talking about war in the *Seminar on Psychoses*; it was just not the kind of war that Ross would have recognized.

The difficulty of the Lacanian seminars is legendary, but the obscurity of his language acquired a kind of radiance all its own. Claude Lévi-Strauss reminisces about attending Lacan's first seminar in 1964 at the Ecole normale supérieure:

> What was striking was the kind of radiant influence emanating from both Lacan's physical person and from his diction, his gestures. I have seen quite a few shamans functioning in exotic societies, and I rediscovered there a kind of equivalent of the shaman's power. I confess that, as far as what I heard went, I didn't understand. And I found myself in the middle of an audience that seemed to understand.[33]

The magic that Žižek ascribes to *objet petit a* is obviously what is produced by Lacan himself. Understanding the difficulty of the master is the magic that the master creates for his most devoted interlocutors and followers. According to Žižek,

> The Lacanian name for this by-product of our activity is objet petit a, the hidden treasure, that which is 'in us more than ourselves,' that elusive, unattainable X that confers upon all our deeds an aura of magic, although it cannot be pinned down to any of our positive qualities . . . The subject can never fully dominate and manipulate the way he provokes transference in others; there is always something 'magic' about it.[34]

This magic that is beyond our grasp is also one of the material conditions of Lacan's aura. For if Lévi-Strauss testified to his incomprehension, he also saw that his fellow audience members were captured by incomprehensibility, seemed to understand in order to stand in the auratic circle.

Lacan and Warhol also put into practice, at least for a time, a kind of radical affirmation and permissiveness with regard to the fans who because of their growing notoriety were attracted to their persons. There are many accounts of the early Factory, but McShine's is perhaps the most succinct:

> In addition to serving as a studio, the Factory became Warhol's own Hollywood set, and the maestro found himself surrounded by a coterie of acquaintances and friends: jeunesse (some dorés, some tarnished), glamorous transvestites, eager dealers, avid collectors, avant-garde matrons of New York society, prescient young curators, precocious pets and the cunning curious. This cast became the subject of his films . . . Surrounded by the 'beautiful people' and intrigued by his own drawing power, Warhol regarded himself as director and impresario both within and outside the Factory, with the power to invent 'superstars.'[35]

In Roudinesco's description of Lacan's *cabinet* after the founding of his school, the EFP, we can see a peculiar similarity between the two scenes:

> . . . [T]he door at the rue de Lille was open to anyone and without appointment: to members and non-members, to analysands and the 'sick,' to robbers, thugs, psychotics, and the troubled . . . In sum, anyone could show up at his home to discuss absolutely anything . . . Very early on, Lacan contracted the habit of no longer giving appointments at fixed times. He was unable to refuse anyone and anyone could come to his sessions according to his whim or need. The Doctor's house was an immense asylum in which one could move about freely, its doors open from morning to night, among first editions, artistic masterpieces, and piles of manuscripts.[36]

The chaos of their semi-public, semi-private spaces of work and speculation is predicated on the question of the experiment: for Lacan as for Warhol, the question of the unpredictable became a factor of everyday life and everyday work. Age and a confrontation with mortality would decrease their openness, but in the early sixties, the anti-institutionality of their work-sites presents a Utopic idea of work that was more speculative than practical.

Friedrich Kittler highlights Lacan's relationship to recording devices as a condition of the master's difficulty; what the Lévi-Strauss anecdote reveals is the quality of the listening: Lacan's rapt interlocutors also had an effect upon the master's pronouncements. The listening was hardwired to the magic of the Lacanian charisma. That is, Lacan was not only speaking to the tape heads: his performance was a performance for those who bathed in the enjoyment of understanding the incomprehensible.

Both Warhol and Lacan were working through ideas about the principle of repetition, albeit in fantastically different spaces: for Lacan, Freud's theories of repetition had to be amplified by an insistence on the signifier. In order to reinvest language with the radical contingency of the signifier, Lacan undoes the everyday notion of communication by showing that the clinic is a space of exchanges that are irreducible to interpretation on the level of meaning alone. This ostensibly modest lesson, unassimilable by mainstream psychoanalysts, has reshaped certain areas of literary and cultural studies. For Warhol, painting became a space where low-tech strategies of repetition such as silk-screening would replace the authenticating gesture of the artist's hand. Shortly after the success of his first one-man show in New York City, Warhol "retired" from painting.[37] Both Lacan and Warhol represent different faces of masterful opacity in their relationship to recording devices: one baffles because of the complexity of his recorded speech, the other because of the simplicity of his utterances (often punctuated merely by the word "wow"). Both, however, understand that a certain detachment with regard to repetition is necessary in the age of mechanical reproduction, when the effects of the political can only be registered in a negative way.

The subject of popular culture and mass media is the barred subject of politics: the condition of its powerlessness is transformed by its momentary consecration as an object of knowledge. In pointing to the increasing sophistication of consumption of popular culture in academic discourse, Krauss isolates a problem with Cultural and Visual Studies, but what she misses is the institutional frame of her own arguments. A more "correct" reading of Lacan makes no difference in the application of his theories if the historiography of Lacanian reception is neglected. In any case, the legacy of Lacan continues to provoke thought and debate, and his lessons and his career can be analyzed in terms of the allegorical missed encounter with his contemporary, Andy Warhol. The Frankfurt School took the criticism of enjoyment to its very limit by demonstrating that mass culture offered a miniaturized outlet for libidinal release. "Fun" becomes the name of the diminished pleasures that are offered to us. Along with "fun" comes an enervated political sphere.

Criticism is a word related to crisis: the saturation of the visual field with mass-produced images and the technologization of the archives have both led to a crisis in the university itself. Cultural Studies tries to make studying more "fun" by offering easy transgressions of disciplinary and institutional boundaries. Is this perhaps its fatal error? If it is, Krauss' corrective seems no more effective at addressing the critical situation in which we find ourselves. She wants to be more correct than her colleagues, whom she denounces as having offered a false promise of revolution: in so doing, she plays her super-egoic role with gusto, and acts as the fierce guardian of a political orthodoxy whose territoriality can only subsist and persist within the confines of the university. How can we renounce such Pyrrhic victories in order to promote a more experimental, more generous kind of thinking and engagement with history, theory, and aesthetic production? Lacan taught that the discourse of the university is indeed doomed to slavishness, which as we know, has its own pleasures.

LIBRARY, UNIVERSITY OF CHESTER

NOTES

1. See the dossier on "excommunication" in *Television: A Challenge to the Psychoanalytic Establishment*, trans. Denis Hollier, Rosalind Krauss, and Annette Michelson, ed. Joan Copjec (New York: W. W. Norton, 1990).
2. The seminar was given in 1964. The text of the seminar was published in 1973 as *Le Séminaire XI. Les quatre concepts fondamentaux de la psychanalyse* (Paris: Seuil).
3. Benjamin Buchloh, "Andy Warhol's one-dimensional art: 1956–1966," *Andy Warhol: A Retrospective* (New York: Museum of Modern Art, 1989).
4. Andy Warhol, *The Philosophy of Andy Warhol (From A to B and Back Again)* (San Diego:Harcourt Brace, 1975), p. 96.
5. Warhol, *The Philosophy of Andy Warhol*, p. 178.
6. Heinz Hartmann, *Ego Psychology and the Problem of Adaptation* (New York: International Press, 1958).
7. Sherry Turkle, *Psychoanalytic Politics: Jacques Lacan and Freud's French Revolution*, 2nd edn. (New York: Guilford Press, 1992).
8. Buchloh, "Andy Warhol's one-dimensional art: 1956–1966," p. 57.
9. See Liz Kotz, "Words on Paper Not Necessarily Meant to Be Read as 'Art': Postwar Media Poetics from Cage to Warhol" (PhD dissertation, Columbia University, 2001), especially "Conclusion: An aesthetics of the index?" pp. 350–62.
10. Jacques Lacan, "Radiophonie," *Autres écrits* (Paris: Seuil, 2001), p. 407.
11. Heinz Hartmann, *Ego Psychology and the Problem of Adaptation* (New York: International Universities Press, 1958).
12. Frances Stonor Saunders, *The Cultural Cold War: The CIA and the World of Arts and Letters* (New York: New Press, 2000).
13. Edward H. Berman's *The Influence of the Carnegie, Ford and Rockefeller Foundations on American Foreign Policy* (Albany: State University of New York Press, 1983) provides a detailed account of the ways in which the philanthropic organizations, under the rubric of "world peace" studies, worked closely with government agencies to further the agenda of Cold War American foreign policy: foreign students were supported as were foreign elites, specific topics of research encouraged, others dismissed.
14. Laurence Rickels has, throughout his work, insisted upon the radical compatibility of psychoanalysis with mass media, technology and popular culture, but his inversion of the hierarchies of critical theory has proven less consumable than Žižek's: his work on modernity, California, and perversion is more historical and is entirely involved with Freud rather than Lacan. Lacan proves more *popular* with Anglophone theorists of popular culture.
15. Rosalind Krauss, "Welcome to the cultural revolution," *October* 77 (Summer 1996), p. 84.
16. Krauss, "Welcome to the cultural revolution," p. 84.
17. See *Visual Culture: Images and Interpretation*, eds. Norman Bryson, Michael Ann Holly, and Keith Mosey (Hanover and London: Wesleyan University Press, 1994).
18. Gérard Pommier, *La Névrose infantile de la psychanalyse* (Paris: Point Hors Ligne, 1989), pp. 62–3. Author's translation.

19. Friedrich Kittler, "Dracula's Legacy," in *Literature, Media, Information Systems*, ed. John Johnston (Amsterdam: OPA, 1997), pp. 50–1.
20. For more on Warhol's relationship to his tape recorder, see Peter Krapp, "Andy's wedding: Reading Warhol" in *Sensual Reading: New Approaches to Reading in its Relations to the Senses*, eds. Michael Syrotinski and Ian MacLachlan (Lewisburg, Pa: Bucknell University Press, 2001), pp. 295–310.
21. Warhol, *The Philosophy of Andy Warhol*, pp. 94–5.
22. See Laurence Rickels, *The Case of California* (Minneapolis: University of Minnesota Press, 2001).
23. Krauss, "Welcome to the cultural revolution," p. 96.
24. Slavoj Žižek, *Enjoy Your Symptom! Jacques Lacan in Hollywood and Out* (New York: Routledge, 1992), pp. 83–4.
25. I must thank my students in the Basic Seminar class of Fall 1999 at the University of Minnesota for bringing this point home to me.
26. Friedrich Kittler, "Gramophone, Film, Typewriter," *Literature, Media, Information Systems*, ed. John Johnston (Amsterdam: OPA, 1997), p. 45.
27. Friedrich Kittler, "Media wars," *Literature, Media, Information Systems*, ed. John Johnston (Amsterdam: OPA, 1997), pp. 128–9.
28. Slavoj Žižek, *Looking Awry: An Introduction to Jacques Lacan through Popular Culture* (Cambridge, Mass.: MIT Press, 1991), pp. 73–4.
29. Gretchen Berg, "Andy: My True Story," *Los Angeles Free Press* (17 March 1967), p. 3. Quoted in Buchloh, "Andy Warhol's one-dimensional art: 1956–1966," p. 39.
30. Jean-Michel Rabaté, *Jacques Lacan* (New York: St. Martin's Press, 2001), p. 12.
31. This can be translated loosely as "language fails to do justice to . . ." or "I do not have the words for . . ." or more literally, "I am missing the word for . . ."
32. Kristin Ross, *Fast Cars, Clean Bodies: Decolonization and the Reordering of French Culture* (Cambridge, Mass.: MIT Press, 1998).
33. Claude Lévi-Strauss, "Entretien avec J.-A. Miller and A. Grosrichard," in *L'Ane* 20 (January-February, 1985). Quoted in Elisabeth Roudinesco, *Jacques Lacan & Co.: A History of Psychoanalysis in France, 1925–1985*, trans. Jeffrey Mehlman (Chicago: University of Chicago Press, 1990), p. 362.
34. Žižek, *Looking Awry*, p. 77.
35. Kynaston McShine, "Introduction" in *Andy Warhol: A Retrospective* (New York: Museum of Modern Art, 1989), p. 18.
36. Roudinesco, *Jacques Lacan & Co.*, pp. 418–19.
37. McShine, "Introduction," p. 18.

FURTHER READING

Works by Lacan

A detailed chronological list of Lacan's publications and Seminars (with their transcriptions) is available in Elisabeth Roudinesco's *Lacan*, pp. 511–34. Since the focus of this Companion is on English translations, the texts quoted here are available in English. I quote all the titles of the Seminars (one can find a useful summary of Lacan's works in Marcelle Marini, *Jacques Lacan: The French Contexts*, trans. Anne Tomiche (New Brunswick: Rutgers University Press, 1992), pp. 139–249. There is an unpublished and unauthorized English translation of all the Seminars by Cormac Gallagher. The dates given in parentheses in the first section are those of the original publications or, in the case of the Seminars, of the date on which they were held. I do not list the texts that are available in *Ecrits: A Selection*.

(1932) *De la psychose paranoïaque dans ses rapports avec la personnalité, suivi de Premiers écrits sur la paranoïa* (Paris: Seuil, 1975).
(1946) "Logical time and the assertion of anticipated certainty" ("Le temps logique et l'assertion de certitude anticipée") also in *Ecrits*, pp. 197–213, translated by Bruce Fink and Marc Silver, *Newsletter of the Freudian Field* 2 (1988), pp. 4–22.
(1952) "Intervention on transference" ("Intervention sur le transfert") also in *Ecrits*, pp. 215–226, translated by Jacqueline Rose in *Feminine Sexuality, Jacques Lacan and the école freudienne*, edited Jacqueline Rose and Juliet Mitchell (New York: Norton, 1985) pp. 61–73.
(1953) "Some reflections on the Ego," *International Journal of Psychoanalysis* 34, pp. 11–17.
(1953) "The individual myth of the neurotic, or poetry and truth in neurosis" ("Le Mythe individuel du névrose"), repr. in *Ornicar?* 17–18, 1978, translated by Martha Evans, *Psychoanalytic Quarterly* 48, 1979.
(1953–54) *Seminar I: Freud's Papers on Technique* (published in French by Seuil, *Les Ecrits techniques de Freud*, 1975), edited by Jacques-Alain Miller, translated and annotated by John Forrester (New York: Norton, 1998).
(1954–5) *Seminar II: The Ego in Freud's Theory and in the Technique of Psychoanalysis* (published in French by Seuil, *Le Moi dans la théorie de Freud et dans la technique de la psychanalyse*, 1977), translated and annotated by Sylvana Tomaselli and annotated by John Forrester (New York: Norton, 1998).

(1955) *Seminar on "The Purloined Letter"* (*séminaire sur "La Lettre volée"*) also in *Ecrits*, pp. 9–61, translated by Jeffrey Mehlman in *The Purloined Poe*, edited John Muller and William Richardson (Baltimore: Johns Hopkins University Press, 1988) pp. 28–54.

(1955–56) *Seminar III: The Psychoses* (published in French by Seuil, *Les Psychoses*, 1981) *Seminar III, Psychoses*, edited by Jacques-Alain Miller, translated and annotated by Russell Grigg (New York: Norton, 1993).

(1956) with Wladimir Granoff, "Fetishism: the Symbolic, the Imaginary and the Real" in S. Lorand and M. Balint, editors, *Perversions: Psychodynamics and Therapy* (New York: Random House, 1956) pp. 265–76.

(1956–57) *Seminar IV: Object Relations and Freudian Structures* (published in French by Seuil, *La Relation d'objet et les structures freudiennes*, 1984). Forthcoming in English from Norton.

(1957–58) *Seminar V: The Formations of the Unconscious* (published in French by Seuil, *Les Formations de l'inconscient*, 1998).

(1958–59) *Seminar VI: Desire and its Interpretation*, (*Le Désir et son interprétation*), partly translated as "Desire and the interpretation of desire in Hamlet," in *Literature and Psychoanalysis*, edited Shoshana Felman (Baltimore: Johns Hopkins University Press, 1982) pp. 11–52. The *Hamlet* sections are published in *Ornicar?* 24–25 (1981–82).

(1959–60) *Seminar VII: The Ethics of Psychoanalysis* (published in French by Seuil, *L'Ethique de la psychanalyse*, 1986) *The Ethics of Psychoanalysis*, edited by Jacques-Alain Miller, translated and annotated by Dennis Porter (New York: Norton, 1992).

(1960) "Position of the unconscious" ("La Position de l'inconscient"), also in *Ecrits*, pp. 829–50, translated by Bruce Fink in *Reading Seminar XI: Lacan's Four Fundamental Concepts of Psychoanalysis*, edited by Bruce Fink, Richard Feldstein, and Maire Jaanus (Albany: State University of New York Press, 1995) pp. 259–82.

(1960–61) *Seminar VIII: Transference* (published in French by Seuil, *Le Transfert*, 1991).

(1961–62) *Seminar IX: Identification* (*L'Identification*).

(1962–63) *Seminar X: Anxiety* (*L'Angoisse*).

(1963) "Kant with Sade" ("Kant avec Sade"), also in *Ecrits*, pp. 765–90, translated and annotated by James Swenson in *October* 51 (1989) pp. 55–75.

(1964) *Seminar XI: The Four Fundamental Concepts of Psychoanalysis* (published in French by Seuil, *Les quatre concepts fondamentaux de la psychanalyse*, 1973) edited by Jacques-Alain Miller, translated by Alan Sheridan (London: The Hogarth Press and the Institute of Psycho-Analysis, 1977).

(1964) "On Freud's *Trieb* and the psychoanalyst's desire" ("Du Trieb de Freud et du désir du psychanalyste"), also in *Ecrits*, pp. 851–4, translated by Bruce Fink in *Reading Seminars I and II: Lacan's Return to Freud*, edited by Bruce Fink, Richard Feldstein, and Maire Jaanus (Albany: State University of New York Press, 1996) pp. 417–21.

(1964–65) *Seminar XII: Crucial Problems of Psychoanalysis* (*Les Problèmes cruciaux de la psychanalyse*).

(1965) "Homage to Marguerite Duras," *Duras by Duras* (San Francisco: City Lights Books, 1987) pp. 122–9.

(1965–66) *Seminar XIII: The Object of Psychoanalysis* (*L'Objet de la psychanalyse*).

(1965) "Science and Truth" ("La Science et la vérité), opening session of *Seminar XIII*, also in *Ecrits*, pp. 855–77, translated by Bruce Fink, *Newsletter of the Freudian Field* vol. 3, 1–2 (1989) pp. 4–29.

(1966) *Ecrits* (Paris: Seuil). Partly translated as *Ecrits, A Selection*, by Alan Sheridan (London: Tavistock Publications, 1977). A reliable revised translation of *Ecrits, A Selection* has recently been made by Bruce Fink (New York: Norton, 2002). Fink's "Endnotes" are extremely useful (pp. 313–55).

(1966) "Of structure as an inmixing of an otherness prerequisite to any subject whatever," *The Languages of Criticism and the Sciences of Man: The Structuralist Controversy*, edited by Richard Macksey and Eugenio Donato (Baltimore: Johns Hopkins University Press, 1970) pp. 186–201.

(1966–67) *Seminar XIV: The Logic of Fantasy* (*La Logique du fantasme*).

(1967–68) *Seminar XV: The Psychoanalytic Act* (*L'Acte psychanalytique*).

(1968–69) *Seminar XVI: From one other to the Other* (*D'un Autre à l'autre*).

(1969–70) *Seminar XVII: The Reverse of Psychoanalysis* (published in French by Seuil, *L'Envers de la psychanalyse*, 1991).

(1970–71) *Seminar XVIII: Of a Discourse That Would Not Be Pure Semblance* (*D'un discours qui ne serait pas du semblant*).

(1971–72) *Seminar XIX: . . . or worse* (. . . *ou pire*).

(1972–73) *Seminar XX: Encore* (published in French by Seuil, *Encore*, 1975), *On Feminine Sexuality, The Limits of Love and Knowledge 1972–1973. Encore, The Seminar of Jacques Lacan, Book XX*, edited by Jacques-Alain Miller, translated and annotated by Bruce Fink (New York: Norton, 1998).

(1973–74) *Seminar XXI: The Non-Duped Err* (*Les Non-dupes errent*, pun on "les noms du père").

(1974) *Television* (published in French by Seuil, *Télévision*, 1974), edited by Joan Copjec, translated by Denis Hollier, Rosalind Krauss, and Annette Michelson, and *A Challenge to the Psychoanalytic Establishment*, translated by Jeffrey Mehlman (New York: Norton, 1990).

(1974–75) *Seminar XXII: RSI, Ornicar?* 2–5 (1975).

(1975–76) *Seminar XXIII: The Sinthome* (*Le Sinthome*), *Ornicar?* 6–11 (1976–77).

(1976) "Preface" to the English edition of *The Four Fundamental Concepts of Psychoanalysis*, pp. vii–ix.

(1976–77) *Seminar XXIV: L'Insu que sait de l'une bévue s'aile à mourre* (punning on "The failure [or the unknown that knows] of *das Unbewusste* [the unconscious as a misprision] is love"), *Ornicar?* 12–18 (1977–9).

(1977–78) *Seminar XXV: The Time to Conclude* (*Le Moment de conclure*).

(1978–79) *Seminar XXVI: Topology and Time* (*La Topologie et le temps*).

(2001) *Autres écrits*, edited by Jacques-Alain Miller (Paris: Seuil, 2001).

On Lacan – historical, bibliographical, and biographical

Clark, Michael, *Jacques Lacan: An Annotated Bibliography* (New York: Garland, 1998).

Clément, Catherine, *The Lives and Legends of Jacques Lacan*, trans. A. Goldhammer (New York: Columbia University Press, 1983).

Dor, Joël, *Bibliographie des travaux de Jacques Lacan* (Paris: InterEditions, 1983).

Thésaurus Lacan: Nouvelle bibliographie des travaux de Jacques Lacan (Paris: EPEL, 1994).

Macey, David, *Lacan in Contexts* (London: Verso, 1988).

Marini, Marcelle, *Jacques Lacan, The French Context*, trans. A. Tomiche (New Brunswick: Rutgers University Press, 1992).

Nordquist, Joan, *Jacques Lacan: A Bibliography* (Santa Cruz: Reference and Research Services, 1987).

Roudinesco, Elisabeth, *Lacan & Co.: A History of Psychoanalysis in France 1925–1985*, trans. by Jeffrey Mehlman (Chicago: University of Chicago Press, 1990).

Jacques Lacan, trans. Barbara Bray (New York: Columbia University Press, 1997).

Schneiderman, Stuart, *Jacques Lacan. The Death of an Intellectual Hero* (Cambridge, Mass.: Harvard University Press, 1983).

Turkle, Sherry, *Psychoanalytic Politics: Freud's French Revolution* (New York: Basic Books, 1978).

Lacanian journals in English

(a): The journal of culture and the unconscious (San Francisco)

Anamorphosis (San Francisco)

Bien Dire (Norfolk, Va)

Clinical Studies: International Journal of Psychoanalysis (New York)

Journal for the Psychoanalysis of Culture and Society (JPCS) (Columbus, Ohio)

Journal of European Psychoanalysis (Rome)

Lacanian Ink (New York)

Newletters of the Freudian Field (Columbia, Mich.)

Other Voices (Philadelphia, Pa)

Papers of the Freudian School of Melbourne (Melbourne)

Umbr(a): A Journal of the unconscious (Buffalo, NY)

Critical approaches

Adams, Parveen (ed.), *Art: Sublimation or Symptom, a Lacanian Perspective* (New York: The Other Press, 2002).

Adams, Parveen, and Cowie, Elizabeth, *The Woman in Question* (Cambridge, Mass.: MIT Press, 1990).

Althusser, Louis, *Writings of Psychoanalysis, Freud and Lacan*, trans. Jeffrey Mehlman (New York: Columbia University Press, 1996).

André, Serge, *What Does a Woman Want?* Foreword by Frances Restuccia, trans. Susan Fairfeld (New York: The Other Press, 1999).

Apollon, Willy, and Feldstein, Richard (eds.), *Lacan, Politics, Aesthetics* (Albany: State University of New York Press, 1996).

Apollon, Willy; Bergeron, Danielle; Cantin, Lucie; and Hughes, Robert, *After Lacan: Clinical Practice and the Subject of the Unconscious*, edited by Kareen Malone (Albany: State University of New York Press, 2002).

Barnard, Suzanne, and Fink, Bruce (eds.), *Reading Seminar XX, Lacan's Major Work on Love, Knowledge, Femininity, and Sexuality* (Albany: State University of New York Press, 2002).

Barzilai, Shuli, *Lacan and the Matter of Origins* (Stanford: Stanford University Press, 1999).

Benvenuto, Bice, *Concerning the Rites of Psychoanalysis, or The Villa of the Mysteries* (Cambridge, Polity Press, 1994).

Benvenuto, Bice, and Kennedy, Roger, *The Works of Jacques Lacan: An Introduction* (London: Free Association Books, 1986).

Berressem, Hanjo, *Lines of Desire: Reading Gombrowicz's Fiction with Lacan* (Evanston: Northwestern University Press, 1998).

Boothby, Richard, *Freud as Philosophy: Metapsychoanalysis after Lacan* (London and New York: Routledge, 2001).

Borch-Jacobsen, Mikkel, *The Freudian Subject*, trans. Catherine Porter (Stanford: Stanford University Press, 1988).

Lacan: The Absolute Master (Stanford: Stanford University Press, 1991).

Bouveresse, Jacques, *Wittgenstein Reads Freud: The Myth of the Unconscious*, trans. Carol Cosman (Princeton: Princeton University Press, 1995).

Bowie, Malcolm, *Freud, Proust and Lacan: Theory as Fiction* (Cambridge: Cambridge University Press, 1987).

Lacan, London, Fontana, 1991.

Psychoanalysis and the Future of Theory (Oxford: Blackwell, 1994).

Bracher, Mark, *Lacan, Discourse, and Social Change: A Psychoanalytical Cultural Criticism* (Ithaca: Cornell University Press, 1993).

Bracher, Mark; Alcorn, Marshall; Corthell, Ronald; and Massardier-Kenney, Françoise (eds.), *Lacanian Theory of Discourse. Subject, Structure, and Society* (New York: New York University Press, 1994).

Braunstein, Néstor, *La Jouissance: Un concept lacanien* (Paris: Point hors ligne, 1992). Forthcoming in English from Verso.

Brenkman, John, *Straight Male, Modern: A Cultural Critique of Psychoanalysis* (New York and London: Routledge, 1993).

Brennan, Teresa, *The Interpretation of the Flesh: Freud and Femininity* (London and New York: Routledge, 1992).

History after Lacan (London and New York: Routledge, 1993).

Brivic, Sheldon, *The Veil of Signs: Joyce, Lacan and Perception* (Urbana: University of Illinois Press, 1991).

Bugliani, Ann, *The Instruction of Philosophy and Psychoanalysis by Tragedy: Jacques Lacan and Gabriel Marcel read Paul Claudel* (San Francisco: International Scholars Publications, 1998).

Burgoyne, Bernard, and Sullivan, Mary (eds.), *The Klein-Lacan Dialogues* (New York: The Other Press, 1997).

Butler, Judith, *The Psychic Life of Power: Theories in Subjection* (Stanford: Stanford University Press, 1997).

Subjects of Desire: Hegelian Reflections in Twentieth Century France, 2nd revised edn. (New York, Columbia University Press, 1999).

Antigone's Claim: Kinship between Life and Death (New York: Columbia University Press, 2000).

Caudill, David S., *Lacan and the Subject of the Law: Toward a Psychoanalytic Critical Legal Theory* (Atlantic Highlands, NJ: Humanities Press, 1997).

Chaitin, Gilbert D., *Rhetoric and Culture in Lacan* (Cambridge: Cambridge University Press, 1996).

Copjec, Joan, *Read My Desire: Jacques Lacan against the Historicists* (Cambridge, Mass.: MIT Press, 1994).

Copjec, Joan (ed.), *Supposing the Subject* (London: Verso, 1994).

David-Ménard, Monique, *Hysteria from Freud to Lacan. Body and Language in Psychoanalysis*, trans. Catherine Porter (Ithaca: Cornell University Press, 1989).

Davis, Robert Con (ed.), *Lacan and Narration. The Psychoanalytic Difference in Narrative Theory* (Baltimore: John Hopkins University Press, 1983).

The Fictional Father: Lacanian Readings of the Text (Amherst: University of Massachusetts Press, 1981).

Dean, Tim, *Beyond Sexuality* (Chicago: Chicago University Press, 2000).

Dean, Tim, and Lane, Chris (eds.), *Homosexuality and Psychoanalysis* (Chicago: Chicago University Press, 2001).

Derrida, Jacques, *The Postcard*, trans. Alan Bass (Chicago: University of Chicago Press, 1987).

Resistances of Psychoanalysis, trans. Peggy Kamuf and Pascale Anne Brault (Stanford: Stanford University Press, 1998).

Dor, Joel, *Introduction to the Reading of Lacan: The Unconscious Structured like a Language*, edited by Judith Feher-Gurewich and Susan Fairfield (New York: The Other Press, 1999).

The Clinical Lacan, trans. Susan Fairfield (New York: The Other Press, 1999).

Structure and Perversions, trans. Susan Fairfield (New York: The Other Press, 2001).

Dosse, François, *History of Structuralism*, trans. Deborah Glassman (Minneapolis: University of Minnesota Press, 1997).

Dufresne, Todd (ed.), *Returns of the French Freud* (London and New York: Routledge, 1997).

Evans, Dylan, *An Introductory Dictionary of Lacanian Psychoanalysis* (London and New York: Routledge, 1996).

Feher-Gurewich, Judith, and Tort, Michel (eds.), *The Subject and the Self: Lacan and American Psychoanalysis* (Northvale: Jason Aronson, 1996).

Feldstein, Richard; Fink, Bruce; and Jaanus, Maire (eds.), *Reading Seminar XI: Lacan's Four Fundamental Concepts of Psychoanalysis* (Albany: State University of New York Press, 1995).

Reading Seminars I and II: Lacan's Return to Freud (Albany: State University of New York Press, 1996).

Feldstein, Richard, and Sussman, Henry (eds.), *Psychoanalysis and . . .* (London and New York: Routledge, 1990).

Felman, Shoshana, *Jacques Lacan and the Adventure of Insight* (Cambridge, Mass.: Harvard University Press, 1987).

Felman, Shoshana (ed.), *Literature and Psychoanalysis. The Question of Reading: Otherwise* (Baltimore: Johns Hopkins University Press, 1977).

Ferrell, Robyn, *Passion in Theory: Concepts of Freud and Lacan* (London and New York: Routledge, 1997).

Fink, Bruce, *The Lacanian Subject: Between Language and Jouissance* (Princeton: Princeton University Press, 1995).

A Clinical Introduction to a Lacanian Psychoanalysis: Theory and Technique (Cambridge, Mass.: Harvard University Press, 1997).

Forrester, John, *The Seductions of Psychoanalysis* (Cambridge: Cambridge University Press, 1990).

Truth Games: Lies, Money and Psychoanalysis (Cambridge, Mass.: Harvard University Press, 1997).

Gallop, Jane, *Reading Lacan* (Ithaca: Cornell University Press, 1985).

Gherovici, Patricia, *The Puerto-Rican Syndrome: Hysteria in the Barrio* (New York: The Other Press, 2003).

Glowinski, Huguette; Marks, Zita M.; Murphy, Sara; and Nobus, Dany (eds.), *A Compendium of Lacanian Terms* (London: Free Association Books, 2001).

Grosz, Elizabeth, *Jacques Lacan: A Feminist Introduction* (London and New York: Routledge, 1990).

Halpern, Richard, *Shakespeare's Perfume: Sodomy and Sublimity in the Sonnets, Wilde, Freud and Lacan* (Philadelphia: University of Pennsylvania Press, 2002).

Harari, Roberto, *Lacan's Seminar on Anxiety, An Introduction*, trans. Jane C. Lamb-Ruiz (New York: The Other Press, 2001).

How James Joyce Made His Name: A Reading of the Final Lacan, trans. Luke Thurston (New York: The Other Press, 2002).

Harasym, Sarah (ed.), *Levinas and Lacan: The Missed Encounter* (Albany: State University of New York Press, 1998).

Hartman, Geoffrey (ed.), *Psychoanalysis and the Question of the Text* (Baltimore: Johns Hopkins University Press, 1978).

Hill, Philip H. F., *Using Lacanian Clinical Technique – An Introduction* (London: Press for the Habilitation of Psychoanalysis, 2002).

Hogan, Patrick, and Pandit, Lalita (eds.), *Criticism and Lacan: Essays and Dialogue on Language, Structure, and the Unconscious* (Athens: University of Georgia Press, 1990).

Julien, Philippe: *Jacques Lacan's Return to Freud: The Real, the Symbolic and the Imaginary*, trans. D. Beck Simiu (New York: New York University Press, 1994).

Lacoue-Labarthe, Philippe, and Nancy, Jean-Luc, *The Title of the Letter: A Reading of Lacan*, trans. François Raffoul and David Pettigrew (Albany: State University of New York Press, 1992).

Lane, Christopher (ed.), *The Psychoanalysis of Race* (New York: Columbia University Press, 1998).

Laplanche, Jean, and Pontalis, Jean-Baptiste, *The Language of Psycho-Analysis*, trans. D. Nicholson Smith (London: Hogarth Press, 1973).

Leader, Darian, *Why Do Women Write More Letters Than They Post?* (London: Faber & Faber, 1996). Published in the United States as *Why do Women Write More Letters Than They Send? A Meditation on the Loneliness of the Sexes* (New York: Basic Books, 1996).

Leader, Darian, and Groves, Judith, *Lacan for Beginners* (Cambridge: Icon, 1995).

Lechte, John (ed.), *Writing and Psychoanalysis: A Reader* (London: Arnold, 1996).

Leclaire, Serge, *Psychoanalyzing, On the Order of the Unconscious and the Practice of the Letter*, trans. Peggy Kamuf (Stanford: Stanford University Press, 1998).

Lee, Jonathan Scott, *Jacques Lacan* (Amherst: University of Massachusetts Press, 1990).

Lemaire, Anika, *Jacques Lacan*, trans. D. Macey (London and New York: Routledge, 1979).

Leupin, Alexandre, *Jacques Lacan and the Human Sciences* (Lincoln: University of Nebraska Press, 1991).

Luepnitz, Deborah, *Schopenhauer's Porcupines* (New York: Basic Books, 2002).

Lupton, Julia Reinhard, and Reinhard, Kenneth, *After Oedipus: Shakespeare in Psychoanalysis* (Ithaca: Cornell University Press, 1993).

MacCannell, Juliet Flower, *Figuring Lacan: Criticism and the Cultural Unconscious* (Lincoln: University of Nebraska Press, 1986).

The Regime of the Brother: After the Patriarchy (London and New York: Routledge, 1991).

The Hysteric's Guide to the Future Female Subject (Minneapolis: Minnesota, 2000).

Malone, Kareen Ror, and Friedlander, Stephen R. (eds.), *The Subject of Lacan: A Lacanian Reader for Psychoanalysts* (Albany: State University of New York Press, 2000).

Mathelin, Catherine, *Lacanian Psychotherapy with Children: The Broken Piano*, trans. Susan Fairfield, annotated by Judith Feher-Gurewich (New York: The Other Press, 1999).

Metzger, David, *The Lost Cause of Rhetoric: The Relation of Rhetoric and Geometry in Aristotle and Lacan* (Carbondale: Southern Illinois University Press, 1994).

Miller, Jacques-Alain, *Clear Like Day Letter for the twenty years since the death of Jacques Lacan* (New York: Wooster Press, 2002).

Mitchell, Juliet, and Rose, Jacqueline (eds.), *Feminine Sexuality: Jacques Lacan and the Ecole Freudienne* (London: Macmillan, 1982).

Molino, Anthony, and Ware, Christine (eds.), *Where Id Was: Challenging Normalization in Psychoanalysis* (London and New York: Continuum, 2001).

Muller, John P., *Beyond the Psychoanalytic Dyad: Developmental Semiotics in Freud, Peirce and Lacan* (New York and London: Routledge, 1996).

Muller, John P., and Richardson, William J., *Lacan and Language: A Reader's Guide to Ecrits* (New York: International Universities Press, 1982).

Muller John P., and Richardson William J. (eds.), *The Purloined Poe: Lacan, Derrida and Psychoanalytic Reading* (Baltimore: Johns Hopkins University Press, 1988).

Nasio, Juan-David, *Hysteria: The Splendid Child of Psychoanalysis*, trans. Susan Fairfield (Northvale: Jason Aronson, 1997).

Hysteria from Freud to Lacan: The Splendid Child of Psychoanalysis, edited by Judith Feher-Gurewich with Susan Fairfield (New York: The Other Press, 1998).

Five Lessons on the Psychoanalytic Theory of Jacques Lacan, trans. David Pettigrew and François Raffoul (Albany: State University of New York Press, 1998).

Newman, Saul, *From Bakunin to Lacan* (Lexington: Lexington Books, 2001).

Nobus, Dany, *Jacques Lacan and the Practice of Psychoanalysis* (London and Philadelphia: Routledge, 2000).

Nobus, Dany (ed.), *Key Concepts of Lacanian Psychoanalysis* (New York: The Other Press, 1999).

Pettigrew, David, and Raffoul, François (eds.), *Disseminating Lacan* (Albany: State University of New York Press, 1996).

Plotnistky, Arkady, *The Knowable and the Unknowable: Modern Science, Nonclassical Thought and the "Two Cultures"* (Ann Arbor: University of Michigan Press, 2002).

Pommier, Gérard, *Erotic Anger, A User's Manual,* trans. Catherine Liu, foreword by Patricia Gherovici (Minneapolis: University of Minnesota Press, 2001).

Rabaté, Jean-Michel, *Lacan and the Subject of Literature* (Houndmills: Palgrave, 2001).

Rabaté, Jean-Michel (ed.), *Lacan in America* (New York: The Other Press, 2000).

Ragland-Sullivan, Ellie, *Jacques Lacan and the Philosophy of Psychoanalysis* (Urbana: University of Illinois Press, 1986).

   Essays on the Pleasure of Death: From Freud to Lacan (London and New York: Routledge, 1995).

Ragland-Sullivan, Ellie and Bracher, Mark (eds.), *Lacan and the Subject of Language* (New York: Routledge, 1991).

Rajchman, John, *Truth and Eros* (New York and London: Routledge, 1991).

Roazen, Paul, *The Historiography of Psychoanalysis* (New Brunswick: Transaction Publishers, 2001).

Rose, Jacqueline, *Sexuality in the Field of Vision* (London: Verso, 1996).

Roth, Michael S., *Knowing and History: Appropriations of Hegel in Twentieth Century France* (Ithaca: Cornell University Press, 1988).

Roudinesco, Elisabeth, *Why Psychoanalysis?* trans. Rachel Bowlby (New York: Columbia University Press, 2002).

Roustang, François, *Dire mastery: Disciplineship from Freud to Lacan* (Baltimore: Johns Hopkins University Press, 1982).

   The Lacanian Delusion, trans. Greg Sims (Oxford: Oxford University Press, 1990).

Safouan, Moustafa, *The Seminar of Moustafa Safouan,* edited by Anna Shane and Janet Mackintosh (New York: The Other Press, 2002.)

Safouan, Moustafa, and Rose, Jacqueline, *Jacques Lacan and the Question of Psychoanalytical Training* (Houndmills: Palgrave, 2000).

Samuels, Robert, *Between Philosophy and Psychoanalysis: Lacan's Reconstruction of Freud* (London and New York: Routledge, 1993).

Sarup, Madan, *Jacques Lacan* (Hemel Hempstead: Harvester, 1992).

Schneiderman, Stuart (ed.), *Returning to Freud: Clinical Psychoanalysis in the School of Lacan* (New Haven: Yale University Press, 1980).

Schroeder, Jeanne Lorraine, *The Vestal and the Fasces: Hegel, Lacan, Property and the Feminine* (Stanford: University of California Press, 1998).

Seshadri-Crooks, Kalpana, *Desiring Whiteness: A Lacanian Analysis of Race* (London and New York: Routledge, 2000).

Smith, Joseph H., *Arguing with Lacan: Ego Psychology and Language* (New Haven: Yale University Press, 1991).

Smith, Joseph H., and Kerrigan, William (eds.), *Taking Chances: Derrida, Psychoanalysis and Literature* (Baltimore: Johns Hopkins University Press, 1987).

Staten, Henry, *Eros in Mourning: Homer to Lacan* (Baltimore: Johns Hopkins University Press, 2002).

Stavrakis, Yannis: *Lacan and the Political* (London and New York: Routledge, 1999).

Stoltzfus, Ben: *Lacan and Literature: Purloined Pretexts* (Albany: State University of New York Press, 1996).

Sturrock, John, *Structuralism* (1986), 2nd edn. (London: Fontana, 1993), 3rd edn. (Oxford: Blackwell, 2002).

Sturrock, John (ed.), *Structuralism and Since* (Oxford: Oxford University Press, 1979).

Sullivan, Henry W., *The Beatles with Lacan: Rock 'n' Roll as Requiem for the Modern Age* (New York: Peter Lang, 1995).

Taylor, Gary, *Castration: An Abbreviated History of Western Manhood* (New York and London: Routledge, 2000).

Thurston, Luke (ed.), *Re-inventing the Symptom, Essays on the Final Lacan* (New York: The Other Press, 2002).

Van Boheemen-Saaf, Christine, *Joyce, Derrida, Lacan and the Trauma of History* (Cambridge: Cambridge University Press, 1999).

Van Haute, Philippe: *Against Adaptation: Lacan's "Subversion of the Subject,"* trans. Paul Crowe and Miranda Vankerk (New York: The Other Press, 2002).

Vanier, Alain, *Lacan,* trans. Susan Fairfield (New York: The Other Press, 2000).

Van Pelt, Tamise, *The Other Side of Desire: Lacan's Theory of the registers* (Albany: State University of New York Press, 2000).

Verhaeghe, Paul, *Does the Woman Exist? From Freud's Hysteric to Lacan's Feminine,* trans. Marc du Ry (New York: The Other Press, 1999).

Beyond Gender: From Subject to Drive (New York: The Other Press, 2002).

Weber, Samuel, *The Legend of Freud* (Minneapolis: University of Minnesota Press, 1982).

Return to Freud: Jacques Lacan's Dislocation of Psychoanalysis, trans. M. Levine (Cambridge: Cambridge University Press, 1991).

Wilden, Anthony (ed.) *The Language of the Self: The Function of Language in Psychoanalysis* (Baltimore: Johns Hopkins University Press, 1968).

Williams, Linda Ruth, *Critical Desire: Psychoanalysis and the Literary Subject* (London: Edward Arnold, 1995).

Wright, Elizabeth, *Psychoanalytic Criticism: Theory to Practice* (New York: Routledge, 1985).

Psychoanalytic Criticism: A Reappraisal (New York: Routledge, 1998).

Lacan and Postfeminism (Cambridge: Icon, 2000).

Wright, Elizabeth, and Wright, Edmond (eds.), *The Žižek Reader* (Oxford: Blackwell, 1999).

Wyschogrod, Edith; Crownfield, David; and Raschke, Carl A. (eds.), *Lacan and Theological Discourse* (Albany: State University of New York Press, 1989).

Žižek, Slavoj, *The Sublime Object of Ideology* (London: Verso, 1989).

Looking Awry: An Introduction to Jacques Lacan through Popular Culture (Cambridge: Mass.: MIT Press, 1991).

Enjoy Your Symptom! Jacques Lacan in Hollywood and Out (London: Routledge, 1992).

The Plague of Fantasies (London: Verso, 1997).

Žižek, Slavoj (ed.), *Everything You Always Wanted to Know about Lacan (But Were Afraid to Ask Hitchcock)* (London: Verso, 1992).

On Belief (London and New York: Routledge, 2001).

Cogito and the Unconscious (Durham: Duke University Press, 1998).

Žižek, Slavoj, and Dolar, Mladen, *Opera's Second Death* (New York and London: Routledge, 2002).

Zupančič, Alenka, *Ethics of the Real: Kant and Lacan* (London: Verso, 2000).

INDEX

CAMBRIDGE COMPANIONS TO LITERATURE

*The Cambridge Companion to
Herman Melville*
edited by Robert S. Levine

*The Cambridge Companion to
Edith Wharton*
edited by Millicent Bell

*The Cambridge Companion to
Henry James*
edited by Jonathan Freedman

*The Cambridge Companion to
Walt Whitman*
edited by Ezra Greenspan

*The Cambridge Companion to
Henry David Thoreau*
edited by Joel Myerson

*The Cambridge Companion to
Mark Twain*
edited by Forrest G. Robinson

*The Cambridge Companion to
Edgar Allan Poe*
edited by Kevin J. Hayes

*The Cambridge Companion to
Emily Dickinson*
edited by Wendy Martin

*The Cambridge Companion to
William Faulkner*
edited by Philip M. Weinstein

*The Cambridge Companion to
Ernest Hemingway*
edited by Scott Donaldson

*The Cambridge Companion to
F. Scott Fitzgerald*
edited by Ruth Prigozy

*The Cambridge Companion to
Robert Frost*
edited by Robert Faggen

*The Cambridge Companion to
Eugene O'Neill*
edited by Michael Manheim

*The Cambridge Companion to
Tennessee Williams*
edited by Matthew C. Roudané

*The Cambridge Companion to
Arthur Miller*
edited by Christopher Bigsby

*The Cambridge Companion to
Sam Shepard*
edited by Matthew C. Roudané

CAMBRIDGE COMPANIONS TO CULTURE

*The Cambridge Companion to Modern
German Culture*
edited by Eva Kolinsky
and Wilfried van der Will

*The Cambridge Companion to Modern
Russian Culture*
edited by Nicholas Rzhevsky

*The Cambridge Companion to Modern
Spanish Culture*
edited by David T. Gies

*The Cambridge Companion to Modern
Italian Culture*
edited by Zygmunt G. Baranski
and Rebecca J. West